LOCATING PRIVACY IN TUDOR LONDON

Locating Privacy
in Tudor London

LENA COWEN ORLIN

OXFORD
UNIVERSITY PRESS

OXFORD
UNIVERSITY PRESS

Great Clarendon Street, Oxford OX2 6DP

Oxford University Press is a department of the University of Oxford.
It furthers the University's objective of excellence in research, scholarship,
and education by publishing worldwide in

Oxford New York

Auckland Cape Town Dar es Salaam Hong Kong Karachi
Kuala Lumpur Madrid Melbourne Mexico City Nairobi
New Delhi Shanghai Taipei Toronto

With offices in

Argentina Austria Brazil Chile Czech Republic France Greece
Guatemala Hungary Italy Japan Poland Portugal Singapore
South Korea Switzerland Thailand Turkey Ukraine Vietnam

Oxford is a registered trade mark of Oxford University Press
in the UK and in certain other countries

Published in the United States
by Oxford University Press Inc., New York

British Library Cataloguing in Publication Data

Data available

Library of Congress Cataloging in Publication Data

Data available

Typeset by Laserwords Private Limited, Chennai, India
Printed in Great Britain
on acid-free paper by
Biddles Ltd., King's Lynn, Norfolk

ISBN 978–0–19–922625–2

1 3 5 7 9 10 8 6 4 2

For Phyllis Rackin
Legendary Fair Woman

Acknowledgments

THIS project began in 1986, when, with a travel grant from the National Endowment for the Humanities and the help of trip planner and navigator Glenn Orlin, I studied surviving examples of Elizabethan and Jacobean domestic architecture. Or it began in 1990, when I attended one of the paleography seminars led by Laetitia Yeandle at the Folger Shakespeare Library. Or in 1998, when the British Academy funded a residency at the Canterbury Cathedral Archives and Library. Then again, it began in 2001, when Georgianna Ziegler shared with me her catalogue of the Berger Collection of British art, and I came upon a portrait known as 'Lady Ingram and her Two Boys'. Or in 2002, when I proposed a new name for the painting at a conference in honor of Phyllis Rackin. Or in 2003, when Carole Levin encouraged the idea of a book with alternating chapters of cultural history and case study.

Of course, Glenn and Laetitia and Georgianna and Phyllis and Carole are only the start of it. For their support of my research I am also grateful to Christy Anderson, A. R. Braunmuller, Cynthia Herrup, and Bruce Smith. I have profited from conversations about the archives with Peter Beal, Peter Blayney, Loreen Giese, Vanessa Harding, John A. W. Lock, Alan H. Nelson, Catherine Richardson, and David Harris Sacks. Judith Bennett read the first chapter; Carole Levin read the whole. In London I have relied on Russ McDonald, Lois Potter, and especially Patricia Tatspaugh. At home I owe more than can be said to Leeds Barroll, Lynda Boose, William C. Carroll, Anthony B. Dawson, Margo Hendricks, Nancy Elizabeth Hodge, Jean E. Howard, James R. Siemon, and Georgianna Ziegler. Harry Berger, Jr., Natalie Zemon Davis, Betty Jo Teeter Dobbs, Richard Helgerson, Phyllis Rackin, Alan Sinfield, Joan Thirsk, and Stanley Wells are also continuing sources of inspiration.

I would like to thank the John Simon Guggenheim Memorial Foundation for a Fellowship, the National Endowment for the Humanities for a Senior Fellowship, and the University of Maryland Baltimore County for making research leaves possible. I have benefited from residencies at the Center for Advanced Study in the Visual Arts at the National Gallery of Art, the Rockefeller Foundation's Bellagio Study and Conference Center, and the Yale Center for British Art. I am grateful for travel grants from the English-Speaking Union of Washington, DC (the Helene Gladstone Williams Award) and from UMBC's Research Initiative Fund.

I am deeply indebted to the staffs of the following institutions (as they were when I consulted them): the Bethlem Royal Hospital and Archives, especially Colin Gale; the Bodleian Library, especially Oliver House and Steven Tomlinson; the British Library; the Canterbury Cathedral Archives and Library, especially David Pilcher and Michael Stansfield; the Centre for Kentish Studies, especially Michael Carter and Helen Orme; Christie's South Kensington, especially Marijke Booth; Christ's Hospital, especially Elizabeth Bridges and Tony Hogarth-Smith; the Clothworkers' Company of London, especially Alexandrina Buchanan and David Wickham; the Corporation of London Record Office, especially Jim Sewell; the Denver Art Museum, especially Jessica Fletcher, Carole Lee Vowell, and Timothy Standring; the Drapers' Company of London, especially Penelope Fussell; the Essex Record Office; the Family Records Centre; the Heinz Archive at the National Portrait Gallery in London, especially Matthew Bailey and Paul Cox; the Lambeth Palace Library, especially Clare Brown; the Leicestershire Record Office; the London Guildhall Library, especially Stephen Freeth; the London Metropolitan Archives; the Museum of London, especially Mark Bills and John Schofield; the National Archives of the United Kingdom (the Public Record Office), especially James Travers; the West Sussex Record Office, especially Alison McCann; and the Yale Center for British Art, especially Melissa Gold Fournier, Michael Hatt, and Amy Meyers. I have also relied upon the owners and staffs of many sixteenth- and seventeenth-century houses, and especially Jill Harris and Marice Kendrick at Boughton Monchelsea Place in Kent. My research base is the Folger Shakespeare Library, and I am grateful to Director Gail Kern Paster, Librarian Richard Kuhta, Reading Room Supervisor Elizabeth Walsh, Curator of Books and Exhibitions Rachel Doggett, Curator of Art and Special Collections Erin Blake, Reference Librarian Georgianna Ziegler, and Reading Room staff Harold Batie, LuEllen DeHaven, Rosalind Larry, and Camille Seerattan.

My most recent debts are to the wise and wonderful Andrew McNeillie and to Jacqueline Baker at Oxford University Press. Those of longest standing are to the best of fellow travellers, Glenn.

Contents

List of Illustrations

Note on Conventions

Spelling, capitalization, and punctuation are silently modernized for early modern sources. Dates are given Old Style, but with the new year taken to begin on 1 January rather than 25 March.

List of Abbreviations

BCB	Bridewell Hospital, Bethlem Royal Hospital Archives and Museum
BL	British Library
Bodley	Bodleian Library
CCAL	Canterbury Cathedral Archives and Library
CKS	Centre for Kentish Studies
CLRO	Corporation of London Record Office
CPR	Calendar of Patent Rolls
CSPD	Calendar of State Papers Domestic
Drapers'	Drapers' Company of London
ERO	Essex Record Office
ESRO	East Sussex Record Office
FSL	Folger Shakespeare Library
GL	Guildhall Library of London
Lambeth	Lambeth Palace Library
LRO	Leicestershire, Leicester, and Rutland Record Office
LMA	London Metropolitan Archives
PRO	Public Record Office of the National Archives
SBT	Shakespeare Birthplace Trust Records Office
WSRO	West Sussex Record Office

Introduction: Doors

LIKE ALL historical projects, this is an attempt to reopen a door that time has closed. Some of the simplest of things, things so long held trivial that only in the last few decades have they come to the scholarly forefront, are those that seem most securely locked away from us. These are quotidian matters of work and leisure, production and consumption, community and controversy, horizons and boundaries. How can we recover the manner in which the peoples of the past apprehended not only epochal moments but also their ongoing daily existences? Is it possible for us to register some of the many differences occasioned by their ages and genders, stations and locations, backgrounds and aspirations, beliefs and personalities? What can we know of the ways in which they related to their built environments and personal possessions, when they felt comfort and where they exercised control? Do there remain points of access to the events they would have kept hidden from their contemporaries and which history has so far worked to conceal from us, too? Every question I want to ask has to do with how those long gone lived their private lives.

The particular subjects of inquiry in this book are among the most fugitive. Personal privacy takes many forms: interiority, atomization, spatial control, intimacy, urban anonymity, secrecy, withholding, solitude. In the Tudor age, we have been given to understand, such things constituted brave new worlds of experience. After all, in his commanding survey of private life in the west, Philippe Ariès pays tribute to early modern England as the very 'birthplace of privacy'. He speaks specifically of the popularization of diaries, letters, and autobiographies—in France at this time, he says, 'there is nothing comparable'—and of how such texts witness 'the determination of some people to set themselves apart'.[1] These are, of course, statements not only about the past but also about our evidence for such narratives as we construct about it in the present. My narrative differs, because my evidence does.

---

[1] Philippe Ariès, 'Introduction', to Roger Chartier (ed.), *A History of Private Life*, iii. *Passions of the Renaissance*, trans. Arthur Goldhammer (Cambridge, Mass.: Belknap Press of Harvard University Press, 1989), 5.

In sixteenth-century England, personal writings were more often symptoms of privacy than expressions of it. Henry Machyn's mid-1550s London journal, for example, tells us a great deal about his times but very little about his inner life. We would not call it a 'diary' were we not so eager to find early instances of the genre. Other accounts from the period seem to document literacy, leisure, discipline, and conventional piety rather than to betray innermost thoughts—by which, of course, we really mean unconventional thoughts. Like some of Ariès's further indicators for privacy, such as sumptuary laws and duels, surviving texts are biased to the social elite. The autobiography and spiritual meditations of Lady Grace Mildmay, the personal and astrological observations of John Dee, the daily examinations of Lady Margaret Hoby, the religious journal of Richard Rogers, and the commonplace book of John Manningham are all products of privilege.[2] It is not until the seventeenth century that we encounter the life writings of memorandist Martha Moulsworth, turner Nehemiah Wallington, tailor Leonard Wheatcroft, shopkeeper Roger Lowe, seaman Edward Barlow, farmer William Coe, and others.[3] Compared to them, sixteenth-century authors occupy a rarified demographic. Their status is at cross purposes with the impulses that brought many scholars to this field of focus in the first place: interest in the modest and middling rather than the great and powerful, in women as well as men, in those who worked rather than those with inherited wealth, and in people unable or unwilling to 'set themselves apart' through self-recordation.

[2] *The Diary of Henry Machyn, Citizen and Merchant-Taylor of London, from A.D. 1550 to A.D. 1563*, ed. John Gough Nichols, Camden Society 42 (1848); Linda Pollock, *With Faith and Physic: The Life of a Tudor Gentlewoman, Lady Grace Mildmay, 1552–1620* (New York: St Martin's Press, 1993); *The Private Diary of Dr. John Dee*, ed. James Orchard Halliwell, Camden Society 19 (1842); *The Diaries of John Dee*, ed. Edward Fenton (Charlbury: Day Books, 1998); *The Private Life of an Elizabethan Lady: The Diary of Lady Margaret Hoby, 1599–1605*, ed. Joanna Moody (Phoenix Mill: Sutton, 1998); *Two Elizabethan Puritan Diaries by Richard Rogers and Samuel Ward*, ed. M. M. Knappen (Chicago: American Society of Church History, 1933); John Manningham, *The Diary of John Manningham of the Middle Temple, 1602–1603*, ed. Robert Parker Sorlien (Hanover, NH: University Press of New England for the University of Rhode Island, 1976).

[3] *My Name was Martha: A Renaissance Woman's Autobiographical Poem*, ed. Robert C. Evans and Barbara Wiedemann (West Cornwall, Conn.: Locust Hill, 1993); Paul S. Seaver, *Wallington's World: A Puritan Artisan in Seventeenth-Century London* (Stanford: Stanford University Press, 1985); *The Courtship Narrative of Leonard Wheatcroft, Derbyshire Yeoman*, ed. George Parfitt and Ralph Houlbrooke (Reading: Whiteknights, 1986); *The Diary of Roger Lowe of Ashton-in-Makerfield, Lancashire, 1663–74*, ed. William L. Sachse (New Haven: Yale University Press, 1938); *Barlow's Journal of his Life at Sea in King's Ships . . . from 1659 to 1703*, ed. Basil Lubbock (London: Hurst & Blackett, 1934); *Two East Anglian Diaries, 1641–1729: Isaac Archer and William Coe*, ed. Matthew Storey, Suffolk Records Society 36 (1994). But see Margaret Spufford on the continuing bias to Puritans and dissenters: 'The urge to write autobiography in itself defines an exceptional man' ('First Steps in Literacy: The Reading and Writing Experiences of the Humblest Seventeenth-Century Spiritual Autobiographers', *Social History* 4 (1979), 407).

Physical apartness, too, plays a critical role in most histories of private life, including that of Ariès and his collaborators.[4] While for them England did not in this instance take the lead, as it did in personal literatures, it certainly participated in the transformations of domestic interiors that were to have their most celebrated expression in the closet or study. The early modern phenomena of private areas and private literatures are related in popular understanding, because the small enclosed chamber—a room of one's own—has long been assumed to be the condition of possibility for thinking and writing. The two also share connotations of luxury, the closet seemingly as lavish with space as the diary is with time. This association may represent the misplaced influence upon our imagination of the Italian *studiolo*, which survives in places like Mantua and Urbino as a perfect jewel box for the pursuits of contemplation and creativity. But there were other types of closet in England, just as there are sources of private knowledge other than the personal writings that were produced in them. In this book, both the closet and a seventeenth-century family memoir are endpoints, subjects of the concluding chapter, rather than initial concerns. Important as they are to the history of private life, there were alternate forms of privacy that were powerfully at issue in their own time and that can be rediscovered only in their own terms. The more controversial privacies often involved not intellectual autonomy—itself a product of elite subjectivity—but, rather, disruptions of community and interruptions of social knowledge. Through the door opened by investigation into legal and municipal records, the privacies that first showed themselves to me were publicly contested ones.

This is an attempt to recreate the cultural landscape of private life that unfolded on the other side of that door. There are uncharted sectors as well as familiar landmarks, and while many pathways are recognizably purposeful, others may seem indirect. I have allowed them to be shaped by the contours of the evidentiary terrain, because this book is as much about where we locate our sources on privacy as it is about where early moderns located their experiences of it. In view of the limitations and self-selectedness of personal writings, I have turned to material culture and institutional archives: merchant-class portraiture, buildings and floor plans, household furnishings and personal goods, and documents from parish churches, ecclesiastical courts, charitable organizations, livery companies, and records offices. Such texts have their own interests, and these must be decoded, but they are also rich in information that we have feared to be irrecoverable. My guide through this new territory is a forgotten woman, a sixteenth-century city wife of the 'middling' sort

---

[4] Ariès, 'Introduction', iii. 6–7, and see also Orest Ranum, 'The Refuges of Intimacy', in *A History of Private Life*, iii. 207–29.

named Alice Barnham. When I set out I did not know how far I would be able to follow before losing sight of her. Despite the undoubted difficulties of pursuing women in history, though, Alice has proved to be a reliable and generous travel companion, seeing me through to the last chapter. Some of her trails diverged and some crossed, but this is true to an account that should never be told in a linear way, as a story of steady and deliberate progress.

A MAP

Chapter One, 'The Search for Lady Ingram', opens the case study of a lost woman writer, a self-chronicler in fewer than seventy surviving words. These were recorded on one of the earliest family group portraits of the Tudor age, dated to 1557. 'Lady Ingram and her Two Boys' is an example of what has been called a 'speaking' portrait for its textual inscriptions, which seem to introduce its three sitters by addressing the viewer directly. As is characteristic of personal expression in the sixteenth century, however, the painting withholds as much as it shows forth. Archival detection is required to make the connection between Lady Ingram and Alice Barnham, who was the wife of prosperous draper Francis Barnham and mother of Martin, Steven, Anthony, and Benedict Barnham. The painting represents its principal subject in the act of writing, or rather, because she is rendered having just penned one line and pausing before going on to another, in a moment of contemplation. With this depiction of inwardness, 'Lady Ingram and her Two Boys' may represent the invention of a 'thinking' portrait. This is a subject for subsequent chapters, as well: how, in an age that we understand to have been restrictive for women, did this one find her 'speaking' voice? And where did she locate the experience of *interiority* to which the painting bears witness?

Chapter Two, 'Rebuildings', initiates the book's second major through line, which is a cultural history of household space. W. G. Hoskins, remarking an early modern revolution in domestic architecture, termed the period between 1570 and 1640 the 'Great Rebuilding' of England. At the elite level, as described especially by Mark Girouard, this involved design ideas from the Continent.[5] One way of explaining the breadth of the Rebuilding is in terms of the trickling-down of aspiration, as workmen, servants, suppliers, provincial neighbors, and guests encountered the architectural achievements

---

[5] W. G. Hoskins, 'The Rebuilding of Rural England, 1570–1640', *Past and Present* 4 (1953), 44–59; Mark Girouard, *Robert Smythson and the Elizabethan Country House* (New Haven: Yale University Press, 1983).

of great country houses. Equally important were an expanding economy with fixed rents and rising incomes, opportunities for 'new' men to buy land in the wake of the post-Reformation redistribution of former church properties, and a proliferation of consumer goods at all market levels. In a change that is said to have had as many implications for social organization as for spatial reorientation, homes became less centered on the medieval great hall. Most architectural historians conclude that higher levels of personal privacy resulted from the greater number of rooms in early modern houses, and most follow Hoskins in believing that the desire for privacy motivated them. For these scholars, there would be small mystery to the inner life revealed in the painting of 'Lady Ingram and her Two Boys'; it conforms to those larger narratives of the Renaissance that involve the discovery of the individual and the privatization of domestic space. But, this chapter argues, there are other ways of understanding the differences between medieval and Rebuilt homes. Many of the changes identified by Hoskins brought members of the early modern household into closer proximity, and the projects described by Girouard turned family rooms into showpiece spaces. The *atomization* of the new domestic environments had multiple and varied consequences. Privacy was not as ruling a motivation for the architectural innovations of the Great Rebuilding as has long been imagined, and not as dominant an effect.

Chapter Three, 'Alice Barnham in the Rebuilt World', brings together the themes introduced in the first two chapters: the story of an individual Tudor woman and her experience of the Great Rebuilding. Hoskins traces the architectural revolution in rural areas and provincial towns; Girouard concentrates on the prodigy houses of the countryside. Change impacted London, too, most famously in the urban palaces of royals and peers but also in corporate homes such as the halls of the great livery companies. Because apprentices, journeymen, and small tradesmen marked various stages of their careers in these buildings, they were important agents for the democratization of new design standards. Drapers' Hall was as much an artifact of the Great Rebuilding as was the city dwelling place of Alice and Francis Barnham. The two structures shared other spatial systems, as well. Ironically, however, our best evidence of a preclusive practice comes from the civic and not the domestic sphere. The home parlor was an adaptable room, serving both for the family's leisure activities and as a reception area for guests and visitors. But the corporate parlor, sheltering closed meetings to which only a handful of company officers had access, was already inflexibly established as a site for confidential discussions, secret elections, and closely-held records. It had a coercive role within the corporate hierarchy as the prerogative of the all-male Company elite, who enacted and exerted their patriarchal authority in displays of *spatial control*. For all their built affinities, institutional and residential structures differed in this crucial respect. The privacy performed so conspicuously and so confidently in Drapers' Hall was largely unavailable in the multipurposed, bi-gendered, contested, and negotiable domestic sphere.

Chapter Four, 'Boundaries', further diagnoses the levels of privacy experienced within households and between neighbors. London's living spaces, for example, were subdivided under demographic pressure, and people found themselves sharing walls, chimney stacks, water supplies, cesspits, and a great deal of personal intelligence. While the overcrowded capital might seem to have been an extreme case for shared space and boundary violations, in fact there are reports from throughout England of the surreptitious knowledge that resulted from the overhearings, eavesdroppings, and informed deductions that accompanied lives lived in close proximity. In courts from every ecclesiastical diocese, for example, witnesses deposed that they had observed others' transgressive liaisons through 'holes' in party walls. These peepholes have generally been dismissed as legal fictions, but there is irrefutable evidence that in fact the occasions for surveillance, voyeurism, and accidental observations were many. They represent the refusal of neighbors to be denied the traditional prerogatives of familiarity. Ecclesiastical courts, which policed moral behavior, generated evidence of moral infractions—that was their specialty. These reports, though, are mere symptoms of how much private information was in circulation in early modern society. Had other courts, such as those of quarter sessions, similarly taken down witness depositions *in extenso*, we would have had evidence of the many kinds of secrets that were aired in early modern society, in addition to those regarding sexual *intimacy*.

Chapter Five, 'The Chronicles of Francis Barnham', proceeds from the point of view of a civic officer in London in the 1560s and 1570s, for whom the gathering of private information was not a personal matter but a social imperative, essential to accepted methods for maintaining public order. As a leader of the Drapers' Company, governor of the Court of Bridewell, and member of the city's Court of Aldermen, Alice Barnham's husband Francis was charged to keep the peace and prosecute wrongdoing, and he seems to have subscribed fully to the belief that there were important cultural uses for intercepted knowledge. The Reformation is usually related to advancements in privacy because of its emphasis on the examined life. A different story emerges here, among institutions strongly committed to the deterrent effect of shared intelligence and public discipline. The various courts on which Francis Barnham sat worked against what we otherwise have been encouraged to imagine as a high degree of urban *anonymity*. These institutions had their own concerns with public 'fame'. Nor was Francis Barnham himself exempt from the mechanisms of a surveillant society. More than most private writings of the period, the public records reveal his interests, personality, and motivations.

Because Francis Barnham was the commissioner and censor of many of the records in these cases, it can also be argued that they can be compiled into the accidental autobiography of a man who had no intention to 'set himself apart' in ways that historians of private life have traditionally valued.

Chapter Six, 'Galleries', investigates the cultural meanings of the most revolutionary space of the new Elizabethan architecture. The ostensible purpose of the long gallery was to provide for sheltered walking during inclement weather. To this end, it was kept uncluttered by furniture, and its long walls were hung with tapestries and paintings to provide visual interest. Perhaps because it was so extravagantly spacious and lavishly ornamented, it soon eclipsed the great hall as the area of highest status; when the Countess of Shrewsbury was visited by Elizabeth I's delegate at Hardwick Hall, she chose to receive him in her long gallery. There, however, she discovered a collateral effect in this showpiece space, which was that, at one far end of the gallery, she was unable to eavesdrop on an exchange taking place at the other end. Episodes such as these are windows into a lost world-view. Where we tend to focus on privacies that are sexual (those of the bedchamber), bodily (those of the water closet or privy), or intellectual (those of the study), it is apparent that a great deal of early modern cultural anxiety coalesced also around the social privacy of confidential conversation. In interrogations that were conducted in connection with the Ridolfi Plot of 1569–71, it is possible to trace a detailed spatial history centered on the long gallery. For William Cecil and his agents, its use seems to have given cause for alarm. With regard to treason, intention was as much at issue as event, and merely by arranging to meet in such a room people betrayed their treacherous desire for *secrecy*. The pursuit of privacy was inherently suspicious, and there were sophisticated registers for behaviors in space that betrayed such dangerous ambitions as those associated with the Ridolfi conspirators.

Chapter Seven, 'The Barnhams' Business Secrets', shows Francis Barnham to have been a subject of central-government investigation, in connection with the charge that he violated the 1571 Statute against Usury. For all the evidence amassed against him, a great deal went unreported, not only because some witnesses were reluctant to testify fully but also because agents of the Court of Exchequer neglected to log such crucial information as the disposition of the case. Only in seemingly unrelated documents in Drapers' Hall is it possible to learn the Exchequer's determination. If one jeopardy of the inquiry is the prudence of Barnham's borrowers, another is the economy of the records, which were compiled for their own practical purposes and without our interests in mind. The case of *Queen* v. *Barnham* also provides a first clue that Alice Barnham was herself a businesswoman who dealt in the ribbons and fringes that have been called 'narrow ware'. While the family may have had good cause to keep Francis's loans private, they would have had no reason to suppress evidence of Alice's career. The loss of her public identity is a trick of history, one that was perpetrated on all the silkwomen of the sixteenth century. Women trading in these luxury commodities did not organize themselves or form a guild, and thus for them there is no institutional records base such as that for Francis Barnham's Drapers' Company. The chapter illustrates that some things which we take to have been secret in fact appear so only to us, having been produced inadvertently and posthumously by the more indifferent *withholdings* of the past. Gaps in the archives that have survived to us now create the misleading illusion that they were created deliberately then, imputing to the past a higher level of privacy than in fact it enjoyed.

Chapter Eight, 'Closets', concerns another space that was added in great numbers in the early modern period and that has long been uniquely associated with the history of privacy. The chapter demonstrates that although there was certainly a proliferation of working spaces—associated as we might expect with papers, property documents, and books—it was even more common to find closets devoted to the secure storage of valuable goods, which could include plate, currency, jewelry, spices, and medicines. Nor were they always designed with solitude in mind; we find closets fitted out like bedchambers and some that served conversational groups as parlors might do. They were defined not by their contents, nor by their size, but simply by their closure. Like overgrown chests, they were safely kept locked. Here again, intention is at issue: the personal privacies that were discovered in these small chambers were often, as for long galleries, unanticipated effects of spaces built for other purposes. An instance of this sort of accidental privacy is provided in a closet at Boughton Monchelsea Place in Kent, which was fitted out with cupboards and storage bins but which in an early inventory also had writing implements. In this room meant for objects, in other words, an early occupant had perhaps discovered the subjectivity that we associate with authorship. Boughton Monchelsea was inherited in 1613 by the grandson of Alice Barnham, who himself authored a family memoir. This chapter thus ends where most discussions of personal privacy begin: with the topic of self-recordation and the kinds of privacy associated with *solitude*.

As is apparent from this overview, the book features two acts of recovery: one, the past uses of domestic space and the other, the private life of a merchant-class Tudor woman. These represent an attempt to balance the generalizing with the particularizing, cultural history with case study. The pursuit of spatial history, in even-numbered chapters, seems almost irresistibly to produce narratives of architectural revolution, and design change is usually described in terms of stately building, European influence, aristocratic culture, and abstract theory. The odd-numbered chapters are intended as counterweights, compensating for the historiographic heft of elite subjects by continually regrounding the project in the middling, the material, and the concrete. Occasionally there are emigrations from one track to another: John Shute, for example, features as author of the first English treatise on architecture in Chapter Two and resurfaces briefly in Chapter Three as a contributor to the ornamentation of Drapers' Hall; Ralph Treswell prepares a survey of Barnham family property in Chapter Three, returns as a principal source on the crowded conditions of London housing in Chapter Four, and then illustrates the terms of construction for closets in Chapter Eight; Francis Barnham appears outside his track in Chapter Six when he carries to his fellow drapers the Queen's message about the fourth Duke of Norfolk's treason trial and also funds her armed response to rebellion.

More importantly, Chapters Two and Three are about the Great Rebuilding; Chapters Three and Four, about boundary negotiations in the public and private spheres; Chapters Five and Six, about private knowledge and public order; Chapters Six and Seven, about social strategies for deciphering hidden intent. Finally, Chapter Eight discusses among the many possible incarnations of the early modern closet one that survives in a Barnham family home and one in which was preserved a Barnham family chronicle. Despite these crossovers, I would like to think that some readers will feel free to disassemble the book and follow one track alone, or one before the other. Chapter Eight is the conclusion for either and both.

THE ARGUMENT

The notions that personal privacy is something desirable and something progressive are at least implicit, if not explicit, in most writings on the subject. For Ariès, privacy achieves recognizable contours in the sixteenth century; for Hoskins, it is a cause of the Great Rebuilding; for Girouard's followers, an obvious consequence of early architectural design. I have focused on the three named authors because I have been so heavily influenced by them and also because I finally found myself having to empty out their assumptions and start afresh—not proceeding from a known definition of personal privacy in contemporary lexicons but instead seeking the particular valences that had most purchase on common culture in Tudor England; not presuming that all varieties of privacy shared similar trajectories over the course of the century but instead recognizing that each aspect moved at an individual pace and sometimes in an unexpected direction; not supposing that privacy was a prime motivation for early moderns but instead learning that in their complicated lives other objectives were more urgent.

In terms of content, this is the most important argument of the book: privacy inspired an uneasy mixture of desire and distrust. There are countless instances of individuals actively seeking privacy for their own personal reasons, as we would expect. But there is also an abundance of evidence for communal resistance to privacy, as we might not have. What we would think of as improvements in privacy were seen from some perspectives as encroachments. For many persons such 'progress' represented an unwanted change to cultural habits of long standing. Furthermore, we must understand the degree to which society organized itself around the principle of preventing privacy. Curiosity was authorized—indeed, mandated—as a condition of order. For this reason, the book is more occupied with ways in which privacy was thwarted than ways in which it advanced.

This is not to deny that the sixteenth century was a time of change for the history of privacy; it is to say that the story was more equivocal than is generally recognized. For example, the principal manner in which England differed from France—which had 'nothing comparable' in the way of personal expression—was that Henry VIII broke with Rome and founded a national church. England was also unlike other reformed countries in the dizzying pace of its theological transitions: Roman and then English under Henry, more radically reformed under Edward VI, Catholic again under Mary I, and finally Anglican under Elizabeth I. It was the switchback course of official religion, more than any particular variety of doctrine, that created the mid-century space in which all persons of faith were also necessarily persons of private conscience. During one reign or another all were heretics; there were Henrician martyrs, Marian exiles, Elizabethan recusants, and radical sectarians. Privacy is usually associated with the Reformation emphases on direct engagement with scripture, self-examination, and personal accountability for spirituality. At the same time, however, the Reformation was responsible for important deprivatizations of moral experience, as is discussed at greater length in Chapter Five. Offenses that had been confined to the confessional as matters kept secret between a person and his priest, with the priest setting conditions for absolution, were brought into the comparative open of the ecclesiastical courts, with their many church officials, witnesses, competing reports, and testimonies transcribed and shared out. Punishments were public, as well, whether as penance performed in the parish church or as display made at the pillory of a market scaffold. In this way the Reformation worked to stimulate the flow of information about personal and family matters. The symptoms of Protestant privacy may be more familiar to us than are the countervailing forces of public policing.

Another governing paradigm that this study challenges is the predominance of political interpretations. Indeed, it is primarily in political terms that privacy *has* a spatial history. When Foucault wrote that 'a whole history remains to be written of spaces', he added that this 'would at the same time be the history of powers', and, in consequence, the effects of interiors are most often discussed in terms of the disciplines they exert, the senses of license they create, the ownerships they attract.[6] Undeniably, these are aspects of domestic development; I pursue them in Chapter Three. But there are other, antecedent stories, about how the meanings of space were tested and how their agencies were explored *before* they came to be fully realized in performances of hierarchy and exclusion. My interest in these earlier processes accounts for my emphasis on the accidental effects of new structures.

Not unrelatedly, the dominant discourse of this book is economic. Thus, in Chapter Two I quarrel with conventional narratives of the Great Rebuilding, which begin with evidence for household expansion rather than with the proliferation of domestic goods that is evident in the same probate inventories used to document room counts. The underlying logic of most architectural histories is that those who had more chambers required more possessions to fill them. But we may have gotten the causal relationship for these two phenomena exactly backwards: instead I would suggest that early moderns began to accumulate more personal possessions and then needed more spaces in which to keep them. Except in such eccentric cases as long galleries, rooms were given definition by their furnishings. So, the specialization of function that is often remarked for Renaissance homes may have followed from the particularization of purpose for different kinds of tables, chairs, and, especially, chests. Similarly, in Chapter Five, I emphasize profit motives among the London aldermen rather than their desire to contain disorder; in Chapter Seven, the business success of Alice Barnham as key to her private authority; in Chapter Eight, the closet as an overgrown chest, more implicated in the anxiety to secure valuables than in any wish to establish the personal privilege of solitude.

To set out to write a 'history of powers' is also substantially to predispose the gendering of the results, and one important aim of the book is to tell history through early modern women as much as through men. The case study of Alice Barnham does not recover an 'ordinary' life; she, her husband, and her sons were too successful and too wealthy for that. But nonetheless she can be located in the stratum of society known as 'middling', and in fact the family biography is threaded through with decisions made in disdain

---

[6] Michel Foucault, 'The Eye of Power', in *Power/Knowledge: Selected Interviews and Other Writings, 1972–1977*, ed. and trans. Colin Gordon (New York: Pantheon, 1980), 149.

of the sorts of status of which history has most often taken note. Francis Barnham's first career placement was in the Royal Household with the Lord Steward, but he left a life at court determined to become a merchant instead. Francis and Alice married their son Martin into a family whose principal member, Edward Wotton, had notoriously rejected a knighthood even though it was strenuously urged upon him by Elizabeth I; he preferred his provincial independence to palace attendance. Insisting that his merit was sufficient, Martin Barnham himself refused to purchase a knighthood as so many others did when James VI came to the English throne. By that time, the widowed Alice had already declined her own opportunity to become a Lady by making a second marriage with the prosperous Sir Thomas Ramsey. To these reasons the Barnhams have not been better known we can add that they were rich but not phenomenally rich, important but not exceptionally important, controversial but not outrageously controversial, and philanthropic but not famously philanthropic. Francis Barnham escapes mention even in urban histories of sixteenth-century London. He never achieved the position below which scholarly attention seems rarely to dip, that of Lord Mayor, having died before the usual rotations of aldermanic seniority brought him to that office (and thus to the knighting that would routinely have been awarded).

If Alice Barnham's life cannot be said to have been ordinary, it may yet be termed in many ways representative. Here, her story is built out of the institutions that shaped it, and in this has broad implications for other middling-sort women of the sixteenth century. Alice Barnham was not the only city wife to attend livery-company dinners, to read the admonitory legends of malefactors at the Cheapside pillory, to foster an orphaned child, or to partner in her family's advancement. The nature and events of urban life that are detailed here, as matters of public record, are evidence that others shared Alice's mental and material worlds. Those in search of historical significance will note that she and her husband were at the center of many epochal events and developments. She was an early adherent of the new religion, faithful even during the trying reign of Mary I; Francis profited from trade in an increasingly cash-based economy; the couple were beneficiaries of the redistribution of church properties that followed from the Reformation; they used their city fortune to achieve country-house gentility for their firstborn son. Their biographies can be fitted into influential arguments regarding the rise of the middle class, the origins of a proto-capitalist economy, the growth of individualism, the role of literacy in culture—and also, here, the uneven progress of personal privacies. At the same time, however, they cannot be fully contained by such arguments. In the astonishing amount of information that has survived about them, the Barnhams exceed conventional historical paradigms. The thick description of succeeding chapters goes to show how complicated their lives were, how particularized, and how unconformable to any number of well-established theories about early modern society and the boundaries between public and private spheres, the regulatory interests of city fathers, and, especially, the role of women. This book aims to make early moderns knowable in ample and specific ways and thus to constitute an argument about the politics of detail.

Finally, though, the life of Alice Barnham is of historiographic value not only because its ingredients were not peculiar to her but also because it is *accidental*: she had made no previous claim on our attention. For those who have accepted that women were confined to what is imagined to have been a strictly delimited and infungible private sphere, it is all the more corrective that the life of Alice Barnham, as indeed the central argument about privacy in this book, proceeds from public records. The heart of the project is in the churchwardens' accounts for St Clement Eastcheap, the minute books of the London Drapers' Company, the repertories of the London Court of Aldermen, the reports of the royal Court of Exchequer, the records of Bridewell and St Thomas's Hospital, the property surveys of Christ's Hospital and the Clothworkers' Company, the deposition books of various Consistory Courts, and other institutional papers. Not all of these are public in a technical sense, as being housed in the National Archives or a county records office; the Drapers' accounts, for example, are still held in Company hands. But they are nonetheless of a different category of document from the sort that were generated in a domestic context, by members of a family, for personal use.

Diaries and autobiographies are problematic not only for their demographic biases but also for their relative scarcity—though the two types of narrowness are not unrelated. There is a material connection between the status of diarists and the survival of their diaries, because great aristocratic families had evidence rooms and attics in which many sorts of papers have been preserved. It is telling that while a providential narrative authored by Alice Barnham's son Martin is lost, the family memoir of her grandson is recoverable (even if only in later copies); he was the first in his family to establish himself in a country house inherited by members of his direct line. In fact, records of all classes have spatial histories. Institutions like the Drapers' Company, the Corporation of London, or the Consistory Courts had their own muniments storage, and in the comparative security of the more public sphere an astonishing wealth of documents was protected. Much of this project has been a simple matter of going where such records remain, to learn what they have to say on topics for which they have been underexploited.

FINDING THINGS OUT

Had the title not already been taken, this book might have been called 'The Pleasure of Finding Things Out'.[7] Again it is a phenomenon that can be located in two registers. On the one hand, there is the pleasure of the past, vividly communicated in witness testimonies to alert observations, accidental overhearings, and all the violations of privacy with which this study is occupied. The social mandate for mutual surveillance gave full license to early moderns indulging their inquisitiveness about others. On the other hand, there is my pleasure in the present, as I found answers to so many of my questions about the vanished particulars of Tudor daily life.

I wanted to know what book Martin Barnham was reading in the family painting, what dinner was served to Alice Barnham on 15 November 1569, what it meant to Francis Barnham that he was a governor of the 'bawdy' hospital, what happened to a foundling left on the Barnham doorstep, and what was inscribed on the lost monument that once stood in their parish church of St Clement Eastcheap. I was curious about the purposes Bess of Hardwick found in building, what Tobias Robinson saw through the peephole into Thomas Towne's kitchen, what the fourth Duke of Norfolk said to Roberto Ridolfi in his long gallery, and what Richard Bellasis hid in the wall by his stairs. I discovered that Francis Barnham was a sociable man as well as a successful one, that Barbara Champion was a forceful woman, that Sir Warham Sentleger had a vindictive streak, and that Alice Barnham was as capable of keeping her own counsel as her portrait suggests. I encountered countless readjustments to some unthinking assumptions: for example, that election to the lord mayorship of London represented not a level of personal popularity but rather a mere advancement in aldermanic seniority, that there were many men besides Thomas Gresham who deserved credit for the Royal Exchange (Francis Barnham among them), that the desperate need of landed gentlemen for ready cash was a nearly irresistible incitement to usury in the period, that while sixteenth-century women had lost the old medieval monopoly on silkwork there were still some who flourished in the trade, and that privacy was not always an object of desire.

The pleasures that I have indulged attach to the purpose of honoring under-represented lives: by depicting how richly textured they were, by illustrating how much more information has survived about them (especially in public records) than we have been led to believe, and by demonstrating some ways

---

[7] Richard P. Feynman, *The Pleasure of Finding Things Out: The Best Short Works of Richard P. Feynman*, ed. Jeffrey Robbins (Cambridge, Mass.: Perseus, 1999).

in which research in this period can proceed from evidence as well as from intuition. The political convictions that underlie much contemporary theory have been essential in provoking us to concern ourselves with the occupations and preoccupations of ordinary people and everyday existence. Theory is also vital for bridging gaps left in the historical record. Sometimes, though, we anticipate gaps that do not exist, and so resort to abstract theory, which is by its nature generalizing, when we might persist in the search for particularizing evidence. Thus, while theory has informed my approach, showing me how to read closely and also, often, against the grains of my documents, I find that they lead me to quarrel with some of theory's most familiar paradigms, especially about gender and power. Finally, this will read like a records-based study, densely argued as a matter of principle, to show how complex early modern lives were and how inductive it is possible to be even about the foreign country of the Tudor past. Much remains to be rediscovered, if we open unfamiliar doors.

1

The Search for Lady Ingram

I was born the 7 of September on a Sunday 1523, turned from that I was
unto that ye see Anno Domani 1557.

So READS the central legend of a portrait known as 'Lady Ingram and her
Two Boys', one of the earliest family groups from England (see Fig. 1.1).
Positioned over the head of each of the painting's persons is a textual plaque.
The labels for the children could be entries in a family chronicle: 'Martin
was born the 26 of March at 9 of the clock before noon in Anno Domani
1548', and 'Steven was born the 21 of July on a Sunday at night and 10 of
the clock Anno Domani 1549'.[1] The inscription for the principal figure seems
to abbreviate her own natal history in order to hint instead that an occasion
motivated this painting, although the precise nature of the 'turn' of 1557 goes
unspecified. And while the use of the first-person singular produces the effect
of an authorizing subjectivity, it serves also to suppress the sitter's identity.
Thus an apparent act of self-display is in the end an act of self-ambiguation.

Those who have been content with her traditional denomination of 'Lady
Ingram'—though I am not one of them—assume that her mysteries can be
solved in speculation about the unseen 'Lord Ingram'. Where, they ask, is
this family's husband and father? The nameless 'I' wears black; perhaps she
has been recently widowed. 'Martin' holds open a Book of Proverbs printed
in the vernacular, and the date of the painting falls between 1553 and 1558;
it may be that Lord Ingram was a reformist refugee to Europe, a Marian

---

[1] Inscriptions are corrected from *600 Years of British Painting: The Berger Collection at the
Denver Art Museum* (Denver: Denver Art Museum and the W. M. B. Berger Charitable Trust,
1998), 45 (where Lady Ingram's birthday is mistakenly given as '30 September' rather than
'7 of September'). In private conversation, Caroline Barron points out that the syntax was
traditional in family Books of Hours. See also the earliest surviving English sampler, worked by
Jane Bostocke in 1598: 'Alice Lee was born the 23 of November being Tuesday in the afternoon
1596' (Donald King and Santina Levey, *The Victoria and Albert Museum's Textile Collection:
Embroidery in Britain from 1200 to 1750* (London: V&A Publications, 1993), fig. 47). For the
opportunity to study the portrait, I am grateful to Berger Collection Curator Timothy Standring
and his former assistant, Anne Odell.

Figure 1.1 One of the earliest family group portraits from England, known as 'Lady Ingram and Her Two Boys'. Dated 1557. Inscribed 'STEVĒ WAS BORNE THE .21. | OF IVLI ON A SONDAY AT | NIGHTE AND .10. OF THE CLOKE | Å. DŇI .1549.'; 'I WAS BORNE THE .7. OF SᴱPTEMBER | ON A SONDAY .1523. TORNID | FRŌ THAT I WAS VNTO THAT | YE SE. Å. DŇI 1557.'; and 'MARTIN WAS BORNE THE .26. | OF MARCHE AT .9. OF THE | CLOKE BEFORE NOVNE IN | Å DŇI 1548.'

exile. Cataloguers for the Denver Art Museum, where the painting is now held, surmise that the inconjugate woman 'looks to her Protestant faith for guidance in raising her two young sons' on her own.[2] To test such conjectures, as this chapter does, is also to contest our assumptions about the contingent position of women in Tudor society. It is, further, to confront our limited expectations for what we can recover of individual female lives. Given the selective habits of the archives, with all their biases to fathers, husbands, and sons, an account of the missing Lord Ingram is necessarily a point of departure. But to make his biography an end point would be to subsume Lady Ingram's existence into that of her husband's as thoroughly as did the early modern doctrine of coverture. His absence from her life may not be the only way of accounting for his absence from her portrait.

Certainly Lady Ingram positions herself within the familial context to which the Denver cataloguers respond. She leans back slightly from the waist to yield a forward plane of the painting to her sons and, through the fall of her upper arms, to form the silhouette that integrates three clustered bodies into a single visual mass of consanguinity. But where we might have expected her to pull her children closer in a genealogically demonstrative embrace, her lower arms reach instead towards the paper before her. With this pose she asserts a double role for herself, penwoman as well as mother. On the unfolded sheet one line is legible, and she appears poised to begin another with a freshly dipped quill. In the foreground, projecting as far as possible into the sphere of the spectator, is an open case with its niches for reservoirs of ink, stores of paper, quills, and the tools for trimming them.[3] As a performer of literacy Lady Ingram seems also to confirm the meanings of her first-person address: she is patron in the project of portraiture, deviser of the painting's superimposed plaques, author (if only of something under seventy words), and incidental autobiographer. The painting's effects of independent agency are not at odds with her unpartnering.

The project to locate Lady Ingram's personal authority occupies this chapter and four others. Here, the first objects of inquiry are the obliquities she has herself perpetrated in her portrait: the unstated name, the unacknowledged spouse, the unconventional pose, the unexplained 'turn', the undefined significance of 1557, the unshared thoughts. For all but the last there are things to be known, even if sometimes the knowable things do not resolve

---

[2] *600 Years of British Painting*, 45.

[3] The writing case of tooled and gilded leather is a modest version of Henry VIII's leather-and-velvet covered writing box (*c.*1525), on view at the Victoria and Albert Museum and shown in Simon Thurley, *The Royal Palaces of Tudor England: Architecture and Court Life, 1460–1547* (New Haven: Yale University Press for the Paul Mellon Centre for Studies in British Art, 1993), 99 (fig. 130).

themselves into simple explanations. As for the ideas that seem to tremble, only just realized, at the nib of her quill—these will perdurably remain her secrets. 'Lady Ingram and her Two Boys' can be classified as a 'speaking' portrait, like others from the period, because of its narrativized plaques.[4] But the painting seems to aspire also to be a 'thinking' portrait, and in this is more extraordinary. Capturing that pregnant moment just before contemplation is realized through articulation, 'Lady Ingram and her Two Boys' strives to represent its subject's experience of interiority. In its blend of the forthcoming and the withholding, the painting is an undiscovered locus of privacy for the Tudor era.

A MISLABELED LADY

The search for 'Lady Ingram' begins with five clues to her identity. Three of these are the biographical plaques which, infra-red reflectography proves, were original to the portrait.[5] For Lady Ingram, the authentication is ultimately of little consequence. Her birth predates the 1538 regulation for documenting baptisms, marriages, and deaths in English parish registers, those most useful sources for genealogical research.[6] With the loss of her name to her first-person mode of address, the plaque offers little help in the mission to rediscover her. The same cannot be said, however, for those of her sons. These contain the crucial information of two given names and two birth dates which fall within the compass of the earliest surviving church registers.

The fourth clue is external to the painting but closely allied with it, a strip of paper once affixed to the back of the wooden panel. This seems to have been lost in 1998, a year in which the portrait came up for sale at Christie's among the 'principal contents' of a Kentish manor house called Boughton Monchelsea Place, was purchased by William and Bernadette Berger for their extraordinary collection of British paintings, was deposited in the Denver Art

[4] Douglas Chambers, ' "A speaking picture": Some Ways of Proceeding in Literature and the Fine Arts in the Late-Sixteenth and Early-Seventeenth Centuries', in John Dixon Hunt (ed.), *Encounters* (London: Studio Vista, 1971), 28–57. For this reference I am grateful to Tarnya Cooper.

[5] Three textual forms are simulated in the portrait: engraving on the plaques, printing in Martin's book, and handwriting on Lady Ingram's sheet of paper. With some overpainting evident, especially on the last, Timothy Standring and Jessica Fletcher, Denver Art Museum Conservator, authorized and conducted the test of the plaques' authenticity.

[6] In 1538 Thomas Cromwell ordered all baptisms, marriages, and burials recorded. In 1598 all registers were ordered recopied on parchment, with the option of going back only to 1558 (F. G. Emmison, *Archives and Local History*, 2nd edn. (Chichester: Phillimore, 1974), 52).

Museum, and in the course of its travels underwent restoration to correct for the pronounced bowing of its boards. According to the Denver catalogue, the lost tag identified 'Grandmother, Lady Ingram and her two boys'. Christie's has preserved a photograph of the label, and in fact it read, in a seventeenth-century scrawl, 'Great Grandmother Lady Ingram & her two Boys'.[7] This is of course the source of the name that has been given to the portrait, but it is important to note that it is one generation further removed from the subjects than is generally known.

The fifth clue is the painting's place of origin, Boughton Monchelsea, located near Maidstone in Kent (see Fig. 1.2). Until the portrait was auctioned off in 1998, it hung in the front staircase there. Boughton is a medieval house that was greatly expanded by its Tudor owner, Robert Rudston. Rudston's is the first of three family names from its early modern history. When his son died without a male heir in 1613, Boughton passed to his daughter's child, Sir Francis Barnham. Barnham's granddaughter, who inherited the house in 1685, married a man named Rider, and there were Riders in residence until 1887. The portrait could have come to Boughton at any time between its completion in the mid-sixteenth century and photographic records of it on the main stairs in the mid-twentieth. One owner enlarged the Boughton collection of paintings as recently as 1923, for example.[8] With so few clues, however, it is nonetheless worth investigating whether the history of the painting could have coincided with those of the house and its Rudston, Barnham, and Rider occupants.

In 1786, Boughton was inherited by Ingram Rider, a name which in itself testifies to important connections between an early family in possession of the great house and the family of name on the portrait. The association can be traced back to the 1660s, when Arthur Ingram, as a 42-year-old widower in London, married the 17-year-old Anne Lowfield, and when Anne's widowed mother Hannah, 38, soon thereafter became the second wife of Sir Robert Barnham. Sir Robert, then 47, was heir to the house's first Barnham, father-in-law to its first Rider, and kin to an Ingram. The last affiliation was probably

---

[7] I am grateful to Timothy Standring for his file notes on provenance. See also the Christie's South Kensington catalogue for 21 January 1998. Marijke Booth of the Christie's Archives Department kindly provided a photograph of the lost label.

[8] Thomas Philipot, *Villare Cantianum: or Kent Surveyed and Illustrated* (London: 1659), 84–5. Will of Belknap Rudston (3 June 1613), PROB 11/121, fos. 463ᵛ–464ᵛ. House guidebooks printed during the ownerships of Michael Winch and Charlie Gooch (I am grateful to Mr Gooch's secretary Jill Harris). Arthur Oswald, 'Boughton Monchelsea Place, Kent', *Country Life*, 20 June 1963: 1489–93 and 27 June 1963: 1552–5 (for which I am grateful to current owner Marice Kendrick). In private correspondence, Karen Hearn notes that a modern owner of Boughton collected many of its paintings, especially from the 1923 sale of the contents of Eyotes Court (Kent).

Figure 1.2 Boughton Monchelsea Place, near Maidstone in Kent. Built of hard local ragstone between 1551 and 1575 by Robert Rudston (and gothicized with new glazing and battlements around 1790, probably by Ingram Rider).

reinforced by later unions, as the name 'Ingram Rider' implies, and any Ingram who married into the family in possession of Boughton could have brought the painting along as an Ingram heirloom. But, inasmuch as the earliest Ingram with any tie to the house, Arthur, came from a line of sixteenth- and seventeenth-century Johns, Williams, and Roberts—not a Martin or Steven among them—it seems highly unlikely that he was descended from the 'Lady Ingram' of the portrait. Further, because the first Ingram to achieve a knighthood did so in 1613, there was in fact no 'Lady' Ingram until then. For these reasons, the complex kinships of the Ingrams and the Riders undoubtedly explain nothing more than the way in which the name 'Lady Ingram' came eventually to be attached to a portrait of someone else. Because the seventeenth-century tag added to the back of the painting cannot be reconciled to the sixteenth-century plaques that were original to it, in other words, the label constitutes yet another of those countless instances in which the descendants of early moderns misidentified and also falsely ennobled their ancestors.[9]

The histories of painting and house do intersect in 1613, when Boughton was inherited by Sir Francis Barnham. Sir Francis's father Martin Barnham was baptized in the London church of St Mildred Poultry on 27 March 1548, the day after the birth date inscribed for the 'Martin' of the painting. Martin Barnham's younger brother Steven was baptized, also in St Mildred Poultry, on 27 July 1549, six days after the birth date of the 'Steven' in the painting. The names are sufficiently unusual (especially in tandem), the dates sufficiently proximate (because there was always some delay between healthy birth and church baptism), and the connection with Boughton Monchelsea sufficiently strong that it is therefore possible for the first time to identify the 'two boys' of the portrait as Martin and Steven Barnham. The painting may have come to Boughton Monchelsea as early as 1613, when Martin's son took possession of the house, only for the central figure to be mislabeled by one of his many descendants as 'Lady Ingram'.[10] The name long lost is that of Alice Barnham.

[9] Standard genealogical sources make no reference to Tudor Ingrams named Martin or Steven. For Ingram-Lowfield-Barnham connections, see *London Marriage Licences, 1521–1869*, ed. Joseph Foster (London: Bernard Quaritch, 1887), 84, 742. For Sir Arthur Ingram (knighted 1664), see A. R. Maddison (ed.), *Lincolnshire Pedigrees*, Publications of the Harleian Society 51 (1903), 540–1. The more famous Sir Arthur Ingram, London's Controller of the Customs (knighted in 1613) had a father Hugh, brother William, and sons Arthur, John, Simon, and Thomas. Tarnya Cooper notes that Tudor portrait inscriptions 'are quite frequently unreliable and many date from at least three generations later' ('A Painting with a Past: Locating the Artist and the Sitter', in Stephanie Nolen (ed.), *Shakespeare's Face* (Toronto: Piatkus, 2002), 237).

[10] GL Ms 4429/1. Martin had eleven children and his heir Sir Francis, fourteen. I distinguish Francis Barnham from his grandson by referring to the latter as 'Sir Francis' throughout.

Alice Barnham was born into a large and important family in Chichester, West Sussex. Her mercer father, William Bradbridge, was three times mayor of this ancient cathedral city. Two of her brothers were high-ranking ecclesiasts. As one of the youngest of William's fourteen children, Alice grew up in a well-established tradition of civic prominence and public service which perfectly positioned her for her adult life.[11] She married Francis Barnham, a draper who became first Alderman and then, in 1570, Sheriff of London. As is further demonstrated below, his record of business and community activities in the 1550s suggests that he was in residence with his family throughout the reign of Mary I, when the portrait was painted, and he did not die until nearly twenty years afterwards, in 1576. The Barnhams had four children. In addition to Martin and Steven there were Anthony and Benedict, not shown in the portrait because they were not born until 1558 and 1559, respectively. The story of the two generations was a familiar one: Francis made a merchant fortune in London and Martin and Steven became country gentlemen. For the last quarter of the sixteenth century, Alice herself chose to remain a city widow. Having been born ten years to the day before Elizabeth I, she narrowly outlived the last of the Tudors, dying in May 1604 at the age of 80. Since only Martin and Steven survived her, the painting that shows the three of them together may have had a bittersweet resonance for her into the last years of her very long life.[12]

As an urban wife of the mid-sixteenth century, the historical Alice Barnham is immediately more remarkable than a mythical 'Lady Ingram' could ever have been. But her identity is not the last of her mysteries. Speculations about Francis Barnham's absence would seem to be discredited by the fact that he was certainly alive in 1557 and probably living in London. This does not mean there is nothing more to learn about her life from his career.

---

[11] Alice Bradbridge's brother Augustine was Chancellor (1560–2) and Treasurer (1562–7) of Chichester Cathedral. William the younger succeeded him as Chancellor (1562–71) until made Bishop of Exeter (1571–6); he was chosen to translate the Books of Moses for the Bishops' Bible. See William Bradbridge in the *Oxford DNB*; Steven Barnham in *The House of Commons, 1558–1603*; William Durrant Cooper, 'Former Inhabitants of Chichester', *Sussex Archaeological Collections* 24 (1872), 74; and Felicity Heal, 'Clerical Tax Collection under the Tudors: The Influence of the Reformation,' in Rosemary O'Day and Felicity Heal (eds.), *Continuity and Change: Personnel and Administration of the Church in England, 1500–1642* (Leicester: Leicester University Press, 1976), 97–113.

[12] Dates are: Francis, born *c*.1515, buried 23 May 1576; Alice, born 7 September 1523, buried 14 May 1604; Martin, baptized 27 March 1548, died 12 December 1610; Steven, baptized 27 July 1549, buried 18 January 1608; Anthony, baptized 18 March 1558, death date unknown; Benedict, baptized 2 June 1559, buried 27 April 1598. I am grateful to Carole Levin for noting that Alice Barnham shared a birthdate with Elizabeth Tudor.

THE DRAPER'S WIFE

If the private painting is emptied of any reference to Francis Barnham, the public records are gratifyingly full. He was affiliated with London establishments that left voluminous archives: not only the parish church of St Mildred Poultry (where he was churchwarden in 1554 and 1555) and, later, the parish church of St Clement Eastcheap (where in 1576 he was buried), but also the Company of Drapers (where he was made free of the city in 1541), Bridewell and St Thomas's Hospitals (where he sat on boards of governors in the 1560s and 1570s), and the Court of Aldermen (to which he was elected in 1568).[13] Corporate and institutional accounts document the civic standing that followed from Francis Barnham's entrepreneurial success.

In Tudor terms it was a 'new' life, the kind we associate with such conspicuous signs of ambition and achievement as the acquisition of property, an application for arms, a family chronicle, a portrait, a funerary monument.[14] All are aspects of Francis Barnham's life story, though he was himself absent from the painting of his wife and sons, and the memoir awaited a grandson. Around 1630, Sir Francis Barnham wrote a 'character' of his father Martin that throws off information about his grandfather Francis, as well.[15] Sir Francis

---

[13] A catastrophic loss is the Drapers' Court Minute Book for 1561–7 (apparently discarded for water damage). Other lost records include Tudor churchwardens' accounts and vestry minutes for St Mildred Poultry and St Clement Eastcheap; city apprenticeship records destroyed by fire in 1786 (except for a rare contemporary copy of registers for 1551–3, when Barnham freed his first apprentice; see *Register of Freemen in the City of London in the Reigns of Henry VIII and Edward VI*, ed. Charles Welch (London: London and Middlesex Archaeological Society, 1908), 107); membership rosters for the Common Council in the 1550s and 1560s; Sheriff's Court Rolls for 1570–1; Bridewell Minute Books for June 1562 to March 1574 (also incomplete during Barnham's first term as governor); early Merchant Adventurers' Company accounts (apparently transferred to a European head office; see Jean M. Imray, 'The Merchant Adventurers and their Records', in Felicity Ranger (ed.), *Prisca Munimenta: Studies in Archival and Administrative History Presented to Dr. A. E. J. Hollaender* (London: University of London Press, 1973), 229–39, and Anne F. Sutton, 'The Merchant Adventurers of England: Their Origins and the Mercers' Company of London', *Historical Research* 75 (2002), 25–46); and early accounts of the Russia Company (destroyed in 1666; see T. S. Willan, *The Early History of the Russia Company, 1553–1603* (Manchester: Manchester University Press, 1956), pp. v, 19). The Treasurer's Week Book of St Thomas's Hospital for 1569 is inaccessible at this writing, pending conservation.

[14] See e.g. Lawrence Stone, *The Crisis of the Aristocracy, 1558–1641* (Oxford: Clarendon, 1965), esp. 712–13.

[15] 'A Copy of an Original Manuscript of Sir Francis Barnham, Knight' was edited by T. Barrett Lennard from an eighteenth-century copy now in the Essex Record Office, Ms D/DL/229; see *The Ancestor* 9 (1904), 191–209. Subsequent references are to my edition, 'The Character of Sir Martin Barnham', incorporating readings from a seventeenth-century copy, Ms Bodley 10, in James Dutcher and Anne Lake Prescott (eds.), *Renaissance Historicisms* (Newark: University of Delaware Press, 2008).

represented himself as an oral historian, gathering family legends from his grandmother, father, and uncles. The first of his sources was Alice Barnham.

On Francis Barnham's tomb, Alice recorded that her husband was aged 60 when he died in 1576.[16] Thus he was born in 1515 or 1516. His father Steven self-identified as a yeoman in his will. According to his great-grandson, Steven had been Groom of the Privy Chamber to Henry VIII, but the family estate was depreciated when he took a second wife 'merely for love'. By Sir Francis's standards, thus, Francis received but a 'small portion'. He was placed in the Royal Household with the Lord Steward but, again in the words of Sir Francis, found this to be 'a slow way of preferment'. Within two years Francis Barnham left the Court of Henry VIII and apprenticed himself to a London draper.[17] It would seem that he had recognized both the surer source of liquid wealth in early modern society and the ways in which power flowed from it.

With the Drapers' Company, Francis's record in the institutional archives commences. His first master was a man named William Pratt who died before the apprenticeship was completed. Francis was then 'set over', or transferred, to Richard Champion, an exemplary mentor. Champion, a member of the Merchant Adventurers' and North-West Passage Companies, was to serve as Master of the Drapers, Sheriff of London, and Lord Mayor of London, following which, as was customary, he was knighted. Francis was on pace to be elected mayor, and so to be knighted himself, when he died in 1576. His younger brother Thomas followed him to London and was bound to Champion in his turn, but he was never to achieve comparable success. Thomas may have been less capable, but, Sir Francis notes, the second son also had the disadvantage of a smaller portion with which to launch a city career.[18]

---

[16] See n. 42.

[17] Will of Steven Barnham (28 October 1550), PROB 11/34, fos. 2^v–3^r. Sir Francis gives his great-grandfather the status of 'Esquire'. In surviving registers for 1551–3 (*Register of Freemen*), men from gentle and yeomen families represented 39 per cent of admissions to all city companies, 51 per cent to the twelve great companies, and 85 per cent to the Drapers' Company; many who made great fortunes were the second sons of country gentry (Steve Rappaport, *Worlds within Worlds: Structures of Life in Sixteenth-Century London* (Cambridge: Cambridge University Press, 1989), 24, 305–6, 308, 311). Barnham was placed at Court 'in the way of the green cloth'—that is, in service to the Steward of the Royal Household (*OED* for 'green cloth').

[18] Sir Francis says that his grandfather 'bound himself apprentice to a good merchant in London with whom he served out his years', but for Pratt's death in 1539 and Barnham's 'setting over', see Drapers' M.B.1/B, fo. 336^v, and *Roll of the Drapers' Company of London*, ed. Percival Boyd (Croydon: J. A. Gordon at the Andress Press, 1934), 148. For Champion, Alfred B. Beaven, *The Aldermen of the City of London*, 2 vols. (London: E. Fisher for the Corporation of the City of London, 1908–13), i. 92, 200, and ii. 35; and Tom Girtin, *The Triple Crowns: A Narrative History of the Drapers' Company, 1364–1964* (London: Hutchinson, 1964), 154–5. Barnham was of average age at binding (Rappaport, *Worlds*, 295, 297). As mayoral 'elections' were rotational rather than honorific, Barnham would have been elected mayor in 1578 had he lived (Frank Freeman Foster, *The Politics of Stability: A Portrait of the Rulers in Elizabethan*

Francis Barnham completed his apprenticeship on 23 November 1541 and took his oath on the Drapers' New Testament, with two of the Company's four wardens as witnesses. His brief tenure in the Royal Household had not delayed him beyond the usual age for being made free of the city; he was 25 or 26 when he became 'Francis Barnham, citizen and draper' and was enfranchised both politically and economically.[19] Livery companies were far from restrictive in the careers they sheltered; in Drapers' records, for example, we find a member of the fellowship 'occupying bookbinding'. The Company's chief attraction was not an association with the cloth trades but instead its corporate stature, third in the city following the Mercers and Grocers, and thus a superior power base for an ambitious man.[20]

For his part, Francis was among those described by the Drapers as 'no retailer'. He was also a member of the Merchant Adventurers' Company, which prohibited him from keeping an 'open shop or showhouse'. Hence he was one of 327 merchants in London (by John Strype's count for 1561), and he shared in outfitting ships and negotiating trade agreements with others who 'ventured' their goods and capital outside England. Export seems to have been a fairly exclusive focus throughout his career; he was not named among the importers in a surviving port book for 1567 and 1568, for example, and the Surrey and Hampshire clothiers he remembered in his will were probably suppliers for goods he sold abroad. Though Sir Francis emphasized that his grandfather 'had a very extraordinary reputation in those foreign parts where he traded', this did not necessarily involve him in international travel—except

London (London: Royal Historical Society, 1977), 63; Ian W. Archer, *The Pursuit of Stability: Social Relations in Elizabethan London* (Cambridge: Cambridge University Press, 1991), 21; and Beaven, *Aldermen*, ii. 38–40). Sir Francis notes Thomas's smaller portion. Francis bypassed Bachelor offices, proceeding directly to the livery's Court of Assistants, his brother did not (Drapers' M.B.7, p. 38). Thomas was nominated to the livery in 1559 (M.B.7, p. 149) but achieved no higher status.

   [19] Drapers' W.A.3, 1541–2, fo. 1[r]. Entry fees were 3s. 4d. to the Wardens, 8d. to the Clerk, and 4d. to the Beadle (A. H. Johnson, *The History of the Worshipful Company of the Drapers of London*, 5 vols. (Oxford: Clarendon, 1914–22), ii. 74). Freedom involved 'paying scot [taxes] and bearing lot [office-holding]' (Rappaport, *Worlds*, 36). Men were generally not admitted before the age of 26 (ibid. 49, and see 295, 297). Valerie Pearl estimates for the seventeenth century that 75 per cent of London's adult male householders were freemen ('Change and Stability in Seventeenth-Century London', *London Journal* 5 (1979), 13–14).

   [20] Drapers' W.A.5, 1569–70, fo. 8[v] for the bookbinder, and note there 'hosiers and tailors of this Company' and another draper 'occupying [em]broidery,' fos. 7[r], 9[r]; see M.B.1/B, fo. 314[r] for drapers' apprentices complaining they had not been taught 'to sew and shape'. For the Drapers, see Johnson, *History*; Girtin, *Triple Crowns*; and N. B. Harte (ed.), *The New Draperies in the Low Countries and England, 1300–1800* (Oxford: Oxford University Press, 1997). On 'occupational mobility' and the appeal of the great companies, see Rappaport, *Worlds*, 110–17, 96, 303. Some merchants rose to civic standing in lesser companies, but as their careers advanced they might switch affiliation to one of the greater ones for its advantages of material and human resources (Frank Foster, *Politics*, 44).

perhaps during his apprenticeship. Thereafter, he would have dispatched his own apprentices as factors, or commercial agents.[21]

In 1553, Francis joined 239 other Londoners in financing what Sebastian Cabot promoted as an attempt 'to discover isles and lands unknown'. Gentlemen may have held ambitions to explore and colonize, but merchants such as Barnham concentrated on commerce. The expedition eastwards aimed less at the import of Oriental goods than at the discovery of new export markets, and it succeeded in opening trade relations with Muscovy. According to Richard Hakluyt, English goods had been found to be 'in small request with the countries and people about us and near unto us', but Russia was even less commercially advanced, fertile ground for the re-export of European wines, spices, cloths, and paper products. In 1555 the Muscovy adventurers incorporated as the Russia Company, with Francis Barnham as a charter member. Later, in 1562, members of the Company inaugurated the trafficking of African slaves in the West Indies.[22]

Sir Francis writes that 'shortly' after Francis was made free of the city, 'he married Alice Bradbridge'. It may instead have been a matter of several years. The ceremony most likely took place in her home parish in Chichester, for which surviving church registers date back only to 1558. She was a single woman in October 1543, when her father wrote a will requiring his eldest son to contribute £10 towards her marriage portion. This will was not emended before William Bradbridge's death in 1546. That Francis and Alice may have

---

[21] Drapers' M.B.7, p. 163. For Barnham's commercial profile, see T. S. Willan, *The Muscovy Merchants of 1555* (Manchester: Manchester University Press, 1953), 46, 79. John Strype, *A Survey of the Cities of London and Westminster . . . Written at First in the Year MDXCVIII by John Stow*, 2 vols. (London: 1720), ii. 291. Drapers were wardens of the Merchant Adventurers' Company (Girtin, *Triple Crowns*, 85). For their ordinances see W. E. Lingelbach, 'The Internal Organisation of the Merchant Adventurers of England', *Transactions of the Royal Historical Society* NS 16 (1902), 19–67; for their dominance of overseas trade, Robert Brenner, *Merchants and Revolution: Commercial Change, Political Conflict, and London's Overseas Traders, 1550–1653* (Princeton: Princeton University Press, 1993). See also *The Port and Trade of Early Elizabethan London: Documents*, ed. Brian Dietz, London Record Society 8 (1972); and Dietz, 'Overseas Trade and Metropolitan Growth', in A. L. Beier and Roger Finlay (eds.), *London, 1500–1700: The Making of the Metropolis* (London: Longman, 1986), 115–40. On factors, see Willan, *Studies in Elizabethan Foreign Trade* (Manchester: Manchester University Press, 1959), 4, 12.

[22] *CPR: Philip and Mary*, ii. *1554–1555*, 55–9. For Barnham in the Russia Company, see Richard Hakluyt, *The Principal Navigations, Voyages, Traffiques, and Discoveries of the English Nation*, 12 vols. (Glasgow: James MacLehose, 1903–5), iii. 108–18; Hakluyt quotes Clement Adams on English trade woes on the Continent, ii. 239. See also Willan, *The Early History of the Russia Company*, and Elspeth M. Veale, *The English Fur Trade in the Later Middle Ages*, 2nd edn., London Record Society 38 (2003). On the motives for ventures, see Theodore K. Rabb, *Enterprise and Empire: Merchant and Gentry Investment in the Expansion of England, 1575–1630* (Cambridge, Mass.: Harvard University Press, 1967), esp. 35. Barnham was an Assistant of the Russia Company in 1569 (*Muscovy Merchants*, 79). On the slave trade, see Hakluyt, *Principal Navigations*, x. 7–8.

wed as late as 1546 or 1547 is probably confirmed by the birth of their first son, Martin, in 1548. Francis would have been 31 or 32 at the time, old enough to have been married before or to have spent several years on the Continent (though Sir Francis mentions neither possibility). Alice would have been 23 or 24, a not untypical age for first marriage in a woman of her class.[23] Describing the Bradbridge family as 'about that time extinct in the heirs male, and the estate in a manner wholly spent or transferred to daughters', Sir Francis may have been overeager to exonerate his grandfather from the charge of himself marrying 'merely for love'. At least three of Alice's six brothers were still alive. Still, the match was far from impractical. Francis and Alice commenced their married life with a joint, total worth of £1,000. By the time of Francis's death the couple had achieved rental incomes of £1,000 annually and in addition a 'great personal estate' of movable assets (according to Sir Francis).[24]

In a first formal recognition of this aptitude for earning, Francis Barnham was admitted to wear the Drapers' livery on 9 July 1550. At the time there were fifty-five livery men, or drapers of substance (and three times as many yeomen, or small traders and journeymen). The numbers of the livery were in decline, and by 1558, with just forty-three, the Drapers were increasingly concerned at the 'sore decay' of those willing to assume administrative roles, invest in Company activities, and answer calls for assessments and loans. Francis Barnham not only drew upon the standing of the Company but also, in his growing wealth and ability, helped sustain it.[25] In 1554, he was chosen

[23] Will of William Bradbridge (13 October 1543), WSRO STC 1/5, fo. 90. *The House of Commons, 1558–1603* (for Benedict Barnham) repeats a false genealogy that Alice was the widow of a man named Marnay at marriage to Francis Barnham; this may reflect confusion with the 1604 marriage of Francis Barnham (probably the son of Thomas Barnham) to the widow Anne Muns (*London Marriage Licences, 1521–1869*, 84). In 1556 the London aldermen complained of those who 'marry themselves as soon as ever they come out of their apprenticehood'; Rappaport says most waited two or three years (*Worlds*, 326, 327). If Francis had a prior marriage, it was childless. According to Sir Francis his great-grandfather came from Barnham in Suffolk and his great-grandmother from Hampshire; Barnham willed funds to improve roads near Southwick in Hampshire but nothing for Suffolk. Curiously, the Sussex town of Barnham is just a few miles from Chichester, and a merchant family of that name lived in Chichester in mid-century (see WSRO CHICTY/AY/122). William Bradbridge had connections there, leaving the Barnham parsonage lease to his son Nicholas and a vestment to the parish church.

[24] Augustine Bradbridge's will was proved in 1567 (WSRO STC 1/10, fo. 326ᵛ); Nicholas Bradbridge's, in 1548 (WSRO STC 7, fo. 57). William the younger died in 1578. Willan values Barnham's personal property at probate as worth more than £2,200 (*Muscovy Merchants*, 79).

[25] Drapers' M.B.4, fos. 73ᵛ, 74ʳ; Girtin, *Triple Crowns*, 128. 'Originally a fraternity of equals', the Drapers 'gradually became divided into a privileged Livery and an aspiring Yeomanry', notes former Company archivist A. K. Sierz (in his MS calendar of Drapers' holdings, p. 33). Yeomen (or Bachelors), were householders (shopkeepers) and journeymen; Rappaport observes that the lines could have been drawn differently (liverymen and householders as against journeymen, *Worlds*, 221); this would have been to a less oligarchic effect. He estimates that two-thirds of

one of the Drapers' Renters, responsible for collecting rents on the Company's extensive holdings, authorizing expenditures for needed repairs, securing building materials 'at the most advantage', and overseeing other property maintenance. Renters retained Company income as a fund from which to make disbursements, but the office required Barnham to be sufficiently liquid to cover expenses if they outpaced earnings.[26]

On 6 August 1558, Richard Champion presided over the meeting in which the Company elite selected their master and four wardens for the following year, naming Francis Barnham as most junior officer. By tradition, the Third Warden was a man who had never been preferred to office before, and the Fourth was chosen for his unusual potential from among 'the younger sort of the livery'. From this point forward, Francis was a life member of the Drapers' Court of Assistants, the executive body of the Company which enrolled new apprentices, supervised admissions to the freedom of the city by patrimony and redemption as well as by apprenticeship, and selected those who were elevated to the livery. The Assistants were responsible for arbitrating disputes between members of the Company and between masters and apprentices, punishing misbehavior, and organizing Company dinners. They monitored business standards in the city, surveyed Company goods and properties, awarded tenancies, administered charities, and, on demand, provided the Crown with food subsidies and armed soldiers. In 1560 and 1564, Francis audited the Wardens' Accounts. In 1566 he was selected First Warden of the Drapers.[27]

Francis's muscular administrative career with the Drapers proceeded from his growing wealth. The Company had more worries than a shrinking livery:

all liverymen achieved leadership in their companies (ibid. 359). Decline of the livery has been attributed to civic duties, obligatory loans, and disaffection with oligarchy (Girtin, *Triple Crowns*, 129, 149; Johnson, *History*, ii. 71–2, 118). For a modifying view, see Joseph P. Ward, *Metropolitan Communities: Trade Guilds, Identity, and Change in Early Modern London* (Stanford: Stanford University Press, 1997), ch. 4. Barnham paid an extra fine (20s.) for entering the livery without having served as warden of the Bachelors (Johnson, *History*, ii. 193, 290, 303; Rappaport, *Worlds*, 227). Frank Foster describes the new popularity of 'office skipping', bypassing lower offices 'to accelerate rising to the higher ones' (*Politics*, 57).

[26] Drapers' M.B.5, fo. 32[r], M.B.6, fo. 10[r], and, for Barnham's records, Drapers' R.A.4, 1554–5. In January 1556 he and his fellow Renter John Broke made their accounting. See also Drapers' M.B.7, p. 211, and M.B.9, fo. 3[v] and, for the Renters' Oath, Johnson, *History*, ii. 292–3. In 1556 Renter William Beswicke was found in arrears, Drapers' M.B. 5, fo. 91[r].

[27] Drapers' M.B.7, pp. 102–3, 109; see also W.A.4, 1558–9. There were fifteen to thirty-five Assistants (present and former wardens) and about 570 liverymen and Bachelors (Johnson, *History*, ii. 194, 196). On wealth and seniority as prerequisites, see Rappaport, *Worlds*, 263, 354, 356; on the importance of mentors, ibid. 349. See also Johnson, *History*, ii. 217–18. For Barnham's audits, see Drapers' W.A.4, 1559–60, and W.A.5, 1563–4. The Minute Book for Barnham's First Wardenship has not survived (although the Wardens' Accounts do, Drapers' W.A.5, 1566–7).

while the top-ranked Mercers had ninety-nine merchants, the second-ranked Grocers had fifty-seven, and the fourth-ranked Haberdashers had fifty-one, the third-ranked Drapers had only twenty-nine merchants in 1561. For so powerful a fellowship, the competitive field was surprisingly small; Barnham's rise was correspondingly swift. In the records for various levies and loans, where drapers were listed by seniority but assessed by financial capability, Barnham's fiscal precocity was conspicuous. While still a liveryman, in 1556, he gave one pound 'for the erection of Bridewell to be a house of occupations for the poor'; the only others to contribute as much were members of the Court of Assistants. For a loan to Philip and Mary in 1558, when Barnham had not yet been elected Fourth Warden, he paid even more than many Assistants, supplying fifty pounds. In short order, moreover, he was also a leading financial figure citywide. In Privy Council records of loans 'taken up in the same city to her Majesty's use' in 1570, he was one of London's fifteen most affluent and responsive civic leaders. A royal bond was payable to Francis Barnham in the amount of £1,278 in mid-1570 (by late-1571, interest brought the Crown's debt to him to £1,432).[28]

Men such as Barnham launched their municipal careers as churchwardens, a role Francis served in the parish of St Mildred Poultry from 1554 to 1556.[29] The next important office for most merchants was a governorship in one of the three great charitable institutions that had been founded during the reign of Edward VI. Christ's Hospital housed and educated orphans; the other two were more notorious. The illnesses treated at St Thomas's Hospital were so often venereal that it was known as the 'bawdy' hospital, and Bridewell, established to correct and employ petty malefactors, prosecuted vice crimes especially and so was called the 'bawdy court'. Francis served the Bridewell from 1559 to 1561, St Thomas's Hospital from 1564 to 1570, Bridewell again from 1572 to 1574, and then St Thomas's from 1574 to 1576. At Bridewell he

---

[28] For the number of merchants see Strype, *Survey*, 291. Rappaport confirms that Company assessments were progressive (*Worlds*, 276–7). For wheat and corn assessments of one pound in 1551, one mark in 1554, and five marks in 1560, see Drapers' M.B.1/C, fo. 505^r; M.B.5, fo. 27^v; M.B.7, p. 253. For the Bridewell, Drapers' W.A.4, 1555–6, fo. 4^{r-v}. For the loans, Drapers' M.B.7, p. 78, and W.A.4. 1557–8, fos. 14^v–15^r; for the bonds issued every six months for two years (£1,278 on 1 December 1569, £1,261 10s. on 16 May 1570, £1,351 on 22 December 1570, £1,432 on 31 May 1571), see *Acts of the Privy Council of England*, ed. John Roche Dasent et al., 32 vols. (London: HMSO, 1890–), viii. 53–60; CLRO Rep. 17, fo. 89^v. Benbow interprets this as four bonds totaling £5,342 (rather than a single loan extended with a partial repayment in 1570 and then with compiled interest), but see Frank Foster, *Politics*, 138.

[29] GL Ms 4429/1. Barnham follows the career path charted by Nancy Lee Adamson, 'Urban Families: The Social Context of the London Elite, 1500–1603', University of Toronto Ph.D. dissertation (1983), 219. On churchwardens' duties, see Frank Foster, *Politics*, 31–2. For Barnham there were thirteen years between the freedom and the churchwardenship; Foster says the average was sixteen years (ibid. 69).

saw a steady stream of accused pimps, bawds, prostitutes, runaways, thieves, dice-players, and ruffians. Discipline was less an issue at St Thomas's, except with respect to the resident staff, and although the review of patient admissions, discharges, and work placements required constant attention, there was also a great deal of administration regarding the hospital's properties, fund-raising, and provisioning. As Treasurer of St Thomas's from 1567 to 1569, Francis paid employee salaries and maintained a 'Week Book' for rents received and supplies purchased.[30]

From the time he joined the Drapers' livery in 1550, Francis was also eligible for election to London's chief legislative body, the 212-member Common Council. This group set taxes, nominated two candidates for mayor (for review by the Crown), selected one of the city's two sheriffs (the Upper Sheriff was appointed by the mayor), and chose London's four members of Parliament. Because its own election records are sketchy for this period, it is difficult to know when Francis joined the Council, though he seems certainly to have been a member by October 1558, when he collected assessments known as 'fifteenths' for the Crown. In 1561 he represented four wards for a mayoral commission on poor relief, and he was explicitly identified as a Commoner on 12 January 1565, when he was named to the delegation of eight city officials who asked the Company of Merchant Taylors to cede their rights in a plot of land recently bequeathed them. The property joined on Lombard Street, for 'time out of mind' the established meeting place for merchants in the city, and all involved wished to maintain the 'ancient name' of that street for a burse 'to be more fair and costly builded in all points than is the Burse of Antwerp'. The petition failed, but the great enterprise went forward on

---

[30] On the significance of governorships, see Frank Foster, *Politics*, 60. Elections for all hospitals are recorded in the Christ's Hospital Court Minute Books, GL Ms 12806/1 and 12806/2; see also LMA H01/ST/A/001/001, H01/ST/A/001/002, and H01/ST/A/001/003; and CLRO Rep. 16, fo. 502[v] and Rep. 18, fo. 430[r]. John Howes, *A Brief Note of the Order and Manner of the . . . Three Royal Hospitals*, ed. William Lempriere (1582; London: privately printed, 1904); E. M. McInnes, *St Thomas' Hospital* (London: George Allen & Unwin, 1963); and F. G. Parsons, *The History of St Thomas's Hospital*, 3 vols. (London: Methuen, 1932). For St Thomas's, Barnham audited Treasurers' Week Books and purchased fish, butter, cheese (8 January 1563, LMA H01/ST/A/001/001, fo. 66[v]); beef and mutton (29 January 1563, H01/ST/D/01/001, fo. 149[r]); and wheat (29 January and 17 December 1569, H01/ST/D/01/002, fos. 108[r], 136[v]). St Thomas's was funded principally through rents from royal land grants. Barnham conducted property surveys, served on manor courts, and sold lumber (21 February 1564, H/01/ST/A/001/001, fo. 79[v]) and a wood 'to the most profit' (30 August 1568, H/01/ST/A/001/002, fo. 89[r]). The St Thomas's governor who was the most senior member of the Common Council was Treasurer (31 December 1561, H01/ST/A/001/001, fo. 43[r]). See H01/ST/A/001/002 for Barnham as Treasurer, paying staff; buying food, clothing, and medical and housekeeping supplies; and supervising building repairs. He was to 'disburse and lay out of his own purse . . . (if need shall so require)' (H01/ST/A/001/003, fo. 106[v]).

another site nearby. In 1566 Barnham contributed five pounds to the building of the Royal Exchange.[31]

Francis was last listed as a Common Councillor on 23 November 1568, just days before his election (on 14 December 1568) to the executive branch of government as Alderman for the ward of Farringdon Without the Walls. The city's twenty-six aldermen had preeminent authority for social order, good business practices, and public health. They enforced regulations from the Crown (especially regarding the raising of 'loans' and militia), monitored the urban population of strangers and foreigners, managed epidemics of the plague, fixed prices for bread and fish, supervised cloth sales, protected the interests of London orphans who were the children of free men, adjudicated disputes between trade companies, and punished libelers and transgressors. The economic skills of the aldermen were employed in provisioning the city, a sufficiently delicate business that the man who scouted for them in Northamptonshire in 1573 was advised to make his inquiries 'in the most secretest and politickest ways he can'.[32] In his first year on the Court Francis was delegated to call on the Earl of Leicester regarding a city appointment, to petition Lord Wentworth regarding Bridewell lands, to resolve a dispute between freemen waterbearers and foreign waterbearers, and to investigate the rental value of a deceased citizen's lands. Later, he consulted on the purchase of properties in Whitefriars, helped install protectionist regulations for the Company of Minstrels, and took part in an internal investigation of charges brought against other members of the Court. In the course of his years in office, he mediated dozens of two-party disputes.[33]

His ward, Farringdon Without, was the largest and most unruly in London, with a sizeable population of the poor in its crowded and troubled alleys. There,

---

[31] CLRO Journ. 17, fos. 100^r, 126^v, 127^r, 311^v. On the burse, see GL Ms 34010/1, pp. 154–61 (partially transcribed in Charles M. Clode, *The Early History of the Guild of Merchant Taylors*, 2 vols. (London: Harrison, 1888), i. app. 28); and Jean Imray, 'The Origins of the Royal Exchange', in Ann Saunders (ed.), *The Royal Exchange*, London Topographical Society 152 (1997), 20–35. For the Council, see Frank Foster, *Politics*, 50; Rappaport, *Worlds*, 174. For Barnham's contribution, CLRO Journ. 19, fo. 15^v.

[32] CLRO Rep. 16, fos. 413^r, 430^v; Drapers' M.B.8, fo. 54^v; and Beaven, *Aldermen*, i. 157, ii. 38. For a sample letter of election to the Court, see CLRO Journ. 17, fo. 99^r. On aldermen see Frank Foster, *Politics*, 37, 38, 50–3. Archer emphasizes that the legislative authority of the Council was 'circumscribed' by the aldermen (p. 19). See CLRO Rep. 18, fos. 59^v–60^r (8 September 1573) for provisions to be procured by grocer Blase Saunders (for whom see also Ch. 5).

[33] CLRO Rep. 16, fo. 458^r (22 March 1569) for Leicester, normally a matter for senior aldermen (Frank Foster, *Politics*, 82); Rep. 16, fos. 474^r, 474^v (10 May 1569, 17 May 1569) for the Bridewell; Rep. 16, fo. 504^{r-v} (21 September 1569) for the Waterbearers; Rep. 16, fo. 506^v (7 October 1569) for Pyke's land; Rep. 17, fo. 397^r (18 November 1572) for the Whitefriars; Rep. 18, fos. 170^r, 179^v–180^r (4 and 18 March 1573) for the Minstrels; Rep. 18, fo. 96^v (28 October 1573) for impropriety. Two members of the Court were generally assigned to mediate disputes and report back to the full board.

Francis convened courts of wardmote, presided over monthly inquests into vagrancy and disorder, and conducted regular perambulations. In February 1570, Francis Barnham and his deputies were explicitly required by the Court of Aldermen to use their 'good discretions and wisdom [to] take some good order' there. Under normal circumstances he might have presented Joan Muggleston at the Bridewell for being a 'common bawd', but in June he called her before his fellow aldermen in evidence of his disciplinary initiative. In January 1572 he summoned the principal landlords of his alleys to Guildhall. They were prohibited from replacing any tenants who died, so that normal attrition might work to depopulate their tenements. A few months later one of Barnham's constables was empowered to imprison men who refused to serve their turns at watch. In April 1573 Francis secured permission to build a new 'cage' or jail in his ward; in July he was authorized to lock up all the denizens of Salisbury Alley and Whitefriars who were found to 'offend and be disobedient to the rulers of the city'; in August he closed all the Salisbury Alley shops maintained by 'foreigners' (Londoners who were not citizens). Francis had life tenure as an alderman, but he also had a right of reassignment when vacancies arose on the Court. He owed Farringdon Without at least three years, and few men did as many. After five years, in September 1573, he finally executed his 'ancient prerogative' and switched to a quieter office, becoming alderman for Tower ward.[34]

The Drapers' Company preferred to draw its Masters from those members who were aldermen. Thus, in September 1569, immediately following his 1568 election to executive office, Francis was made Master of the Company and presided over the meetings of its Court of Assistants. He was tapped for a second term as Master in 1571.[35] In the intervening year he served as Upper Sheriff of London and Middlesex, chosen by Lord Mayor Sir Rowland

---

[34] On population in extramural parishes, Archer, *Pursuit*, 12–13. CLRO Rep. 16, fo. 529^v (9 February 1570) for Barnham's charge; Rep. 17, fos. 21^r, 24^v (6, 8 June 1570) for the bawd (see also on this subject Rep. 17, fo. 131^v); Rep. 17, fos. 425^r, 427^v, 428^r (15, 20 January 1572) for alley landlords Margaret Hawkins and (renowned philanthropist) Thomas Smith; Rep. 17, fo. 345^r (10 July 1572) for constables; Rep. 18, fo. 1^r (16 April 1573) for the cage; Rep. 18, fo. 48^r (23 July 1573) for jailings; Rep. 18, fo. 54^r (8 August 1573) for the shop shuttings. In 1573 Barnham surveyed 'the order and estate of the poor' in the Farringdon Without parish of St Sepulchre, Rep. 17, fo. 424^r (13 January 1573). For his 'ancient prerogative' to switch wards, see Rep. 18, fo. 74^r and, on 'translation', Beaven, *Aldermen*, i. 240–1. The term for Farringdon Without was originally two years (as for all other wards), but between 1479 and 1550 five men left without completing it; in 1550, the tenure was extended to three years because, says Beaven, of the 'difficulty of finding a suitable person for that Aldermanry' (ii. p. xxi). For the shorter tenures of others, including two aldermen who paid large fines (200 marks and £520) to be discharged of their duties entirely, see ibid. i. 156–7.

[35] Drapers' M.B.8, fos. 72^r–73^v, 156^v–158^r. Of more than 500 men who began their careers in the early 1550s, only fourteen became masters of their companies (Rappaport, *Worlds*, 359).

Heyward. Each sheriff chaired a court that adjudicated charges of trespass, theft, dishonest trade, and debt, and each supervised a compter, or debtors' prison. The office collected fines paid into its poor boxes and revenues generated by the city scavenger; during Francis's term scavenger Anthony Stringer defaulted and was threatened with imprisonment (even though Sir Thomas Gresham testified on his behalf). In addition to his judicial and enforcement responsibilities, a sheriff was required to attend all meetings of the legislative and executive branches of city government (the Court of Common Council and the Court of Aldermen, respectively), as well as those of the city's superior court, the Court of Hustings. As chief Officer of the Peace, he might be called upon for such matters of state as Francis's charge, 'by virtue of the Queen's Majesty's token', to retrieve from 'one Hide's house' papers that had belonged to Sir Thomas Revell.[36]

In the dense documentation of Francis Barnham's civic calendar, comparatively little remains concerning his merchant activities. His success may be best evidenced in the capital he was able to invest and compound through a steady program of land speculation in London, Middlesex, Surrey, Kent, Essex, Dorset, and Wales. In February 1565, for example, the Barnhams purchased the manor of Bobulo in Essex. They resold it just two weeks later to Sir William Cordell, Master of the Rolls for the Court of Chancery and a former member of Mary I's Privy Council. In October 1565, Francis and Alice bought other lands in Essex and then, a year and a half later, sold them to John Southcote, a justice of the Queen's Bench. In purchases in January and June 1568 they acquired the two manors of Bilsington in Kent. These they retained as Martin Barnham's principal legacy. In September 1569, Francis made Martin co-recipient of an enormous twenty-one-year grant of royal lands, rents, and tithes offered in consideration for reversion to the Crown of a property Francis co-owned with James Blount, Lord Mountjoy.[37]

Information also survives about the men Francis trained over the course of his career, though this, too, is incomplete. He took his first apprentice sometime

---

[36] Drapers' M.B.8, fos. 112^v, 121^r. *The Practise of the Sheriff's Court* (London: 1657); Thomas Lewis, *On the Constitution, Jurisdiction, and Practice of the Sheriffs' Courts of London* (London: A. Maxwell, 1833). See also CLRO Rep. 16, fo. 510^v (28 October 1569) for poor boxes; Rep. 17, fo. 156^r (29 May 1571) for tolls; Rep. 17, fo. 216^r (23 October 1571) for Stringer; Rep. 17, fo. 124^v (17 March 1571) for Revell. In 1547, at age 7, Revell became a royal ward; he was later involved in many lawsuits to recover the lands of his father and stepfather.

[37] Will of Francis Barnham (25 April 1575 with codicil of 1 April 1576), PROB 11/58, fos. 76^v–78^r. He bequeathed property in London, Surrey, Essex, and Wales. See National Library of Wales Roll 306 and Peniarth DC 27 and DE 3; Edward Hasted, *The History and Topographical Survey of the County of Kent*, 4 vols. (Canterbury: Simmons & Kirkby, 1782), ii. 67, 454; John Hutchins, *The History and Antiquity of the County of Dorset*, 4 vols. (Westminster: John Bowyer Nichols, 1861–70), ii. 308, 500, 710; *CPR: Elizabeth I*, iii. *1563–1566*, nos. 1269, 1285; see also no. 1006 and *CPR: Elizabeth I*, iv. *1566–1569*, nos. 657, 1125, 1831, 2638.

between September 1543 and September 1544; there were at least thirteen more. As alderman Barnham supervised two or three deputies who lived in his ward, a beadle, and ten or twelve constables; as sheriff he housed several court officers, including his sergeant. Scattered in other documents we find John Dale, his butler; Edmond Wright, an underbutler; and Henry Newton, journeyman. In *An Essay of Drapery* (1635), William Scott was to explain the interlocking roles of affluence, community service, and personal staffs in the period: 'Wealth being gotten, their minds may with more diligence intend the public affairs, having enough to maintain servants to perform the domestic.'[38]

Scott omits Francis's most important confederate. Tudor homiletic literature insisted that the early modern household was a 'commonwealth', with the wife as an 'under-officer'.[39] In fact, establishments such as the Barnhams' were more analogous to corporations, and Francis's rise would not have been possible without Alice's full partnership. Although women were excluded from the governance of the Drapers, the role of Company 'sisters' was recognized in social placements that were as finely calibrated as were those of male members of the fellowship. With each advance in Francis's career, Alice's status rose, especially when he joined the livery in 1550, was granted a coat of arms in 1561, and was elected Sheriff in 1570. For his shrieval inauguration at the Guildhall, she had 'eight or ten' elite Drapers' wives to attend her progress. She was to assume the honorific 'worshipful'.[40]

---

[38] Percival Boyd's *Roll of the Drapers' Company* is inaccurate for Barnham's apprentices. See in Drapers' archives: W.A.3, 1543–4, fo. 4ʳ, M.B.5, fo. 13ʳ, and W.A.4, 1552–3, fo. 1ʳ (and also *Register of Freemen*, 107, for John Kydd); W.A.3, 1546–7, fo. 4ᵛ, M.B.5, fo. 66ʳ, and W.A.4, 1555–6, fo. 1ʳ (Thomas Bye); W.A.4, 1553–4, fo. 3ᵛ (Humfrye Chaffrye); W.A.4, 1553–4, fo. 4ʳ and W.A.5, 1565–6, fo. 2ʳ (William Bennett); W.A.4, 1553–4, fo. 4ʳ (John Dawborne); W.A.4, 1555–6, fo. 2ʳ (William Garway); W.A.4, 1558–9, fo. 2ᵛ and W.A.5, 1565–6, fo. 2ʳ (Thomas Herdson); M.B.8, fo. 55ʳ (and CLRO Rep. 16, fo. 437ʳ, William Willyns); M.B.8, fo. 133ᵛ and W.A.5, 1570–1, fo. 1ʳ (Richard Chester); M.B.8, fo. 173ʳ and W.A.5, 1571–2, fo. 3ʳ (Bryan Luntley); M.B.9, fo. 2ʳ and W.A.5, 1574–5, fo. 3ʳ (Henry Swynerton); M.B.9, fo. 12ʳ (John Bodley); W.A.5, 1578–9, fo. 5ᵛ (Thomas Hyll); W.A.5, 1580–1, fo. 6ᵛ (Lawrence Manfield). For Dale, see Drapers' M.B.8, fo. 124ᵛ; for Wright, M.B.8, fo. 165ᵛ; for Newton, CLRO Rep. 18, fo. 64ʳ; for sheriffs' sergeants, CLRO Rep. 17, fo. 155ʳ, and Stow (1603), p. 538; for aldermen's officers, GL Ms 2463. William Scott, *An Essay of Drapery (1635)*, ed. Sylvia L. Thrupp, Kress Library of Business and Economics 9 (Boston: Harvard Graduate School of Business Administration, 1953), 32.

[39] See e.g. John Dod and Robert Cleaver, *A Godly Form of Household Government* (London: 1598), sig. B1ʳ; Henry Smith, *A Preparative to Marriage* (London: 1591), sig. E7ᵛ.

[40] Thrupp says that 'in London tradition' officers in the important guilds were 'entitled . . . to be addressed thereafter as worshipful' (Scott, *Essay*, 3); Johnson associates the title with the end of Elizabeth's reign (*History*, ii. 199–200). Alice used it on her father's memorial brass in 1592. See also *Grantees of Arms Named in Docquets and Patents to the End of the Seventeenth Century*, ed. Joseph Foster and W. Harry Rylands, Publications of the Harleian Society 66 (1915), 16. For the Barnham arms, see L. R. A. Grove, 'Archaeological Notes from Maidstone Museum: Bilsington', *Archaeologia Cantiana* 86 (1971), 220. For Alice's attendants, see Drapers' M.B.8, fo. 124ᵛ.

Een burghers wijf

Een burghers rijck wijf

Een iongste dochter

Een boer zoo d gaen.

Figure 1.3 Drawing of two English merchant's wives (to the left), from Lucas de Heere, 'Corte Beschryuinghe van Engheland, Schotland, ende Irland', *c.*1574.

She enjoyed economic incentives, as well, with an experience of prosperity that is reflected in her early order of a portrait and in the fur-trimmed velvet gown she wears in it; ten or twenty years later, the rich merchants' wives sketched by Lucas de Heere were still to be seen in her forward-looking fashion (see Fig. 1.3).

In de Heere's companion drawing of a London mayor, liveryman, and alderman (see Fig. 1.4), we find a generic stand-in for the husband who is missing from Alice's family painting. Francis's absence in 1557 can only have been pictorial, for he was certainly not in international exile during the reign of Mary I (from July 1553 to November 1558). He bound his third, fourth, and fifth apprentices between September 1553 and September 1554—a significant business expansion for a single year. He resolved a legal controversy with fellow draper William Beswicke (over custody of a jeweled pendant) in February 1554. He contributed to the Company's loan to Mary in March 1554. He was churchwarden for St Mildred Poultry from March 1554 to March 1556, for which his participation was required each Sunday. He was Renter for the Drapers from September 1554 to September 1555, collecting incomes throughout the year and submitting his accounts at the end of January 1556. In November 1555 he freed his second apprentice; between September 1555 and September 1556 he bound his sixth. In April 1556 he was involved in an unspecified dispute with former apprentice John Kydd. In July 1556 he participated in a 'search' through the city for false measures in the cloth trade. In November 1556 he purchased property from the Earl of Arundel. In 1557 he stood suretor for a loan from the Chamber of the city. In the summer of 1557 Alice conceived their fourth child, Anthony, who was born the following March. In April 1558 Francis paid another royal assessment. Between September 1558 and September 1559 he bound a seventh apprentice. In October 1558 he was one of Philip and Mary's collectors, gathering 'fifteenths' in six wards.[41] Alice Barnham's husband was highly visible in public accounts for the mid-1550s.

These documents were also the medium of his self-expression. With no formal, ongoing relationship to any record-keeping institution, however, Alice constituted herself in a different and less transparent genre of evidence. The amount of information that is available about Francis throws a contrastive light on the mysteries perpetrated by 'Alice Barnham and her Two Boys'. As Francis's life partner, Alice shared in the phenomena that are understood to have fueled the early modern market for portraiture. These associate a wider impulse to self-memorialize with the development of a proto-capitalist economy, with the wealth attained by the middling sorts who were eventually to be recognized as a bourgeois class, and with the individualism that is understood to have proceeded from a democratization of opportunity. If

---

[41] Drapers' M.B.5, fo. 25[r–v], for Beswicke; Drapers' M.B.5, fo. 79[v], for Kydd; Drapers' M.B.5, fo. 90[v], for the search; CLRO Hustings Roll 248/95 (18 November 1556), for Arundel; Mark Benbow, 'Index of London Citizens Involved in City Government, 1558–1603', for surety; GL Ms 4429/1, for Anthony's baptism; Drapers' W.A.4, 1557–8, fos. 14[v]–15[r], for assessment; CLRO Journ. 17, fo. 100[r], for fifteenths.

Figure 1.4 Drawing of an English mayor, alderman, and liveryman, from Lucas de Heere, 'Corte Beschryuinghe van Engheland, Schotland, ende Irland', *c*.1574.

Alice was motivated in these social and economic ways, however, it was only in the most general terms. None of the specific milestones she might have been expected to commemorate—Francis's advances, his offices, his armorial achievement—dates to 1557. Thus none explains why this painting was commissioned or what 'turn' she observed in her own history. But knowledge of Francis's career adds different shadings to Alice's representation without him. While the key to the portrait does not lie in Francis Barnham's death or exile, neither can it be located in his accomplishments.

PUBLIC PERFORMANCES

The painting of 'Alice Barnham and her Two Boys' had private meanings. This seems evident not only from its persistent obscurities but also by comparison with other artistic commissions in which Alice publicly positioned herself as the wife of an illustrious man. Sometime between 1576, when Francis died, and 1588, when she gave a 'standing gift' to the parish church of St Clement Eastcheap, she built what is described in *A Survey of London* as a 'fair tomb on the north side of the choir, made into the wall'. Though this was destroyed in the Great Fire, its inscription was preserved by Anthony Munday in the 1617 continuation of the *Survey* and in a manuscript record of monumental London epitaphs compiled about 1638. Both transcriptions were products of a Tudor preoccupation with genealogy and nationhood which also lay behind the ecclesiastical regulation of 1598 requiring the recopying of parish registers and, even earlier, the royal proclamation of 1560 warning zealous iconoclasts that tomb-breaking would 'darken' the 'true understanding of divers families in this realm'. Thus we know that Francis Barnham was celebrated as citizen, alderman, and sheriff of the city, and that Alice described herself as his spouse and a member of the Bradbridge family 'of immortal memory': 'Francisci Barneham, Ciuis, Senatoris, Vicecomitis Londinensis. Alicieque Vxoris suae è Bradbrigeorem Familia aeternae memoriae. Vixit Annos LX. Obijt X° Maij. 1576. Filios genuit Martinum. Stephanum. Antonium. Benedictum.' In 1604, if her wishes were honored, Alice was interred 'in the same vault wherein the body of my said late husband doth lie'.[42]

There is no recovering how architectural the Barnham family tomb may have been, how sculptural, or how colorful. Among London's remaining memorials are the badly damaged stone figures of Sir Thomas Rowe and his wife, once shown kneeling as if in prayer in a Hackney chapel 'on the south side of the choir' where Rowe said he 'commonly' sat (1569). Alice may also have known the busts of Percival and Agnes Smallpace, which were

---

[42] GL Ms 977/1, fo. 53a–b. John Stow and Anthony Munday, *A Survey of London* (London: 1617), 406 (Munday also gives Benedict's inscription, pp. 406–7); GL Ms 4783. I am grateful to Clare Brown for a scan of Lambeth Ms 1485, fo. 103[r]. On parish registers, see n. 6. Proclamation quoted by Nigel Llewellyn, *Funeral Monuments in Post-Reformation England* (Cambridge: Cambridge University Press, 2000), 218. Alice specified her burial in her will (7 December 1598), PROB 11/104, fos. 53[r]–54[r].

mounted together in a stone frame and affixed to a wall of St Bartholomew the Great (1589). More commonly, civic figures were displayed along with their entire families as collections of painted sculptures sheltered in shallow niches. At St Helen Bishopsgate there were Sir Andrew Judd, with three wives and six children (1558), and alderman William Bonde, with one wife and seven children (1576). Alice's principal inspiration may have been the now-lost memorial to her husband's mentor, which was so imposing that Barbara Champion required permission from the church of St Dunstan in the East to remove three pews 'for the setting up of a new monument there'. When inaugurated as Master of the Drapers in 1571, Francis led a procession to St Dunstan and rewarded the sexton 'for opening the church door to see Sir Richard Champion's tomb'.[43]

In connection with the monument that honored her husband's life and career, Alice Barnham herself comes into clearer focus as an independent agent. She made an annual grant of £7, in perpetuity, to the parishioners of St Clement Eastcheap (paid out of the rents of buildings she owned on Bishopsgate Street). She directed that the parish clerk and the sexton should annually receive 2s. 6d. and 1s. 8d., respectively, 'to sweep and keep clean the tomb of Francis Barnham late Citizen and Alderman of London'. She established a reserve fund of 8s. 6d. to accumulate 'in a chest in the said parish church to be bestowed in and upon repairing of the said tomb when need shall require'. The remaining sums constituted straightforward philanthropy: to thirteen 'honest, godly poor parishioners', two shillings' worth of bread each Sunday, for an annual total of £5. 4s.; to the senior churchwarden, 3s. 4d. to distribute the bread; and to a preacher, £1 to deliver three sermons a year. For as long as she lived, Alice Barnham reserved the right to dispense bread to persons she herself selected for their 'poverty, honest life, and godly conversation'. While the Great Fire frustrated her provisions to maintain the family monument, a weekly dole was awarded in her name down through the nineteenth century.[44]

---

[43] Llewellyn gives illustrations for Rowe (*Monuments*, 6; see also 48), and Smallpace (ibid. 227). See also Sir Thomas Offley at St Andrew Undershaft (*c.*1592). For a photographic record of Sir Rowland Heyward's monument (*c.*1594), once at St Alphage London Wall, see Edward Geoffrey O'Donoghue, *Bridewell Hospital: Palace, Prison, Schools* (London: John Lane the Bodley Head, 1923), following 228. Heyward named Francis Barnham Sheriff and is mentioned in Barnham's will. For Champion, see GL Ms 4887, p. 189, and Drapers' D.B.1, fo. 106^v. Francis was remembered in Champion's will with a cloth gown and a ring; Alice, with a cloth gown (22 November 1568, PROB 11/50, fo. 169^{r-v}). His wife Barbara Champion gave each a gown (15 October 1576, PROB 11/58, fos. 200^r–202^r).

[44] GL Ms 977/1, 'The Gift of Alice Barnham sometimes the wife of Francis Barnham, Alderman, at a vestry holden this 20th day of October 1588', fos. 53a–b; 'An abstract or direction for the Churchwardens of St Clements, London' (regarding the 'gift of Mistress

She was enough of a public figure to have come to the attention of Anthony Munday. In his 1617 edition of the *Survey of London* she appeared as one of forty-three 'citizens' wives deserving memory for example to posterity'. (Francis was not among the 143 men listed, despite his own charitable bequest to Christ's Hospital.) Alice was honored for her £20 legacy to poor students of divinity at the universities of Oxford and Cambridge. Munday may not have known that her will also specified gifts of £120 for start-up loans to young merchants in Chichester; £10 to poor persons in Chichester, £5 to those in Southwick in Hampshire, and £5 to others in her father's home parish of Shingleton in Sussex; £5 each to the poorest prisoners in Newgate, the King's Bench, and the White Lion; £10 to secure releases from the two debtors' prisons in London; £10 to children in Christ's Hospital; £4 for bread and meat in Bedlam; and £5 to the poor in the parish of St Mildred Poultry. Like the tomb in St Clement Eastcheap, her benefactions confirmed her acceptance of the civic responsibilities that followed from personal wealth. (In 1577, when newly widowed, she paid the very high subsidy rate of £250.)[45]

Some years after installing the memorial to her husband and her married family, Alice Barnham remembered her parents and her natal family. Her commemorative brass is the only sixteenth-century monument remaining in Chichester Cathedral (see Fig. 1.5). William Bradbridge had directed that he was to be buried 'in the procession way . . . under two stones which be ready wrought, one to be laid upon me and the other to be set in the pillar at my feet, next to Saint George's Chapel'. Alice's plaque, about twenty inches square, shows a man and a woman kneeling as if in the chapel off the columned south aisle (the 'procession way') of the cathedral, facing each other across a casket

Alice Barnham and Benedict Barnham', fo. 56[b]); and 'A Brief Account of the Substance of the Standing Gifts Belonging to this Parish', 371–4. Benedict added £3 to the fund. Agents of his heirs—the second Earl of Castlehaven, the Countess of St Albans (Alice Bacon), her second husband Sir John Underhill, Sir William Soame, and Lady Constable—appear regularly, making payments. See also GL Ms 977/4 and 981/2, for nineteenth-century churchwardens' accounts, and GL Ms 3656, 'Account of the Bread given away on Sunday at St Clements Church left by Alice and Benedict Barnham' (1834–5). See also Ian W. Archer, 'The Charity of Early Modern Londoners', *Transactions of the Royal Historical Society*, 6th ser., 12 (2002), 223–44.

[45] I am grateful to Donna Hamilton for Munday's revision of *Survey* (1617), 205, 209. In her will of 7 December 1598 (PROB 11/104, fos. 53[r]–54[r]), Alice remembered her surviving sons, a sister, friends and relatives, servants including 'Ellis my cook' and Joan Whittington and, with black funerary gowns, 100 poor mourners. *Two Tudor Subsidy Assessment Rolls for the City of London: 1541 and 1582*, ed. R. G. Lang, London Record Society 29 (1993), 262, for a £210 tax in 1582. I am also grateful to Alan H. Nelson, who documents £250 in 1577 and £80 in 1599; see <http://socrates.berkeley.edu/~ahnelson/>, accessed 1 May 2007. Munday notes Benedict Barnham's gift to London prisons, *Survey*, 200.

Here vnder lyeth the bodies of Mr William Bradbridge
who was thrice Maior of this Cittie, and Alice his wife, who
had vj sonnes & viij daughters, which Willm deceased, 1 5 4 6.
&c this stone was finished at ye charges of ye worshll Mrs Alice Barn
ham widow one of ye dau:trh of ye said Wm Bradbridge, & wife of the
worshll Mr Francis Barnham deceased shrive & Aldrmã of Londõ in 15 70
FYNYSHED IN IVLY 1 5 9 2   A V B

Figure 1.5 Memorial brass to William and Alice Bradbridge, Chichester Cathedral, West Sussex. Commissioned by Alice Barnham, dated 1592. Inscribed 'Here vnder lyeth the bodies of Mr William Bradbridge who was thrice Maior of this Cittie, and Alice his wife, who had vj sonnes & viij daughters, which Willm deceased. 1546. &c this stone was finished at ye charges of ye worsh^{ll} Mrs Alice Barnham widow one of ye dau^{trh} of ye said Wm Bradbridge, & wife of the worsh^{ll} Mr Francis Barnham decased shrive & Ald^{r}mã of Londõ in 1570 Fynyshed in Ivly 1592 A B.'

topped with two open testaments. Behind the man kneel six boys; behind the woman, eight girls, replicating in two dimensions the sculptural arrangement of so many London monuments. The family insignia, a pheon, is suspended centrally against a great leaded window.

Here under lyeth the bodies of Master William Bradbridge, who was thrice Mayor of this City, and Alice his wife, who had six sons and eight daughters, which William deceased 1546, etc. This stone was finished at the charges of the Worshipful Mistress Alice Barnham, widow, one of the daughters of the said William Bradbridge and wife of the Worshipful Master Francis Barnham, deceased, Sheriff and Alderman of London in 1570. Finished in July 1592. A. [pheon] B.[46]

The twice-rendered Bradbridge pheon represents the sort of familial 'bona fides' that Robert Tittler says were important in civic art. On tomb as well as plaque, Alice's identification of herself as Francis Barnham's wife was a bona fide of another, particularly gendered sort. Had she thought of her own portrait as a public artifact, she would have repeated the conventional credentials there, as well. Instead, she undoubtedly anticipated a fashion that was satirized in the 1598 *Entertainment . . . at Mitcham*: 'every citizen's wife . . . must have her picture in the parlor'.[47] Hanging her painting in her Eastcheap home, Alice would have had no cause to name or explain herself to the persons who were certainly its intended viewers, her husband and sons.

PRIVATE COMPOSITIONS

Is it only in our visual imagination that Francis Barnham haunts his wife's portrait? In the verbal texts of the painting, Alice addresses us in her own voice as sole author and patron. The graphic composition, though, can seem to be at odds with her words. Seeing her through the filters of artistic convention and gender theory, we may conclude that Alice has herself raised her husband's ghost simply by her three-quarter turn. She adopts the pose traditionally associated with women in double portraits and family groups, one she accepted for her mother, too, in commissioning the Chichester brass. Our sense of absence is conditioned by designs like that for the 1563 *Whole Book of Psalms* (see Fig. 1.6), where the patriarch is displayed in commanding solitude while his wife and children cluster deferentially opposite him. They exhibit the same pronounced directionality as Alice, Martin, and Steven. The configuration is so familiar that it might seem unavoidable that we should feel that 'Alice Barnham and her Two Boys' lacks a necessary counterweight. No husband occupies the space to our left, holding his wife in her proper

[46] Will of William Bradbridge (13 October 1543), WSRO STC 1/5, fo. 90. See C. E. D. Davidson-Houston, 'Sussex Monumental Brasses, Part II', *Sussex Archaeological Collections* 77 (1936), 130–94 (esp. 132–4); and Mary Hobbs (ed.), *Chichester Cathedral: An Historical Survey* (Chichester: Phillimore, 1994). The brass is 22 3/8 inches wide by 20 3/4 inches high, set in a stone frame 24 1/2 wide by 23 1/4 high. Margaret Hannay has pointed out (in private conversation), that the pheon is generally associated with the Sidney family.

[47] Robert Tittler, 'An Actor's Face? The Sanders Portrait in Context', in Stephanie Nolen (ed.), *Shakespeare's Face* (Toronto: Piatkus, 2002), 226. *Entertainment . . . at Mitcham* cited by Eric Mercer, *English Art, 1553–1625* (Oxford: Clarendon, 1962), 165.

Figure 1.6 A householder and his family in a patriarchal pose. From *The Whole Book of Psalms*, printed by John Day in 1563.

location at his sinister or (as Harry Berger, Jr., terms it) 'lesser' side, claiming the authority to present her to the viewer, and mediating between his family and the world.[48] Merely by looking toward her right Alice may seem to submit to the idea of male supervisory privilege.

Thus, it is not surprising that 'Alice Barnham and her Two Boys' has occasionally been reimagined in ways that would fulfill its patriarchal potential. It might be a fragment, for example. Francis can so easily be pictured standing to Steven's right, correcting for an obvious compositional imbalance, rescuing Alice's second son from his precarious position at the panel's outer edge, and assuming pride of place. The reconstruction seems sufficiently plausible that Denver conservators have searched for evidence of it, but they detect no broken glue marks to betray a detached board. This would have had to have been split off early, both before a paper tag was tacked to the back referring to just three figures ('Great Grandmother Lady Ingram & her two Boys') and also

[48] Tarnya Cooper (Nolen, *Shakespeare's Face*, 238); Harry Berger, Jr., quoting Mariët Westermann, in 'Artificial Couples: The Apprehensive Household in Dutch Pendants and *Othello*', in Lena Cowen Orlin (ed.), *Center or Margin: Revisions of the English Renaissance in Honor of Leeds Barroll* (Selinsgrove, Pa.: Susquehanna University Press, 2006), 127.

before the oak began to warp. The panel is now so symmetrically bowed that an additional plank to the left would mandate one more to the right, positioning a hypothetical family of four even more asymmetrically than is the extant group of three. But if there was never a place for Francis in Alice's painting, it may be that he occupied the other half of a 'pendant'. Twinned images are most familiar for displaying spouses alone; by report of a descendant, Alice's son Martin and her daughter-in-law Judith had their companion paintings done in this fashion.[49] Less likely, but not unexampled, were representations of the husband in one frame and the wife and children in another. Short of a new discovery, there is no sure way of knowing whether 'Alice Barnham and her Two Boys' was once matched with a painting of 'Francis Barnham'.

Even the possibility puts more pressure on how we read female portraiture, however. In this respect, the case of Mary Neville, Lady Dacre, is instructive (see Fig. 1.7). For a painting dated between 1555 and 1558, she, too, is turned in the direction now associated with secondary status, though her panel is not a fragment and no pendant counterpart exists. Dacre is depicted, like Alice, with the literary impedimenta of a contemplative mood. Alice might have inhabited this more opulent setting had she in fact been 'Lady Ingram'. Where Alice stands against an austere brick wall, Dacre sits in an armchair before rich tapestries. And where Alice has an unframed window, Dacre displays a miniature of her deceased first husband. Thomas Fiennes, ninth Baron Dacre, was so eminent a Henrician courtier that he helped bear the canopy over Jane Seymour's funeral bier and, with the third Duke of Norfolk, accompanied Anne of Cleves on her nuptial journey through Kent. This did not save him from execution in 1541, however, when he was found guilty of having joined a poaching raid in which a keeper was killed. Confiscation of his properties left Lady Dacre destitute until an act of Parliament restored her dower.

By the time she had her portrait painted, Dacre had made her third marriage to Francis Thursby and had added six children to those fathered by the ninth Baron.[50] Still, she seems to have had no interest in recognizing Thursby as her pictorial counterpart. Engaged in the battle for full restitution of the Dacre lands and incomes, she defined herself strictly in terms of her first and most

---

[49] Scott Reyburn calls the portrait 'just under half of a superlative family group portrait whose left hand side must have originally contained Lord Ingram, possibly with his daughters' ('The High Price of Falling for Lady Ingram', *Antiques Trade Gazette*, 7 February 1998, 24–5). For the painting's integrity, I am grateful to Timothy Standring and Jessica Fletcher of the Denver Art Museum. Portraits of Martin and Judith Barnham are described in the 'recollection' of Martha Buckle in the 'Nork House' file, Heinz Archive of the National Portrait Gallery, London.

[50] Sir Thomas Barrett-Lennard, *An Account of the Families of Lennard and Barrett Compiled Largely from Original Documents* (privately printed, 1908), 194–6, 197–9, 205–7. Through her second marriage to John Wotton, Dacre came to have kinship ties to the Barnhams. Her granddaughter Elizabeth married Alice's grandson Sir Francis (ibid. 152).

Figure 1.7 Portrait of Mary Neville, Lady Dacre, shown with a painting of her deceased first husband Thomas Fiennes, 9th Baron Dacre, at age 24. Signed HE, *c.*1555–8.

important union. Though Dacre adopted the 'sinister' three-quarter view, she turned towards a simulacrum and commemorated the partner who could no longer be painted from the life. For her, the pendant pose would never be completed with an opposite number. When she finally succeeded in reclaiming the family's lost honors, moreover, in 1559, she celebrated the achievement

Figure 1.8 Portrait of Mary Neville, Lady Dacre, and her son Gregory Fiennes, 10th Baron Dacre. Signed HE, dated 1559. Inscribed 'ÆTATIS XXXVI', 'M.D.LIX', and 'ÆTATIS XXI'.

by commissioning another painting (see Fig. 1.8). This she shared not with her third husband but instead with her Dacre heir, the Tenth Baron. In a further variation on tradition, she assumed the dominant position, to the left, and placed her son on the right.[51] The Dacre portraits demonstrate that in fact the 'sinister' posture could accommodate a variety of compositional and relational possibilities.

Each of the Dacre paintings bears the inscription 'HE', now presumed to stand for Hans Eworth. Eworth, a Low Country expatriate who maintained a studio in Southwark from about 1549, placed his initials on only a few of the portraits that have been attributed to him. 'Alice Barnham and her Two Boys' is unsigned, but it has been described as being in the style of Eworth if not from his hand. Thus it is especially pertinent that Roy Strong discusses the earlier painting of Dacre without in any way entertaining the idea that it

---

[51] My interpretation differs from that of Elizabeth Honig in 'In Memory: Lady Dacre and Pairing by Hans Eworth', in Lucy Gent and Nigel Llewellyn (eds.), *Renaissance Bodies: The Human Figure in English Culture c. 1540–1660* (London: Reaktion, 1990), 60–85.

Figure 1.9 Portrait of Thomas Cromwell. By Hans Holbein the Younger, *c.*1532–3.

may have been a pendant. Nor does he read the composition in terms of the dependent tradition for wives. Writing in 1965, effectively in a pre-feminist moment, Strong instead describes the composition as having been 'lifted' from Holbein's portraits of such substantial figures as Thomas Cromwell (see Fig. 1.9).[52] It should go without saying that Cromwell's painting has never

---

[52] Eworth has been suggested by Marc Weiss (quoted by Reyburn); and in Berger collection file notes, courtesy of Standring. See also Mercer, *English Art*, 166–72; Roy Strong, *Hans Eworth:*

been taken to imply either a missing counterpart or its sitter's subordinate station. All speculations about absence and loss in Alice's painting respond to the 'sinister' implications of a familiar composition—those of the *Psalms* housewife—rather than to the personal power that could also, and more famously, be concentrated in her pose—as in the Cromwell portrait. Only our own commitment to a victim's discourse for women can account for the fact that one analogy now seems more immediately relevant than the other.

As Harry Berger, Jr., emphasizes, 'sitters, painters, and images imitate prior sitters, painters, and images'. To take on board what Berger terms the 'redundancies' of artistic representation is to recognize that both the Barnham family and Lady Dacre (in her earlier commission) may have been inserted into an artist's pre-existent visual formula, each one flexible enough to allow for a pendant should it ever be required and each employed even if, as in Dacre's case, it seems to have been antithetical to the subject's circumstances. Elizabeth Honig suggests that the 'notion of woman as one-half of a married couple' was 'so deeply rooted' that 'in Tudor portraiture women portrayed singly are posed according to the conventions of pair portraiture'; certainly, it is tempting to spin out the symbolic resonances of a subject put in a highly conventionalized position, constrained by the traditional roles and restricted representations available to early modern women.[53] But so politically overdetermined a reading is finally difficult to sustain, especially if we broaden our interpretive base. Countless Tudor men, both seated and standing, were painted in the sinister position: Cromwell, Erasmus, Stephen Gardiner, Cardinal Reginald Pole, Archbishop William Warham, Matthew Parker, Sir William Petre, Sir William St Lo, Sir William Cavendish, Sir Thomas Tresham, Sir Edward Stafford, Sir Edward Hastings, and more. The pendant of Sybil and John Scudamore, as also that of Lady Anne and Sir Thomas Cornwallis, reverse what we think to have been the rule, showing wives on the left and husbands on the right. In their pendants, Sir Nicholas and Lady Dorothy Wadham, Sir Henry and Lady Mary Sidney, Sir Henry and Lady Dorothy Townshend, Sir John and

---

A Tudor Artist and his Circle (Leicester: Museums and Art Gallery, 1965); and Karen Hearn (ed.), *Dynasties: Painting in Tudor and Jacobean England, 1530–1630* (London: Tate Publishing, 1995), 63–76. Mercer says that Eworth's later 'female subjects are more individualized and have more force than his men' (*English Art*, 168). Strong compares Dacre's pose to those of Holbein's Erasmus and Archbishop Warham (*Hans Eworth*, p. x). Alice might also have looked to Chichester, where Lambert Barnard (d. 1568) was cathedral muralist and his son Anthony and grandson Lambert were also painters. See Edward Croft-Murray, *Decorative Painting in England, 1537–1837*, 2 vols. (London: Country Life, 1962), i. 23–5, 95–7, 153–5, 193, 275; Ellis Waterhouse (ed.), *The Dictionary of 16th and 17th Century British Painters* (Woodbridge: Antique Collectors' Club, 1988), 20.

[53] Berger, 'Artificial Couples', 127; Honig, 'In Memory', 64.

Figure 1.10 Portrait of Richard Wakeman. Attributed to Hans Eworth, dated 1566. Inscribed 'WHY VANTIST THOWE THY CHANGYNG FACE OR | HAST OF HYT SVCHE STORE | TO FORM A NEWE OR NONE THOWE HAST OR NOT LYK^E | AS BEFORE | AETATIS XLIIII | M.D. LXVI.'

Lady Joan Thynne, and Sir Thomas and Lady Margaret Kytson adopt identical rather than reciprocal postures, all facing to their right. Richard Wakeman and his wife Joan Thornbury, in a pendant produced by Hans Eworth in 1566, assume the more familiar, complementary stance (see Figs. 1.10 and 1.11). But both paintings display poetic inscriptions that directly address the viewer, and Thornbury, even though placed on the right, 'speaks', like Alice, in the independent voice of the first-person singular.[54]

'Alice Barnham and her Two Boys' may respond to compositional habits rather than to conventions for wifely submission. In fact, its painter may originally have developed these standing postures for parent and principal heir. Mark Bills points out that together, poised between the window and the writing box, Alice and Martin make a perfectly balanced pair. If Steven was added to a design for two sitters, this would explain not only his marginal placement but also the mishandlings of scale that have produced his oddly outsized head.[55] Thus, the principal structural irregularity of 'Alice Barnham and her Two Boys' may finally involve the second son rather than the unseen husband.

The Barnham, Dacre, and Thornbury paintings are all related stylistically, showing the hand or influence of Eworth, but they are also connected ideologically, displaying Tudor women who expressed their autonomy even from within the institution of marriage. Dacre's motives in portraiture seem clear, especially when the focus on literary activity and loss, in her earlier portrait, is contrasted to the emphasis on regained wealth and restored lineage, in the later one. Alice Barnham's purposes are more obscure, though it remains an open question whether or not this was her intent. She cannot have foreseen that within three generations a member of her family would mislabel her as 'Lady Ingram'. Nor that, 450 years later, other viewers would have so little evidence for the interior life of Tudor women that they would wish she had been more exoteric about the 'turn' hers took in 1557.

TURNED THREE WAYS

We can never be sure of the nature of Alice Barnham's self-proclaimed transformation 'to that ye see', but there are guesses to be made. Three

---

[54] For access to photographs of paintings not often reproduced, I am grateful for the collections of the Heinz Archive at the National Portrait Gallery in London, the Courtauld Institute of Art at Somerset House, and the Jennings albums and Photograph Archive at the Yale Center for British Art. See also Honig on the Wakeman portraits, 'In Memory', 71–8.

[55] Mark Bills, Curator of Paintings, Prints, and Drawings at The Museum of London, in private conversation.

Figure 1.11 Portrait of Joan Thornbury, Mistress Wakeman. Signed HE, dated 1566. Inscribed 'MY CHYLDHODDE PAST THAT BEWTIFIID MY FLESSHE | AND GONNE MY YOVTH THAT GAVE ME COLOR FRESSHE | Y AM NOWE CVM TO THOS RYPE YERIS AT LAST | THAT TELLES ME HOWE MY WANTON DAYS BE PAST | AND THERFORE FRINDE SO TVRNES THE TYME ME | Y ONS WAS YOVNG AND NOWE AM AS YOV SEE. | AETATIS XXXVI | M.D. LXVI.'

hypothetical narratives are essayed here; they proceed from Barnham family history, Tudor religious upheavals, and early ideas of portraiture.

First Turn

Alice Barnham had four children.[56] Martin, christened on 27 March 1548, was the subject of his son Sir Francis's affectionate memoir. Martin's public history was solid and respectable: there were three years at St Albans Hall in Oxford, a brief placement in service to a lawyer, and then five years at Gray's Inn. He used his legal training as a Justice of the Peace for Kent from 1580 and then as High Sheriff of Kent in 1598. He was knighted on James I's coronation day (as also was his son Sir Francis). Meanwhile, in 1572, Martin had made a tactical marriage into a family with ties to the Drapers' Company, the new religion, and country life. Ursula Rudston's maternal grandfather was Sir Edward Wotton of Boughton Malherbe in Kent; her paternal grandfather, Sir John Rudston, was a draper and former Lord Mayor of London. Ursula's father Robert Rudston purchased Boughton Monchelsea Place in 1551 and then lost it in 1554 for collaborating in Wyatt's Rebellion against Mary I. Thomas Wyatt was executed, but Rudston was released from the Tower and, in 1555, allowed to buy back his estate. Moving from city commerce to provincial gentility, the Wottons and the Rudstons had established a pattern of advancement that the Barnhams were to achieve with Martin's generation.

The wedding of Alice's oldest son was celebrated in Kent. Sir John Wotton, 'who was then a young courtier, brought a masque thither of gentlemen of quality', according to Sir Francis (see Fig. 1.12). Martin and Ursula Barnham lived at Boughton Monchelsea until their heir was born, in 1576, when they removed to Hollingbourne Parsonage. Ursula died in childbirth within three years, and her second son survived her by only ten days. For eight months Martin lived variously at Boughton and with his mother until, in 1580, he married the daughter of another London draper and future Lord Mayor. With Judith Calthorp he had ten more children. The oldest, his firstborn daughter, he named Alice. Martin negotiated excellent marriages for all his offspring. Sir Francis's wife, Elizabeth Lennard, was daughter of Sampson Lennard and

[56] In *County Genealogies: Pedigrees of the Families of the County of Kent* (London: Sherwood, Gilbert & Piper, 1830), 394–5, William Berry assigns Alice a daughter Ethelred, who married William Cleybroke. His probable source was Hasted, *History*, ii. 466. But London parish registers show Alice baptized just the four sons also named on her husband's tomb. See Robert Cooke's *Visitation of London, 1568*: Francis's brother Thomas had a daughter Awdrey who married William Clebroke (H. Stanford London and Sophia W. Rawlins (eds.), Publications of the Harleian Society 109, 110 (1963), 145).

Figure 1.12 A private banquet and a masque, in a detail from 'The Life and Death of Sir Henry Unton'. Artist unknown, *c*.1596. According to Angela Cox, the musicians play the flute, lute, cittern, bass-viol, pandora, and violin; masquers represent Mercury, Diana with six attendant ladies, and ten cupids.

Margaret Fiennes, Lady Dacre (and granddaughter to Hans Eworth's subject). Alice was matched to Sir Robert Honeywood, and other daughters married Sir George Chute and Sir Christopher Buckle; Honeywood and Buckle had been Martin's wards. As an 'old gentleman' and an 'old lady', Martin and Judith had their companion portraits painted in 'three-quarters length', both dressed in black and both with prominent ruffs. In his will, Martin asked his wife 'often to think upon me, and to remember the loving, familiar, and secret speech and communication that have passed between her and me'. He advised his son that Judith had 'with great respect to my credit, kept my house as profitably as any woman in Kent could do'.[57] Martin outlived his mother by six years, dying in 1610. According to Peter Clark, the merchant's son had 'played the part of a local compounder so well that . . . he was indistinguishable from any other middling gentleman'.[58]

Benedict, baptized on 2 June 1559, made a spectacular career in the city. Sir Francis Barnham was to complain that his grandfather was so 'much carried by the sway of his affections' as to have provided unusually well for the youngest of the four children. Like Martin, Benedict had an elite education at St Albans Hall (see Fig. 1.13). With this, with greater start-up capital than his father had had, and with the advantage of his widowed mother's connections and partnership, he enjoyed a more precipitous rise. In 1589, aged just 30, he paid the very high subsidy rate of £220 (among the top twelve in the city) and was a Member of Parliament for Minehead. Two years later, he was elected Third Warden of the Drapers' Company, Under Sheriff of London, and then Alderman of Bread Street ward. He was Master of the Drapers' Company in 1592 and again in 1596. Members of the Queen's Privy Council recognized him as a leading citizen when he was asked to consult on a proposed tax of the city. In 1597 he was returned to Parliament for Yarmouth. There is no knowing what more he might have achieved had he not died in 1598 at the age

[57] Some aspects of Martin Barnham's life are known only from his son's 'Character' of him, like the report of the wedding masque. For corroborating evidence of other aspects, see *The Register of Admissions to Gray's Inn, 1521–1889*, ed. Joseph Foster (London: Hansard Publishing Union, 1889), 37, 86; CKS Q/M/SR, 1594–1604 *passim* (Commissions of Peace); *The Progresses, Processions, and Magnificent Festivities of King James the First*, ed. John Nichols, 4 vols. (London: J. B. Nichols for the Society of Antiquaries, 1828), i. 205, 214, and 215 (Martin's knighting); Beaven, *Aldermen*, ii. 24, 169 (*inter alia*); and Hasted, *History*, i. p. xcii; ii. 466–7, 468–9. I am indebted to Colin Richmond for a paper on John Rudston presented to the Seminar in Medieval and Tudor London History at the Institute of Historical Research in 2004. Sir Edward Wotton was Ursula Rudston's maternal grandfather and her step-grandfather (his daughter by his first marriage, Anne Wotton, married Ursula's father Robert Rudston, and his wife by his second marriage was Sir John Rudston's widow). Wotton famously refused a knighthood, as reported by Richard Dering (quoted in *The Progresses and Public Processions of Queen Elizabeth*, ed. John Nichols, 2 vols. (London: John Nichols & Son for the Society of Antiquaries, 1823), i. 334. See also Izaak Walton, *The Life of Sir Henry Wotton* (York: 1796), sig. A3[r]. For the Calthorps, see Beaven, *Aldermen*, ii. 40 (*inter alia*). Frank Foster notes that while some London aldermen married their children into gentle and noble families, most preferred to maintain city connections (*Politics*, 99). For Elizabeth Lennard, see Sir Thomas Barrett-Lennard, *An Account*, 216–17; *The House of Commons, 1558–1603*, for Sampson Lennard. For Honeywood, GL Ms 4783. For the Buckle portraits, see n. 49. Will of Sir Martin Barnham (2 February 1611), PROB 11/117, fos. 61[r]–63[r].

[58] Peter Clark, *English Provincial Society from the Reformation to the Revolution: Religion, Politics and Society in Kent 1500–1640* (Hassocks: Harvester, 1977), 127. Patricia Hyde and Michael Zell count 121 Kentish gentry families in 1574 (Michael Zell (ed.), 'Governing the County', in *Early Modern Kent, 1540–1640* (Rochester, NY: Boydell & Brewer, 2000), 20).

Figure 1.13 The front of Albans Hall, Oxford University, with a fanciful group portrait of 'principal persons', including Benedict Barnham. From the 'Oxford Almanac', engraved by Vertue, 1748. Front row, left to right: the Abbess of Littlemore, who lost her tenure with the Dissolution; Dr. Owen, Henry VIII's physician and recipient of a new charter; Robert de St Alban, thirteenth-century founder; Henry VIII; Thomas Wolsey, with staff inverted to represent lost power; Benedict Barnham, with a plan of the north front as he built it; Thomas Lamplugh, Archbishop of York in the seventeenth century; Narcissus Marsh, Archbishop of Dublin and Principal of Alban Hall in the seventeenth century; William Laud, Archbishop of Canterbury in the seventeenth century, with a drawing of Merton College Chapel.

of 38. In his will he left a hundred pounds for another monument to be erected in the parish church of St Clement Eastcheap, 'close to my father's, to be made of such fashion as it shall best please my mother and wife'. Churchwardens there still made reference to 'Master Benedict Barnham's pew' in 1622.

With Dorothy Smith, daughter of the Queen's silkman, Benedict had eight children. Of the four who lived to adulthood, all were girls, and each inherited an estate befitting the daughter of a nobleman. Among the Drapers alone, eight different men were made responsible for £300 apiece for each child. Further evidence of Benedict's extraordinary wealth lies in the marital history of his survivors. With her second marriage his widow rescued the ruined estate of Sir John Packington; her third husband was the first Viscount Kilmorey and her fourth the first Earl of Kellie. The daughters were matched with the second Earl of Castlehaven (as his first bride, not the notorious second wife), Sir William Soame, Sir John Constable, and Sir Francis Bacon. The 45-year-old Bacon 'was clad from top to toe in purple' for his 1606 nuptials to the 13-year-old Alice. Her namesake grandmother, then two years dead, had been entrusted with the child's early rearing by the terms of Benedict's will. 'To whom also I would refer the managing of all my estate', Benedict had added, though he finally chose to relieve the older Alice 'of such weight and trouble' in consideration of her age. He required his executors to 'be to my mother in all things pleasing, giving her no just cause of offense', for 'I protest before God I have found her a most rare and loving mother and a good and just woman.'[59]

Alice Barnham's second son, Steven, was baptized on 27 July 1549. He was a merchant who, like his brothers, was made free of the Drapers' Company by patrimony (in 1572). He joined the livery in 1576. In 1601 he served as Member of Parliament for Chichester, undoubtedly through Alice's connections. On a Parliamentary committee regarding bequests to Christ's Hospital, St Thomas's Hospital, and the Bridewell, he demonstrated a continuing family interest in the London charitable institutions. His first wife, who died in 1592, was Anne Patrick; his second, Anne Dawkes, was a merchant's widow and Alice's

---

[59] *The House of Commons, 1558–1603* for Benedict Barnham; the *Oxford DNB* for Benedict Barnham; Beaven, *Aldermen*, ii. 44, 174 (*inter alia*); Johnson, *History*, iv. 647; Drapers' M.B.10, fos. 274ᵛ, 275ʳ, 281ʳ. For the 1589 subsidy, see Cooke, *Visitation of London, 1568*, 161; for family births and deaths, GL Ms 4783; for his will (29 May 1598), PROB 11/91, fos. 304ʳ–309ʳ; for his wife's second marriage, *The Letters of John Chamberlain*, ed. Norman Egbert McClure, 2 vols. (Philadelphia: American Philosophical Society, 1939), i. 54, 243; ii. 86–7. See also the nuncupative 1584 will of Dorothy Barnham's father, Ambrose Smith, declaring that he would give her 'nothing' (20 June 1584, PROB 11/67, fo. 108ʳ⁻ᵛ). Frank Foster notes that in 1591 thirteen sheriffs declined the office (*Politics*, 61); this goes to explain Benedict's early election. He then had to surrender his Third Wardenship of the Drapers' Company as too inferior for a sheriff; see Johnson, *History*, ii. 216 n. 1. Willan gives his personal estate at probate as £14,614 (*Muscovy Merchants*, 79). See also Cynthia B. Herrup on 'one of London's greatest fortunes', *A House in Gross Disorder: Sex, Law, and the 2nd Earl of Castlehaven* (New York: Oxford University Press, 1999), 11–12; Lisa Jardine and Alan Stewart, *Hostage to Fortune: The Troubled Life of Francis Bacon, 1561–1626* (London: Phoenix Giant, 1998), 288–91; R. B. Jenkins, *Henry Smith: England's Silver-Tongued Preacher* (Macon, Ga.: Mercer University Press, 1983), 7; and the unreliable Alice Chambers Bunten, *Life of Alice Barnham (1592–1650), Wife of Sir Francis Bacon* (London: Page & Thomas, 1919). Benedict's firstborn daughter, Alice, died before she was 4; the same day he buried her he baptized the Alice who would marry Bacon. He willed his mother £500, among other remembrances.

neighbor. Steven named his only son Martin and the oldest of his three daughters Alice. In another tribute to his mother, he called his third child Bradbridge. Much of his wealth was made in land speculation, often in partnership with Alice during her widowhood. He bought Denne Manor in Horsham, Sussex for £1,250, for example, and sold it just five years later for £5,500. He also purchased two other Sussex manors and retired to that county, dying in Southover as an 'esquire' in 1608. Among the rich goods he left his 'loving wife' were a ring with a diamond, worth over £6; another with 'a great blue Oriental sapphire', worth £12; and a third with a three-carat diamond, worth £50.[60]

For Alice Barnham's remaining child, Anthony, there is no history beyond his baptism in St Mildred Poultry on 18 March 1558—by her reckoning 18 March 1557—and the 'sway' of Francis Barnham's affections to Benedict may in fact have been rooted in grief for Anthony's recent death. Anthony's burial is not recorded either in London or in Alice's childhood parish in Chichester, although there, where the earliest registers commence in 1558 with the start of the new year on 25 March, it may have narrowly missed documentation. Were he not sent at birth to Sussex kin, he may have been dispatched to a nurse elsewhere in the provinces in hopes of sparing him the influenza epidemic then raging in London; the custom was to bury a newborn in the parish of its death. If the painting of 'Alice Barnham and her Two Boys' was motivated by the loss of a third, however, this is a tragedy she chose not to memorialize directly. Nor did she record Anthony's death on the family tomb built between 1576 and 1588, long after a 1568 visitation listed the Barnhams as having just the three children Martin, Steven, and Benedict.[61]

Intimations of mortality may nonetheless suffuse the portrait. The trope 'this is what I have become'—'turned from that I was unto that ye see'—is not far removed in implication from 'this is what I will become', the message of *memento mori*. Thirty years later, in 1587, Joyce Frankland exposed a conflicted anguish in her own unusually explicit 'speaking' portrait: 'Alas, my

---

[60] *The House of Commons, 1558–1603* for Stephen Barnham; Benbow for Stephen Barnham; Drapers' M.B.9, fo. 68ᵛ (liveryman); GL Ms 4783; and *London Marriage Licenses, 1521–1869*, 85 (indicating that Dawkes lived in St Clement Eastcheap). For property purchases with Alice Barnham, see Ch. 7. Will of Steven Barnham (November 1607), PROB 11/111, fos. 80ʳ–81ʳ; see also 'Inquisitions Post Mortem. Temp. Henry VII, James I and Charles I', ed. F. W. T. Attree, *Sussex Archaeological Collections* 52 (1909), 104.

[61] Cooke's *Visitation of London 1568* lists Benedict as 'third son' (p. 145). Anthony is described as having 'died sans issue' in *The Visitations of Kent*, ed. W. Bruce Bannerman, Publications of the Harleian Society 74 and 75 (1923 and 1924), 81–2. For the influenza epidemic of 1557 and 1558 see Rappaport, *Worlds*, 71, 95. Parish registers for St Botolph Aldgate (GL Ms 9234) show 'chrisomers' (children who died in the earliest months of infancy) buried in the parish of their deaths, not of family residence.

son died too quickly; he perished too soon. Fate, why do you insult me? Just as you have deprived me of a son I am more blessed with many offspring.'[62] There is little to tell us precisely when in 1557 or 1558 Alice posed for her own painting: was it before her third pregnancy, when she had 'quickened', or after the likely death of Anthony in the last days of the turning year? Though she chose to commission a reminder of the 'blessings' she experienced with Martin and Steven, there may indeed be an absence at the heart of 'Alice Barnham and her Two Boys'. If so, it was not the conjugal one first imagined for her.

Second Turn

Speculation about the missing 'Lord Ingram' proceeds from the religious and political histories of mid-sixteenth-century England, but it may be that the painting should be read in the light of Alice's spiritual biography rather than in the shadow of her unseen husband's. Francis, so thoroughly occupied with his mercantile ventures—including the business of dealing with the Court, its buying power, and its demand for loaned funds—was an unlikely Marian exile. The act of religious dissent depicted in this painting puts Alice, not Francis, at the heretical center.

Alice's son Martin is shown opening a small volume in which it is possible to decipher the running head of a popular Protestant text, *The Proverbs of Solomon*, and there are sufficient hints of verse to establish not only that he reads from the second chapter of Proverbs but also that he consults the metrical translation of 1549 attributed to Thomas Sternhold: 'My son receive ye these my words, the which shall be right wise.'[63] In dialogue with the lesson she has set her firstborn child for his private study of the vernacular scriptures,

---

[62] I am grateful to Tarnya Cooper, who discussed this portrait and translated its Latin inscription at the Seminar in Medieval and Tudor London History at the Institute of Historical Research, 2004. Frankland's only son William died in 1581, having been thrown from a horse; Alexander Nowell, Dean of St Paul's, advised: 'Comfort yourself, good Mistress Frankland, and I will tell you how you shall have twenty good sons' (quoted by Fred Thompson, *Sons of Joyce Frankland: Some Record of the Boys of Newport Grammar School, Essex*, i. *1588–1945* (Saffron Walden: Old Newportian Society, 1979)). Frankland endowed Gonville and Caius College, Cambridge, where her portrait hangs, and in 1588 founded the Free Grammar School of Newton, Essex.

[63] *Certayne Chapters of the Prouerbes of Salomon drawen into metre by Thomas Sterneholde, late grome of the Kynges Majesties Robes* (London: 1549–50; STC 2760) subsequently reissued as *Certayn Chapters taken out of the Prouerbes of Salomon . . . translated into metre by J. Hall, Which Prouerbes of late were imprinted and vntruely entituled to be of T. Sternhold* (London: 1550; STC 12631). See Philippa Tudor, 'Protestant Books in London in Mary Tudor's Reign', *London Journal* 15 (1990), 19–28: 'Reading was seen as an integral part of protestant worship in Marian London' (p. 21).

Alice writes to request 'That we all may receive the same.' She accepts the biblical testament even as Solomon urged his son to do.[64]

Her grandson Sir Francis Barnham, himself a moderate Puritan, described Alice as 'a constant professor of the true religion' especially during 'those times of persecution' to which her portrait dates. The report has the ring of credible personal testimony. His father Martin recalled to him how he (Martin) was 'divers times carried by his mother' (Alice) to hear John Bradford preach from prison, 'from whom he received many pious and profitable instructions'. A compelling spokesman for the new religion during the reign of Edward VI, Bradford was jailed within a month of Mary I's accession. He spent nearly two years in the Tower and in the King's Bench in Southwark, writing, studying with fellow Protestants Thomas Cranmer, Nicholas Ridley, and Hugh Latimer, and also publicly sermonizing to the crowds of the faithful who gathered. Francis Barnham's fellow draper, William Chester, 'wept' as he performed the shrieval duty of leading Bradford to the stake on 31 June 1555. Londoners gathered at four o'clock in the morning to ensure that the execution would not go unwitnessed. Martin was 5, 6, and 7 years old at the time of Bradford's imprisonment, so his mother's Protestant pilgrimages would have been among his first and most powerful memories.[65]

The Barnham family memoir demonstrates that the 'turn' of the portrait does not mark what might be thought to be the most significant moment in any personal religious history, that of conversion. Alice's frequent recourse to hear John Bradford preach between 1553 and 1555 shows her to have been a committed reformist well before 1557. Still, the events that succeeded Bradford's burning may have further focused her convictions. Mary I's government was particularly bloody in the southeast of England, where the bishop in Alice's hometown of Chichester was the queen's personal confessor and the Romanist Nicholas Harpsfield was Archdeacon of Canterbury. Out of 288 Marian executions for heresy, 41 took place in Sussex, with the Cathedral city among the first three sites for public display of the new order. There were also many burnings in Kent: on 16 January 1557 Matthew Bradbridge was killed in Ashford, on 18 June 1557 Joan Bradbridge was martyred in Maidstone, and on 19 June 1557 a woman known only as 'Bradbridge's widow' died in Canterbury (she was, Foxe noted, 'thought to be with child'). Even if she did not herself know the martyrs with whom she shared her maiden name, Alice may have been acquainted with others of the reformers

---

[64] Restoration is more evident here than in any other part of the painting; it is possible that overpainting has obscured the descender of a long *s* and remade an *o*, in which case the phrase would have read 'That we *also* may receive the same' rather than 'That we *alle*'.

[65] See the *Oxford DNB* for John Bradford. For Chester, see Susan Brigden, *London and the Reformation* (Oxford: Clarendon, 1989), 604.

who were imprisoned and examined; the diarist Henry Machyn recorded the burnings in London of three men and two women in April 1557, three men in November 1557, and one man and one woman in December 1557. With some famous exceptions, those executed were persons with few material resources or influential friends; William Bradbridge, by contrast, had the wherewithal to flee to safety on the Continent.[66] But the absence of a brother who had been head of Alice's family until her wedding, responsible for her contract negotiations and marriage portion, would have compounded whatever grief she suffered as fellow Londoners and fellow Bradbridges died in 1557. There were many ways in which the persecutions would have been personal to her.

'To the reformers', says Susan Brigden, 1550s London became the 'idolatrous capital of an ungodly Queen', and they believed their souls to be as much at risk as their safety. From exile in Europe, Rose Hickman wrote to a kinswoman who remained behind: 'you stay', she declared, 'for covetousness and love of your husband's life and goods, but I fear the Lord's hand will be upon you for it'.[67] The unparticularized landscape seen through the window in Alice's painting was conventional in Low Country portraits from about 1460 and could easily have been executed in a London studio by an expatriate such as Hans Eworth. But the distinctively molded bricks of the background, too thin and dark to be of English workmanship, might more plausibly have been copied at the site of their production. This, according to Derek Keene, was Flanders.[68] While the figures of Alice and her sons may have been imported into an old, stock background that had survived their portraitist's relocation to London, the three may equally have been painted before a Flemish wall.

---

[66] John Howes notes that the Bishop of Chichester delivered the sermon at Mary I's coronation (*Brief Note*, 68). See also M. J. Kitch, 'The Reformation in Sussex', in id. (ed.), *Studies in Sussex Church History* (London: Leopard's Head, 1981), 77–98, esp. 94–6; Edward T. Stoneham, *Sussex Martyrs of the Reformation*, 3rd edn., rev. G. Seamer (Burgess Hill: Protestant Alliance and Sussex Martyrs Commemoration Council, 1967); and Zell. Perhaps because of the marginal status of the Sussex martyrs, confirmed in private conversation with East Sussex Record Office Senior Archivist Christopher Whittick, the principal sources on the subject remain John Foxe (*Foxe's Book of Martyrs Variorum Edition Online*, Version 1.1 (<www.hrionline.ac.uk/johnfoxe>, accessed 1 May 2007): 1570 edition, Book 12, pp. 2155, 2165, 2167) and John Knox ('The Names of the Martyrs', in *A Brief Exhortation to England for the Speedy Embracing of the Gospel* (London: 1559), 109–26). In his *History and Antiquities of Maidstone, The County-Town of Kent* (London: privately printed, 1741), William Newton gives 'John', not 'Joan' Bradbridge (p. 125). See also *The Diary of Henry Machyn, Citizen and Merchant-Taylor of London, from A.D. 1550 to A.D. 1563*, ed. John Gough Nichols, Camden Society 42 (1848), 131, 157–8, 161. For William Bradbridge's exile, see the *Oxford DNB* for William Bradbridge.

[67] Brigden, *London*, 559, 560. Other reformists felt morally obliged to remain in London as witnesses and as resisters of their 'ungodly Queen'.

[68] I am grateful for this information from Derek Keene, in private correspondence.

This alternate history for Alice Barnham would imagine her on the Continent in 1557, perhaps for a visit to her brother William in the earlier months of her third pregnancy, perhaps after giving birth.[69] Were such a scenario true, there would be no mystery to Francis's pictorial absence; he remained in London pursuing the aggressive business expansion that began in the first year of Mary's reign, as he took on three new apprentices and joined in financing the Muscovy expedition. Rose Hickman would have called his ventures 'covetous' and would have believed, as Alice may herself have come to do, that Anthony's death was a sign that 'the Lord's hand' was upon the Barnhams. If she fled to the Low Countries, then the portrait may have been the gift she sent Francis from exile, reassuring him of the physical health and spiritual progress of Martin and Steven.

Alice turned 34 in 1557, when the Venetian ambassador to London wrote that 'there were no Catholics in England under the age of thirty-five'; Francis was older. He seems nonetheless to have had reformist sympathies of his own. He was a governor of the Edwardian charitable institutions which replaced the lost religious houses of Catholic England, and he remembered Christ's Hospital in his will. He also made testamentary bequests to the poor parishioners of French and Dutch churches in London.[70] During the Marian years, thus, he may have shared with Alice a double life. In the city, the practical requirements of economic ambition drove his transactions with the regime in power. At home, the painting made a statement of opposition. With its incriminating text from the Protestant *Proverbs*, 'Alice Barnham and her Two Boys' must have been held private for caution's sake.

Even though Francis's commercial activities and royal loans would have helped ensure his family's safety, nothing could fully have mitigated Alice's spiritual suffering as her brother emigrated and Bradford was burned. From the evidence of the memoir and the portrait, Alice Barnham's convictions were put under pressure through all the years between 1553 and 1558. In 1557 she was not to know that it would be only a matter of months before she would see the end of these ingredients for personal crisis—the contaminations of an ungodly London, the victimization of Protestants, her professed allegiance to a dangerous faith, her family's commerce with a Catholic court, and tension between her religious beliefs and their economic practices.

---

[69] If *after* Anthony's birth, then Alice was in Flanders in 1558, retroactively referring to his birth in 1557, and his probable death, as having 'turned' her.

[70] Brigden cites the Venetian ambassador, *London*, 618, and also notes Mary's opposition to the London hospitals, p. 622. That there were Drapers with reformist beliefs is suggested by their admitted ownership of subversive books; see ibid. 595.

Third Turn

In one of the earliest English autobiographies, Thomas Whythorne recorded that he first had his own portrait painted around 1550. Twelve years later he returned to the same artist and sat again, like others who 'cause their pictures or counterfeits to be painted from time to time to see how time doth alter them'. Comparing his two portraits, Whythorne observed in the later one 'the long and fullness of my beard, the wrinkles on my face, and the hollowness of mine eyes; and also that as my face was altered so were the delights of my mind changed'. Whythorne was then 'above thirty years of age and growing toward the age of forty, at the which years begins the first part of the old man's age'. At the time of her painting, Alice had not only achieved her years of maturity but had also just passed the life landmark of 33, the age of Jesus at death.[71]

From this perspective, her legend supplies all the information we need in order to understand that the 'turn' may have been merely the commonplace one of time. 'I was born the 7 of September . . . 1523,' wrote Alice, 'turned from that I was unto that ye see Anno Domani 1557.' Hence, 1557 found her much altered from the day of her birth in 1523. There is a similar conceit in the inscription on Joan Thornbury's portrait (see Fig. 1.11), part of a pendant painted by Hans Eworth in 1566 when Thornbury was 36:

> My childhood past, that beautified my flesh,
> And gone my youth that gave me color fresh.
> I am now come to those ripe years at last,
> That tells me how my wanton days be past.
> And therefore, friend, *so turns the time me,*
> *I once was young and now am as you see.*[72]

In Alice's portrait the 'fresher' faces of her sons set off the way in which her own has 'ripened' with age. This would account for the progressive etiolation of skin tones in the painting, with Alice rosy-cheeked, the firstborn Martin pale as a pearl, and the younger Steven so exsanguine as to appear ghostly.

---

[71] Thomas Whythorne, *The Autobiography of Thomas Whythorne*, ed. James M. Osborn, Modern Spelling Edition (London: Oxford University Press, 1962), 115–17. I am grateful to John A. W. Lock for this reference and to Cynthia Herrup for the suggestion that an early modern surviving the age of 33 might have marked the date with reference to the death of Jesus.

[72] Emphasis added; cited by C. H. George, 'Parnassus Restored, Saints Confounded: The Secular Challenge to the Age of the Godly, 1560–1660', *Albion* 23 (1991), 434. In private correspondence, Mr George referred me to Eric Mercer, *English Art*, 168 and pl. 51. Paul Cox of the Heinz Archive at the National Portrait Gallery, London, provided Thornbury's married name. I am also grateful to David Wallace, who pointed out in private conversation that the penultimate line scans if 'time' is given the medieval pronunciation of two syllables; the meaning is understood to be that 'the time turns me'.

Alice may have perceived no need to further define the turn 'from that I was' to 'that ye see'. The notion that portraits captured moments in time was surely already as familiar as was suggested, some years later, in Shakespeare's *Twelfth Night* (1.5.204–6). There, Olivia is finally persuaded by Viola/Cesario to throw off her mourning veil; 'we will draw the curtain', she says, alluding to the common practice of mounting a painting behind its own cloth hangings, 'and show you the picture'. She exposes her face as Whythorne might have done his 'counterfeit', and, adding 'Look you, sir, such a one I was this present', emphasizes the necessary saturation of portrait by temporality.[73] With current referent following hard on past tense, Olivia recognizes that in the very instant of its completion a painting disengages from the subject in whom time's effects continue. Thus it assumes a memorializing aspect: it is not what is but 'that ye see'.

Just what Alice *meant* for us to see remains even now a matter for speculation. She may have recognized merely the effects of time; unarguably she represented her motherhood and her godliness. These two attributes are linked, as it happens, in Whythorne's defense of portraiture. A visual record, he observed, is good for people to 'leave with their friends, especially with their children, if they have any that be young'. When the children 'come to years of discretion' they can consult the painting: 'though their fathers be dead, yet may they see what manner of favor they had; and also thereby put in mind that, if they left a good report of their virtues behind them, they may embrace and follow the same'. For Alice, mothers, too, could model the 'virtues' of spiritual education, as she does for Martin and Steven. The themes of family and faith, featured so prominently in the completed portrait, correlate closely to those of infant mortality and religious persecution, among the hypothetical motives for its commission. These are also the broad interpretive coordinates for some of our most familiar narratives about epochal change in the post-Reformation private sphere: the glorification of companionate marriage and family affect, the impetus to self-examination and personal belief.

Still, there may yet be more to Alice's story than these usual suspects for subjectivity. The painting is a product of its moment—'this present', according to Olivia. The archives, however, project Alice into other settings and later life stages. Subsequent chapters look to the material culture of the domestic arena, her social experiences in the mercantile community, Francis's

---

[73] William Shakespeare, *Twelfth Night*, in *The Norton Shakespeare Based on the Oxford Edition*, gen. ed. Stephen Greenblatt (New York: W. W. Norton, 1997). Mercer notes contemporary 'insistence on the facial likeness', as for the 1554 portrait of and by Gerlach Flicke: 'Such in appearance was Gerlach Flicke when he was a painter in the City of London. This he painted from a mirror for his dear friends that they might be able to remember him after his death' (translated from the Latin by Mercer, *English Art*, 165).

role in local governance, and their joint ventures in the new economy. The first of these, her home environment, is again a matter on which the painting is provocatively enigmatic. Alice inhabits neither the placeless obscurity of Joan Thornbury nor the overfurnished interior of Lady Dacre. The masonry behind her, whatever its origin, succeeds in creating a receptive context for her textual inscriptions, with their implied agencies and ambiguated identities. And the untrimmed window, bare of moldings and glazing, only heightens the impact of the fantastic landscape it frames. With a gaze directed at the middle distance and a focus turned inward—not toward a putative pendant husband, not toward the son with whom she is in textual dialogue, not toward the viewers she also addresses—Alice Barnham seems occupied with an active internal life that has its pictorial analogue in the bird taking flight behind her. There is only so much she is willing to tell us, only so much she will show. The portrait represents interiority as resistance: an unstated name, the unexplained turn, and, most of all, her unshared thoughts.

2

Rebuildings

AT LEAST since 1577, when William Harrison remarked that 'every man almost is a builder', Tudor England has been known to have experienced a housing revolution. Our own understanding of the nature of that revolution has taken its shape from the near-seamless merge of two different approaches to the topic. First, from the fields of social and economic history, W. G. Hoskins recognized quantitative archaeological evidence for extraordinary improvements in standards of living at the vernacular level. Hoskins documented so much new construction in the period and so many modernization projects that he termed 1570 to 1640 the years of a 'Great Rebuilding'. He described medieval houses transformed by their vertical segmentation, with old, open interiors divided into two stories and with the prolific addition of stairs, chimneys, windows, and fuller fittings and furnishings. New homes were built to this more atomized pattern, with smaller rooms of particularized purpose. And second, from the realm of architectural connoisseurship, Mark Girouard made elite building a locus of important socio-cultural meaning as well as radical design change. His sophisticated, qualitative analysis of works projects by sixteenth-century 'architecter and surveyor' Robert Smythson drew on both archival and visual remains. Girouard emphasized the impact upon status building of High Renaissance ideas from the Continent, with rediscovery of the classical orders and the widespread adoption of other elements from Serlio, du Cerceau, and Palladio. In his telling, architecture first acquired a professionalized aspect during the development of England's early 'prodigy' houses.[1]

Some of the research conducted for this chapter first appeared in ' "The Causes and Reasons of all Artificial Things" in the Elizabethan Domestic Environment', *Medieval and Renaissance Drama in England* 7 (1995), 19–75; and *Elizabethan Households: An Anthology* (Washington, DC: The Folger Shakespeare Library, 1995).

[1] William Harrison, *The Description of England*, ed. Georges Edelen (Ithaca, NY: Cornell University Press for the Folger Shakespeare Library, 1968), 279. W. G. Hoskins, 'The Rebuilding of Rural England, 1570–1640', *Past and Present* 4 (1953), 44–59. Mark Girouard, *Robert Smythson and the Elizabethan Country House* (New Haven: Yale University Press, 1983).

Other important sources for this chapter include: Malcolm Airs, *The Tudor and Jacobean Country House: A Building History* (Phoenix Mill: Alan Sutton, 1995); Clive Aslet and Alan

Hoskins's more audacious thesis has also been the more controversial, as critics have contested the date range he proposed, noting that there

Powers, *The National Trust Book of the English House* (Harmondsworth: Viking in association with the National Trust, 1985); Maurice W. Barley, *The English Farmhouse and Cottage* (London: Routledge & Kegan Paul, 1961); Barley, *Houses and History* (London: Faber & Faber, 1986); Olive Cook, *The English House through Seven Centuries* (1968; Woodstock, NY: Overlook, 1983); Nicholas Cooper, *Houses of the Gentry, 1480–1680* (New Haven: Yale University Press for the Paul Mellon Centre for Studies in British Art in association with English Heritage, 1999); Girouard, *Life in the English Country House: A Social and Architectural History* (New Haven: Yale University Press, 1978); Maurice Howard, *The Early Tudor Country House: Architecture and Politics, 1490–1550* (London: George Philip, 1987); Matthew Johnson, *Housing Culture: Traditional Architecture in an English Landscape* (Washington, DC: Smithsonian Institution Press, 1993); Eric Mercer, *English Vernacular Houses: A Study of Traditional Farmhouses and Cottages* (London: HMSO, 1975); Timothy Mowl, *Elizabethan and Jacobean Style* (London: Phaidon, 1993); L. F. Salzman, *Building in England Down to 1540, A Documentary History*, 2nd edn. (Oxford: Clarendon, 1967); John Schofield, *Medieval London Houses* (New Haven: Yale University Press for the Paul Mellon Centre for Studies in British Art, 1995); Simon Thurley, *The Royal Palaces of Tudor England: Architecture and Court Life, 1460–1547* (New Haven: Yale University Press for the Paul Mellon Centre for Studies in British Art, 1993); and Trudy West, *The Timber-Frame House in England* (Newton Abbot: David & Charles, 1971).

I am also grateful to the owners and managers of the houses I have visited. In Avon: Bristol Red Lodge; in Berkshire: Dorney Court; in Buckinghamshire: Chenies Manor House; in Cambridgeshire: Longthorpe Tower; in Cheshire: Bramall Hall, Churche's Mansion, Dorfold Hall, Dunham Massey White Cottage, Gawsworth Hall, Handforth Hall, Little Moreton Hall, Lyme Park, and Peover Hall; in Cornwall: Cotehele House, Lanhydrock, Prideaux Place, Tintagel Old Post Office, and Trerice House; in Cumbria: Levens Hall, Sizergh Castle, and Townend; in Derbyshire: Bakewell Old House, Bolsover Castle, Eyam Hall, Haddon Hall, Hardwick Hall, and Hardwick Old Hall; in Devon: Boringdon Hall, Bradley Manor, Buckland Abbey, Cadhay, Compton Castle, Prysten House, Shute Barton, Whitechapel Manor, and Yarde; in Dorset: Athelhampton House, Fiddleford Manor, Forde Abbey, Purse Caundle Manor House, Sandford Orcas Manor, Sherborne Castle, and Wolfeton House; in Essex: Audley End, Gosfield Hall, Ingatestone Hall, Layer Marney, Paycocke's, and St Osyth's Priory; in Gloucestershire: Berkeley Castle, Chavenage, Horton Court, Owlpen Manor, Stanway House, and Whittington Court; in Hampshire: Breamore House, Southampton Medieval Merchant's House, Southampton Tudor House, and The Vyne; in Herefordshire: Cwmmau Farmhouse, Hellen's Much Marcle, Hereford Old House, Kinnersley Castle, and Lower Brockhampton; in Hertfordshire: Hatfield House and Picotts End; in Kent: Arden's House, Boughton Monchelsea Place, Cobham Hall, Eyhorne Manor, Godinton House, Hever Castle, Ightham Mote, Knole, Leeds Castle, Old Soar Manor, Penshurst Place, Quebec House, and Stoneacre; in Lancashire: Astley Hall, Gawthorpe Hall, Hall-i'th'-Wood, Rufford Old Hall, Samlesbury Hall, Smithills Hall, Towneley Hall, and Turton Tower; in Leicestershire: Donington-le-Heath Manor House and Lyddington Bede House; in Lincolnshire: Aubourn Hall, Burghley House, Doddington Hall, and Gainsborough Old Hall; in London: Charlton House, Charterhouse, Crosby Hall, Ham House, Queen's House, and Sutton House; in Merseyside: Speke Hall; in Norfolk: Blickling Hall, Felbrigg Hall, Oxburgh Hall, and Yarmouth Tudor houses; in North Wales: Aberconwy House, Gwydir Castle, Penarth Fawr Medieval House, Plas Mawr, and Powis Castle; in Northamptonshire: Canons Ashby, Deene Park, Holdenby, Kirby Hall, Lyveden New Bield, Prebendal Manor House, Rockingham Castle, Rushton Triangular Lodge, Southwick Hall, and Sulgrave Manor; in Nottinghamshire: Holme Pierrepont Hall and Wollaton Hall; in Oxfordshire: Ashdown House, Broughton Castle, Chastleton House, Greys Court, and Mapledurham House; in Shropshire: Benthall Hall, Moat House, Stokesay Castle, Upton Cressett Hall, and Wilderhope Manor;

were pronounced regional variations and successive waves of rebuilding.[2] No one, however, has disputed his bald assertion that a desire for privacy motivated the compartmentalizing changes he observed. 'We must look for the cause of the Great Rebuilding', said Hoskins, 'in the filtering down to the mass of the population, after some two centuries, of a sense of privacy that had formerly been enjoyed only by the upper classes. Privacy demands more rooms, devoted to specialised uses.' Although Girouard warned that 'it would be a mistake to see country-house history in terms of greater and greater privacy', his studies of Smythson and of life in the English country house have nonetheless been widely assumed to have advanced the argument. Thus, both interpretive streams inform the common conviction that persons of all social registers experienced higher levels of privacy in the sixteenth century. We might not have accepted Hoskins's explanatory paradigm so willingly, or have overinterpreted Girouard, had our narratives of the Renaissance not been lastingly imprinted by Burckhardtian notions about the discovery of the individual and of domestic life. Roger Chartier, for example, extends the

in Somerset: Barrington Court, Farleigh Hungerford Castle, Gaulden Manor, Glastonbury Tribunal, King John's Hunting Lodge, Lytes Cary, Montacute House, and Stoke-sub-Hamdon Priory; in South Wales: Llancaiach Fawr Manor, St Fagan's Castle, Tretower Court, Quay Hill Tudor Merchant's House, and buildings at the Welsh Folk Museum; in Staffordshire: Ford Green Hall, Moseley Old Hall, Stafford Ancient High House, and Tamworth Castle; in Suffolk: Christchurch Mansion, Helmingham, Kentwell Hall, buildings in Lavenham, Melford Hall, and Otley Hall; in Surrey: Carew Manor, Great Fosters, Hampton Court Palace, Loseley Park, and Whitehall; in Sussex: Alfriston Clergy House, Anne of Cleves' House, Bodiam Castle, Danny, Filching Manor, Glynde Place, Great Dixter, Michelham Priory, Parham Park, Sackville College, St Mary's, buildings at the Weald and Downland Open Air Museum, and West Hoathly Priest House; in Warwickshire: Baddesley Clinton, Coughton Court, Lord Leycester's Hospital, Packwood House, and the properties of the Shakespeare Birthplace Trust; in West Midlands: Aston Hall, Blakesley Hall, and Oak House; in Wiltshire: Avebury Manor, Great Chalfield Manor, Lacock Abbey, Littlecote, Longleat, Sheldon Manor, and Westwood Manor; in Worcestershire: buildings at the Avoncroft Museum of Buildings, The Greyfriars, Harvington Hall, and Worcester Commandery; in Yorkshire: Burton Agnes Hall, Burton Constable Hall, Calverley Old Hall, East Riddlesden Hall, Norton Conyers, Oakwell Hall, Shibden Hall, Temple Newsam, Wilberforce House, and York Treasurer's House. I benefited from conversations with my sometime traveling companions, Glenn Orlin, Nancy Elizabeth Hodge, and Catherine Belsey. In this chapter, information without direct sourcing derives either from personal observation in these houses or from their (often anonymous) guidebooks.

    [2] See e.g. R. Machin, 'The Great Rebuilding: A Reassessment', *Past and Present* 77 (1977), 33–56. Derek Portman argues that Hoskins's Rebuilding 'extended over the whole of southern and midland England and much of the north' but that in some places, including the East Midlands, it did not commence till after the Restoration ('Vernacular Building in the Oxford Region in the Sixteenth and Seventeenth Centuries', in C. W. Chalklin and M. A. Havinden (eds.), *Rural Change and Urban Growth, 1500–1800: Essays in English Regional History in Honour of W. G. Hoskins* (London: Longman, 1974), 138–9). In *The Great Rebuildings of Tudor and Stuart England* (London: UCL, 1994), Colin Platt uses the plural advisedly in concluding that Hoskins's Great Rebuilding 'never happened' as a national and uniformly periodized phenomenon. He nonetheless finds the theory 'still persuasive' (p. vii).

thesis to what seems an unexceptionable conclusion: 'the new concept of the individual had an important influence on the definition of private space in the early modern era.'[3]

Alice Friedman, an obvious heir to Girouard in her study of Smythson-designed Wollaton Hall, embraces Hoskins's thesis. A 'desire for greater privacy was the motive' for the Great Rebuilding, she states. As she reads it, further, Wollaton gives evidence of the 'gradual and generalized retreat' of leading families to exclusive spaces, with upper-level rooms, in particular, being 'less accessible' and therefore 'more private'. In an analysis of gentry housing as a leading-edge sector for architectural change, Eric Mercer attributes the much-discussed 'decline' of the medieval great hall to the fact that that large open space was not 'capable' of providing newly longed-for comfort and privacy. Maurice Howard similarly asserts that whereas the activities of great households had once been 'concentrated' in the multi-functional hall, in Tudor times, in a 'move towards greater privacy', they were dispersed into 'rooms specially built and furnished for one purpose'. Thus, the 'increasing value placed on privacy in this period' was made possible by 'architectural changes'. At the highest levels, according to Simon Thurley, the power which had been consolidated by the Crown 'aggravated' the monarch's desire to 'remove himself from the Court'; 'important architectural consequences' followed from Henry VIII's 'increasing need for privacy'. The most recent of influential authors on the subject, Nicholas Cooper, is also the most emphatic: 'The common link between the evolution of chambers, hall and parlours was in the increasing provision made in every part of the house for privacy and exclusivity.' There was, he says, 'a mental climate that was increasingly concerned with the cultivation of the individual and with the enjoyment of privacy as a good'.[4]

This chapter does not quarrel with the practice of interweaving the strands of argument initiated by Hoskins and Girouard. Whether the symptoms of architectural revolution are improvements in modest housing or innovations in status building, all demonstrate profound consciousness of and ambitions for the Tudor domestic environment. Here, however, these material events are deliberately disengaged from previously unchallenged interpretations of their

---

[3] Hoskins, 'Rebuilding', 54; Girouard, *Life*, 11; he characterizes the eighteenth century as the time of the greatest personal privacy. Roger Chartier, 'Introduction' to 'Forms of Privatization' in id. (ed.), *A History of Private Life*, iii. *Passions of the Renaissance*, trans. Arthur Goldhammer (Cambridge, Mass.: Belknap Press of Harvard University Press, 1989), 165.

[4] Alice T. Friedman, *House and Household in Elizabethan England: Wollaton Hall and the Willoughby Family* (Chicago: University of Chicago Press, 1989), 179, 151. Eric Mercer, 'The Houses of the Gentry', *Past and Present* 5 (1954), 15. Howard, *Early Tudor Country House*, 108. Thurley, *Royal Palaces*, 37. Cooper, *Houses of the Gentry*, 273, 300.

genesis. Can it indeed be said that a desire for privacy motivated the hall's decline, purpose-specific rooms, the construction of chimneys and stairs, a proliferation of household goods and furnishings, redesigned floor plans and elevations, domestic investment? Mercer accepted this cause for many aspects of the Rebuilding of England, but he also, and in the present context most cogently, maintained that 'although we may allow a development to be logical, it is not logic that causes the development. Logic does no more than solve the problems that the development raises.'[5] Rarely is change as rational, as responsive, as schematic, and as evolutionary as it can be made to seem by abstract argument. In what follows, some of the more important reformations of the early modern spatial surround are reviewed as prelude to a subject to be considered here and then in other chapters, as well: material privacy, but as a problematic.

THE GREAT REBUILDING

Accounts of the Great Rebuilding which are focused on elite architecture generally emphasize that the early sixteenth-century market in real estate, which had been comparatively stagnant, received the sudden infusion of hundreds of important properties. This was in consequence of the Dissolution of the monasteries. The late-medieval Church had owned as much as a third of the country, but in 1536 the Crown commandeered its smaller religious houses. Larger abbeys and monasteries followed in 1539, and college chantries and chapels in 1545 and 1547. Hoskins had a term for the Dissolution, too: the 'Great Plunder', the 'greatest transference of land in English history since the Norman Conquest'. Especially radical was the fact that the Crown did not retain the seized estates among its own holdings. It redistributed most of them to members of the gentry and nobility, at first in reward and then for a fee.[6]

New owners of the transferred properties were often slow to settle on them. Mercer Robert Palmer, for example, was granted a Sussex estate for a fine of £1,255. 6s. 5d. But the building of Parham Park did not begin until 1577, when

---

[5] Mercer, 'Houses of the Gentry', 30.

[6] Barley, *Houses and History*, 131; W. G. Hoskins, *The Age of Plunder: The England of Henry VIII, 1500–1547* (London: Longman, 1976), 121. See also Joyce A. Youings, *The Dissolution of the Monasteries* (London: George Allen & Unwin, 1971); Youings, *Sixteenth-Century England*, The Pelican Social History of Britain (Harmondsworth: Penguin Books, 1984); Stanford E. Lehmberg, *The Reformation Parliament, 1529–1536* (Cambridge: Cambridge University Press, 1970); and Walter C. Richardson, *History of the Court of Augmentations, 1536–1554* (Baton Rouge: Louisiana State University Press, 1961).

his son inherited. With reason to fear that former church holdings might eventually be restored to their original use, many awardees were content merely to gather income from pre-existing rents and from the sale of such resources as timber. They were also willing to demolish monastic structures so that architectural salvage could be put to use in other works projects. Early raiders were the King's surveyors, who in 1537 used roofing lead and forty windows from Rewley Abbey as they remodeled Hampton Court. Between 1546 and 1550 John Haydon built his Devon seat, Cadhay, with stone from the College of Priests at Ottery St Mary and with 'all manner of glass, iron, timber, stones, tomb-stones, tile stones, and paving tile' from Dunkeswell Abbey. Worked stone from abbeys at Bromehill, Ixworth, Thetford, and Bury St Edmunds were purchased by Sir Thomas Kytson for Hengrave; Sir Nicholas Bacon used materials from St Albans for Gorhambury. Even the wooden angels terminating the ceiling hammerbeams in the great hall at Rufford may have been recovered from a suppressed monastery. When an estate retains the name of its source, like Buckland Abbey, Lacock Abbey, or Forde Abbey, this is often the sign of an owner who was, by contrast, sufficiently bold to occupy an ecclesiastical site immediately.[7] Monastic guest houses and abbots' lodgings were among the most advanced residential buildings for their time, readily and sometimes irresistibly adaptable to domestic use.

A further aspect of the Dissolution was that it halted the Church's own construction programs. And while Henry VIII was a builder, his children were not. Elizabeth I relied on her noblemen to create appropriately lavish settings for her seasonal progresses; Christopher Hatton famously described Holdenby as a 'shrine' for 'that holy saint'—the Virgin Queen—'to whom it is dedicated'. Thus, whereas in France royal and ecclesiastical palaces continued to set the architectural pace, in England design ambitions, building materials, and skilled workers were focused on private homes.[8] Great men were reminded, often in vain, that they should 'Let your house be too little for a day or two, rather than too great for a year.' Had he been more interested in upper-end residences, Hoskins might have observed another species of evidence for the housing revolution, which was that familiar forms of complaint about extravagant apparel were newly adapted to the censure of dwelling places, too. Philip

[7] Guidebooks for Parham Park, Cadhay, and Rufford Old Hall. For Cadhay see also Airs, *Tudor and Jacobean*, 133–4. Airs discusses Hengrave, Gorhambury, and reluctance to build on church lands, pp. 29–30. For Hampton Court, see *The History of the King's Works*, iv. *1485–1660 (Part II)*, ed. H. M. Colvin, John Summerson, et al. (London: HMSO, 1982), 132.

[8] Hatton, Letter to Sir Thomas Heneage (1580), quoted by Airs, *Tudor and Jacobean*, 21. As early as 1789, Arthur Young contrasted the 'diffusion of comfort in the houses of private people' in England to 'the concentrated magnificence in public works' in Italy (quoted by Lawrence Stone and Jeanne C. Fawtier Stone, *An Open Elite? England, 1540–1880* (Oxford: Clarendon, 1984), 297).

Stubbes inveighed against contemporaries with 'gorgeous houses, sumptuous edifices, and stately turrets' in which they lived 'like mighty potentates'. In 1644 Sir Edward Coke was dismayed that Parliament had still not passed an act against 'excess of building' even though it was 'a wasting evil'.[9]

Instead, Hoskins emphasized the larger demographic and economic changes that fueled a Great Rebuilding among more modest men. In the sixteenth century, population totals began finally to approach the historic high of 1300, before the worst devastations of plague. At last there was again a need for buildings that had been left abandoned in years of depopulation, but these were now found to be 'decayed houses', with 'pits and cellars left uncovered' and many walls 'feeble' and likely to collapse, according to the so-called 'Rebuilding Statutes' of the 1530s and 1540s. To be habitable, vacated structures required renovation. In the meantime, technology had advanced, so refittings were generally done to new standards. Hoskins describes the use of coal rather than wood for home heating, as well as the availability of cheap window glass. He notes also that prices for produce began to rise even as rents remained fixed, meaning that many small farmers had more surplus income than had previously been the case; M. W. Barley agrees that by mid-sixteenth-century laborers 'could afford to improve their way of life'.[10]

Admittedly, there was no single remaking of the countryside in the Elizabethan and Jacobean years. The phenomena Hoskins identified are most visible in the southeast, where men who made or inherited London fortunes were likely to relocate—as did Martin Barnham and his kin by marriage, John Rudston and Edward Wotton. The north and the west were slower to change. Furthermore, the physical evidence which Hoskins took pains to honor is partial and sometimes misleading. Those without discretionary wealth lived in substandard housing that has long since disappeared. With their vanished walls has gone proof of the enforced persistence of one-roomed and single-storied

---

[9] For 'let your house be too little', I cite Sir William Wentworth's 1604 'Advice to his Son' (from *Wentworth Papers 1597–1628*, ed. J. P. Cooper, Camden Society 4th ser., 12 (1973), 14), though the injunction was so common as to be proverbial. Nicholas Cooper indicates that it was still current a half-century later ('Rank, Manners and Display: The Gentlemanly House, 1500–1750', *Transactions of the Royal Historical Society* 6th ser., 12 [2002], 300). Stubbes quoted by Frederick Hard (ed.), *The Elements of Architecture by Sir Henry Wotton* (Charlottesville: University Press of Virginia for the Folger Shakespeare Library, 1968), p. lx. Coke's *Third Part of the Institutes of the Laws of England: Concerning High Treason and Other Pleas of the Crown* (1644; London: 1660), 201. For complaints about ostentatious building see also Whitney R. D. Jones, *The Tudor Commonwealth, 1529–1559* (London: Athlone, 1970), 93–4.

[10] On population, see esp. Hoskins, *Age of Plunder*, 4–6, also citing the Parliamentary Acts of 1534 and 1542. Robert Tittler speculates on the connection between these statutes and Hoskins's 'Great Rebuilding' ('For the "Re-edification of Townes": The Rebuilding Statutes of Henry VIII', *Albion* 22 (1990), 602). On surplus income, see Hoskins, 'Rebuilding', 50, 53; and Barley, *English Farmhouse*, 124.

houses. R. Machin describes the artifacts of the Rebuilding as objects of *over*building. There was a 'medieval preference for impermanent building', he says, and the mystery is why this changed in the early modern period.[11] But his argument does not convincingly negate that of Hoskins, who recognized that in fact there were a number of fourteenth- and fifteenth-century houses built so substantially that they still stand today, but with the second stories, partition walls, chimneys, and staircases that were introduced in the sixteenth century during what he memorably called a 'Great Rebuilding'.

Essentially, surviving structures constitute anecdotal evidence—though Hoskins would presumably not have identified them as such. Besides 'look[ing] over hedges', however, he also delved into archives, where he found ample documentation that early moderns were themselves aware of their transformed environs. William Harrison, for example, marveled that 'never so much hath been spent in a hundred years before as is in ten year of our time . . . and he that hath bought any small parcel of ground, be it never so little, will not be quiet till he have pulled down the old house (if any were there standing) and set up a new after his own device'. If there were not some truth to his observations, there would have been no need for a statute of 1589, ordering that anyone who raised a new home was required to have at least four acres of land. The problem was 'the erecting and building of great numbers and multitudes of cottages, which are daily more and more increased in many parts of this realm'. An unlikely further source on the subject is the Consistory Court of London, where depositions were taken about Woodford, a provincial parish to which many Londoners resorted each summer. Laboring men were being displaced by these wealthier newcomers who demolished cottages in order to build 'great houses'. The Woodford deponents described processes now known as suburban 'gentrification' and 'mansionization'.[12]

Hoskins's detractors are concentrated on empirical evidence. Finally, the reason his thesis has nonetheless persisted is because it seems unarguably to be true to contemporary perception. He recognized an aspect of Tudor material life that was crucially informing of its mental world. As an intimation of common culture, moreover, anecdotal evidence can be profoundly suggestive. There are stories like that of Londoner Eleanor Peerson, who was so deeply invested in her home in Aldersgate Street that she rejected a suitor in 1566

---

[11] On Rebuilding in the southeast, see Barley, *Houses and History*, 226. On survivals and losses, ibid. 245 and Mercer, *English Vernacular Houses*, 2, 27. Machin, 'Great Rebuilding', 55.

[12] Hoskins, 'Rebuilding', 44. Harrison, *Description*, 279. On the Cottages Act, see Hoskins, 'Rebuilding', 49, and Barley, *English Farmhouse*, 59. On gentrification, GL Ms 9189/1, fos. 9ᵛ–16ᵛ. The Consistory was concerned with enlargement of the parish church to accommodate population growth (then in Essex, now part of Greater London); where three or four people had formerly resided, gentlemen lodged households numbering fifteen and more.

because he asked her to move to his place. Her stubborn refusal 'pleased' John Strete 'as well as though she had beaten him about the ears with her fist', and betrothal negotiations were broken off. It is an open question whether her motivation was as reported, but the fact remains that house pride was presented as a credible pretext. In Townend, in the west country, Susannah Rawlinson agreed to wed George Browne only if his home was entirely rebuilt. The stipulation was written into their marriage contract. The ways in which early moderns could identify with their living space is especially apparent in their wills. Thus, John Turner of Great Waltham directed in 1592 that 'after my decease, my wife shall build up at her cost one kitchen house' to his specifications. Essex husbandman Thomas Hayward stipulated that his wife was to construct 'a dwelling house of forty-four foot long and eighteen foot broad between the sills, with two [gable] walls'. There was to be 'ceiling all over, and the house to be double story, the nether story to be seven foot and the upper story five-and-a-half foot between joints, with the wideness also of sixteen inches between stud and stud of each story'. (Hoskins would have noted with interest that two levels were called for in 1568, rather than an open hall.) Suffolk yeoman Hugh Butcher, having assembled 'window timber' before his death in 1620, willed that one window was to be 'made and framed' in his own bedchamber and another in his parlor.[13]

For upper-class builders, too, spatial intentions rose to the level of deathbed preoccupations. In 1601, for instance, the north-country knight Richard Brakenbury directed that 'My will is that my executors [are] to proceed with the finishing of Selby house.' In 1617, Sir Edward Pytts ordered £2,000 to be set aside for building at Kyre Park 'according to the plot remaining in Chaunce's hands drawn by my dictation'. Sir Thomas Holt reserved £1,000 for landscaping at Aston Hall in the West Midlands in 1637. His banqueting houses were originally to have imitated structures he had admired at Campden House in Gloucestershire but were latterly to follow 'a plot which I have now made'. Sir John Thynne's will of 1579 specified that 'if I happen to die before I have fully finished the buildings of my house at Longleat', the executors should 'cause or procure my said house at Longleat to be fully and perfectly

---

[13] Stoneleigh might be a classic instance of Rebuilding as Hoskins described it; see N. W. Alcock, *People at Home: Living in a Warwickshire Village, 1500–1800* (Chichester: Phillimore, 1993). Deposition of John Strete, *Eleanor Peerson* v. *Rose Hytchins*, GL Ms 9056, fos. 26ʳ–27ʳ. Rawlinson and Browne cited by Bill Rollinson, 'A Guide to Townend' (National Trust, n.d.). Will of John Turner (1592), F. G. Emmison, *Elizabethan Life: Home, Work and Land* (Chelmsford: Essex Record Office, 1991), 5. Will of Thomas Hayward (1568), *Essex Wills (England)*, ii. *1565–1571*, ed. F. G. Emmison (Boston: New England Historic Genealogical Society, 1983), no. 689. Will of High Butcher (1620), *Wills of the Archdeaconry of Suffolk, 1620–1624*, ed. Marion E. Allen, Suffolk Records Society 31 (1989), no. 77.

finished and builded in all things as well inwardly as outwardly according as I have appointed'.[14]

Longleat was a project with many directors, including Smythson, but the principal vision was surely Thynne's. Records show him deciding that walls from the first floor up need be only two bricks thick, ordering the timber for doors and wainscotting to be well seasoned before their working, requiring brick chimney stacks to be rebuilt in stone, supervising the design for an overmantel, selecting the hinges and staples for a door, and having trees cleared to give an unimpeded view of the most accomplished elevation of its age. It was both strictly regular and astonishingly rich in interest, massive in contour but delicate in detail (see Figs. 2.1 and 2.2). For Girouard, Longleat comes 'as near as anything in England in the sixteenth century to a truly Renaissance house', and Nicholas Cooper calls it 'the most revolutionary house of its age'. It evolved through four stages of construction—the third mandated by a devastating fire—and each, says Maurice Howard, was 'more radical' and also 'more coherent in design'. At first Thynne adapted some minor Carthusian buildings to create twenty-seven dwelling rooms (1547–53); then he constructed an additional wing and refaced old ones to create a symmetrical block with Gothic moldings and a 'bristling' skyline (1553–67); after the fire he built to an entirely different, larger scale, with more windows and eight staircase turrets (1567–72); and finally he wrapped the whole in the disciplined façade for which he is now famous (1572–80).[15] The process of trial, error, correction, and heady invention was as consuming as Thynne's will suggests.

Thynne's neighbor William Darrell satirized his protracted quest for perfection, speaking as if in the voice of Longleat itself: 'But now see him that by these thirty years almost with such turmoil of mind hath been thinking of me, framing and erecting me, musing many a time with great care and now and then pulling down this or that part of me to enlarge sometime a foot, or some few inches, upon a conceit, or this or that man's speech, and by and by beat

---

[14] Will of Richard Brakenbury (1601), *North Country Wills . . . 1558 to 1604*, ii, ed. John William Clay, Publications of the Surtees Society 121 (1912), no. 152. Will of Sir Edward Pytts cited by John Summerson, *Architecture in Britain, 1530 to 1830*, 7th edn. (Frome: Penguin Books, 1983), 60; Airs, *Tudor and Jacobean*, 156. Will of Sir Thomas Holt excerpted by Oliver Fairclough, *The Grand Old Mansion: The Holtes and Their Successors at Aston Hall 1618–1864* (Birmingham: Birmingham Museums and Art Gallery, 1984), 66. Will of Sir John Thynne quoted by Girouard, *Robert Smythson*, 53; this will of 1579 was superseded before Thynne's death in 1580.

[15] Frank Jenkins, *Architect and Patron* (London: Oxford University Press, 1961), 11; see also David Burnett, *Longleat: The Story of an English Country House* (London: Collins, 1978), 19, 20, 28; Airs, *Tudor and Jacobean*, 42–3, 85; Cook, *English House*, 79. Girouard, *Robert Smythson*, 41; Cooper, 'Rank, Manners, and Display', 295. Howard, *Early Tudor Country House*, 184; for the stages of construction, I follow Girouard, *Robert Smythson*, 42–50.

Figure 2.1 The symmetrical façade of Longleat, near Warminster in Wiltshire. The building was conceptualized 'in the round', with all four elevations designed to the same discipline.

Figure 2.2 A corner of the elevation at Longleat, showing the rich detailing of its execution and the movement evoked by its advancing and receding bays.

down windows for this or that fault here or there.' Two years later, William Harrison used uncannily similar terms to describe the restlessness of all elite Rebuilders: 'It is a world to see, moreover, how divers men, being bent to building and having a delectable vein in spending of their goods by that trade, do daily imagine new devices of their own to guide their workmen withal, and those more curious and excellent always than the former. In the proceeding also of their works,' he continued, 'how they set up, how they pull down, how they enlarge, how they restrain, how they add to, how they take from, whereby their heads are never idle, their purses never shut, nor their books of account never made perfect.'[16]

Where Thynne was still reinventing Longleat on his deathbed, Bess of Hardwick was said to have believed she would not die as long as she was building. 'After a lifetime's experience' at Chatsworth, Owlcotes, Worksop, and Hardwick Old Hall, says Girouard, she 'clearly set out to create the perfect

---

[16] Darrell quoted by Girouard, *Robert Smythson*, 76, from *The Records of the Building of Longleat*, Canon Jackson's 3-vol. scrapbook of original documents and copies of manuscript materials. Thynne was also described as 'infesting' Edward Seymour, Duke of Somerset, with 'plats and forms and many a subtle thing'; Girouard, ibid. 41. Harrison, *Description*, 277. Machin points out that 'Harrison's comments relate largely to Essex and Kent' ('Great Rebuilding', 40).

house', and accomplished it at Hardwick (New) Hall.[17] Edward Pytts acquired a ruined castle at Kyre Wyard in 1586. He had remade it by 1595, but, after redeveloping a London townhouse and absorbing city tastes and influences, returned to his Worcestershire seat for a second overhaul. Sir Christopher Hatton began Kirby even before completing Holdenby. Sir Thomas Tresham remodeled Rushton Hall and Lyveden and did his most original work at Lyveden New Bield and the allegorical Triangular Lodge. In the Bacon family the rebuilding urge was contagious across the generations: at Gorhambury Sir Nicholas destroyed a house he had purchased in 1561 and used the materials for a new house begun in 1563; in 1617 Sir Francis left Gorhambury standing but erected Verulam nearby. Sir William Cecil supervised Burghley, Theobalds, and Cecil House in the Strand; his son was responsible for two more London residences, Cranborne House, and a £38,000 project at Hatfield, where extant structures were deemed good only for stables. Sir William Petre bought the Essex manor of Ingatestone in 1539 and immediately pulled down the 'old house', which he described as 'scant meet for a farmer to dwell upon', before building anew. Sir Francis Willoughby inherited a house in a valley but razed it to position Wollaton Hall on a hilltop. Sir Henry Hobart purchased Blickling in 1616 but preserved only part of it as he created a more impressive residence.[18] Bess and her compatriots would not have started fresh were they not measuring themselves against new standards and styles that were features of a Great Rebuilding.

WHAT BESS OF HARDWICK BUILT

The legacy that haunted early modern status building was the idea of the castle, notionally an impregnable stronghold with its residential functions centered on the communal life of the great hall. In 'To Penshurst', Ben

---

[17] Thynne's last will omits the clause about finishing the house, but Girouard shows that while he spent £1,140 in 1568, between £627 and £930 for each of the next nine years, and £596 in the fifteen months between October 1578 and December 1579, between January 1580 and his death in May 1580 he had already spent £491 more. A descendant notes that 'some of the towers' were left unfinished; Thynne's son completed these and also installed the screen and wainscotting in the hall (Girouard, *Robert Smythson*, 53). Hardwick's tomb credits her with Chatsworth, Hardwick, and Owlcotes, but she also contributed to the design of Worksop. Having lost Chatsworth in a hostile split from her fourth husband, George Talbot, Earl of Shrewsbury, she immediately set about rebuilding her birth home, Hardwick Old Hall, working on it from 1584 to 1591. Even before it was finished she began the nearby Hardwick (New) Hall in 1590; she moved in on 4 October 1597 (Girouard, *Robert Smythson*, 112, 144–5).

[18] Airs, *Tudor and Jacobean*, 20–2. F. G. Emmison, *Tudor Secretary: Sir William Petre at Court and Home* (Cambridge, Mass.: Harvard University Press, 1961), 27.

Jonson panegyrized a fourteenth-century building that was unfortified but that otherwise retained all the signifying elements of the form (see Fig. 2.3). Traditionally, the hall was a vast space to accommodate feudal retainers in eating and sleeping; Penshurst's is 62 ft long and 39 ft wide. It was necessary to build high in order to build large, and the complementary nature of footprint, elevation, and population meant that the hammerbeams and crown-posts of the medieval roof were often carved, painted, and gilded to draw an admiring eye to their lofty location. Penshurst is so tall a hall at 60 ft that in 1471 a local man was hired to catch hawks there. The most efficient way to warm large numbers of people was with a central fire, and Penshurst still retains the octagonal tiling and curbing of its hearth, along with a set of Tudor firedogs. Directly overhead, at the peak of a great hall's roof, stood a cage-like contraption with slats that could be opened to vent smoke or closed to shut out rain. Penshurst's louver no longer survives, though its former presence can be detected. The most important of the hall's sparse furnishings were long dining tables with boards that could be removed to clear the room or placed directly on the ground as sleep surfaces. Penshurst has the oldest remaining examples of the medieval trestle table. Windows were positioned high over fixed benches and wall hangings, their sole purpose to admit light. Only the high-end bay, or oriel, allowed the outward view that was the perquisite of the medieval lord. His own table rested on a raised platform; at Penshurst the dais stands six inches above the main floor. When chimneys were eventually added in halls, it was often at the dais, opposite the oriel, further distinguishing the members of the principal family and their honored guests from the retainers and subordinates served by the hearth.[19]

The most notable design characteristic of the great hall was its imbalance, beginning with its rectangular shape and including all its means for endowing one end, the dais, with importance. Even on the external façade, the high end was indicated by the oriel. Matthew Johnson emphasizes the relationship between asymmetry of design and asymmetry of status, and indeed it was undoubtedly the great hall's proficiency in spatializing social hierarchy that accounted for its continuing resonance in post-medieval culture. The room was entered at one short end by means of a corridor which stretched the full width of the typical building, from front door to back (see Fig. 2.4). This was known as the 'screens' passage for the partial wall that divided the throughway from the hall and concealed the traffic of servants, providers, and petitioners.

---

[19] For general information on the great hall, see the sources listed in n. 1. For Penshurst, see also house guidebooks and Don E. Wayne, *Penshurst: The Semiotics of Place and the Poetics of History* (Madison: University of Wisconsin Press, 1984). The hall was built for a London draper, Sir John de Pulteney, four times Lord Mayor of London, in 1341; see Nigel Nicolson, *Great Houses of Britain* (New York: Putnam, 1965), 27. A louvre survives at Gainsborough old Hall.

Figure 2.3 The great hall at Penshurst Place, in Kent, looking from the dais toward the central hearth, the screen, and the minstrels' gallery.

The screen's two openings, which permitted access to the hall, were matched across the corridor by doors to the pantry and buttery. Space was structured so that any newcomer was directed from the front portal, into the passage, and then into the hall only after a ninety-degree turn through one of the screen's entry points as through triumphal arches. The placement of the dais at the opposite end of the hall originally had a security function. In latter days, however, the long view was designed mainly to impress. The feudal functions of the hall had been abandoned for centuries; in the 1360s, *Piers Plowman* had already complained of the lord who forsook the dais to eat 'by himself | In a privy parlor . . . Or in a chamber with a chimney.'[20]

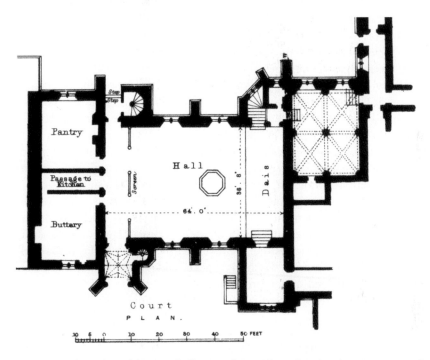

Figure 2.4 Floor plan of the great hall at Penshurst Place, showing the entrance porch, the screens passage, the hearth, the dais, and, across the screens passage, pantry and buttery.

---

[20] Johnson, *Housing Culture*, 57. Girouard says that the 'ceremonial function' of the medieval hall was 'perfected when a musicians' gallery was built over' the screens passage (*Life*, 38). Langland quoted by Nathaniel Lloyd, *A History of the English House from Primitive Times to the Victorian Period* (1931; London: Architectural Press, 1975), 48. See also *Civil and Uncivil Life* (1579), in *Inedited Tracts: Illustrating the Manners, Opinions, and Occupations of Englishmen during the Sixteenth and Seventeenth Centuries,* ed. William Carew Hazlitt (London: Roxburghe

In the sixteenth century there were a few great men who revived the medieval rituals of dining in state, like the lords Burghley and Ellesmere. The hall at Rufford was still a principal dining room in 1620, fully furnished with tables, cupboards, forms, stools, cushions, cloths, hangings, and paintings. At Raglan Castle, the Earl of Worcester ate at the dais into the 1620s; not until 1689 did his family move to a 'little parlor' to dine. But generally the head of household was content for the hall to enact the symbolic function of establishing his 'dignity' without requiring his appearance. Gentlemen might convene manor courts in their halls; yeomen located their economic activities there; and for laborers it continued to be a primary living space. But in the principal room of the great house, with every structural element celebrating the dais, the dominant mode was absence. At Nonsuch Palace, forty yeomen of the guard served dinner to an empty high table each day, while musicians played. The platters presented so ceremonially were then removed to the privy chamber where Elizabeth awaited them, unseen by the court. In the 1550s, forty visitors were fed in the hall at Ingatestone daily, along with thirty household servants; perhaps at Christmastide, when tenants, laborers, and villagers were hosted on successive days, Sir William Petre might himself preside from the dais. Sir Christopher Hatton visited Holdenby rarely—just 'once in two years', said Barnabe Riche—but he arranged that the hall should meet its obligations without him, making 'daily provision' for passing 'strangers' and for 'any nobleman with his whole train that should hap to call in of a sudden'.[21]

The hall's continuing role in the domestic imaginary is suggested by how many houses were named for the space: Astley, Aston, Blickling, Burton Agnes, Cobham, Doddington, East Riddlesden, Felbrigg, Gawthorpe, Gosfield, Hardwick, Hengrave, Ingatestone, Kentwell, Kirby, Levens, Melford, Oakwell, Oxburgh, Peover, Rufford, Rushton, Speke, and Wollaton were all called 'Halls'. No one valued halls more than the arrivistes who had not inherited them. Sir Robert Hesketh, born a bastard, finally achieved his Rufford estate

---

Library, 1868), on entertainment 'first in the hall, next in your parlor, or, if you keep that manner or estate, in your great chamber' (p. 39).

[21] On old-fashioned state, see Girouard, *Life*, 82; on absence, Cooper, *Houses of the Gentry*, 275. For manor courts, Cooper, ibid. 284–5 (noting that at Owlpen Manor a separate court was built so that manor activities could be removed from the family's hall); on the halls of yeomen and laborers, Mercer, 'Houses of the Gentry', 22–3 (emphasizing that the hall was important to courtiers for self-presentation and yeomen for business, but not to gentry and laborers). Nehemiah Wallington still used his hall for family dining; see Paul S. Seaver, *Wallington's World: A Puritan Artisan in Seventeenth-Century London* (Stanford: Stanford University Press, 1985), 24, 76. For Elizabeth, see Girouard, who quotes from Thomas Platter's 1599 travel diary (*Life*, 110). For Ingatestone, Emmison, *Tudor Secretary*, 29, 123. Barnabe Rich, *Barnabe Riche His Farewell to Military Profession*, ed. Donald Beecher (Ottawa: Dovehouse Editions for Medieval and Renaissance Texts and Studies, 1992), 131–2.

in the late 1520s. He then manufactured a medieval hall, complete with hammerbeam roof, a grand coving over the dais, and benching behind the high table—with a recess for his chair of state. Though there was never a hearth, a chimney was added well after this first build. In 1536 Richard Rich used the nave of the Augustinian priory of Little Leez for his great hall; Sir Richard Grenville was to do the same with the dissolved abbey church of Buckland in 1576. William Cecil insisted on having an old-fashioned hall at Burghley House, a rival to Penshurst at 68 ft long and 30 ft wide. It was over 60 ft tall, with a double hammerbeam roof that was thoroughly anachronistic in 1555. At Barrington Court, a gentrifying merchant so respected the ancient ceremony of the hall that around 1560 he placed a lavabo (for the washing of hands) in his screens passage. At Montacute, a hall built in the 1590s by Sir Edward Phelips still had tables and forms in a 1638 inventory. At Hatfield, Robert Cecil's 1608 rebuilding project included a hall and the refectory tables made for it. Tudor halls were built nostalgically at Burton Agnes, Charlecote Park, Compton Winyates, Cowdray, Gawthorpe, Hengrave, Lyme Park, Melford Hall, Wilderhope Manor, and Wollaton; Stuart halls at Aston, Audley End, and Northampton House. At Baddesley Clinton a medieval hall fell into disuse, but in the 1580s a new one was built and furnished with a 22-ft-long table; a similar process had already happened at Knole.[22]

Rufford aside, veneration for the great hall rarely extended to medieval recreations, and Penshurst is rightly celebrated for having so uniquely retained its fourteenth-century aspect. Elsewhere, old halls were given early modern makeovers which have often survived to the present day. Chimneys were the most notable additions, and windows were often enlarged, as at Adlington and Broughton Castle, but there were important restylings, as well. At Knole the hall was enhanced between 1605 and 1608 with a new oak screen, minstrels' gallery, overmantel, and wainscotting. Also added, however, were elements of what has been called the room's 'decline': a plaster ceiling and frieze. Knole, in other words, no longer had a 'tall' hall, nor did Aston, Baddesley Clinton, Barrington Court, Buckland Abbey, Burton Agnes, Felbrigg, Ingatestone, or Montacute. All these were built from the first with, above them, rooms which shared the hall's central location in the house and which competed with it for prestige. At Broughton, Canons Ashby, Little Moreton, and The Vyne, old halls were ceiled so that rooms could be added directly overhead. Thynne built a two-story hall at Longleat that was surmounted by a third level, but

---

[22] Cook remarks the persistence of the designation 'Hall', *English House*, 48. For Little Leez, see Airs, *Tudor and Jacobean*, 27; for others, see house guidebooks. Some religious sites were particularly attractive *because* they had naves that could be converted to halls.

he attempted to disguise this compromise with the old forms by constructing false hammerbeams.[23]

The hall declined in the face of new ways for communicating status, not only in grand rooms on upper levels but also in the presentational modes of the Renaissance exterior. A series of bird's-eye views can make this transformation, too, look progressive and schematic (see Figs. 2.5–2.8). In medieval castles such as Berkeley, domestic quarters were built within massive and intimidating walls; houses such as Kempsford were no longer fortified but still faced resolutely inward; at Toddington, the disappearance of

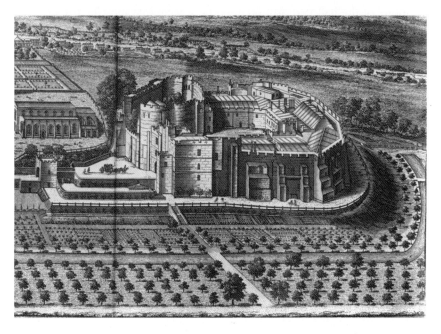

Figure 2.5 A bird's-eye view of Berkeley Castle in Gloucestershire, showing domestic quarters built against the perimeter wall of the fortress. Engraved 1712.

---

[23] The hall at Broughton Castle was ceiled by 1554; that at The Vyne, not till the seventeenth century. But compare Oakwell, where a single-storied hall was built in the 1580s by John Batt. During his grandson's 1630s rebuilding, the upper level was removed to create a tall hall with two-storied windows (though with a gallery for communication between upper rooms). To further medievalize the space, the younger Batt moved the fireplace originally built between the hall and the cross passage, positioned the new chimney on an outer wall, and added a screen with two arched openings. Some lesser homes were untouched by the new standards; Mercer cites Bristows in Surrey, which had a hall open to the roof and which was described as 'new-built' in 1637, and Bents in Cheshire, also with an open hall, but probably from even later in the seventeenth century (*English Vernacular Houses*, 27).

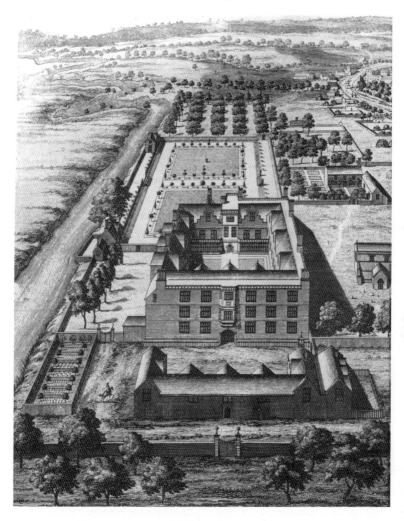

Figure 2.6 A bird's-eye view of Kempsford in Gloucestershire, showing the influence of the castle form on the courtyard house. Engraved 1712.

a closing wing converted the central yard into an open forecourt; and, finally, Smythson-designed Doddington represented the thorough extroversion of the Tudor home. The public façades of the sixteenth century developed under the influence of Continental designs, which in their stringent symmetry were incompatible with vernacular tradition. Athelhampton encapsulates the problem (see Fig. 2.9): the Tudor range has perfectly balanced windows and

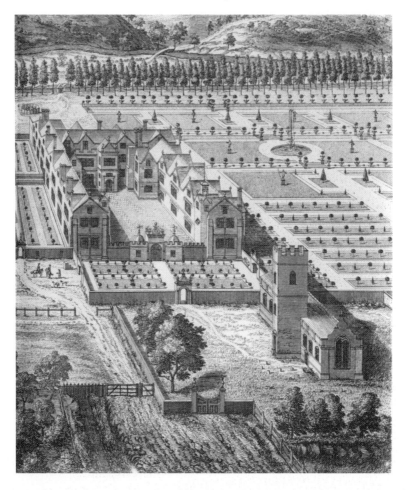

Figure 2.7 A bird's-eye view of Toddington Hall in Gloucestershire, showing the courtyard house in transition to an outward-looking plan. Engraved 1712.

gables, but the fifteenth-century core retains the medieval irregularities of an oriel at the location of the dais and a side entrance into the screens.

Segregating traffic, focusing the visual perspective, and maintaining a respectful distance from the high end of the hall, the screens passage seemed an inseparable element of the ceremonial style. At Wollaton, Smythson moved the hall back from the façade, creating a string of forespaces to mediate between a fashionable central doorway and the customary off-center entrance to the screens. More ingeniously, at Burton Agnes he created an exterior porch and designed the oriel to match it. Both extrusions were constructed squarely

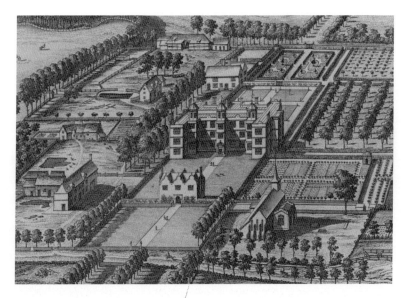

Figure 2.8 A bird's-eye view of Doddington Hall, near Lincoln in Lincolnshire, showing a Smythson-designed outward-looking house. Engraved by Johannes Kip, 1708.

Figure 2.9 Athelhampton House, near Dorchester in Dorset, with a symmetrical Elizabethan wing (to the left) married to an asymmetrical fifteenth-century hall house (to the right, with oriel and porch into the screens passage).

Figure 2.10 Burton Agnes Hall, near Driffield in East Yorkshire, with the porch matched to the oriel and the entrance door tucked to one side to create a symmetrical front façade.

and of three stories, with matching window treatments and identical frontal displays. The only difference between the two was a door hidden in one side of the porch which led directly into a screens passage sited in the usual way (see Fig. 2.10). The same trick for mating asymmetrical hall to symmetrical façade was performed at Chastleton, Wroxall Abbey, and Aston Hall. A variation at Audley End featured two equilibrious porches, one for the screens and one for the house's great stairs. Elsewhere, as early as 1530, the builders of Sutton Place near London had abandoned such temporizing strategies and introduced a medial entrance into the hall; the same was done at Holland House in 1605 and Blickling in 1616. Gawthorpe (1600–5) relegated its old-style hall into an ignominious rear corner, where it could not disturb a more modish front.

The solution which was to have the most momentous consequences, however, appeared at the resolutely symmetrical Hardwick in 1599 (see Fig. 2.11). Working with Smythson, Bess of Hardwick turned the hall on axis, so that those who used the centered entrance found themselves immediately at the midpoint of what was in effect the screens passage, stretching across the front of the house rather than crossing its depth. The low screen was little more than a classically columned interjection, a distant echo of its original form. The viewer's eye was drawn not to the end wall but to one side, where an

Figure 2.11 The symmetrical façade of Hardwick Hall, near Mansfield in Derbyshire.

overmantel featured real antlers affixed to its plasterwork stags. Hardwick also disdained the display of pantry and buttery which had traditionally reassured visitors of a house's hospitality.[24] And the signal turn of direction was delayed until, at the far end of the hall, the visitor encountered her fantastic 'river of stairs', which led to two withdrawing chambers, low and high great chambers, Bess's bedchamber, the 'best' bedchamber, and the long gallery. Status accrued not to seating on a dais but instead to arrival at these upper spaces with their costly imported furnishings, portraits of eminent Elizabethans, wainscotting, fireplaces featuring alabaster statues of Justice and Mercy, a painted plaster frieze of the court of Diana, and tapestries of Ulysses and of Gideon. The hall that Bess built was reduced to little more than an outsized throughway to more important state rooms, and it was sufficiently influential that by 1663 Balthazar Gerbier could refer to 'the hall of a private house' as 'serving for the most part but for a passage'.[25] Thus liberated from the formal tyrannies of

[24] Henry Wotton, writing much later, nonetheless observed that 'though all the other petty offices . . . may well enough be so remote, yet by the natural hospitality of England the buttery must be more visible' (*The Elements of Architecture* (London: 1624), sig. I4ʳ). Cooper notes that 'The low-end entry became not only irrelevant but also inconvenient when the hall's purpose was solely to enable the owner, his immediate family and his polite visitors to enter the house on their way to the rooms they habitually used' (*Houses of the Gentry*, 285).

[25] For Hardwick, see especially Girouard, *Robert Smythson*, ch. 4, and also his very substantive Hardwick guidebook for the National Trust. Balthazar Gerbier, *Counsel and Advice to all Builders* (London: 1663), sig. B5ᵛ.

the medieval past, early modern great houses developed their own systems for communicating ambitions and meanings.

THE INVENTION OF ARCHITECTURE

The old craft traditions, with native skills and knowledge passed from father to son or master to apprentice, were insufficient to elite Rebuildings. To remodel Hampton Court, Henry VIII employed Germans Robert Schenk and Henry Blaynston for architectural and painted decorations, Frenchmen James Mercaden and Robert Sande for wainscotting, another Frenchman called 'Richard' for 'antik heads', a painter named John de la Mayn who may have been Italian, and the Dutchman Galyon Hone for window glass.[26] Increasingly, however, Continental influences were exerted through print media. Thomas Tresham owned the architectural treatises of Alberti (1512 and 1533), Labacco (1552), Cataneo (1554), du Cerceau (1559 and 1576), de l'Orme (1561 and 1568), Vignola (1563), de Vries (1563 and 1566), Bullant (1564), Palladio (1570), and Serlio (1575 and 1584). Francis Willoughby had two volumes by du Cerceau as well as others by Alberti, Vitruvius, Serlio, Palladio, Vignola, and de l'Orme. Thomas Smith held five different editions of Vitruvius in his own extensive collection. Cecil learned of Philibert de l'Orme's 1561 *Nouvelles Inventions pour Bien Bastir* from Smith, while engaged in building Burghley House in 1568, and he wrote to the English ambassador in Paris to procure a copy.[27]

   These works importantly provided ideas, and they also served as the media of articulation between builders and their teams. The lead man at Burghley House, Roger Ward, was highly experienced, but a letter he wrote to Cecil in 1556 suggests the difficulties he and other workers faced as they sought to fulfill the wishes of their employers: 'I do understand your pleasure is to have three lukon windows for your inner court . . . I shall desire you to draw your meaning how and after what fashion you would have them to be made in all points both the wid[th] of the light and also the height of the same, with the fashion of all the molds that doth belong thereunto and in

---

[26] *History of the King's Works*, 133. Low Country glaziers had already been employed at The Vyne in the early 1520s. Girouard observes that 'It would be a mistake to underrate the continual influence exerted on the buildings of the time by foreign craftsmen and foreign publications' (*Robert Smythson*, 18).

[27] Airs, *Tudor and Jacobean*, 36–7 and Girouard, *Robert Smythson*, 15 (for Tresham); Friedman, *House and Household*, 32–3 (for Willoughby); Jenkins, *Architect*, 10 (for Smith); Lloyd, *History*, 91 (for Cecil). Lucy Gent says that book catalogues demonstrate English familiarity with European treatises (*Picture and Poetry, 1560–1620: Relations between Literature and the Visual Arts in the English Renaissance* (Leamington Spa: James Hall, 1981), 74).

what place you would have them to stand, and your pleasure known I shall do the best it lieth in me to do.'[28] The *Nouvelles Inventions* may eventually have facilitated this part of the process of building Burghley. In his will, Sir Edward Pytts required 'my chief mason, workman, and surveyor of the work', John Chaunce, to return to his heirs 'one book of architecture' through which he had presumably communicated his vision for Kyre Park. William Arnold, described as 'wonderfully sought, being indeed the absolutist and honestest workman in England', was known to have used Flemish pattern books, and Smythson seems to have studied du Cerceau. The results are everywhere apparent. The porch at Felbrigg; an arch at Blickling; chimney hoods at Bolsover, Wollaton, Hardwick, and Burghley—all are copied from Serlio. Kirby Hall incorporated elements of Serlio, of Hans Blum's *A Description of the Five Orders* (1550), and also two pilasters from the title page of the first English architectural volume, by John Shute.[29]

Shute was a London painter-stainer who, in 1550, was sent on a tour of Italy by the Earl of Northumberland and other wealthy builders. Thirteen years later he published *The First and Chief Grounds of Architecture*, declaring that he was 'stirred forward to do my duty unto this my country wherein I live and am a member'.[30] This was one symptom of a naturalizing process that also took more concrete and, for purists, adulterating forms. Thynne required decades of experimentation, at first mingling medieval English motifs with Renaissance European ones, before finally achieving the discipline that now distinguishes Longleat. By contrast, Sir Thomas Smith's Hill Hall is described by Maurice Howard as having indulged all the 'conflicting attractions and possibilities presented by a wealth of source material'. In effect, it displayed on its façade the catalogue of Smith's large library. William Harrison's boast—'our workmen' are 'comparable in skill with old Vitruvius, Leon Battista, and

---

[28] Ward quoted by Jenkins, *Architect*, 23–4. Knowledge was traditionally transmitted orally and by demonstration, but also with plans and sketches: William Horman observed that 'he is not worthy to be called master of the craft' of building 'that is not cunning in drawing and portraying' (*Vulgaria* (London: 1519), sig. Rr5ᵛ). John Thorpe inherited drawings from his mason father, and Robert Smythson was bequeathed drawings that he subsequently left to his own son and that later came to his grandson. The 1546 will of John Multon listed 'all my portraitures, plats, books with all other my tools and instruments', and in 1562 mason Cornelius Brownstone left his apprentice 'all my plats and patterns'. In 1579, William Cure divided his 'patterns' between his son and his son-in-law. A sketchbook in the possession of a family of plasterers stretches over 150 years of work, begun by one man around 1575, continued by a son born in 1612, and augmented by the grandson born in 1639. See Airs, *Tudor and Jacobean*, 51–4, 151.

[29] Pytts quoted by Summerson, *Architecture*, 60; Arnold by Airs, *Tudor and Jacobean*, 154. For examples of Continental elements in English construction, see especially Girouard, *Robert Smythson*, 14; Aslet and Powers, *National Trust Book*, 74–5; and Summerson, *Architecture*, 51.

[30] John Shute, dedicatory epistle 'To the Most High and Excellent Princess Elizabeth', *The First and Chief Groundes of Architecture* (1563) in facsimile reprint, ed. Lawrence Weaver (London: Country Life, 1912).

Serlio'—documents the currency of these names in English culture rather than a world-class architectural proficiency. Indeed, a visiting Mantuan sniffed that 'as for the rooms, there is no imaginable order, as the English merely look to convenience'. Tudor builders were 'pirates rather than disciples', says Girouard, seeking inspiration for the part rather than the whole, adopting details with which to ornament their surfaces rather than plans for the massing of blocks fronted by those surfaces.[31]

'The likes of Smythson drew the elevation first and thought of the rooms afterwards', notes John Harris. As yet there was no place for the radical genius of Inigo Jones, who was able 'to think of a building inside-out, so that, for example, the windows of an elevation would fit the room inside symmetrically'. In the sixteenth century, the new symmetry was often a fashionable veneer applied to structures that obeyed their own independent imperatives. The great hall was uniquely resistant to such mismatching because its syntax was so inflexibly codified, but more versatile spaces were more yielding ones. If the requirements of interior and exterior were in conflict, a pantry might sport the same bay window as a parlor. At Longleat, chamber windows which are so impressive on the elevation reached to ceiling height internally (and were later blocked at the top for practical purposes). Hardwick has windows that light two separate stories simultaneously. At Barrington Court, the rear of the house is a false wall of windows; behind them stands the great kitchen fireplace. Wardour also has windows placed before chimney stacks, and Westwood Manor has oriel windows built against turret stairs.[32]

The idea that form should follow function, already emergent in Continental treatises, excited little interest in England. Sir Francis Bacon declared that while houses should be 'uniform without', they should be 'severally partitioned within', thus suggesting that there was no need to design buildings which were what Rudolf Arnheim calls 'frankly informative'. Henry Peacham asserted that 'the greater vanity you show in your invention, the more you please'.[33] The disarticulation of interior and exterior was, if anything, a source of

---

[31] Howard, *Early Tudor Country House*, 195. Harrison, *Description*, 199. Letter of Annibale Litolfi, a Mantuan in England during Mary I's reign, quoted by Ian Dunlop, *Palaces and Progresses of Elizabeth I* (London: Jonathan Cape, 1962), 88. Girouard, *Robert Smythson*, 18.

[32] John Harris, *The Design of the English Country House, 1620–1920* (London: Trefoil Books and the American Institute of Architects Foundation, 1985), 15. See also, *inter alia*, Girouard, *Robert Smythson*, 54, 81, 153. Ingatestone is another, 'fairly early' example 'of imposing an outward, superficial uniformity upon a building, the essential internal arrangement of which was still largely medieval and asymmetrical in composition' (Emmison, *Tudor Secretary*, 28–9).

[33] Francis Bacon, 'Of Building', in *The Essayes or Counsels, Civill and Morall*, ed. Michael Kiernan (Cambridge, Mass.: Harvard University Press, 1985), 136. Rudolf Arnheim, *The Dynamics of Architectural Form* (Berkeley: University of California Press, 1977), 102. Peacham (1612) quoted by Margaret Jourdain, *English Decorative Plasterwork of the Renaissance* (London: B. T. Batsford, 1926), 3.

pleasure for the spatial secrets and surprises it produced. In the Tudor years, notions of symmetry were never as regular and austere as they were to become under the influence of the more intellectual Jones. Instead, this was an exuberant architecture, enlivened by projecting and receding bays, great spiraling chimneys, densely textured surfaces, and contrasting colors. Girouard says that Hardwick can be described either as 'romantic' or as 'ruthless', but it is in either case 'a perpetual delight, so simple is it, so ingenious, so obvious, so effective, as one walks round and watches the masses group and regroup, contract and spread out, advance and fall away . . . shifting from the full weight and splendour of the main elevations to the view from the side, when the house shuts up narrow and bears down with the race and speed of a ship in full sail'.[34]

Hardwick was recognized in its own time as an architectural event. So was Henry VIII's earlier Nonsuch Palace, 'as important a source' as any pattern book, according to John Summerson (see Fig. 2.12). Cecil supplemented his print collection with drawings of the Escorial in Spain, Trinity College in Dublin, various drainage systems and gardens, and also two plans of Longleat. He and England's other great builders shared ideas and competed over craftsmen. Thynne commissioned a carver Sir William Sharington had employed at Lacock Abbey. Sir William Cavendish wrote to Thynne for the loan of his own 'cunning plasterer', known to have made 'diverse pendants and other pretty things' at Longleat; Bess of Hardwick, then Cavendish's widow, was still hoping to employ the same plasterer five years later. Robert Lyminge and his full Blickling crew, bricklayer Matthews, glazier Linacre, and plasterer Stanyan, were reassembled at Felbrigg. Sir Thomas Tresham was anxious to contract masons 'else haply they may be bespoken in Sir John Stanupp's work this summer, and know not I where to have so good workmen'. When Sir Edward Pytts died in 1618, his son got John Chaunce to make a four-year commitment to Kyre Park.[35]

Cecil, Thynne, Hardwick, Tresham, and others like them constituted a cohort of gentry builders who were created by such sixteenth-century phenomena as the Dissolution of the monasteries, new money, changed household

---

[34] Girouard, *Robert Smythson*, 149–52.

[35] Summerson, *Architecture*, 84; for Nonsuch, see also John Dent, *The Quest for Nonsuch* (London: Hutchinson, 1962); and *History of the King's Works*, 179–205. On Cecil, Girouard, *Robert Smythson*, 13; on Thynne, Cavendish, and Bess, Airs, *Tudor and Jacobean*, 75, 77. Felbrigg from guidebook. Tresham quoted by Friedman, *House and Household*, 35. The great chamber chimney piece at Montacute (Somerset) is similar to others at Wayford Manor, Cranborne Manor House, Wolfeton House, and Stockton House (Somerset, Dorset, and Wiltshire); all may have been designed by William Arnold. Jourdain finds shared plaster molds for early seventeenth-century friezes and ceilings at Bromley-by-Bow Palace and Bury Hall, at Bury Hall and the Tottenham Vicarage, at Albyns and Broughton Castle, at Little Strickland Hall and Barton Kirk (*English Decorative Plasterwork*, 17).

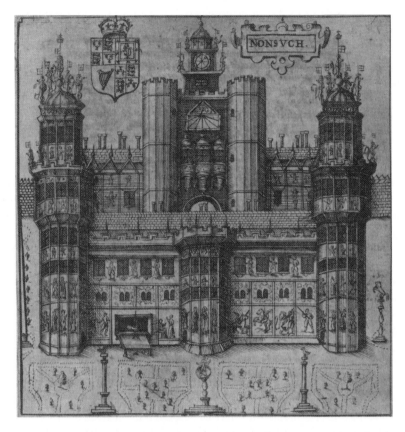

Figure 2.12 Nonsuch Palace, from John Speed's map of Surrey in his atlas, *The Theatre of the Empire of Great Britain*. Engraved 1610.

structures and practices, and a national discourse about architectural designs and standards. They were the first such generation; they were also the last. Praising the 'care and direction of old Gabriel Moore', who 'so fitly adjoined' new wings at Chantmarle to old ones, in 1612 Sir John Strode was one of the earliest to refer to his head workman as 'a skillful architect'—though he also insisted that Moore was employed 'only to survey and direct the building to the form I conceived and plotted it'. In 1570, John Dee had an idea of the architect as 'neither smith, nor builder, nor, separately, any artificer', but he admitted that as he wrote there were few in England capable of being 'the head, the provost, the director, and judge of all artificial works'. Over the course of the later sixteenth century, however, men with the talent and interest to be what Dee called 'true' architects came to the forefront. Smythson's burial monument names him 'Architecter and Surveyor unto the most worthy house of Wollaton with divers others of great account', and Lyminge was described in the parish of his death as 'the architect and builder of Blickling Hall'.[36] The professionalization of domestic construction was another change more lastingly associated with the name of Inigo Jones, but it had its roots in a cult of celebrity that emerged as builders sought the services of that handful of contractors who had educated themselves in Serlio, du Cerceau, and Shute.

At least as important as the circulation of ideas among England's gentry builders was the way in which their ideas spread through other tiers of sixteenth-century society. Each major construction project was a public exhibition of new designs. It was also an incubator of specialized technical knowledge and an incentive to local economic growth. Henry VIII was so impatient to rebuild Hampton Court in the summer of 1534 that he employed forty-nine masons, fifty-two carpenters, as many bricklayers, thirteen joiners, nine plumbers, twelve sawyers, four plasterers, and 141 laborers, some conscripted. These men developed skills they could take to other rebuildings. (The market value of royal association is suggested by John Hethe, describing molds he bequeathed to his son as those 'I served the King withal'.) Many Tudor prodigy houses required the initiation of brickworks, iron foundries, plaster firms, and glass manufactures, all staffed by laborers who outlived the original project and sometimes established themselves as regional resources for chimney stacks, firebacks, ornamental ceilings, and glazed windows. The business of furnishing a great house similarly enlarged the provincial repertories of woodworkers from carpenters and coopers to, in addition, sawyers, turners, and joiners. Country craftsmen learned to produce beds, tables, chairs, stools, and cupboards to upper-class standards. There were such household linens as tablecloths, napkins, sheets, and cushion covers to be woven, stitched, worked, mended, and laundered. For cooking implements, potters, metalworkers, smiths, and tinkers were needed. Local folk also cultivated newly fashionable fruits and vegetables such as artichokes and oranges. They brought their produce, meats, fish, and specialist condiments to the doors of the gentry, often succeeding in inaugurating regular channels of provision. Great houses gave steady employment to estate administrators, domestic servants, stable

---

[36] Strode quoted by Airs, *Tudor and Jacobean*, 34. John Dee, Preface to *The Elements of Geometry of the Most Ancient Philosopher Euclid of Megara*, trans. H. Billingsley (London: 1570), sig. D4^{r-v}. For Smythson, see Girouard, *Robert Smythson*, 83; for Lyminge, the Blickling guidebook. In 1567, Elizabeth sent the emperor of Russia an 'architecter', a doctor, an apothecary, and other expert advisers; *Calendar of the Manuscripts of . . . the Marquess of Salisbury . . . Preserved at Hatfield House*, 24 vols. (London: 1883–1976), i. no. 1140 (pp. 347–8). On the professionalization of architecture, see especially Jenkins, *Architect*.

workers, and gardeners, as well as occasional trade to repairmen, midwives, wet-nurses, and travelling players.[37]

The much-lamented decline of the hall did not mean that great houses ceased to relate to their environs. The principal terms of association began to shift, however, from a patronage system to one of economic exchange, from the offer of hospitality to the promise of consumption. Here, the changing nature of these engagements is itself less at issue than are the sheer number of early modern men and women whose spatial imaginations were enlarged by their encounters with the elite achievements of the Great Rebuilding.

RETHINKING DISTINCTION

Prodigy houses were uncommon events. Not many Elizabethans were able to build so lavishly, and, among these, fewer still were willing to do so. But the rarified strand of architectural history pursued by Mark Girouard shares one important theme with the broadly inclusive thesis put forward by W. G. Hoskins: across all social registers, it is said, Rebuilt houses had more spaces, and these had specialized identities. Larger room counts and particularized room uses are the grounds from which discussions of early modern privacy generally proceed.

Again, the starting place is the hall. The poorest cottages would have had *only* a hall, a space for shelter, cooking, eating, working, storage, and sleeping. In remoter regions there remained rural 'longhouses' which made rudimentary distinctions between human and animal quarters: on one side the hall, on the other the byre, with a through-passage from front to back creating a buffer between the two. According to M. W. Barley, the crucial change in the

---

[37] This discussion was inspired by Victor Skipp, *Crisis and Development: An Ecological Case Study of the Forest of Arden, 1570–1674* (Cambridge: Cambridge University Press, 1978), 63–4, 70–1. Barley adds that 'What was going on at Wollaton between 1580 and 1588 must have been widely known over the east Midlands, for the stone came from Ancaster or thereabouts in Kesteven, and tenants of Sir Francis Willoughby were employed to carry building materials from a wide area' (*English Farmhouse*, 57). For Hampton Court, see *History of the King's Works*, pp. 129 ff. Will of John Hethe (1552) quoted by Margaret Jourdain, *English Decoration and Furniture of the Early Renaissance (1500–1650)* (London: B. T. Batsford, 1924), 105; he probably referred to work at Nonsuch. Brick was a Tudor fad; Barley gives the example of a London vintner, George Herbert, who built a brick house in a stone and timber region (*Houses and History*, 179–80). On the economic development motivated by country houses, see Joan Thirsk, 'England's Provinces: Did They Serve or Drive Material London?' in Lena Cowen Orlin (ed.), *Material London, ca. 1600* (Philadelphia: University of Pennsylvania Press, 2000), 97–108. For an example of the economic function of a great house, see Emmison, *Tudor Secretary*, esp. 125, 146–7, 151, 156, 158–9, 215.

subsistence dwelling of the early modern era was the addition of a median wall that converted the passage into part of the residential space and thus reified the identities of stable and home. From this all the other events of Hoskins's Great Rebuilding can be traced in their most schematic forms. The hall had originally been open to the rafters, with a gap at the peak to vent smoke from the domestic hearth or hob. In the sixteenth century a chimney might be constructed, making it possible not only to close the roof but also to insert beams carried across the new through-passage wall. At the animal end these could support stored hay and equipment. In the living area boards might be laid on them, left loose so that goods could be accessed by a ladder inserted at any point. Eventually, the boards might be nailed down and a staircase constructed. A second opening in the chimneystack might provide heat at the loft level. If a gable were extruded, this upper room would receive natural light from an added window. Eventually, farm animals might be moved to an outbuilding so that even more dwelling space could be reclaimed. With certain tell-tale signs of its origins suppressed, like the narrowing of a door built wide for the passage of cattle and the closing of a ground-level aperture for flushing animal wastes, the longhouse might assume the appearance of any regular cottage, two rooms up, two down. In place of hall and byre were a kitchen, a parlor, and sleeping chambers, distinct in degree but not in kind from the Rebuildings Hoskins reported for more prosperous, middling-sort Elizabethans.[38]

As described, the sequence seldom varies: a tall hall made single-storied; upper-level chambers created; and structural staircases, chimney openings, and windows added to provide access, heat, and light. By the 1550s, southern farmers and yeomen had ceased constructing open halls. The same was true in the north by the turn of the century. The pace of conversion for medieval halls differed. At Hookwood Manor in Surrey the floor for a second level was inserted in 1571. At Kite House in Kent a second story was constructed in 1574 and a fireplace built four years later. At Trout's Farm in Surrey an

---

[38] Barley, *English Farmhouse*, 164–5. On the longhouse, see also Barley, *Houses and History*, 161–2; and Mercer, *English Vernacular Houses*, 37. In 1656 Daniel King recalled that in the early seventeenth century Cheshire farmers still 'had their fire in the midst of the house, against a hob of clay, and their oxen also under the same roof' in the early 1600s; transhumance did not entirely die out in the north until 1700 (quoted by Barley, *English Farmhouse*, 119–20). In 1656 a longhouse was built at Throwleigh, and as late as 1663 another at Walkhampton was finally enlarged by the addition of a parlor wing and staircase; these were remarked because they were exceptional (Mercer, *English Vernacular Houses*, 40). For examples of surviving longhouses, see Hendre'r-ywydd Uchaf-Clwyd and Cilewent at the Welsh Folk Museum. For an example of loose floorboards, see the 1604 will of Elizabeth Jenyson, which refers to 'all the boards which shall be then unlaid and unnailed' (*Wills and Inventories from the Registry at Durham, Part IV*, ed. Herbert Maxwell Wood, Publications of the Surtees Society 142 (1929), 3–6).

old hall was demolished and replaced by a two-storied structure in 1581. At Hunt Street Farm in Kent renovations of 1595 created three levels in an old open hall. Improvement was often slowest in parish-dependent parsonages; in Somerset, three examples of tall halls survived through the reign of Charles I. A Devon clergyman complained in 1680 that he had 'a great hall floored with earth, no chamber over it'. Revealing his awareness of the rectory's exceptional backwardness, he spoke to otherwise ubiquitous change.[39]

Victor Skipp's analysis of inventories from the Arden area demonstrates that in the mid-sixteenth century 86 per cent of peasant families lived in houses of three rooms or less, 8 per cent in four or five rooms, and only 6 per cent in six or more rooms. By the last quarter of the century, however, 23 per cent had six or more rooms, and in the first quarter of the seventeenth century only 24 per cent remained in houses of one to three rooms, while 31 per cent now lived in six or more rooms. By mid-seventeenth century there were still 24 per cent in one to three rooms but the number in at least six rooms had more than doubled to 64 per cent. The average had moved from two-and-a-half rooms in the mid-sixteenth century to six-and-a-half in the mid-seventeenth. Derek Portman similarly demonstrates for the Oxford region that in 1640 there were twice as many homes with three or more rooms as in 1600, while, at a somewhat higher economic level, those with seven rooms quadrupled in the same period. Once more there is anecdotal evidence supporting these statistics. The probate documents of Essex yeoman William Payne referred to 'two new chambers over the hall', of Newcastle merchant Robert Atkinson to 'the new chamber above the hall', and of Essex tailor Robert Burges to 'the furthest chamber that was last made'.[40]

As homes became more complex, their rooms required grouping or sequencing. In cities and towns, where a premium was placed on ground space, household functions had long been distributed vertically. There were a shop at

---

[39] In middling homes, hobs were perhaps more common than hearths: the fire was placed against a wall, with above it a hood of timber and plaster or clay over an ironwork structure. The hearth was inconvenient for cooking, and so was most likely to persist in the halls of houses large enough to have separate kitchens with chimneys. See Mercer, *English Vernacular Houses*, 5–6; Barley, *English Farmhouse*, 63–4; and Barley, *Houses and History*, 233 (for the Devon clergyman), 253–5. As early as 1500, a house in Maidstone, Kent was 'to be lofted over' (Barley, *English Farmhouse*, 43), and according to Mercer, 'by the late sixteenth century two-storeyed houses were standard throughout the southeast' (*English Vernacular Houses*, 28). The hall of The Gables in the East Midlands was not chambered over until about 1700 (Barley, *English Farmhouse*, 84–5). Cooper is the source of the term 'tall hall'.

[40] Skipp, *Crisis*, 62–3; Portman, 'Vernacular Building', 152. Will of William Payne (1567), *Essex Wills (England)*, ii. no. 655. Inventory of Robert Atkinson (1596), *Wills and Inventories from the Registry at Durham, Part II*, ed. William Greenwell, Publications of the Surtees Society 38 (1860), no. 117. Will of Robert Burges (c.1571), *Essex Wills (England)*, iii. *1571–1577*, ed. F. G. Emmison (Boston: New England Historic Genealogical Society, 1986), no. 102.

ground level, family living areas one flight up, bedchambers above, and garrets for work and storage as well as additional sleeping. Such organizational modes were newer to country building. An intriguing Tudor innovation was the 'lobby house', where a massive chimney in the center of the floor plan effectively bisected the building. Incoming traffic was channeled by the brick stack: to one side the parlor, where guests were received; to the other the kitchen, with its ongoing household business. A third mode of discrimination was effected between front and back. Even great medieval houses had been 'single pile', that is, only one room deep, as was appropriate to courtyard plans especially. But when the early modern house became more compact it also became more dense; Hardwick is an important example of a 'double pile' house, with its rotated hall crossing the depth of two rooms. In smaller houses, the same effect was accomplished when service 'outshuts', or lean-tos, were constructed along rear walls and then eventually reconstructed for permanent incorporation into the domestic fabric. In this plan, service rooms shifted to the rear.[41]

Distinctions of function most often effected a dichotomization of leisure and labor. In poor and middling establishments, where every member of the household worked, this did not at first initiate a physical separation of master from servants, male from female. If there were distance and division, they were products of elite architecture. Much has been made, for instance, of Henry VIII's suite of apartments: guard chamber, presence chamber, privy chamber, bedroom, withdrawing chamber, closet, stool chamber. Each space represented a progressively more controlled level of access to the monarch, a sequence which had its imitators in other upper-class settings; Sir Thomas Leigh, who inherited and rebuilt Stoneleigh Abbey in 1571, required three state bedrooms, each with its own withdrawing and inner chambers. The dominant story in middling houses, however, had less to do with parlors and dining chambers—though there were new numbers of these—than with the vastly expanded inventory for services: not only kitchen, buttery, and pantry, but also rooms set aside for brewing, dairying, cheese making, apple storage, laundry, and any number of variations that were specific to different regions and industries. This kind of spatial complexity seems more focused on the order required to achieve productivity than on the social hierarchy and seclusion generally associated with specialization.[42]

[41] On the lobby house and the double-pile house, see Mercer, *English Vernacular Houses*, 61–2, 73. An example of the lobby house survives at the Weald and Downland Open Air Museum in Sussex (the 'Pendean' Farmhouse, originally from Midhurst).

[42] On royal suites, see Howard, *Early Tudor Country House*, 28, and Thurley, *Royal Palaces*, 135–43. For Stoneleigh, Geoffrey Tyack, *The Making of the Warwickshire Country House, 1500–1650*, Warwickshire Local History Society Occasional Paper Number 4 (July 1982), 41.

Hoskins has had his most powerful influence upon our understanding of architectural history, although in fact he made brief reference to a parallel narrative of the Great Rebuilding involving 'a remarkable increase in household furnishings and equipment'. For all except the indigent, he stated, there was 'more of everything and better of everything, and new-fangled comforts (like cushions and hangings) as well'. William Harrison was again a crucial source for him, reporting not only that 'every man almost is a builder', but also of those who 'do yet find the means to obtain and achieve such furniture as heretofore hath been unpossible'. Harrison describes tapestries and silver in the homes of noblemen, 'whereby the value of this and the rest of their stuff doth grow to be almost inestimable', and lavish displays of plate, pewter, brass, and linens in the houses of gentlemen and merchants. But whereas 'in time past the costly furniture stayed there' among the wealthier citizens, 'now it is descended yet lower, even unto the inferior artificers and many farmers'. Fixed rents and rising prices, which are said to have produced surplus income for rebuildings, featured also in the history of movable goods, according to Harrison: 'by virtue of their old and not of their new leases', lesser men 'have for the most part learned also to garnish their cupboards with plate, their joint [joined] beds with tapestry and silk hangings, and their tables with carpets and fine napery'.[43]

For goods, our primary records base is the probate inventory. Although these documents produce information about room counts, they do so only incidentally, in the course of providing finding guides for the chattels which are their real concern. A survey of post mortem materials in the Arden demonstrates an explosion of personal possessions at every economic level: up 289 per cent among the wealthy, 275 per cent among the 'substantial', 310 per cent among the middling sort, and 247 per cent among the peasantry. In 1560 Oxfordshire farmer Edward Kempsale had a house with two rooms and goods worth less than £20. Twenty-eight years later Thomas Gyll, with similar holdings of land, animals, and equipment, lived in a house with four rooms and possessions inventoried at over £67. While less than a fourth of Kempsale's real worth was invested in his household possessions (farm stock counted for three-quarters), Gyll's linens and tableware made up half the value of his estate. Gyll had twenty-eight pieces of pewter and five silver spoons where Kempsale had just six trenchers. It is also possible to compare Gyll's thirteen-and-a-half pairs of sheets to Kempsale's three, Gyll's six coverlets to Kempsale's one, and Gyll's four tablecloths to Kempsale's two. Only Gyll had the pillows and pillowcases

---

[43] Hoskins, 'Great Rebuilding', 44, 49. Harrison, *Description*, 200.

which to Harrison so importantly constituted a revolutionary 'amendment of lodging'.[44]

For this alternate discourse of the Great Rebuilding, an essential strand of argument has long been associated with the name of Joan Thirsk. 'A list can be compiled', says Thirsk, 'of 106 different articles mentioned by contemporaries in the sixteenth century as foreign imports which Englishmen seemed to regard as indispensable.' One early cataloguer was Sir Thomas Smith, enumerating 'glasses as well looking as drinking as to glass windows, dials, tables, cards, balls, puppets, penhorns, inkhorns, toothpicks, gloves, knives, daggers, ouches, brooches, aglets, buttons of silk and silver, earthen pots, pins, points, hawks' bells, paper both white and brown, and a thousand like things'. Smith was alarmed at the 'inestimable treasure' being paid out for 'trifles' brought 'from beyond the seas'. In 1549 he suggested two solutions to trade imbalance. First, luxury goods might be 'clean spared'. This was not to be; as Thirsk has demonstrated, a 'consumer society' was already under way. Noblemen, gentlemen, yeomen, and merchants possessed 'an almost encyclopedic body of knowledge' about commerce in the lengthening inventory of goods which had crossed the threshold from curiosities to popular commodities.[45]

Smith's second suggestion was that fashionable foreign items might be made 'within the realm' instead. The development of new English industries was as significant a sixteenth-century phenomenon as the expansion of international trade. By 1580, according to Thirsk, there were well-established initiatives in thread-making, iron founding, woad growing, stocking knitting, alum mining, and flower growing, as well as the production of the most popular New Draperies. This both kept more wealth in England, as Smith had urged, and also advanced the trickling-down of wealth. Many of the men who launched manufacturing ventures created works projects to educate and employ the poor. In turn, earned wages helped establish a new consumer base. The industry was actively responsive to the less moneyed markets, producing an 'infinite variety of designs and qualities, and at many different prices'. Thus,

[44] Skipp, *Crisis*, 70; *Household and Farm Inventories in Oxfordshire, 1550–1590*, ed. M. A. Havinden, Historical Manuscripts Commission 10 and Oxfordshire Record Society 44 (London: HMSO, 1965), 30–2, 48–9, 248–9. Early sixteenth-century inventories list cattle first, then personal possessions. By 1633, according to Skipp, household goods are recorded first in every inventory in the Arden, without exception.

[45] Joan Thirsk, *Economic Policy and Projects: The Development of a Consumer Society in Early Modern England* (Oxford: Clarendon, 1978), 49, 106, 119. Thomas Smith, *A Discourse of the Commonweal of This Realm of England, Attributed to Sir Thomas Smith*, ed. Mary Dewar (Charlottesville: University Press of Virginia for the Folger Shakespeare Library, 1969), 63–4. See also Jean-Christophe Agnew, *Worlds Apart: The Market and the Theater in Anglo-American Thought, 1550–1750* (Cambridge: Cambridge University Press, 1986); and Chandra Mukerji, *From Graven Images: Patterns of Modern Materialism* (New York: Columbia University Press, 1983).

many of the most popular 'luxury' goods appeared in cheap versions that were attainable even by middling and laboring families.[46] Wall hangings constitute a classic example; tapestries, imported from the Netherlands, were so expensive that even Bess of Hardwick bought used sets from Sir William Newport, covering his Hatton-family arms with her own insignia painted on cloth patches, and transforming his does into Hardwick stags by means of painted antlers. William Sheldon founded an English tapestry works, but he did not entirely succeed in keeping English wealth at home. His small looms could not produce the large pieces that elite buyers continued to commission abroad. Meanwhile, however, itinerant craftsmen produced painted and stained cloths that made it possible even for laborers to add color, design, and narrative to their walls.[47]

The decline of the great hall is usually ascribed to changing social and household structures. But there is another, more object-oriented story here, too. While the hall had permanent features such as the dais, the high table, and benches fixed to the walls, other tables were disassemblable, and forms and stools were easily pulled aside. The adaptability and versatility of the hall, as much a part of its nature as its asymmetry, were unconformable to emerging preferences for more settled surroundings. A 1575 inventory from Lacock Abbey shows that the hall was fitted out with furniture and hangings worth £8. 17s. 4d. But goods in the parlor were worth more than £20 and those in the gallery nearly £46. In various bedchambers were furnishings appraised at over £18, £21, £23, £53, and £56 (reflecting the high valuation of linens and textiles). Similarly, a sixteenth-century inventory from Beddington lists hall furnishings at 13s. 6d., while both the parlor and the great chamber had contents assessed at more than £20 apiece. At Speke in 1624, there were chambers with goods worth over £50 and £34 and a parlor worth almost £21. Even the 'little parlor' had objects valued at £8. 11s. 2d., while those of the hall totaled just £5. 18s. 8d.[48]

---

[46] Smith, *Discourse*, 65; on new industries, Thirsk, *Economic Policy*, 24–50, 161, 173. Thirsk takes a longer view than Hoskins, emphasizing the range of goods that developed between 1550 and 1800 (p. 106). But she says that 'throughout the 16th century wages lagged behind prices, and the labouring family's demand for non-essential consumer goods was negligible. . . . In the seventeenth century the incomes of the lower classes improved' (173).

[47] Girouard's Hardwick guidebook (rev. edn. of 1989), 58–9. E. A. B. Barnard, 'Part I: The Weavers', and A. J. B. Wace, 'Part II: The Tapestries', 'The Sheldon Tapestry Weavers and Their Work', *Archaeologia*, 78 (1928), 215–314. For painted cloths, see especially Barley, *English Farmhouse*, 42. For just one of many examples of a husbandman with 'hangings in the chamber' and 'stained cloths in the hall', see the will of John Sayer (1571), *Essex Wills*, iii. no. 588.

[48] 'Inventory of Sir Henry Sharington: Contents of Lacock House, 1575', ed. Thelma E. Vernon, *Wiltshire Archaeological and Natural History Magazine* 63 (1968), 72–82. This was not a probate inventory but is probably more complete, as it does not omit legacies and implements that were often considered 'standards', such as hall tables. For Beddington, see Howard, *Early Tudor Country House*, 112. 'A Speke Inventory of 1624', ed. E. B. Saxton, *Transactions of the Historic*

Early 'moveables' were essentially 'transportables'. The chest was valued for its ability to secure clothes, linens, plate, and other treasures for easy conveyance. As goods multiplied, however, storage units grew more diversified and more stationary. The derivatives of the chest included not only cases for books, papers, and jewels, but also livery cupboards, aumbreys, and dole cupboards for food; court cupboards to display plate; buffets, sideboards, and kitchen dressers for other tableware; and presses for clothes and linens. Another innovation was furniture purpose-built for its setting. At Lacock Abbey Sir William Sharington commissioned Italianate stone tables which were carved specifically for his banqueting tower. A square table at Grey's Court has an inscription that, translated from the German, reads 'Felix Brunner had me made in the year 1584; in this house I must stay.' In the early Tudor years those with more than one residence often had a single set of furnishings which they took from house to house. This changed over the course of a century. In the 1640s it was remarked that the Crown now owned eight 'standing palaces'—that is, palaces with furniture that did not move with the king. The monarchy had accumulated enough goods to furnish all these buildings and also to deposit furniture, armor, plate, and tapestries in vast storerooms at the Tower. By 1585 one area there was already set aside just for surplus bedsteads.[49]

Domestic goods exerted a perceptible pressure on the early modern housing market. In 1570 the parish church of St Michael Cornhill allowed Steven Rowlansson to hold a lease just 'to lay in his household stuff for one whole year, though he do dwell abroad himself'. Testators who worried about houseroom for their bequests included husbandman Richard Bridge, leaving his daughter 'one little solar to lay her stuff in until she marry', and Margaret Smith, specifying that her son should have a locked chamber for 'the household stuff that I give to him'. George Carey, second Baron Hunsdon, wrote Sir William More in 1596 that he had kept 'my armour and other stuff that I have' in Arundel House. But the building was part of the Lady Arundel's jointure, and the Earl had just died; 'thereby I am forced to seek for some other place to lay my stuff in'. He thought of the Blackfriars: 'Understanding that you

Society of Lancashire and Cheshire 97 (1945), 106–43. For problems with inventories as evidence, see my 'Fictions of the Early Modern English Probate Inventory', in Henry S. Turner (ed.), *The Culture of Capital: Property, Cities, and Knowledge in Early Modern England* (New York: Routledge, 2002), 51–83, esp. 63–73. Lacock and Speke seem to reflect fully furnished halls, as they mention large tables.

[49] On chests, Jourdain, *English Decoration*, esp. 263; *Jacobean Household Inventories*, ed. F. G. Emmison, Publications of the Bedfordshire Historical Record Society 20 (1938), 16–18; and Emmison, *Elizabethan Life*, 9. Greys Court guidebook. On standing palaces, Barley, *Houses and History*, 169; for the Tower, Dunlop, *Palaces*, 58–9.

have already parted with part of your house to some that means to make a playhouse of it, and also hearing that you mean to let or sell your other house', perhaps More had surplus space that Hunsdon could use.[50]

Most telling are Rebuilding projects that did not follow Hoskins's tidy sequence in full. At Synyards in Kent, a tall hall was subdivided in the late sixteenth century. Decades passed before the upper rooms were heated, suggesting a more pressing need for storage space than for separate bedchambers. M. W. Barley contests the prevailing hypothesis even for the old one-roomed longhouse, demonstrating that when upper lofts were first added they were used for garnering corn, malt, apples, bacon, cheeses, and wool—not, he says, for 'the comfort or privacy of sleeping upstairs'.[51]

Implicit in many approaches to the living conditions of the middling sort is the idea that the consumer revolution was a lesser story than was that of the Great Rebuilding. For Richard Carew, however, the histories of buildings and their furnishings were thoroughly intertwined. Writing in the 1580s, he described backward conditions in the west country, where within recent memory Cornishmen had dwelled in houses with 'walls of earth, low thatched roofs, few partitions, no planchings [floorboards] or glass windows, and scarcely any chimneys, other than a hole in the wall to let out the smoke. Their bed, straw and a blanket; as for sheets, so much linen cloth had not yet stepped over the narrow channel between them and Britain. To conclude, a mazer [wooden cup] and a pan or two comprised all their substance.' But, Carew observed, 'most of these fashions are universally banished, and the Cornish husbandman conformeth himself with a better supplied civility to the Eastern pattern'. He assumed that 'civility' involved goods provision as well as Rebuilt spaces.[52]

---

[50] *The Accounts of the Churchwardens of the Parish of St Michael, Cornhill, in the City of London, from 1456 to 1608*, ed. William Henry Overall (London: private printing by Alfred James Waterlow for the Vestry, 1868), 236. Will of Richard Bridge (1586), *Essex Wills: The Archdeaconry Courts, 1583–1592*, ed. F. G. Emmison (Chelmsford: Essex Record Office, 1989), no. 199. Will of Margaret Smith (1563), *Essex Wills (England)*, i. *1558–1565*, ed. F. G. Emmison (Washington, DC: National Genealogical Society, 1982), no. 559. Letter of George Carey, Folger Ms L.b.38; he also campaigned to prevent the development of the Blackfriars as a playhouse.

[51] For Synyards, see Lloyd, *History*, 197. There was also resistance to the loss of a hearth. See the 1601 case of Thomas Hinde, presented in an Essex manor court because he lit a fire in a room with no chimney (cited in Emmison, *Elizabethan Life*, 3) and the 1696 case of Christopher Banister, disciplined for endangering an almshouse with his 'nastiness and loathsomest' when he lit wood on an open hearth rather than use the coals provided for his chimney (cited by Ian W. Archer, *The History of the Haberdashers' Company* (Chichester: Phillimore, 1991), 134–5). Barley, 'The Use of Upper Floors in Rural Houses', *Vernacular Architecture* 22 (1991), 20–3.

[52] Carew quoted by Barley, *English Farmhouse*, 113.

The matter of houses and belongings has never been put as a chicken-and-egg question—which came first?—presumably because it has seemed natural to assume that people who acquired more rooms assembled the goods to fill them. But a competing logic would make an argument that is at least as compelling: people who accumulated more possessions needed space in which to employ, store, display, and enjoy them. A resonant anecdote out of Loseley House in Surrey involves a 1556 inventory which lists 'things new bought'. These objects had not been sorted into their spaces because the spaces did not yet exist. In 1562 William More began to rebuild his house, adding the chambers in which his possessions finally found useful locations.[53] There may also be some symbolic significance to the fact that the 1529 statute requiring probate inventories of moveables considerably predated Hoskins's 1570 start date for the Great Rebuilding. Hoskins declared that 'privacy demands more rooms, devoted to specialised uses'. Perhaps it is as important to say that more personal property demands more rooms.

THE PROBLEM OF PRIVACY

Hoskins was occupied primarily with laying out the evidence for an early modern housing revolution, although he also sketched some ways of accounting for it. He wrote, for example, of fixed rents and surplus income. As Jules Lubbock has observed, however, discretionary funds need not have been spent on housing. Hoskins pointed, further, to dramatic population growth over the course of the sixteenth century. But he himself argued that this was at first a consequence of improved living conditions and only later and secondarily a reason that houses were further enlarged. Finally, he emphasized technological advances like the use of coal and cheaper window glass. With this, privacy seems to have become inextricably implicated in all discussions of the motivating forces for material change. Access to heat and light made possible 'small, separate rooms', Hoskins explained. For him and for others, the connections between specialization and privacy are so self-evident that the terms have become constant companions. The shift from 'multifunctional' halls to rooms designed 'for one purpose' was, according to Maurice Howard, a 'move towards greater privacy'. Nicholas Cooper says that inventories 'confirm an overall impression of increasing specialisation in the uses of rooms and a concomitant increase in the attainment of privacy'. For example, earlier bedchambers had 'doubled as sitting rooms, and the gradual separation of

---

[53] More cited by Cooper, *Houses of the Gentry*, 275.

functions is the clearest evidence of increasing desire for privacy'.[54] It seems that no one has questioned the precise articulation of these two phenomena. Was privacy an effect of particularized spaces? If so, what kind of privacy? And was it an intended effect?

Most writers on the subject use that slippery word 'increasing'. There are assumptions, first, that privacy is a desirable state; second, that it was arrived at by positive evolutionary change; and, third, that early modern privacy evolved away from a more primitive, medieval style of life that was public or communal.[55] However, a thoroughly convincing case might be made that the medieval courtyard house, focused exclusively in upon itself behind its self-enclosing walls, was in fact more private in nature than was the early modern compact house, which appeared eager to engage with viewers and was also needier of their approval and admiration. This may seem a fairly abstract argument about architectural character and its meanings, but the conditions of social engagement produced by the two modes were also materially different. In the courtyard house, servants' lodgings were usually ranged in the outer wing at maximum distance from the hall and principal solar. In the compact house, they were brought under the same roof as those of the head family, so that each group lived less privately, being in closer proximity to the other.[56]

Our notion of the medieval household is dominated, as were medieval houses, by the great hall. It is invariably described as a multipurpose room for communal use. If it is imagined apart from its built context, this is its nature. In its relations with other domestic spaces, however, the hall also had separationist agencies. As Cooper himself recognizes, 'the open hall provided a physical barrier between the high and low ends on all but the ground floor'. At one end of the hall stood the residential block with ground-level parlor and upper solar connected by their own staircase; at the other end a service block

---

[54] Jules Lubbock, *The Tyranny of Taste: The Politics of Architecture and Design in Britain, 1550–1960* (New Haven: Yale University Press for the Paul Mellon Centre for Studies in British Art, 1995), 56–7. Hoskins, 'Great Rebuilding', 53, 55. Howard, *Early Tudor Country House*, 108. Cooper, *Houses of the Gentry*, 273–4; elsewhere, Cooper suggests that 'evolving civility showed itself in the desire for greater privacy and in the need for more rooms' ('Rank, Manners and Display', 297).

[55] Girouard argues against the notion that change is evolutionary and progressive: 'The point which [Nicholas Cooper] fairly makes—the growing emphasis on privacy and personal expression as against community and hierarchy, which led to the decay of the great hall—help to explain the development of the late Elizabethan and Jacobean house but not the Caroline house which followed it, in which self-expression is curtailed in favour of a standard [compact] model' ('Suitable for all men of dignity: Domestic Architecture and the Reaction against Elizabethan and Jacobean Individualism', review of Cooper's *Houses of the Gentry* and Simon Thurley's *Whitehall Palace*, *Times Literary Supplement*, 16 June 2000, 20–1).

[56] Platt points out that 'In the double-pile house, the servants once accommodated in the ranges of the outer court slept above the family quarters in the garrets' (*Great Rebuildings*, 41).

with kitchen, pantry, and buttery below, secondary (servant) chambers and storage lofts above, and its own internal means of communication. Cooper discusses this arrangement strictly in terms of inconvenience; passage between the upper rooms of the two blocks was possible only by descending one flight of stairs, crossing the hall, and then climbing another. Matthew Johnson describes the same arrangement to assert that the tall hall had 'centralizing functions'.[57] They can as easily be seen as segregating. The medieval hall divided the household's communities, establishing clearly demarcated—in effect more private—spheres for both.

Staircases in the medieval house tended to display their genealogy. Because they functioned as ladders had done, many were single-purposed. They joined one floor to another without regard for other possible connections. Maurice Howard discusses stair turrets that might link two upper levels exclusively; at Coughton Court, for example, the turret is an empty space at ground level because it was intended for use only between higher floors. Elsewhere, a tower might provide access from ground to roof, with no openings into intermediary chambers. One foreign ambassador reported a private meeting with Elizabeth I, achieved when he was conducted from a courtyard 'up some secret stairs' that led directly 'into a hidden chamber'. Occasional stairs such as these acted to inhibit movement as much as to facilitate it, and in this had highly privatizing functions. In the sixteenth century, by contrast, main stairs were constructed at Hardwick, Hatfield, Knole, Aston, and many other great houses.[58] These were important architectural and decorative features in their

---

[57] Emphasis on the 'decline of the hall' persists in early modern discussions, even though Girouard correctly points out that the space was 'past its prime by 1400', in most cases two centuries before the developments associated with the Great Rebuilding (*Life*, 31). Cooper, *Houses of the Gentry*, 282; Johnson, *Housing Culture*, 56.

[58] Howard, *Early Tudor Country House*, 85–7. Walter H. Godfrey notes that in late-medieval houses, for lack of corridors, circular stairs were 'placed wherever required for occasional use' (*The English Staircase, an Historical Account . . . to the End of the XVIIIth Century* (London: B. T. Batsford, 1911), 5; see also 7). At Dartford a nunnery was converted to a royal residence with four winding staircases: from the king's privy kitchen to his dining chamber, from the queen's privy kitchen to her dining chamber, from the king's privy chamber to his garden, and from the queen's privy chamber to her garden (*History of the King's Works*, 70). See for a contrary opinion Platt, *Great Rebuildings*, 153. Frank E. Brown notes that 'access relations . . . evolve precisely to facilitate, and to inhibit, movement as required for practical and social purposes. If two spaces accommodate functions that are intimately related, it is highly likely that a plan arrangement will be developed that permits direct passage from one to the other. Conversely, if two rooms have distinct and unrelated uses, then access will probably be directed through other spaces, and a direct connection may be prohibited even when the two rooms are next to each other' ('Continuity and Change in the Urban House: Developments in Domestic Space Organisation in Seventeenth-Century London', *Comparative Studies in Society and History* 28 (1986), 567). Elizabeth's meeting reported in *Queen Elizabeth and Some Foreigners, Being a Series of Hitherto Unpublished Letters from the Archives of the Hapsburg Family*, ed. Victor Von Klarwill, trans. T. H. Nash (London: John Lane, 1928), 182. Henry VIII was so proud of the stairs at

own right, but it should be understood that central staircases rationalized a medieval form of privacy out of existence.

There is one further way in which the early modern house was effectively less private than its predecessors. In many late-medieval homes, bedrooms were furnished with their own garderobes. The fifteenth-century lodging ranges at Gainsborough Old Hall and Chenies Manor House had repeating, highly standardized facilities. Each chamber was provided on the outer wall with a brick stack that housed both a chimney, with its tunnel opening to vent smoke on the roof, and a privy, with a ground-level trap for removal of accumulated waste.[59] These arrangements, which conduced to high levels of privacy, vanished from new building by the mid-sixteenth century. Cooper points to the design 'difficulty of incorporating a garderobe projection into an elevation that was increasingly regular and symmetrical'. He also finds a way to accommodate his dominant argument, saying that garderobes were less necessary when householders shared their bedchambers with servants rather than other family members and when early modern closets created private space for close stools. However, sleeping arrangements did not change as rapidly as he implies, and closets were not always attached to bedchambers. Records emphasize instead that it was difficult and expensive to empty garderobe shafts.[60] Between cleansings, they emitted foul odors. Privacy may well have been sacrificed not to design but to the more urgent concern of olfactory annoyance.

The difficult issue of motivation lies also at the heart of discussions about purpose-specific spaces. As has already been suggested, these may have developed out of desires other than privacy, including the will to impose order on possessions and activities. When the first emphasis is put on goods, then rooms can be seen as a strategy for managing anxiety about goods.[61] For most early moderns, after all, the highest degree of particularization was associated with storage and service rooms. Later chapters consider in detail the more elite spaces of the Great Rebuilding, long galleries and closets. Here, however, the problem with reflexive associations of privacy and atomization can be briefly suggested with reference to the parlor. Although it is understood

Bridewell Palace that in 1528 he posed there to receive the papal legate (*History of the King's Works*, 58).

[59] I am grateful to Lieutenant Colonel MacLeod Matthews for a private tour of the lodging range at Chenies Manor House with its row of privies (which are not usually open to visitors).

[60] Cooper, *Houses of the Gentry*, 297−8. Sir John Harington defends the invention of the water closet with reference to privy odors in *A New Discourse of a Stale Subject Called the Metamorphosis of Ajax* (London: 1596).

[61] Arnheim notes that 'the more complex the structure, the greater the need for order' (*Dynamics*, 178).

to have replaced the 'multifunction' hall, it was itself a multipurpose space. Cooper said that medieval bedchambers 'doubled as sitting rooms'; so did early modern parlors. Inventories show them fitted out with both beds and dining tables. Even rooms that are generally thought to have been highly 'specialized' were, in fact, far more flexible than is often admitted. William Wentworth describes his father confined to bed during a serious illness, 'in that chamber which now is used for the dining chamber'.[62]

Finally, it is impossible fully to reconcile discussions of increasing privacy with those of the decorative intent of elite builders. Located above the great hall in order to derive importance from a central location, the new rooms of the Great Rebuilding were showpiece spaces. They featured wainscotting in an endless variety of patterns, plaster ceilings with dramatic pendants and molded foliate forms, colored and gilded friezes, imported tapestries and their painted imitators, embroidered cushion covers and bedhangings, window curtains and Turkey-work table carpets. Overmantels displayed biblical themes such as the story of David (at Montacute), the marriage of Tobias and Sarah (for Chatsworth, now at Hardwick), and the judgment of Solomon (at Barrington Court); there were also literary and mythological motifs including the judgment of Paris (at Montacute and Wolfeton), Apollo and the Nine Muses (for Chatsworth, now at Hardwick), Orpheus charming the beasts (at Haddon Hall), and a scene from Ovid's *Metamorphoses* (at Broughton Castle). A single overmantel at Levens Hall showed the five senses, the four elements, the four seasons, Samson, and Hercules. At Wolfeton, Hope and Justice framed images of the three ages of man, and Faith and Hope were joined by orientalized figures and New World natives. Burton Agnes had overmantels with Faith, Hope, and Charity; the Dance of Death; and Patience, Truth, Constance, and Victory. The Nine Worthies, a popular theme combining classical, Old Testament, and Christian heroes, appeared in plaster friezes (at Aston Hall) and a corridor-long wall painting (at Harvington). Most prevalent of all were displays of coats of arms in stained glass and carved stone and on iron firebacks.

In the medieval house there was one space meant to impress: the great hall. In the Renaissance house there might be a dozen that were designed and decorated for public consumption. The prolific ornamentation of the early modern home is usually understood to represent a mode of self-expression—in other words, it is taken to constitute yet another species of evidence for prevailing narratives

---

[62] Cooper, *Houses of the Gentry*, 273; see the example of Anne Reade Thorneworke cited by D. G. Vaisey (ed.), *Probate Inventories of Lichfield and District, 1568–1680*, Staffordshire Record Society, 4th ser., 5 (1969), 4. In 'Sir William's Account of the Providences Vouchsafed his Family' (1607), William Wentworth refers to an upper-level room (*Wentworth Papers*, 28).

about the invention of the individual in the Renaissance. But this argument, too, can be turned on its head, inasmuch as these were exhibitionist spaces, aimed at self-display rather than self-discovery.[63]

Great builders seem always to have been conscious of their audiences. The pattern at Hampton Court, for example, was for tapestries to be taken down when the Queen was not in residence. Arras would be rehung for foreign visitors, though, to ensure that they could 'see the magnificence of the same'. Wollaton was so strenuously exhibitionist that the Willoughbys could not afford to live there except when entertaining; otherwise, they occupied their less ostentatious homes, which were not as expensive to operate. Both at Hatfield and at Hardwick, older family buildings were maintained nearby for supplemental lodgings. Thus the show houses could be constructed to smaller scale, with every space purpose-built to impress. Hatfield had two sets of furnishings so that the most elegant ones would not be spoiled by regular usage, and at Knole, too, there were suites brought out only for distinguished visitors. John Spencer of Durham referred in his will to 'such furniture as there is in the house to serve the Queen'.[64] None of this luxury was intended for the private enjoyment of the principal family. Like all status building, that of early modern England was a public performance.

Despite all the regionalized revisions and periodizing qualifications to which it has been subjected, the larger notion of a Great Rebuilding endures. It has too solid an evidentiary base in surviving structures, parliamentary statutes, and, especially, common culture. This chapter takes issue with that aspect of the phenomenon which has hitherto gone unexamined—its meaning, as construed both in its motivations and its effects. If sixteenth-century buildings were less self-absorbed than their medieval predecessors; if, instead, elite Rebuildings were devoted to display; if upper rooms, too, were decorated for public reception; if central staircases universalized access to bedchambers; if the formerly discrete populations of the principal family and its service

---

[63] Even Cooper admits that the hall oriel 'seems to be an early manifestation of the desire which informs much of the development of the house in the sixteenth century: the apparently contradictory wishes both to attain privacy and to display it' (*Houses of the Gentry*, 276).

[64] For tapestries see Dunlop, *Palaces*, 60, 90; for Wollaton, Friedman, *House and Household*, 155; for Hatfield, Girouard, *Life*, 115. The practice at Knole accounts for the survival of so much furniture there, including the late seventeenth-century 'King's Bed'. Will of John Spencer (1600), *Wills and Inventories from the Registry at Durham, Part III*, ed. J. C. Hodgson, Publications of the Surtees Society 112 (1906), 176–7. Joyce Youings asks: 'Was it not in order to avoid the expense of entertaining all and sundry in the manner of their ancestors that the aristocracy gradually learned from the gentry and the wealthier merchants the virtues of family privacy?' (*Sixteenth-Century England*, 381).

workers were brought into closer contact in double piles; if homes at all social levels abandoned the segregating zone of the tall hall; and if the early modern explosion of consumer goods provided a more urgent need for specialized spaces than did any desire for withdrawal or seclusion, then the material history of privacy is not, after all, a settled one.

3

Alice Barnham in the Rebuilt World

WERE this a conventional biography of Alice Barnham, a study of her material world would detail the landmarks of London as she surely knew them: Whitehall in the west and the Tower in the east, symbolic of court culture and royal power; St Paul's Cathedral, dominant on the central skyline even without the steeple lost in 1561; the Thames, crossed by the busy water traffic that Francis Barnham routinely joined in making his way to St Thomas's Hospital in Southwark; Cheapside, periodically transformed by the passage of the city's ceremonial processions; the great gates in the old walls, some opening to fields spread with drying linens; the meat market at Smithfield, where Alice may have seen John Bradford martyred; the parish churches of St Mildred Poultry and St Clement Eastcheap, with their records of her family's life passages; the Royal Exchange, for the construction of which Francis lobbied and to which he contributed five pounds; Newgate and the compters, objects of Alice's charity; and Guildhall, site of such municipal occasions as the feast which celebrated the Barnhams as Master and Mistress Sheriff.

But this chapter, a case study in urban and middling-sort experiences of the Great Rebuilding, is focused more narrowly on Alice's domestic frames of reference. Through her husband's offices and her own spousal 'sisterhood' in the Drapers' Company, she was exposed to the widest possible range of city living spaces and household customs. There were the tenements thrown up in the alleys of Francis's ward of Farringdon Without the Walls, the many modest rental properties he inspected for the Drapers' Company, and also the Company's own urban mansion. Drapers' Hall is part of an architectural history most often told in terms of country or 'prodigy' houses. The parallel story of the great houses of London, one largely lost to the fire of 1666, includes not only metropolitan estates in private hands, such as Somerset House and Arundel House, but also those in corporate ownership. Company halls, equally implicated in the competitions of self-representation and status associated with the Great Rebuilding, were media through which innovation was transmitted to the large populations of their merchants, traders, craftsmen, and apprentices. Thus Drapers' Hall played a highly significant role in the democratization of new design ideas and standards of living. In their own removing and remodelings, the Barnhams exemplified the way in which the effects of the building revolution trickled down. For them, Drapers' Hall was a native model of material aspiration, as much an event as were Nonsuch and Longleat and Hardwick.

No change is ever painless, however, and the same was true of material reinvention. Dislocated during an improvement project, quarreling with their workmen over the charges, the Drapers registered the vexations that shadowed the Great Rebuilding. Francis and Alice Barnham found their own home renovations a source of neighborhood controversy. And the dispossession of Roger Sadler, a Drapers' tenant who had overinvested in the new climate of material competition, makes a cautionary tale about the economic hazards that could be engaged through status housing. These disputes both localize the Rebuilding in London and carry the story forward into some of its lesser-known disseminations and its discontents.

A livery hall and a family home may seem to belong to different orders of things. In this period, when there had not yet developed elaborate concepts or conventions of institutional building, they shared not only an architecture but also many ways of being in that architecture.[1] If the Company's vanished hall represents a genre of unacknowledged landmarks in architectural history, their archives are an unexploited resource on spatial processes, an astonishingly rich store of detail on civic social life and also on other ways in which Tudor men and women related to their built environments. Family papers, unvaryingly cryptic on the subject, make overmuch room for a free play of speculation about the uses and jurisdictions of the domestic surround. The Drapers' minute books, by contrast, are so journalistic that they might be sites for anthropological field research.

As much as any great house, for example, Drapers' Hall—a former monastic property, a former elite residence—was a locus of hospitality and festivity. The private residence of the Barnhams was, similarly, an epicenter of public functions: mercantile transactions, metropolitan governance, community standing, municipal ceremony, boundary negotiations, local charity. For Francis and Alice Barnham, who expressed their upward mobility by undertaking the type of renovations associated with elite architecture, the impetus for rebuilding cannot have been that desire for domestic privacy which has

---

[1] For the similarity of private homes and Company Halls, compare their inventories (generally, probate inventories for families and regular surveys by some livery companies—e.g. the records of the Cutlers' Company for 1586, 1608, and 1618 (GL Ms 7164) and the Tallow Chandlers' Company for 1559 and 1563 (GL Ms 6152/1, fos. 69^r–70^v and 105^v–107^r)). Company halls were distinguished from those in private residences mainly by the addition of Company insignia and business implements such as beams (to weigh merchandise).

generally been imputed to all early moderns. They required a platform for activities that advertised and advanced their success and status.

The new concept of privacy that does emerge from the Company records is an instrument of oligarchy in the Tudor *public* sphere: the development, by mid-sixteenth century, of the corporate parlor as an exclusionary space. While the parlor of the domestic arena was a room of changeable purpose, in Drapers' Hall it was a dedicated site for the secret acts of regulation and patronage conducted by the Company's officers. Their choreographies of the open and the closed were more ritualized and more coercive than was possible in any household, and they followed from acts of withdrawal, exercises of spatial privilege, and differentiations by gender. All the machineries of institutional authority were used to defend this advance in spatial control, a rare and delicate commodity in Tudor culture—and a privacy to which Alice Barnham was not privy.

DRAPERS' HALL AND THE GREAT REBUILDING

The London Drapers joined the Great Rebuilding in 1543. They moved to a new Company Hall, trading up to a property dislodged from its longtime owner by the Dissolution of the monasteries. They were already substantial landowners. As early as 1538, members of the Drapers' Court of Assistants had discussed the investment opportunities occasioned by Henry VIII's seizure and redistribution of church holdings. At that point, anxiety about the new order of things prevailed. The situation appeared sufficiently volatile that they concluded they should not be 'hasty' in entering the newly expanded property market. When in 1541 they received a large bequest from Sir John Rudston (grandfather to Martin Barnham's first wife), they elected to invest it not in suppressed lands but instead in a property known as 'the Herber', which had belonged to Margaret Pole, Countess of Salisbury, before she was attainted for treason.[2]

By 1543, however, the Drapers were ready to re-evaluate. For one thing, it now appeared that ecclesiastical lands would not be restored to their former owners. For another, the Drapers had been promised major new investment funds from a former warden of the Company, Thomas Howell. Howell traded

---

[2] Drapers' M.B.1/B, fos. 359^v–362^r, and see Johnson, *History*, ii. 278–82. For reservations about suppressed lands, M.B.1/B, fo. 288^v; for a 1542 decision not to buy lands offered by Sir Richard Cromwell, fo. 350^v. For the Rudston bequest, M.B.1/B, fo. 318^r. In 1540, the Drapers reported annual rental income of £246. 17s. 8d. (M.B.1/B, fos. 310^r–311^v). On the Herber, Johnson, *History*, ii. 67; Girtin, *Triple Crowns*, 118.

goods through Seville, and when he died in 1537 it was a difficult business to extract his £2,700 bequest from Spain. Further challenges resulted from Howell's instructions that the income from his endowment should be used to provide marriage portions for ten orphaned women annually. To manage their greatly expanded philanthropic activities, the Drapers reorganized their rental accounts, with a separate administration for the lands of Howell's large legacy. Despite all these procedural complications, there were benefits, too. The Drapers' most significant property purchase, which included the new Company Hall, came to them, or so it was said, because the king appreciated that future earnings from his holdings would be put to Howell's benevolent uses. When the Drapers were soon thereafter asked to house the Spanish ambassador in the buildings acquired from the Crown, they successfully protested that poor maidens would lose their portions if the Company lost its rents.[3]

The purchase at issue was the London mansion of Thomas Cromwell, formed when he was able to join a large plot on Throgmorton Street to an adjacent one once owned by an Augustine abbey. Cromwell had commissioned royal carpenter James Nedeham to build him a 'large and spacious' head house there, 'in the place of old and small tenements'. Decades later, John Stow was to recall another of Cromwell's improvements: he extended the grounds of his estate by moving his fence northwards twenty-two feet into the garden of Stow's own father. There had been a building on the senior Stow's land, but Cromwell had it 'loosed from the ground', set on rollers, and moved beyond the new property line that he created by digging a trench, laying a foundation, and erecting a high brick wall. 'No man durst go to argue the matter', said Stow, even though his father continued to be assessed the full rent for 'that

---

[3] Lay ownerships of former church properties were reconfirmed in 1554 by 1 and 2 Philip and Mary, cap. 8, 'An Act repealing all statutes . . . made against the see apostolic of Rome since the 20th year of King Henry VIII, and also for the establishment of all spiritual and ecclesiastical possessions and hereditaments conveyed to the laity.' See *The Statutes of the Realm (1225–1713)*, ed. A. Luders et al., 9 vols. (London: Eyre & Strahan, 1810–22), iv. 246–54. See Girtin on Howell's legacy, *Triple Crowns*, 114–15, 150–1. Company officers called on the Spanish ambassador with 'a good dish of meat' and solicited his help 'recovering' moneys held by Howell's executors (Drapers' M.B.1/C, fo. 375^v). Although they used other funds to purchase the Cromwell estate, the King professed himself 'content' with the fiction 'that the revenues and profits coming of the said place shall yearly be given to maids' marriages', as Howell directed (M.B.1/B, fo. 360^r; see also the Assistants' resolution that 'the King's Grace may preserve to what use the revenues of the Lord Cromwell's place shall go unto', fo. 362^r). When housing for the ambassador was secured with a Mistress Cornwallis, the Drapers rewarded her with 40s. for a frock and 10s. for her maid's kirtle (M.B.1/C, fo. 374^v; Johnson, *History*, ii. 66). In 1554, members of Philip's retinue were housed in the halls of livery companies because Londoners refused to lodge them (Susan Brigden, *London and the Reformation* (Oxford: Clarendon, 1989), 556). There were continuing problems administering Howell's legacy; for an instance involving Francis Barnham, see Drapers' M.B.9, fo. 3^r.

half which was left'. Cromwell's properties, including nine buildings as well as the great garden, reverted to the rolls of the Crown's Court of Augmentations when he was executed in 1540. Nearly three years later the Drapers delegated five members of their Court of Assistants to open negotiations with the Treasurer of the Augmentations for Cromwell's former London base.[4]

The Drapers' decision was not easily taken. If the purchase proved 'more pleasant than profitable', and the Company overextended itself, financial burdens would fall on individual merchants. The majority accordingly 'had little mind thereunto', but they were finally persuaded by the few who argued that while one of the Cromwell buildings would serve splendidly for their company hall, the remaining eight could be let to drapers who 'do lack houses to dwell in' in overcrowded London. Some of those present remembered the good rental values of the buildings when they were 'separated', before Cromwell engrossed them into his great estate. In the final concord, the first condition was that these properties should be let only to Company members. There were other provisions: the delegates should offer the Crown 1,700 marks but were authorized to go as high as 1,800 marks (£1,200); the Augmentations should guarantee the use of conduit water and a customary right of way and should verify that all fixtures and fittings would convey with the lands and buildings; and the necessary paperwork should include a valuation of the property by the king's auditor as well as a documents search to verify clear title.[5]

The first stipulation, the policy restricting tenancies, was soon to fall away. By 1550 the Drapers' highest priority was rental profit. The second resulted in an agreed purchase price of 1,800 marks, with 1,000 marks paid down and 800 due within twelve months. For the third, the Drapers were assured that water and access would be maintained—'God forbid else'—and that porches,

---

[4] For Cromwell's estate, see Drapers' M.B.1/C, fos. 376[r]–377[r]; *Letters and Papers... of the Reign of Henry VIII*, ed. J. S. Brewer et al., 21 vols. (London: HMSO, 1864–1932), v. no. 1028, and ix. nos. 66, 172, 259, 862, and 1029; William Phillips Sawyer, 'The Drapers' Company', *Transactions of the London and Middlesex Archaeological Society* 7, Part 1 (1888; printed as an appendix to vol. vi, 1890), 37–64; Mary L. Robertson, 'Profit and Purpose in the Development of Thomas Cromwell's Landed Estates', *Journal of British Studies* 29 (1990), 317–46, esp. n. 10; and Johnson, *History*, ii. 278–81. For Nedeham, H. M. Colvin, D. R. Ransome, and John Summerson (eds.), *The History of the King's Works*, iii. *1485–1660 (Part 1)* (London: HMSO, 1975), 10, 30, 41–3, *inter alia*. Johnson purports to transcribe the Drapers' survey of the new property, but he includes only 'Master Palmer's house', 'Pechi's house', and the Company hall, omitting 'Calverant's house', 'Williamson's house', 'Master Lees's house', two other tenements, and 'Master Roche's house'. John Stow, *A Survey of London* (London: 1598), 140–1; rev. edn. (London: 1603), 180–1.

[5] Thomas North, Treasurer of the Augmentations, approached the Drapers about purchasing Cromwell's estate, Drapers' M.B.1/B, fo. 359[v]. Approval was not as 'immediate' as Girtin suggests, *Triple Crowns*, 118–19; see fo. 361[r]. For terms and negotiations, fos. 359[v]–362[r].

cupboards, presses, tables, forms, benches, shelves, cisterns, breadbins, glass windows, locks, keys, door chains, and bars would remain as implements. But they were not permitted to inventory these items nor even to view the properties: 'It was not the king's honor so to permit them.' Thus they were asked to make the single most important investment of their corporate history for buildings purchased sight unseen.[6] Although the fourth condition was presumably fulfilled, this did not prevent the widow of one Anthony Brisket from laying claim to a portion of the estate thirty years later, in 1574, at that point encumbering the Drapers with considerable legal expense to maintain ownership of their corporate home.[7]

When they finally entered their new premises in July 1543, the Drapers discovered they had Rebuilding projects ahead of them. Disintegrating the estate into its separate residences, they found too few of the privies, chimneys, and storage cellars that Londoners now expected.[8] They retained their former Company Hall on St Swithins Lane, renting it out to a draper for his personal use, but it, too, required major modifications to be brought up to residential standard. The old tall hall had to be 'boarded for a second story'—that is, bisected into two levels—with both floors 'divided into chambers' and new privies added.[9] The use of the building for Company business had artificially prolonged its life as a medieval hall house. As a private home of the mid-1500s, it required vertical division, atomization, and more amenities.

On Throgmorton Street, the Drapers' great gate opened into a paved courtyard. A low, roofed gallery bordered the far (north) side of the yard; in 1555 the Drapers enlarged this loggia, and in 1564 they fitted it out with forty-five feet of benching. A turret with bay windows enclosed the winding stair that led up one flight, as was typical of urban plans, to a great hall on a medieval scale. Even at its raised level, the hall was at least two stories tall, for above the adjoining pantry and buttery was a chamber with a latticed opening that looked down into it. The Company still had corporate uses for this large and impressive space. There were two glazed bay windows, one of which the Drapers relocated from another room, and a round, curtained

---

[6] Drapers' M.B.1/C, fo. 485ʳ; M.B.1/B, fo. 360ʳ⁻ᵛ. As soon as agreement in principle was reached, a view was arranged for 22 March 1543 (fo. 360ᵛ).

[7] For the documents search, Drapers' M.B.1/B, fo. 360ᵛ. The Drapers paid £5. 3s. 4d. for legal counsel regarding Mistress Brisket's suit (W.A.5, 1573–4, fos. 6ᵛ–7ʳ).

[8] They entered in July and celebrated 'the first assembly at our new hall' on 7 August 1543 (Drapers' M.B.1/C, fo. 371ᵛ). The Lord Mayor approved the keeping of court there on 20 October 1543, and on 22 October they surveyed the property (fo. 372ᵛ). In 1568, the Clerk had 'a privy new made within his chamber for his necessity and commodity' and the Porter was given cellar space (M.B.8, fo. 33ᵛ).

[9] Drapers' M.B.1/C, fo. 379ʳ. For later repairs at the Old Hall, see M.B.8, fo. 29ʳ⁻ᵛ and M.B.9, fo. 11ʳ.

clerestory window. A second spiral stair connected the hall to the service rooms at ground level. These included a kitchen with two chimneys, a pastry house with three ovens, a scullery, and two larders. Both street stairs and kitchen stairs were at the far end of the hall from the high table. The Drapers surrounded the staircase doors with wall-mounted morris pikes and halberds.[10]

The religious and political tumults that had brought the Company to the great estate on Throgmorton Street also caused a series of changes within. The fellowship had originally been founded in honor of the Virgin, and old Catholic 'imagery' was brought out of storage when Mary I came to the throne (see Fig. 3.5). In 1559 or 1560, in consequence of the Elizabethan Acts of Uniformity and Supremacy, this wallhanging was retired for the last time. From that point forward, the decorations of the great hall were colorful and self-ceremonializing, but in secular terms. As early as 1558, the Company's arms were executed in stained glass at the high end of the hall and, soon after, on a wall panel. There was also a carving of the arms of England, with colors and gilding executed by John Shute in the early 1560s. The record gives unique evidence of Shute's otherwise obscure career as a painter-stainer after he returned to London from his Italian tour and before he published *The First and Chief Grounds of Architecture*.[11]

While the Drapers were quick to register the religious reversals of the century in the great hall, they were slower to make changes in their parlor, the

[10] The description is based on sources given in n. 4 and on Drapers' M.B.5, fo. 58^v; R.A.5, 1563–4, fo. 10^v; M.B.1/C, fo. 379^v; and R.A.4, 1557–8, fo. 6^v. The Company also maintained an 'armory house' (as of 1560, M.B.7, p. 215; see also R.A.5, 1577–8, fo. 9^v). Above-ground halls were frequent in urban and monastic building.

[11] Although the imagery was removed (Drapers' R.A.4, 1559–60, fo. 6^v), there were still objects such as the crimson velvet cushion 'with the image of the Assumption of Our Lady embroidered', a bequest from a former draper (M.B.7, p. 207). See also Girtin, *Triple Crowns*, 127, 137–9. For the Company arms, R.A.4, 1557–8, fo. 18^r; for a patent search, carving, and painting, W.A.4, 1560–1, fos. 8^r–9^v; for Shute, W.A.4, 1561–2, fo. 6^r. Shute's London career is largely irrecoverable because the earliest records of the Painter-Stainers' Company date from 1623. In 1566 or 1567, the Drapers hired a smith to construct an iron canopy over the arms when they were regilded (R.A.5, 1566–7, fo. 10^r). See also R.A.5, 1578–9, fo. 10^v for 'coloring' of the great hall and R.A.5, 1578–9, fo. 18^v for 'lead colors' on the windows. The high table and stools in the hall were also painted (W.A.5, 1563–4, fo. 5^r; R.A.5, 1576–7, fo. 9^v). For the secularization of the livery companies, see Joseph P. Ward, *Metropolitan Communities: Trade Guilds, Identity, and Change in Early Modern London* (Stanford: Stanford University Press, 1997), 100. There is no evidence that the Drapers displayed portraits of its leading members in this period (as Robert Tittler describes in *Townspeople and Nation: English Urban Experiences, 1540–1640* (Stanford: Stanford University Press, 2001), 17, and in 'An Actor's Face? The Sanders Portrait in Context', in Nolen, *Shakespeare's Face*, 218–20). The sixteenth-century portraits now held by the Company, of William Chester and members of the Lambarde family, were given in 1944 and the 1960s, respectively.

far more private space in which the Company's administrative business was increasingly conducted. Not until 1572 were pre-Reformation hangings finally described as 'contain[ing] divers blasphemies and superstitions to the offense of divers'. They were then 'new stain[ed]'. The parlor had bay windows, a chimney, fashionable 'antic' work painted on the ceiling, its own buttery, and a closet or 'treasure house' in which the Drapers locked their papers. The room was furnished with several tables covered in once-blue cloths redyed a 'sad green'. Officers sat at the head table or 'board' with ledges 'wherein certain ordinances are written for the Master Wardens to look upon'. They had bound copies of royal statutes for ready reference, the books 'fair embossed with latten bosses'. Every year the Clerk purchased an almanac; there was also a large hanging 'table almanac perpetual with pricks and pins' (see Fig. 3.1). A New Testament, used for oath-takings, was cushioned in a red-leather 'purse'. The ivory-handled hammer by which Quarter Day meetings were gaveled to order required periodic repairs; there was also an hourglass with an ivory pillar.[12]

In the mid-1570s the Drapers repaneled the parlor, an undertaking so costly that they scaled back their annual banquets for five years. Some leading members began stockpiling oak as early as June 1573, well before the November 1574 meeting in which the project was officially approved. By September 1575, old wainscotting had been stripped out and joiners were at work building frames for the new panels. For more than six months, meetings of the Court of Assistants were displaced from the parlor to a third space located over the great entrance gate. The Ladies' Chamber had its own chimney, bay windows, privy, and rush floor matting.[13] When the renovations finally ended, there was a dispute over charges—as was

[12] The parlor was located next to the hall and over the outdoor gallery. When the gallery was enlarged in 1555, so was the parlor (Drapers' M.B.5, fo. 58ᵛ). For decor and furnishings, M.B.8, fo. 209ᵛ (superstitious hangings); R.A.5, 1576–7, fo. 9ᵛ (antic work); M.B.7, p. 234; M.B.9, fo. 95ᵛ; W.A.5, 1564–5, fo. 6ʳ; W.A.5, 1566–7, fo. 5ᵛ; and R.A.5, 1566–7, fo. 10ʳ (tables, ledges, and coverings); M.B.7, p. 215 (statutes); W.A.5, 1564–5, fo. 5ʳ and W.A.5, 1566–7, fo. 5ʳ (almanacs); M.B.8, fo. 96ʳ (New Testament); W.A.4, 1561–2, fo. 5ᵛ (ivory gavel); M.B.8, fo. 39ᵛ (hour glass). In Whitehall, a carpet was provided in the Council Chamber 'to cover the table that the oldness of the board be not seen' (quoted by Dunlop, *Palaces*, 69). The Company arms were mounted on the parlor overmantel at least from 1575. In 1584 a protective curtain of reused silk was added; the Assistants soon observed it 'is not durable but staineth with the air and sun', requiring redyeing or replacing (M.B.10, fols. 10ᵛ, 48ᵛ). The latten bosses on the statute books were knob-like ornaments of brass or another mixed metal similar to brass, usually placed on the center of the cover.

[13] The 1555 enlargement of the parlor probably resulted in mismatched wainscotting. For the Assistants' exile from the parlor, Drapers' M.B.9, fos. 25ᵛ, 32ᵛ, 40ᵛ, 44ʳ. Evidence for the privy comes from the order for a new key, R.A.5, 1580–1, fo. 9ᵛ. The room may have been named for a decorative program of wall paintings or wall hangings or for its occasional use by the 'sisters' of the Company (as was the case at Mercers' Hall).

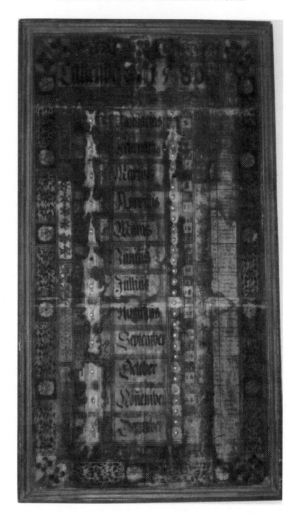

Figure 3.1 This 'table almanac perpetual with pricks and pins', dated 1580, survives in the collections of the Levoca Town Hall, Slovakia. A movable peg is used to mark the desired date.

not uncommon. Four men were brought in to measure, two on behalf of the Drapers and two for the joiners. It was finally agreed that the joiners had installed 674½ yards of wainscotting, which at 7½ shillings a yard totaled nearly £253. The special carving of the Company arms on the overmantel cost an additional 10 marks. The Clerk's painstakingly detailed records regarding materials, labor, and controversy betray the full level of aggravation experienced by those who lived through this Rebuilding project.[14]

A remarkable feature of the Cromwell estate, and equally an object of Rebuilding, was its one-and-a-half-acre garden. The Drapers added herbs planted in knot designs, grass paths for walking, and banks set with roses, gooseberry trees, and privet hedges. Elsewhere in the city, green space was sacrificed to the need for more housing for a burgeoning population, but the Company protected its rare privilege fiercely. The privacy of their bowling alley was secured in 1574 when a brick wall was built 'to stop up the light of the gable end of a house adjoining to the wall of the same garden'—that is, to prevent the residents of a neighboring building from looking into the Drapers' exclusive pleasure grounds. Year after year, the Assistants debated the matters of who should have access to the garden and whether any wives might dry their linens there.[15]

The most valuable of the Company's goods were textiles—napery, table carpets, and cushion covers. There were also banners and streamers that were hung in the hall for feast dinners, carried into the streets for civic processions, and otherwise stored in a press and a settle in the parlor. In 1571 the Company acquired twelve damask counterpanes, six with white thread buttons and white bone lace, six with gold buttons and gold bone lace; the gold lace had to be removed each year for laundering, then reapplied.[16] The Drapers had surprisingly little plate. They had purchased the Cromwell estate only in part with Howell's bequest; for the rest, they gathered funds by first selling some £60 worth of Company plate, then using items worth £115 as sureties

[14] For records detailing the wainscotting project, see Drapers' M.B.8, fos. 222^v, 223^r, 225^r; M.B.9, fos. 4^v, 61^v, 62^v; and R.A.5, 1575–6, fos. 7^v, 17^v–19^v. The old wainscotting was reused in other Company buildings (M.B.9, fo. 32^r). The old stone overmantel, broken during removal, was stored in the cellar in pieces (R.A.5, 1580–1, fo. 18^v).

[15] R.A.5, 1573–4, fo. 25^r. On privacy, light, and overlooking, see my 'Boundary Disputes in Early Modern London', in *Material London, ca. 1600* (Philadelphia: University of Pennsylvania Press, 2000), esp. p. 361. Johnson, *History*, ii. 67–8; Girtin, *Triple Crowns*, 122; and, for renovations and maintenance, Drapers' M.B.1/C, fos. 383^v, 414^r, 428^v; M.B.7, p. 229. For extensive work on water drainage, R.A.5, 1573–4, fo. 23$^{r–v}$. The many entries concerned with washing and drying linens include a prohibition on anything other than Company napery (M.B.5, fo. 81^r); an exception granted 'provided always that the same should be no precedent hereafter to any other' (M.B.7, p. 154); permission given on condition that boards be placed 'to keep the kitchen stones and pavement from breaking' (M.B.7, p. 234); authorization for Assistants so long as 'they hang no dishcloths nor rags nor any other unseemly cloths' (M.B.8, fo. 205^r); and, finally, another general prohibition (M.B.8, fo. 263^v). In 1572 a new door made it easier to bring fertilizing dung into the garden (M.B.8, fo. 205^r).

[16] The Drapers bought two new presses for 'napery, cushions, carpets, streamers, and banners' (Drapers' R.A.4, 1556–7, fo. 6^r and W.A.5, 1567–8, fo. 9^r; for the settle, W.A.5, 1573–4, fo. 4^v). On 28 April 1568 the officers voted to inventory their table linens and make new purchases (M.B.8, fo. 28^r; W.A.5, 1567–8, fo. 9^r). The Clerk's wife usually had the commission to launder Company linens (e.g. M.B.8, fos. 39^r, 176^r). For gold lace, W.A.5, 1570–1, fo. 7^v.

in borrowing from their members, and finally allowing drapers to purchase any pawns they held. Shortly thereafter they sold a last hoard for £190. With forced subsidies to the Crown and loans to the City, their cash flow was so active that there was little to bank in cups and goblets, and by 1571 they had restocked only minimally, with a nest of goblets purchased outright and a few other pieces received as gifts and legacies.[17] At mid-century, their policy was to rely on the wealth of members for funds as required, not to build a corporate reserve in plate.

Buildings and grounds made unceasing demands on any bequests or surpluses. Besides maintaining the Company Hall, the Drapers conducted biennial surveys to monitor their extensive rental holdings. No renovations or repairs could be undertaken without the express approval of the Assistants. Thus they, like all institutional landlords, were regularly visited by petitioning tenants. In 1556, for example, alderman Thomas Lodge asked to extend his lease on a Company house to 'make the best' of the implements he proposed adding. The Assistants decided instead 'that a draper ought to have the preferment', though the new tenant should compensate Lodge for refurbishments already undertaken. In 1584, Henry Walker sought 'license to build up a chimney of new, having now but one chimney in all his house which is in the kitchen, and also to make a window in the chamber'. The Drapers authorized the changes and granted Walker a 'benevolence' of twenty shillings toward his charges. Requests such as these were steady enough throughout London that in 1571 the governors of St Thomas's Hospital established a three-year moratorium to contain their costs.[18] This is another species of evidence for the pandemic that was the Great Rebuilding: the pressure on property holders not only for routine repairs but also to accommodate rising standards. In their rental housing as in their corporate home, the Drapers were of necessity great Rebuilders.

---

[17] In 1571, the Drapers certified that their plate, cash, and moveables together amounted to no more than £53 (Drapers' M.B.8, fo. 163^r). For the sale of plate, Girtin, *Triple Crowns*, 122–3. For inventories of plate, M.B.7, p. 294 (1560) and W.A.5, 1570–1, fo. 10^{r-v}. For bequests of plate, M.B.8, fos. 63^v, 66^r; M.B.9, fo. 20^v; and M.B.10, fo. 43^v. On plate as 'crucial in the ritual of gift-exchange which was the visible cement holding the hierarchy together', see Philippa Glanville, 'Cardinal Wolsey and the Goldsmiths', in S. J. Gunn and P. G. Lindley (eds.), *Cardinal Wolsey: Church, State and Art* (Cambridge: Cambridge University Press, 1991), 134. When the Queen called for a loan of £116. 13s. 4d. in 1575, she 'expressly stated that the burden must not be allowed to fall on individual members of the Company but must be borne by the corporate funds' (Girtin, *Triple Crowns*, 167).

[18] Drapers' M.B.5, pp. 197, 200 (Lodge); Drapers' M.B.10, fo. 17^r (Walker). Renters and Renter Wardens were not themselves empowered to authorize improvements, which were referred to the Assistants. The St Thomas's moratorium excepted only repairs needed to keep buildings 'wind tight and water tight or to keep or uphold any house from falling down', LMA H01/ST/A/001/003, fo. 55^r.

REBUILDINGS AND THEIR DISCONTENTS

The Barnhams were Rebuilders, too—though little else can be discovered about them as householders: they located themselves in St Clement Eastcheap in 1559, conducted a major renovation in 1568, and undertook further refurbishments in 1570. When the Drapers first entered the Cromwell estate they recorded their inspection of each structure. For the Barnhams, by contrast, not even a probate inventory remains. Family wills are wholly uninformative on the subject of domestic arrangements, being occupied with lands, philanthropies, and personal mementos rather than with beds, cupboards, and household necessities. There is, however, evidence of a storage cellar—as was increasingly common in London—because it was mentioned in connection with nine loads of stone and five loads of chalk Francis once sold to the Drapers' Company. The parish register of St Clement Eastcheap refers to a gate, which implies an imposing entrance and a forecourt. Even more unusually, the Barnhams had green space of their own; in Bridewell the witness Ursula ('who hath no surname') testified in the matter of a neighborhood housebreaking that she saw 'one Elizabeth Mat talk with two young men in Master Barnham's garden the same night the robbery was done'.[19]

Among Francis Barnham's holdings was a large Southwark tract which incorporated grounds from the dissolved priory church of St Mary Overy. He left this property not to the 'bawdy' institutions he had helped govern but instead to London's home for orphaned children. Still today there is a 'Barnham Street', just east of the London Bridge Underground station, named in honor of his endowment to Christ's Hospital. For this land that passed out of family hands in 1576 there is again far more information than for their own home, because the bequest was conferred with a collection of deeds and evidences deposited in an institutional archive. These include a series of surveys drawn over many years; the earliest, which may be in the hand of Ralph Treswell, illustrates lands near Horselydown bordered by Mill Ditch, with a house, two yards, a large garden, and a commercial oven (see Fig. 3.2).

---

[19] Because the Barnhams held property in more than one county, their wills were probated in the Prerogative Court of Canterbury, which did not archive inventories. The Drapers bought nine loads of hard stone and five loads of lye and chalk from Barnham; they also paid for 'carrying the said stone out of the cellar at Master Alderman's' (Drapers' R.A.5, 1569–70, fo. 8ᵛ). For the gate, GL Ms 4783/1 (1573); for the garden, BCB-01, fo. 113ʳ (with Francis as governor, the reference in Bridewell to 'Master Barnham's garden' undoubtedly indicates him rather than his brother). Family possessions included two calivers, or light-weight muskets, which the Drapers borrowed for an extravagant 'show' staged for Elizabeth I on May Day 1572 (CLRO Rep. 17, fo. 292ʳ). The Drapers paid for 'new stocking' one of Barnham's calivers and 'mending and trimming' another (Drapers' W.A.5, 1571–2, fo. 11ᵛ).

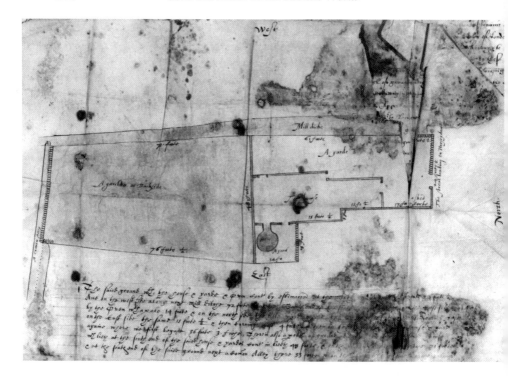

Figure 3.2 Early seventeenth-century survey of property bequeathed by Francis Barnham to Christ's Hospital, showing a house, two yards, an oven, and a garden bounded on the west by Mill Ditch, on the south by 'a common alley', and on the north by 'the street leading to Horseydown'.

As John Schofield has shown, Christ's governors commissioned Treswell to map their property in the early seventeenth century.[20]

The Barnham sketchplan was not bound with other Treswell surveys into their 'Evidence Book' (and thus was not known to Schofield).[21] In 1577 the

[20] PROB 11/58, fos. 76ᵛ–78ʳ. For Horselydown, GL Ms 12918 (three bundles of deeds and documents) and Ms 12919. In *A Brief Note of the Order and Manner of the... Three Royal Hospitals* (1582), John Howes noted that Christ's Hospital was 'chiefly maintained by the liberal devotion of the citizens' (ed. William Lempriere (London: privately printed, 1904), 74). *The London Surveys of Ralph Treswell*, ed. John Schofield, London Topographical Society 135 (1987).

[21] Barnham's gift is referenced in the Christ's Hospital Evidence Book (GL Ms 12850) in connection with rental income from tenant Edward Coosens (£20), but the plans are attached to deeds in Bundle Two of GL Ms 12918. The catalogue of 'Known Surveys of Ralph Treswell', compiled by Ralph Hyde for *London Surveys*, ed. Schofield, 5–7, has also been augmented by Martha Carlin, who shows Treswell (or his son) at work in Horselydown on a simple plan of the open pasture ground there ('Four Plans of Southwark in the Time of Stow', *London*

Court of Aldermen had ruled that all documents relating to this tract should be held apart for a century, ready to 'show and bring forth in any court or courts whatsoever'. A widow named Alice Powlter had made a claim against the hospital. Lewis Stoddard, from whom Francis Barnham purchased the Horselydown lands, died in debt to Powlter's husband for £600. Citing a statute of 1559 that offered redress to those with moneys owed that were otherwise unrecoverable, Powlter demonstrated that she was entitled to some of the rents 'issuing out of the said lands'. About a year after Francis's death it was determined that Powlter and her descendants should recoup £100 at the rate of 20s. per year over the next hundred years. The aldermen also required Christ's to give Powlter £27. 10s. immediately and to clear a £3. 5s. arrearage in rents, but there was otherwise no question of title. The governors were 'quietly to enjoy their lands and tenements aforesaid to them belonging'.[22]

The plot in Southwark was but one of the Barnhams' many investments in a land market propelled into unprecedented motility by the Dissolution. To their portfolio of country property they added such London real estate as three houses on St Clement's Lane (including two that had belonged to the suppressed monastery of Stratford Langthorne in Essex), a mansion on St Botolph Lane, five houses on the Poultry in Cheapside, three residences and two shops in the parish of St Mildred Poultry, two buildings in St Mary Colchurch, and three in the Old Jewry. After Francis's death, on 1 March 1578, Alice purchased two houses on Watling Street. She acquired the properties on Bishopsgate Street which endowed her gift to her parish church.[23]

When first married, the Barnhams had set up housekeeping in the parish of St Mildred Poultry. There they christened their four sons. They made their last appearance in the St Mildred's register on 2 June 1559, when

Topographical Record 26 (1990), 15–56). See also Judith Etherton, 'New Evidence—Ralph Treswell's Association with St Bartholomew's Hospital', *London Topographical Record* 27 (1995), 103–17.

[22] The agreement was formally subscribed in the Aldermen's Repertories as a decision taken privately in 'the Inner Chamber of Guildhall' on 4 April 1577, about a year after Francis Barnham's death (CLRO Rep. 19, fos. 189ᵛ–191ʳ). A copy is included in GL Ms 12918, Bundle One, along with copies of 'An offer towards an agreement made the 15th day of December 1576 by Alice Powlter, widow' and a release from Martin Barnham. The file grew over the next century with the addition of later surveys, but its contents continued to be held apart for the duration of the city's obligation to Powlter.

[23] *CPR: Elizabeth I*, ii. *1560–1563*, 57 (for two messuages on St Clement's Lane, 31 October 1561); *CPR: Elizabeth I*, vii. *1575–1578*, 238; CLRO Hustings Rolls 248/95 for 18 November 1556, 250/175 for 17 July 1560, and 255/70 for May 1567. Some properties were resold. See also *CPR: Elizabeth I*, vii. *1575–1578*, 455, for Alice's properties in Watling Street and GL Ms 977/1, fos. 53a–b, 56b, and pp. 371–4 for Bishopsgate Street.

Benedict was baptized. Just six weeks later, the family had removed to St Clement Eastcheap: on 18 July 1559, the Drapers conducted a survey of Company property and, the Clerk noted, various members 'dined that day at Master Warden Barnham's house in St Clement's Lane'.[24] The lane ran south from Lombard Street, then one of two ancient 'locis of power' in the city, according to Emrys Jones; the other was St Paul's Cathedral. Stow wrote that merchants from 'divers nations' assembled on Lombard Street twice daily until 22 December 1568, when the scene shifted to the Royal Exchange. Though the lobbying effort with the Merchant Taylors had failed, the burse was still within easy range of the Barnham house. And, as early as 1508, the Drapers had acquired eleven messuages, three stables, two warehouses, and two gardens in the immediate area. More likely than not, these were tenanted by Company members who would have made sympathetic neighbors; years later, in 1598, Stow confirmed the character of the area as one 'possessed by rich drapers'.[25]

Of all the possible reasons for the family's relocation, however, the most urgent may have had to do with those self-presentational issues associated with the Great Rebuilding. In 1559 Francis was just weeks away from assuming his first public office as governor of the Bridewell. References to the gate and their garden probably indicate that the family settled in the Abbot of Stratford Langthorne's principal London domicile, which is known to have had a magnificent stone entranceway.[26] The house on St Clement's Lane would seem to have suited the Barnhams' new civic standing; like the Drapers, they had traded up (see Figs. 3.3 and 3.4).

There were housing shortages of all sorts in sixteenth-century London, and members of the Court of Aldermen were as concerned with the scarcity of elite residences as they were with overcrowding in alleys. They issued aggressive prohibitions against the conversion of 'mansion houses' into tenements, ruling

---

[24] GL Ms 4429/1; Drapers' M.B.7, p. 172.   [25] Stow, *Survey*, 156–7, 171.

[26] Jones cited by Nancy Lee Adamson, 'Urban Families: The Social Context of the London Elite, 1500–1603' (Ph.D. thesis, University of Toronto, 1983), 23–5. Adamson emphasizes a third locus, the Guildhall, to describe a 'power triangle' in the sixteenth-century city. The Drapers owned properties in the neighboring parishes of St Clement Eastcheap, St Benet Gracechurch, Allhallows Lombard Street, and St Edmond Lombard Street as early as February 1508, when tenants included Florentine merchants (see the Catalogue of the Drapers' Company Property (St Clement parish), held by the Company) and the abbot of Stratford Langthorne (Drapers' M.B.1/B, fo. 222ʳ). John Schofield notes the abbot's 'exceptional' stone gateway in *Medieval London Houses* (New Haven: Yale University Press for the Paul Mellon Centre for Studies in British Art, 1995), 36. St Clement Eastcheap was not a popular parish for city leaders, according to Frank Foster, *Politics*, 132 n. 1. This may be why the parish church was, as Stow said, 'void of monuments' save for the Barnhams (1598, *Survey*, 171–2).

Figure 3.3 Example of an Elizabethan house at Crutched Friars in London, showing a highly ornamented street front. Drawn by John Thomas Smith, 1792; etched, 1812.

that their own members were to have the 'preferment' of the city's great houses when they came available. In 1584, when a skinner named Stephen Slanye was elected sheriff, he removed for the year to a 'capital messuage' befitting his administrative and social duties. Although Slanye's own home was called

Figure 3.4 Example of the interior in a wealthy London merchant's house, with wainscotted walls, plasterwork ceiling, and an elaborate overmantel. Built by Paul Pindar *c.*1600, the Bishopsgate house was destroyed in 1890. A portion of the façade with an ornate window was salvaged and can be seen at the Victoria and Albert Museum. Drawn by John Thomas Smith, 1792; engraved, 1810.

a 'great house', it was nonetheless insufficient.[27] Francis, by contrast, was able to serve out his shrieval term in the house on St Clement's Lane, which is some indication of its magnificence. When elected, he received the usual 'benevolence' of the Drapers, £33. 6s. 8d. (50 marks) to help set the scene for requisite dinners. Six members of the Court of Assistants personally supervised the 'trimming up' of the Barnham house.[28] As was customary, the Drapers also helped Francis meet his obligation to supply a 'proportion' of plate for his installation feast at Guildhall. He asked for the use of Company napery, as well, an unprecedented request that occasioned a special meeting of the Assistants to consider the matter. On 17 October 1570 four more members of the Court came to St Clement's Lane to 'confer' about 'what part of the said proportion might be had of him and then to provide the rest as they might among the whole Company'.[29]

If the St Clement's Lane property was suitable to a city father, this was undoubtedly in consequence of a Rebuilding project which preceded the refurbishments of 1570 and which was sufficiently controversial to have come before the Court of Aldermen. On 31 August 1568, nine years after

---

[27] CLRO Rep. 13, No. 2, fo. 452^v and, for instances of men charged with subdividing great houses, Rep. 19, fo. 501^r; Rep. 20, fo. 369^v. For Slanye, Mark Benbow, 'Index of London Citizens Involved in City Government, 1558–1603' (deposited in CLRO).

[28] The Drapers presented a 'benevolence' to every elected sheriff; in 1570 they added £2 more than 'the common order in giving' because Barnham was one of their own, to total £10 in gold: Drapers' M.B.8, fos. 125^v–126^r (9 November 1570), and R.A.5, 1570–1, fo. 6^v; for dinners, see M.B.8, fo. 131^r (26 December 1570); and M.B.8, fo. 164^v (26 September 1571). For 50 marks for refurbishment, M.B.8, fos. 116^v, 117^v; W.A.5, 1570–1, fo. 6^v. In 1571, a draper sheriff was given £40 (M.B.8, fo. 160^r; W.A.5, 1571–2, fo. 6^v), but the Company soon voted to return to the old amount (W.A.5, 1572–3, fo. 5^v), and 50 marks was still the operative figure when Benedict Barnham was chosen sheriff in 1591 (W.A.5, 1591–2, fo. 9^v). The sheriff's sixteen sergeants, their yeomen, and six clerks probably did not stay in the Barnham house during his shrieval year, but Stow (1603) says sheriffs also had 'stewards, butlers, porters, and other in household many' (*Survey*, 538). More information survives about mayors' households; see Frank Foster, *Politics*, 85–6; and B. R. Masters, 'The Mayor's Household before 1600', in A. E. J. Hollaender and William Kellaway (eds.), *Studies in London History Presented to Philip Edmund Jones* (London: Hodder & Stoughton, 1969), 95–114.

[29] The Lord Mayor's feast was furnished with nine standing cups, four from Barnham and five from various drapers; twenty goblets and bowls, four from Barnham and sixteen from other drapers; seventy-two beer and ale pots, twelve of them from Barnham; forty salts, fifteen from Barnham; eleven ewers and basins, two from Barnham; a few other pots from drapers; and twenty-four spoons, all from drapers. In addition, the Company provided two damask tablecloths, one diaper tablecloth, two couchers (or cushions), two long damask towels, three dozen damask napkins, and four dozen diaper napkins; Barnham added three dozen damask napkins. The Drapers also paid the beadle's fee for transporting plate, the Clerk's wife for marking and washing table linens, and the clerk for drawing up of 'bills' for the loans of goods. Most items were returned 'incontinent' after the feast, although some drapers' silver remained with the Barnhams for Francis's full year in office. Drapers' M.B.8, fos. 120^r, 123^r, 124^v, 125^r, 126^v, 165^v; W.A.5, 1570–1, fo. 6^v.

the Barnhams had relocated to Eastcheap, a bowyer named Robert Collet complained that their house was 'repugnant' to London's 'good laws and ordinances'. The aldermen often delegated such neighborhood disputes to four experienced builders, the sworn Viewers, so it is surely a measure of Francis's standing that in this case they themselves elected to 'take the pains to view and well consider the new frame or building of Francis Barnham draper in St Clement's Lane near unto Eastcheap for the order, manner, and fashion of the building thereof'. A week later, with the inquiry not yet conducted, Collet reappeared at the Guildhall to demand the names of all those who had promised him satisfaction. The aldermen, unmoved, omitted to bring forward the matter of the Barnham rebuilding until 20 November. They presumably did so then only because Francis was less than a month away from joining their select number (they would have known where he stood in the order of election).

There were three knights among the eleven men who finally visited the 'new frame or building lately erected and made in St Clement's Lane near unto Eastcheap by Francis Barnham'. Disputes regarding matters not consigned to the Viewers were regularly detailed to two or three members of the Court, and most reached resolution without any further mention in Court minutes. This was, therefore, an astonishing group both in number and prestige and, in further evidence of the overt circumspection with which the investigation was conducted, the decision was copied into the Aldermen's Repertory book:

The same building is lawful and tolerable in all things and not repugnant to the good laws, ordinances, and customs of this city saving only we think it good that the upper part or jetty of a round compassed window towards St Clement's Lane aforesaid shall be cut off and be made even with the room next under the same except six or eight inches only for the lead to be sealed and laid upon for defense of the same against the weather. . . . Whereupon the court here ordered and agreed that the said frame being reformed according to the said report shall be quietly permitted to stand and remain in such order as it now is, the allegation of the said Collet to the contrary notwithstanding.

In what may have been an extensive Rebuilding project, the pulling back of the cantilevered window was undoubtedly a token adjustment. After all, every alderman was himself personally concerned with London's limited inventory of status housing. On 25 November, Collet, Francis Barnham, and a Collet supporter named Dove appeared in Guildhall. The three 'were well exhorted and required by the said Court quietly to satisfy and content themselves with the said opinion and judgment', and all 'did willingly assent and agree'.[30]

---

[30] CLRO Rep. 16, fos. 388ᵛ, 392ʳ, 413ᵛ, 419ᵛ–420ʳ, 420ᵛ–421ʳ. On 'round-compassed' or semicircular windows, introduced in royal architecture in the 1530s, see Schofield, *Medieval*

Within a few weeks, Barnham was to be found sitting on the ranking side of the board.

The complaint of Robert Collet has special significance for a theme that has surfaced intermittently in this chapter and that is a chief focus of the next one: property, its ownership, its maintenance, and its uses were sources of endless controversy in early modern England. The expanded land market occasioned by the redistribution of church holdings and the material transformations of the Great Rebuilding are known to have been outlets for the wealth and ambition of 'new' as well as established men.[31] But this is just part of a much larger, though less familiar, story. For many other men and women, there were significant after-effects: the collateral damages of transfer, as alleged in the widow Brisket's claim on Drapers' Hall and Alice Powlter's suit against Christ's Hospital; trespasses across traditional boundaries, as when Cromwell enlarged his garden and the Barnhams extruded their bowed window; and disputed contracts, like the falling out of the Drapers and their joiners over a wainscotting project. Change always occasions discontent, in this arena not only for the principals but also for their tenants, neighbors, and workmen. Whether it is focused on country houses within the splendid isolation of their large grounds or vernacular buildings that have been removed to open-air museums, our architectural imagination tends to approach structures as free-standing objects of analysis. The fact that buildings had dense social lives is especially apparent in London, with its urgent issues of proximity and jurisdiction. These broader repercussions of the Great Rebuilding extended its reach, but they also represent the unacknowledged underside of its received history.

London Houses, 104. For other aldermanic reviews of projecting windows, see CLRO Rep. 17, fos. 166ʳ, 334ᵛ (21 June 1571 and 19 June 1572). They allowed Christopher Draper to build a chimney and an oven on City ground 'to serve his turn withal when he shall come to the honorable office of mayor of this city' (1566); see Charles Lethbridge Kingsford, 'A London Merchant's House and Its Owners, 1360–1614', *Archaeologia* 74 (1925), 137–58 (esp. 144–5). In 1611 James VI and I prohibited urban jetties but allowed oriel or bay windows; in 1618, these, too, were banned; see Jules Lubbock, *The Tyranny of Taste: The Politics of Architecture and Design in Britain, 1550–1960* (New Haven: Yale University Press for the Paul Mellon Centre for British Art, 1995), 28–9. The Barnhams' neighbors on St Clement's Lane were litigious; see Janet Senderowitz Loengard (ed.), *London Viewers and their Certificates, 1508–1558*, London Record Society 26 (1989), nos. 302, 399, 405. In 1573 the aldermen were advised that the parishioners of St Clement Eastcheap had 'impeached' an alley easement; CLRO Rep. 18, fo. 113ᵛ. Barnham, present at the meeting, may have reported his neighbors' trespasses.

[31] T. S. Willan points out 'how many of the property transactions of merchants involved former monastic and chantry lands and houses, not only in the countryside but in the towns as well' (*The Muscovy Merchants of 1555* (Manchester: Manchester University Press, 1953), 51).

EVICTING THE SADLERS

The Rebuilding's casualties included a draper named Roger Sadler. Sadler's financial reverses are exposed in a small collection of documents that may survive because Francis Barnham was an inveterate keeper of records. As Master of the Company in 1570 he was lead signatory to letters revoking Sadler's tenancy in the grandest of the Cromwell buildings.[32]

With a great hall, twenty-two chambers, a long gallery, a cross gallery, a private chapel, a tower, and various closets, garrets, and cellars, the head house was a highly desirable property. There was no other home for which occupation by a member of the Company was as important, because it joined Drapers' Hall through the connecting Ladies' Chamber, where officers held occasional meetings, private dinners, and select suppers. The Master who had advocated purchase of the Cromwell estate in 1543, Sir William Roche, betrayed a personal incentive when he secured the first residency in its most splendid quarters. John Sadler achieved the succeeding tenancy in 1554, in part by paying relocation expenses to Roche's widow to hasten her departure. Thirteen years later his son Roger was named Second Warden of the Company, but, after missing his own election feast, was replaced by Edward Hewar. In September 1567 Roger Sadler was absent for a dinner at which Francis Barnham filled his place.[33] In July 1568 Sadler completed his withdrawal from the Company by announcing that he wished to void his lease.

Martin Calthorp already stood as 'first suitor' to succeed him. Walter Garway also expressed interest in the head house. But with these good prospects established, the Drapers were suddenly thwarted. Sadler changed his mind. Shortly thereafter, he denied his colleagues access to the Ladies' Chamber for a Company dinner. In response, 'it was ordered and enacted that the same should be bolted in until the said Master Sadler might be spoken with'.[34] Sadler then sublet the house to the French ambassador and decamped to Edmonton. He violated policy in not securing the Drapers' approval, but he made an ally of the Lord Mayor, who was involved with the Crown in the

---

[32] What I refer to as 'the Sadler collection' is a group of letters on the topic, found in one of the boxes of 'Miscellaneous Documents' (A.III.151) held by the Drapers' Company.

[33] Drapers' M.B.1/C, fo. 377^r (survey of the head house); M.B.1/C, fo. 543^v and M.B.6, fos. 22^v, 24^r, 30^r (the Sadler tenancy); M.B.8, fos. 2^v–3^v and D.B.1, fo. 68^r (Sadler's withdrawal from the Company).

[34] Drapers' M.B.8, fo. 34^r (Calthorp), 35^v (Garway); see also fo. 120^v on leasing the head house to a draper, providing that he made the Ladies' Chamber accessible. The 'pine door' and doorframe were constructed in 1557 or 1558; Drapers' R.A.4, 1557–8, fo. 6^v. For the bolt, M.B.8, fo. 39^v and R.A.5, 1568–9, fo. 29^v.

difficult business of housing foreign diplomats. Francis Barnham headed the delegation of officers who promised the mayor that they would not revoke Sadler's lease, though they refused to commit this pledge to paper. Later, one of the mayor's men and one of the Drapers' wardens rode to Edmonton to nego-tiate with Sadler, but the stand-off continued until the ambassador departed.[35]

On 21 July 1570, during Francis Barnham's first mastership, the Drapers' officers issued a letter to Sadler which summarized the harm they believed had been done to the Company in consequence of his tenancy: 'you keep in your hands a house of ours', but, with no one in occupation, 'it is already ruin[ed] and still runneth daily more and more in decay and ruin, which we may not nor will not suffer any longer'. Francis and his wardens hoped that their detailed knowledge of Sadler's domestic circumstances would have a sobering effect: even if he were to take up residence again, they wrote, 'your estate being as it is and your family so small, it will scarcely furnish as it ought the one half of the same'. Therefore, 'if you would weigh with yourself aright, you might think as others do that a house of a smaller rent and charge were meeter for you than that house'. The argument for fit proportion went specifically to financial status, for by 'family' the Drapers referred to servants and apprentices as well as immediate kin. Sadler was asked to appear in the Drapers' parlor to be 'certified that we mind not you shall enjoy our said house any longer but that we be fully determined to have such a tenant as both shall inhabit therein and also be of ability to maintain the same'. A transparent threat closed the letter: the Drapers aimed, they said, to 'satisfy you therein with reason, if reason may take place', for 'where by entreaty things are ended with favor, contrarywise, when law endeth them, it is seldom seen any favor to follow'.

The next letter in the Sadler collection, in the hand of draper John Broke, indicates that Sadler's debts included funds borrowed against the estate of orphaned children named Butler. Knowing that Sadler was 'altogether unprovided' to repay them, Broke had himself deposited money into the Butler accounts. He would be sufficiently compensated, he suggested, were he permitted to take over Sadler's lease. Broke reported further that Sadler might be willing to vacate the head house if he were reimbursed both for the relocation moneys he had paid Lady Roche in 1559 and for his Rebuilding expenses in installing some bay windows. Broke was also aware that there was another rebuilder in the Sadler family, and that she remained unreconciled.

When in 1559 Sadler had requested consideration for his wife, he was advised that 'if God should call him', and if Mistress Sadler were to remarry a draper, that draper would be made free of the Company. Her continued occupation of the head house seems then to have been assumed, though

---

[35] Drapers' M.B.8, fos. 77ᵛ–78ʳ.

this, too, was a pledge not committed to paper.[36] Writing in 1570, Broke now suggested that Mistress Sadler, having been led to believe that she had life rights in the property, was 'very loath to forgo the same house'. In an extraordinary revelation of the balance of power in the Sadler marriage, of the recourse she had to an alternate support group of kin and advisers, of the lobby of relations who sought to protect her interests, and of her sense of ownership in the head house, Broke suggested that the Assistants might directly explain matters 'unto [her] and her friends, that she may be satisfied therein at [the Drapers'] mouths'.

By most contemporary formulations, the household was a 'petty commonwealth'. However, this realm of political abstraction was not where the internal jurisdictional dispute over the Drapers' head house was most powerfully engaged. In 1568 the Drapers had warned Mistress Sadler to evacuate her cellar—half was to serve for the beadle's lodgings and half for Assistant Matthew Colclough 'to lay wines in'—and they had also ordered her to restore the wall into which she had introduced a 'warehouse' door.[37] Wives of London's free men were entitled to operate commercially as 'femmes sole', neither responsible for the debts of the other,[38] and Mistress Sadler's need for extensive, easily accessed storage space suggests not only that the head house may have been her place of business but also that her trade flourished even as her husband's declined. For her, in other words, the house was a status location, a place of occupational identity, and a center of economic production.[39]

But with the lease itself silent on her rights as a widow, Francis Barnham and his Wardens saw no need to mediate Mistress Sadler's marriage, her jointure, her commercial activities, or her professional reputation. Again they wrote to Roger Sadler:

These are to advertise you that we have received your letter, answer to ours sent you, in which your letter is contained much more matter than we think requisite to be answered at this time. But to be short in the special points, this may suffice. Whereas you writ you have a grant from this Company of this house for term of your life and

[36] Drapers' M.B.7, p. 136. Sadler was told that his request 'should be considered', but there is no evidence that he was given satisfaction.

[37] Drapers' M.B.8, fo. 53[r] (cellar, 29 November 1568); M.B.8, fo. 33[v] (beadle, 30 June 1568); M.B.8, fo. 61[r] (warehouse wall, 25 April 1569); and M.B.8, fo. 120[v] (Colclough, 27 September 1570). See also R.A.5, 1568–9, fo. 29[r] for construction costs at the beadle's lodgings.

[38] 'A woman that exerciseth a trade without her husband is chargeable without him . . . She may plead as sole, and shall have her law and other advantage by way of plea; and, if condemned, shall be put in prison till she pay the debt. The husband nor his goods in such case shall not be charged nor impeached' (*The Practise of the Sheriff's Court* (London: 1657), 18). See also Marjorie Keniston McIntosh, 'The Benefits and Drawbacks of *Femme Sole* Status in England, 1300–1630', *Journal of British Studies* 44 (2005), 410–38.

[39] The same may have been true for Eleanor Peerson, who had refused a suitor rather than leave her home on Aldersgate Street (see Ch. 2).

the widowhead of your wife, in very deed we find no such grant, as by the copy of the same taken out of our registers and herein sent you it may well appear. And what you have given to my Lady Roche and others for their good will the Company hath had no profit thereof at all, as you right well do know. And as for your building that you writ of, it is to small commodity to the Company or to him that shall hereafter occupy the same. Not a little marveling what moved you to challenge the Company with any injury offered towards you or any others, for you know it hath not been nor is the manner of our proceeding. But we looked rather for some reasonable submission on your part whereby we might have had the better occasion to consider of your estate and poverty, which if you so shall do you shall find at our hands that which to the contrary is not to be looked for. And yet be you assured we will offer you no wrong whatsoever you rashly judge of us. Wherefore we wish you to send us your direct answer hereunto with as much speed as conveniently you may, to the end you give us no further occasion to proceed therein, as we have just cause. And thus fare you well from the Drapers' Hall in London the 28th day of July 1570. Your friends Francis Barnham, William Chester, Martin Calthorp, Robert Diconson, Walter Garway.

A few months later, Sadler at last relinquished the head house. The Drapers awarded it to Broke the mediator. By settling some of Sadler's debts, he could legitimately be said to have ended the impasse. But Broke immediately passed the coveted tenancy to Martin Calthorp, as he had already privately assured the officers he would do. Francis Barnham presumably had a strong hand in negotiating this outcome; Martin Barnham's eventual marriage to Calthorp's daughter goes to suggest that Calthorp was a Barnham confederate, and Broke noted that the lease transfers were 'done by your costs'—that is, the Company had borne the expenses.

Broke was granted occupation of the old Drapers' Hall on St Swithins Lane instead. Thus, one of many Tudor contests for elite urban housing was finally resolved in the interests of balanced books, spatial control, and old-boy cronyism. Sadler's story illustrates the pressures of London's overheated housing market, the scale of living cultivated by new men, temptations to live beyond even merchant means in the capital city, high-stakes rivalries for those urban mansions that survived without subdivision, and, as a further consequence of built ambitions, the public regulation of the private sphere. The Drapers had successfully protected their most profitable investment from one of their own, from further interventions by the Crown's chief officer—and also, it appears, from a city wife.[40] With this they closed off the

---

[40] Drapers' M.B.8, fo. 138^v (Broke requested and was granted lease, 19 March 1571); M.B.8, fo. 143^r (lease to Broke sealed, 7 May 1571); Drapers' A.III.151 (letter from Broke to officers regarding lease arrangements, 5 December 1571); M.B.8, fo. 177^r (Calthorp requested and was granted lease of 40 years, 6 December 1571); M.B.8, fo. 215^v (Calthorp requested extension to 50 years, 11 March 1573); M.B.8, fo. 217^v (50-year lease to Calthorp sealed, 8 April 1573);

fragile trail of evidence for her entrepreneurship. As the Drapers policed some of the jeopardies of the new Tudor economy and of its product, the Great Rebuilding, Mistress Sadler was collateral damage.

ALICE BARNHAM'S SOCIAL SPACE

Alice Barnham may not have held Company status in her own person, but as Francis's partner she had a long history with the fraternal activities that were among its most important member benefits. In a space of near-palatial splendor, middling-sort merchants were introduced to an aristocratic level of extravagance. In this way, too, Drapers' Hall was both an instance of the sixteenth-century's Rebuildings and an agent of further dissemination. At each year's election banquet, for example, the great hall was hung with banners and streamers and the floor was strewn with rushes and sweet herbs. For the parlor, tapestries were rented from Tower of London wardrobes; in 1566, these showed the classical legend of Venus and the biblical story of David. Service was provided by junior members of the Company, two dozen Bachelors in all, and they were required to be 'twenty-four of the comeliest and handsomest men of the yeomanry, decently apparelled'. Often, the musicians brought in were the wind instrumentalists or 'waits' on permanent retainer for the City's sabbath and holiday concerts. The Company's extraordinary 'Dinner Book' (1563–1602) meticulously details purchases of meat, poultry, fish, sugar, spices, fruits, greens, pastries, wine, and ale. The wardens, who hosted, might spend £100 on the night.[41]

Assistants, liverymen, and selected wives and guests were invited to the annual feast, to two or three quarter dinners each year, and to such special functions as funeral repasts for former drapers and their widows.[42]

A.III.151 (letter from Broke to officers mentioning tenancy of old Hall, 8 July 1584). Broke was also Barnham's fellow Renter in 1554–5. Garway died in March 1572. In 1576 the Drapers were still carrying Sadler's debt for a half-year's rent, which Calthorp refused to pay (Drapers' R.A.5, 1575–6, fo. 20[r]).

[41] Election feasts are described annually in the Drapers' Minute Books and Dinner Book; various reports are here pieced together to produce a synthetic narrative, including Drapers' D.B.1, fos. 48[v], 97[r], 112[v] (tapestries); fo. 88[r] (waiters). Barnham took part in the ceremony on 7 August 1558 (M.B.7, p. 103); 7 August 1559 (M.B.7, p. 177); 8 August 1569 (M.B.8, fo. 73[r]), 7 August 1570 (M.B.8, fo. 114[r]); 6 August 1571 (M.B.8, fo. 157[r–v]); 4 August 1572 (M.B.8, fo. 199[v]). On city waits, see also, e.g., CLRO Rep. 17, fo. 174[r]. Compare Peter Brears, *All the King's Cooks: The Tudor Kitchens of King Henry VIII at Hampton Court Palace* (London: Souvenir, 1999).

[42] Each year there might be three quarter dinners, one feast or election dinner, two 'view' dinners (following surveys of Company property), and two 'search' dinners (following reviews

Francis Barnham was eligible to attend the election banquet from 1550, when he was called to the livery. By the late 1560s, he had achieved sufficient stature that a Clerk listing important diners would always name Francis. Though it is surely more a matter of eccentric documentation than anything else, however, the first Barnham to be registered was Alice. This was in 1564, when she was described as seated in the hall at the second table (of three) with ten other women and three of their husbands.[43]

On 15 November 1569 Alice Barnham was named, along with Francis, at a quarter dinner. This time she was placed at the upper end of the western side table, with Drapers' officers and their wives. That same night they supped 'very bountifully' in the more exclusive Ladies' Chamber. On 21 February 1570, Francis and Alice enjoyed a meatless quarter dinner with a first course of boiled Alexander buds (also known as horse-parsley), green salad with hard-cooked eggs, butter, ling fish, green fish, pike, carp, lamprey pies, and custards, and for the second course eels with river lampreys, fried smelts, and tarts. Francis was Master of the Company that year, so he and Alice would also have had the dish of fresh salmon that was served only to those at the high table and the high end of the second table. There was no fish at the quarter dinner of 21 November 1570, when they had one course of boar and mustard, swan, boiled capon, roast capon, baked venison, mince pies, and custard, and then a second course of woodcock, partridge, plover, lark, and marzipan.[44] Also on the Drapers' calendar were search and view dinners (each held twice yearly). Francis did not take part in the view of Company properties conducted on 17 July 1571, but he and Alice attended the dinner, bringing with them their visitor from Kent, Thomas Wotton's second wife Eleanor. Alice and Francis were also present at a two-course dinner following the death of John Lowen's widow on 2 October 1571 (fresh sturgeon was a notable entry on this menu) and another for Walter Garway on 12 March 1572.

Francis Barnham's record of attendance at these and many other Company events is extensive; he understood the uses of institutional ceremony and

---

of standards of measure in the city). There were also occasional dinners, like that hosted for the ambassador of Russia on 29 April 1557 (Drapers' M.B.5, fo. 115[v]; see also Hakluyt, *Principal Navigations*, ii. 358; *Acts of the Privy Council*, vi. 54). The Barnhams attended quarter dinners on 15 November 1569 (M.B.8, fo. 84[r]) and 21 February 1569 (M.B.8, fo. 94[r]); Francis, on 6 June 1570 (M.B.8, fo. 106[r]); 21 November 1570 (M.B.8, fo. 129[r]); and 6 December 1571 (M.B.8, fo. 176[v]). These records are incomplete. The normal vagaries of the records are compounded by the loss of the Drapers' Minute Book for 1561 to 1567.

[43] Drapers' D.B.1, fo. 12[v].

[44] Drapers' M.B.8, fos. 83[v], 84[r], 94[r], 129[r]. At the last, swan was the high-end dish, with goose for others.

conviviality.[45] At the end of his first term as Master, in 1570, he presided over a feast with so many more guests than usual that an ancient ritual had to be modified. The dinner usually served three tables in the great hall, one in the parlor, and another in the Ladies' Chamber. There came a point in the evening when the Master and Wardens were expected to retire briefly to the parlor, which was subdivided by a tapestry hung on fir poles. Behind the arras was an area set aside for them to don ceremonial caps or 'garlands' before processing back to the hall with sword bearers and musicians. In 1570, because the parlor was 'all hanged with arras and guests dining there', with no partition and thus no staging area, the officers made their costume changes in the Ladies' Chamber instead. As Master, Barnham was undoubtedly responsible for the record invitational crowd in the parlor. Evidences are that many of the new guests were women, members of Alice's social circle.[46]

The musical interludes were also expanded that year. In addition to the city waits, there was 'Segar, a Dutchman'. Another unique entry in the Dinner Book notes that in 1570 a wax chandler was commissioned to sculpt 'three standing dishes': models of a boar's head, the arms of the Company, and the helm and crest of the Company. These were carried to the first table in sequence, one for each course, and there were added fees paid for 'them that made the speeches at the bringing in of the boar's head and to the child that took pains therein'—perhaps a boy actor.[47] In the months leading up to the feast, the Drapers also invested in the costliest of their luxury purchases, the 'state', a walnut chair for the most important guest seated at the hall's high table. The crimson velvet cushion for the chairback was embroidered with the Drapers' arms and, like the seat cushion, had silk fringe, tassels, and buttons. The chair was too magnificent for daily use, so the

---

[45] Drapers' M.B.7, p. 110; M.B.8, fo. 154ʳ; M.B.9, fos. 14ᵛ, 19ᵛ, 20ʳ, 21ʳ (Alice noted at the last). For funeral dinners, M.B.8, fo. 166ʳ (Mistress Lowen, 2 October 1571, with Alice noted); M.B.8, fo. 186ᵛ (Walter Garway, 12 March 1572, with Alice noted); M.B.8, fo. 246ʳ (Sir William Chester, 22 December 1573); M.B.9, fo. 6ᵛ (Rose Trott, 17 January 1575). Barnham attended Bachelor dinners as an officer on 22 September 1567, 26 September 1569, and 24 September 1571, appearing also at their audit dinners on 17 October 1569 and 15 October 1571 (Drapers' M.B.8, fos. 3ᵛ, 77ʳ, 164ʳ, 80ʳ, 167ʳ). And see Drapers' M.B.7, p. 172 and W.A.4, 1558–9, fo. 11ʳ; M.B.7, p. 178; M.B.5, fo. 90ᵛ; M.B.8, fos. 97ᵛ, 192ʳ, 196ᵛ, 215ᵛ for search and view dinners hosted by the Barnhams in 1559; 31 July 1559 search dinner at the Cardinal's Hat tavern in Lombard Street; view dinners at Thomas Castell's house on 15 July 1556, the Bishop's Head in Lombard Street on 15 March 1570, William Vaughan's house on 20 May 1572, Master White's house on 8 July 1572, and Anthony Pryor's house on 9 March 1573.

[46] Drapers' M.B.8, fo. 114ʳ. See D.B.1 for e.g. 1567, which specifies a table in the parlor and 'women above in the gallery chamber' (fo. 55ʳ).

[47] Drapers' D.B.1, fos. 96ᵛ, 97ᵛ.

Drapers also bought red satin bags to protect the cushions and a red buckram dustcover for the frame. The officers' ceremonial garlands of embroidered crimson velvet were refashioned that same year: the silver badges showing the Company's arms and the Tudor rose were retained, but those featuring the Assumption of the Virgin were replaced by fleurs-de-lis. The year 1571 also saw the purchase of the twelve damask counterpanes, six trimmed in gold, six white.[48]

Besides procuring these splendors, Francis masterminded a series of countermeasures taken in the face of threats to civic festivity. The first challenge was mounted on 13 February 1570, when the Court of Assistants was 'credibly informed'—most probably by Alderman Barnham himself—that 'the nobility and gentlemen about the Court are much offended at the great number of bucks being consumed in the halls of Companies within London at their feast dinners'. While the hierarchy of foods was less codified than was sumptuary law, venison, swan, and sturgeon were generally understood to be dishes for the privileged. In 1567 the Drapers had consumed forty bucks, with Francis himself setting a record by exploiting his country connections to bring in ten-and-a-half. The venison was cooked into pasties that were distributed to area notables and the membership-at-large but also to the urban poor who knew to wait at the Drapers' gate. Liverymen took some home to their servants and neighbors.[49]

As Master in 1570, however, Barnham presided over an attempt to avoid further courtly disapproval through self-policing. The Assistants ruled that the wardens, who were responsible for supplying bucks for the election dinner, should be known to have limited themselves to ten in total on penalty of a fine of forty shillings. It is surely not a coincidence, however, that at about this time the Drapers began to establish alternate sources of supply in obligatory 'gifts' so that they could maintain their traditional patronage profile in the community. Just two weeks later the Assistants allowed Robert Yoward to sublet his Company-owned shop to Richard Hutton, on condition that Hutton and Yoward would together provide a buck for the feast that year. In July 1570, June 1571, and December 1571, the Drapers granted freedom by redemption to three men who promised three bucks, one buck, and two bucks, respectively. In October 1571, a Mistress Candelers petitioned to reconfirm a lease of

---

[48] Drapers' W.A.5, 1569–70, fo. 9^{r-v} details frame, leather, velvet, satin, buckram, fringe, buttons, tassels, feathers, tacks, nails, and labor (the cushion covering of red Bruges satin was recycled from the 'forepart for a kirtle'). The Lord Mayor sat in the Drapers' State in 1568 and 1570 (M.B.8, fos. 41^{r}, 114^{r}). The refashioning of the badges may confirm Francis's Reformist sympathies (M.B.8, fo. 108^{r}, W.A.5, 1569–70, fo. 9^{r}).

[49] Drapers' M.B.8, fo. 91^{r}; D.B.1, fo. 60^{r}. See also Johnson, *History*, ii. 222, and Ian W. Archer, *The History of the Haberdashers' Company* (Chichester: Phillimore, 1991), 128.

Company property that had been made a year earlier. The Drapers noted that a contracted brace of bucks had not been sent, and the lease was renewed only when the oversight was addressed.[50] Barnham's role can be guessed from the fact that Candelers was kin to Thomas Wotton, into whose family his son was to wed within the year. Wotton both accompanied Candelers to Drapers' Hall and pledged the yearly gift of venison.

Meanwhile, the Company had traditionally set aside ten marks for each quarter dinner. Now, with Barnham still presiding as Master, the Assistants increased the allowance by two marks to £8 total. They formalized a policy of inviting not only the livery and officers but also 'the aldermen's wives and their own wives and also all those widows of our Company whose husbands have been either masters of the Company or wardens'.[51] Alice Barnham was thus ensured a place at the quarter dinners not only during Francis's life but also after.

The restrictions the Drapers had placed upon themselves did not prevent a further crisis on 3 August 1573. The Lord Mayor issued a 'precept' or executive order that no dinners should be held in connection with company elections.[52] The ban would not apply to quarter dinners, but even they were required to be more modest, with outside guests prohibited. The next summer, the Master, Richard Pipe, was absent from a gathering of the Assistants. Francis Barnham took the chair in his stead, and by the end of the meeting the board had approved a new scheme for countermanding the precept. The Drapers would reschedule one of their quarter dinners for the first Monday in August, traditionally the date of their feast dinner. Thus, Company elections would continue to be conducted in connection with a banquet. This creative solution was approved with the provision that the wardens were to invite 'the aldermen and their wives, the Assistants and their wives, the widows whose husbands were of the Assistants', as well as 'the whole livery'. One consequence of the mayor's ruling was that the feast would be funded only at the level of a quarter dinner, recently increased though that amount was. But it was observed for the record that the eight-pound allowance would be supplemented by two bucks supplied by the Drapers' tenant on Colman Street—that is, in effect, by Francis's new kinsman Thomas Wotton.[53]

As leader of the Drapers' Company, Francis Barnham was personally responsible for raising the standards of extravagance at corporate events. His

---

[50] Drapers' M.B.8, fos. 91ʳ, 94ᵛ, 112ʳ, 149ʳ, 174ʳ, 168ᵛ.

[51] Drapers' M.B.8, fo. 93ᵛ. This may have been a formal restatement of standing policy, but Johnson believes it was a justification for raising the allowance at quarter dinners (*History*, ii. 222).

[52] Drapers' M.B.8, fo. 230ʳ⁻ᵛ; see also Johnson, *History*, ii. 223. The regulation proposed by the Board of Aldermen on 24 July 1573 was endorsed by the Common Council (CLRO Rep. 18, fos. 49ᵛ, 52ʳ).

[53] Drapers' M.B.8, fo. 266ʳ⁻ᵛ (14 July 1574).

tastes had been refined among the social circles of other wealthy aldermen and of the country-gentry family into which he married his son. In his will, Francis did not make a bequest of property or plate to the Drapers. Instead he remembered his colleagues in the most characteristic of ways, leaving twenty pounds for his funeral dinner—an amount so generous that unspent funds were used for a second dinner a month after his death.[54] Because Company clerks soon thereafter ceased naming prominent diners at Drapers' events, it is impossible to know how often Alice Barnham took advantage of the policy engineered by her husband, her license to attend election banquets and quarter dinners. But she made one last appearance before the records thin, dining at a 1578 feast when she was two years a widow, and she herself gave twenty marks for a dinner on the day of her burial.[55] Francis Barnham had secured the great hall at Drapers' Hall as his wife's social space.

THE OPEN HOUSE

At first, a 1573 notation in the parish register for St Clement Eastcheap seems to offer a rare glimpse into the private life of the Barnham household: 'Charity of God a child found at Master Alderman Barnham's gate was baptized the 21 of December.' But to conclude that the Barnhams would have adopted the foundling left on their threshold is not to know them, their unsentimental drive toward advancement, or the politics of abandonment in early modern London. Valerie Fildes has estimated that a thousand children were cast out each year, many at the doorsteps of city leaders. Presented in Bridewell, one unwed mother explained that she was advised to leave her newborn 'at some rich man's door and it will be better kept than thou canst keep it'. On St Clement's Lane, charity was less at issue than was Francis's ability to secure a placement in the overburdened city orphanage. Although Christ's Hospital was devised as a death benefit for London's free men, fostering citizens' children left unparented while minors, members of the Court of Aldermen could intervene on behalf of other orphans. Francis was to do so in 1574 for an infant found on the streets in his own Tower ward. With the child left at his very doorstep, however, and in the face of what might have been

---

[54] Drapers' M.B.9, fos. 44^v, 46^{r-v}. Others gave the Company property (Sir John Rudston, Thomas Howell), plate (Sir Richard Champion, Benedict Barnham), textiles, or spice bread—though dinners were not uncommon.

[55] Drapers' M.B.9, fo. 114^r. Alice Barnham willed £13. 6s. 8d. for a Company dinner 'on the day of my burial' (PROB 11/104, fos. 53^r–54^r).

publicly mistaken for a mute paternity claim, he took care to effect a degree of separation, transferring custody to parish officers.[56]

The St Clement churchwardens did not accept the charge to the parish, as they might otherwise have done, following the established custom of placing the foundling with an older woman in the neighborhood. Instead they petitioned Christ's Hospital. Their success implies Francis's good offices behind the scenes; a register book notes the child's admission on 10 January 1574. First appearances to the contrary, the clerk of St Clement Eastcheap had not intended to remark the infant's discovery with a pious tribute to divine mercy. Instead, he recorded a baptismal name of the sort that Ben Jonson was gleefully to satirize. The orphan was entered at Christ's as 'Charity Godd', estimated to be 6 months old. She was put out to nurse with Jane Alcock, probably a countrywoman, as was the hospital's policy for 'sucking children and such as for want of years were not able to learn'. But if Francis and Alice followed the progress of Charity Godd, they would have discovered that within a few months, by 7 August 1574, the infant left at their gate had died.[57] Both remembered Christ's in their wills.

The house on St Clement's Lane was a public landmark, known to Charity's anonymous mother as to other London denizens. Moving there in 1559, the Barnhams had invested in the idea that their home should openly exhibit wealth and standing. Their entrance gate and garden were signs of privilege and prominence. The cantilevered window added so controversially in 1568 was flagrantly modish. Contributions made by the Drapers to the 'trimming up' of the residence in 1570 demonstrate that it was a matter of Company pride, too, that one of their most celebrated members should be visibly represented as befit the ancient dignity of their mystery. The rebuildings were not designed to produce personal privacy; this was the center of Francis's

---

[56] GL MS 4783/1; BCB-01, fo. 207^v. And see BCB-01, fos. 140^r, 167^r; BCB-02, fos. 62^r, 84^v. Valerie Fildes, 'Maternal Feelings Reassessed: Child Abandonment and Neglect in London and Westminster, 1550–1800', in Valerie Fildes (ed.), *Women as Mothers in Pre-Industrial England: Essays in Memory of Dorothy McLaren* (London: Routledge, 1990), 139–79. In 1573, accepting a child at the suit of Lady Mildmay, the aldermen directed two governors of the hospital 'to declare their good wills to gratify her Ladyship in that request, trusting she will not hereafter make the like suit, for that the same house is much charged'. CLRO Rep. 17, fo. 176^v (requests from Lady Mildmay and Earl of Bedford, 17 July 1571); Rep. 17, fos. 262^r (29 January 1572 admission) and 275^r (26 February 1572 admission); Rep. 18, fo. 52^r (30 July 1573 admission); Rep. 18, fo. 151^r (punishment of an abandoner, 9 February 1574); Rep. 18, fo. 288^v (foundling in Barnham's ward, 28 October 1574); Rep. 19, fo. 52^v (child abandoned in the common privy on London Bridge, 8 March 1576).

[57] *Christ's Hospital Admissions*, i. *1554–1599* (London: Harrison, 1937), fos. 35, 38. For Christ's policies, Howes, *Brief Note*, 12–13. Vanessa Harding notes the name 'Job-raked-out-of-the-ashes' for a child found on a cinder heap in 1612 (*The Dead and the Living in Paris and London, 1500–1670* (Cambridge: Cambridge University Press, 2002), 58–9).

business activities and, from the time he was elected to civic office, it was also the site of important municipal functions. For his shrievalty, especially, he required an *over*built house, one large enough for the rounds of dinners he was expected to host and for a staff that Stow described as 'stewards, butlers, porters, and other in household many'.[58]

The rituals of Francis Barnham's 1570 inauguration as Upper Sheriff of the city are rehearsed in extraordinary detail in an appendix to the Drapers' Court minutes for that year. Ceremonies began on Michaelmas Eve (28 September) with oathtakings at the Guildhall. The next afternoon, after a communal Evensong, the two new sheriffs called on Newgate and Ludgate prisons and both compters, for which they now took responsibility and where they received inmate rosters. On the third day, they traveled by barge to Westminster for an installation ceremony before the Queen's Barons of the Exchequer.

Because so many civic leaders were involved as witnesses and attendants, inaugural protocols were unforgiving. Thus, the Drapers' Clerk took special care to note for future reference where 'we did err' when Francis Barnham's sixteen escorts split to form two rows between which he passed as he entered the Guildhall on the first day: correctly, 'the ancients should stand next the State which is at the going up to the Mayor's Court' and 'the youngest of the livery' should 'stand by to the doorward as the Company cometh'. At the Guildhall feast, it was also noted, the Drapers took the more honorific bench fixed to the wall, as representatives of the 'Uppermost Sheriff's Company', while the grocers who were associated with Under Sheriff William Boxe had the detached forms facing them across a long table. Ironically, structural 'pillars bearing out took away the place' for two bench seats for the Drapers.[59]

---

[58] During Barnham's shrievalty he and Alice held dinners for the Wardens of the Drapers' Company (Drapers' M.B.8, fo. 125ᵛ, 9 November 1570); representatives of the four leading livery companies (M.B.8, fo. 131ʳ, 26 December 1570); and men who attended the next sheriff-elect (also a draper) at the end of his term (M.B.8, fo. 164ᵛ, 26 September 1571). They hosted a search dinner on 18 July 1559 (M.B.7, p. 172) and a view dinner in 1558 or 1559 (W.A.4, 1558–9, fo. 11ʳ). Stow (1603), *Survey*, 538.

[59] Drapers' M.B.8: 'The Order of this Company in the Year of Our Lord God 1570 et Anno Regine Elizabeth xijmo Master Francis Barnham Alderman being the Uppermost Sheriff of London Elect of this Company and Master William Boxe the other Sheriff Elect, Being a Commoner Free of the Company of Grocers.' See also M.B.8, fos. 112ᵛ, 118ʳ, 120ᵛ, 121ʳ, 124ʳ. There were more Drapers at the election feast at Guildhall because Lord Mayor Rowland Heyward came from a company with a smaller livery (M.B.8, fo. 124ʳ). Barnham took precedence among the Drapers during his shrieval year; see 'eighteen men of our Company appointed to wait upon' him in their 'velvet coats' when Elizabeth visited the City (R.A.5, 1570–1, fos. 9ᵛ–10ʳ). 'Eight or ten' of the Assistants' wives escorted Alice Barnham to the house of the Lord Mayor where she joined the Lady Mayoress for the procession to Guildhall (M.B.8, fo. 124ᵛ). For a Midsummer's Eve event Barnham requested sixteen Bachelors to attend the Lord Mayor, but they resisted (M.B.8, fos. 149ʳ and 151ᵛ).

One of the most striking features of the civic election ceremonies is how home-based they were.[60] Each morning when Barnham departed his door he had a parade of mounted attendants who also returned him to St Clement's Lane at the end of the day (see Fig. 3.5). On Michaelmas Eve, sixteen members of the Drapers' Company breakfasted with the Barnhams, accompanied Francis to the Guildhall for his oathtaking, and then processed back for a dinner in his house. The next day Francis was escorted to and from the church and prisons. On the third morning a delegation of drapers rode with him from his home to the quay and the Westminster-bound barge. Later the Barnhams entertained the Lord Mayor, a number of aldermen, and the clerks of the Exchequer.

It might seem that the ceremonial cortège enacted ritual functions of transition between the public and private spheres. In fact it worked instead to obscure any such distinctions, to make the family home the first and last of the stations of civic pilgrimage, and thus to initiate its transformation into a municipal headquarters of a particularly prominent sort for the length of Francis's term. The defining symbol of his office was a sheriff's post, prominently erected at his front gate. While his court was convened 'in the west end of Guildhall', others of his official functions may have been conducted in his home; on occasion, for instance, Lord Mayors held hearings at their residences.

Discussing the obligations that accrued to early modern privilege, Jules Lubbock describes life in London as private, in contrast to that in the country. Provincial life was public, he says, because of the necessity of keeping an open house.[61] Of course, this distinction was operative only for landed gentry. In their own sphere, merchant families such as the Barnhams had unrelenting social responsibilities. These were more incumbent upon London's leading citizens even than liberality among provincial gentry, because their mandate was more explicit and the urban calendar so fixed. Here there was small room for the decay of hospitality regularly lamented in country-house life. The prosperity that allowed the Barnhams to participate in the Great Rebuilding carried with it the cost of maintaining an open house. Among all the evidence that theirs was a highly public life, there is little indication that Francis and Alice were motivated by any desire for privacy—except, perhaps, in the commission of a 1557 portrait. By the time they moved to St Clement's Lane, they could safely, publicly, display it in the parlor to which they welcomed city officials and guests.

---

[60] Also emphasized in *The Order of my Lord Mayor, the Aldermen, and the Sheriffs for their Meetings and Wearing of their Apparel throughout the Whole Year* (London: 1568). See CLRO Research Paper 13.7, 'Notes on Sheriffs' Breakfast' (1989).

[61] Lubbock, *Tyranny*, 50. See also my 'Temporary Lives in London Lodgings', forthcoming in *Huntington Library Quarterly*, 2007.

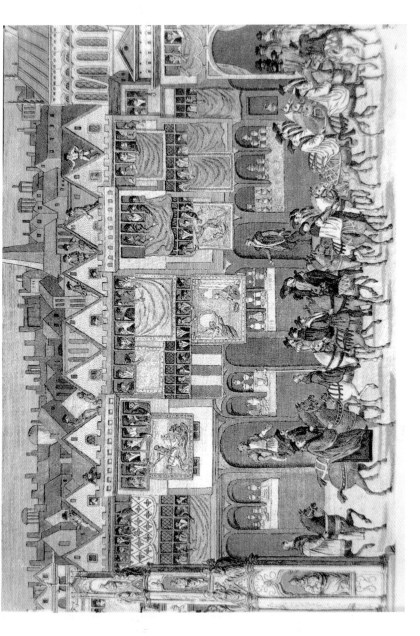

Figure 3.5 A London procession. For this occasion, a royal promenade, goldsmiths set out examples of their wares, and Catholic 'imagery', a tapestry of the Annunciation, was hung from a central window. Detail from 'The Procession of King Edward VI from the Tower of London to Westminster, Feb. XIX, MDXLVII, previous to his Coronation', copied from a now-lost wall painting by Samuel Hieronymous Grimm and engraved by James Basire in 1787.

CLOSING THE PARLOR DOOR

The properties on Throgmorton Street and the house on St Clement's Lane were, equally, manifestations of the Great Rebuilding. Both the Drapers and the Barnhams achieved their ambitious proprietorships in consequence of a land market fueled by the redistribution of former church estates. Drapers' Hall incorporated the holdings of an Augustine abbey; the family home, the urban seat of a provincial Cistercian monastery. The new secular owners, corporate and private, undertook renovation projects to translate their status aspirations into material splendor. These improvements entailed such immediate aggravations as disputes with workmen and complaints from neighbors, but they more lastingly created spaces for lavish civic hospitality. Social occasions were essential to the mechanism of municipal governance. For their members, the Drapers staged quarter dinners which were the Company's principal, ongoing constituent benefit; for their elite, they hosted election feasts, search dinners, and funeral suppers. The Barnhams held their own official and quasi-official functions in their Eastcheap home.

Amid all the designs and functions shared by the two structures, there were also important distinctions which bear directly upon the issues of privacy and of Alice Barnham's place in the Rebuilt worlds of Tudor England. These were at their most visible in the space called the parlor. In private homes, this 'specialized' room had multiple personalities. It could be a bedroom, a dining chamber, or both simultaneously, and it switched identities and functions as required, to suit family exigencies and life passages. The parlor often lodged temporary residents, such as houseguests or the terminally ill. It was the space traditionally set aside for a widow living with her husband's heirs; being located on the ground floor, it gave easy access to the kitchen, yard, and garden. Thus the principal family sometimes ceded the parlor to alternate ownerships. It rotated out of their immediate possession for the residency of an elderly relative and returned to their inventory with her death. When occupied by guests it was a social space; as used by the family, a private one; if reserved to a widow, female. The correlation of widows and parlors, particularly well established in popular culture, may have intersected with the picture-hanging conventions observed in the *Entertainment . . . at Mitcham* for citizens' wives.[62]

The meanings of the parlor in Drapers' Hall were, by contrast, fixed. It had a clear ownership, served highly particularized purposes, and was

[62] 'Every citizen's wife that wears a taffeta kirtle and a velvet hat . . . must have her picture in the parlor' (1598), cited by Mercer, *English Art*, 165.

antithetically gendered. In matters of civic governance, the spatial story of the sixteenth century was the movement of Company decision-making away from the great hall, where ordinances had once required the approval of all the junior members, or Bachelors, and into the parlor, where policies and procedures came to be determined by a small group of selected officers behind closed doors. The Bachelors had long constituted the authorizing base of the Company pyramid, but no more. Now a compound corporate structure evolved, and in its redundant hierarchies the officers of the Bachelors were marginalized by the officers of the livery. As the size of the livery shrank, the top wardenships rotated among a progressively smaller population. Fewer and fewer men had any prospects for command of the populations and perquisites of the parlor. This was to upset a balance that, according to Steve Rappaport, had long proved its effectiveness: younger members of the livery companies had accepted the inequities of hierarchy because they expected to rise. Complaints about the increasingly oligarchic nature of the Company leadership therefore became a recurrent theme, here as in other London livery companies.[63]

Not coincidentally, in Drapers' Hall the most important works project of the century was the wainscotting of a room which was the condition of possibility for the Assistants' more exclusive jurisdiction. During the renovation they removed to the isolated Ladies' Chamber rather than return to the hall. This Rebuilding investment was a bold reminder that the Company's spaces represented the way in which control had been consolidated by power.

The privileged informations of the parlor were highly prized. Members of the Court of Assistants periodically reminded themselves that they were forbidden to take away from their meeting room any 'words spoken secretly in this house'. At times the beadle stood outside the door to prevent eavesdroppers from approaching. Anyone found to have betrayed the names of new officers in advance of their public announcement was fined £10. Assistants could order whippings as well as assess fines, particularly when presented with wayward apprentices. The two men delegated to flog offenders with birch rods were disguised in 'two frocks of canvas like porters and two hoods of the same canvas made after visor fashion with a space for the mouth and for the eyes left open'—all so that, in transparent analogy to executioners,

---

[63] Rappaport, *Worlds*, 359, 387; see also Ward, *Metropolitan Communities*, esp. ch. 4. A. K. Sierz notes that 'The Drapers, originally a Fraternity of equals, gradually became divided into a privileged Livery and an aspiring Yeomanry . . . also known as the Bachelors' (unpublished guide to Company archives, 33). At mid-century the Bachelors complained that with insufficient opportunity to congregate they had difficulty gathering fines and fees (Girtin, *Triple Crowns*, 129; see also Rappaport on the Merchant Taylors, *Worlds*, 229). By 1560 the Bachelors had separate ordinances. The hierarchy was exaggerated because the most ambitious drapers (such as Barnham) 'skipp[ed] lower offices' in the Yeomanry 'to accelerate rising to the higher ones' (Frank Foster, *Politics*, 57).

'they shoulds [*sic*] not be known'.[64] But corporal punishment was only the most conspicuously punitive of the regulatory and disciplinary functions of the parlor; the hierarchy and privilege it reproduced had coercive effects, too. Because apprentices were presented there, oaths were administered, petitioners were received, and disputes were adjudicated, persons of all ranks and both genders traveled in and out of the Company's highest court. But they did so only as allowed—or compelled—by the Assistants, who thus exerted their political prerogative in the most material of ways.

In the elaborate ceremonies of election that stretched over four days each August, the Drapers' Assistants made annual rites of their rights of privacy.[65] Events began with a meeting of the Court of Assistants in the parlor, often on a Saturday. The Company elite held a 'secret nomination' or 'secret election' to designate their officers for the coming year. On Sunday, the parson of St Michael Cornhill came to Drapers' Hall to lead a procession back to the church for an afternoon service. The Draper aldermen went first, then the wardens, the Assistants, and finally the liverymen. In 1569, the places of highest honor were held by Sir William Chester, wearing the Master's chain, and Francis Barnham, in a velvet tippet. During the service Chester sat in the 'uppermost pew' and Barnham, as alderman, in the second row. The next year, Barnham would take precedence. Afterwards, the Drapers enjoyed a potation in their great hall where even the payment of quarterage fees was organized by rank. The First and Second Wardens collected from the aldermen and Assistants; the Third and Fourth, from the livery.[66]

On Monday afternoons the liverymen again donned their fur-trimmed gowns and paraded to St Michael Cornhill. At the annual banquet which followed, an 'open election' would reveal the results of the Saturday selection. As the feasting concluded, the four wardens went to the high table to 'require' the Master to withdraw to the parlor. Behind the 'traverse of arras' hung strictly for the purpose of creating a public effect of privacy, he donned his velvet garland with its silver-gilt badges. He reappeared in the hall, preceded by minstrels, a cupbearer, and a sword bearer, and went to the high table to tender his cap ceremonially to the honored guests, some of the women in attendance, and Drapers who had previously been masters of the Company. These were ruses to prolong the suspense until he crowned the man named

---

[64] Drapers' M.B.1/C, fos. 223[r], 485[v]. Ward describes the beadle protecting 'the secrets of the court', *Metropolitan Communities*, 86. The selection of officers was generally called a 'secret nomination' (see e.g. M.B.8, fos. 71[v], 156[v]). For corporal punishment, M.B.1/B, fo. 246[r]; W.A.5, 1564–5, fo. 6[r] (when the Drapers had to replace one of the gowns); and M.B.8, fo. 52[r].

[65] As for the Drapers' election feast, above, this is a composite account from the Minute Books and D.B.1, fo. 42[r].

[66] Junior wardens helped a new Clerk by identifying members of the Company for him, 'whereby he might prick them as they paid', in 1569 (Drapers' M.B. 8, fo. 72[v]).

Master for the coming year, and drank to him; in 1569, Chester conferred the garland on Barnham.

The four wardens then retired to the parlor in their own ostentatious acts of withdrawal. They reappeared with their garlands and attendants and processed through the hall, making two passes at the high table to do obeisance to the guests. The First Warden pretended to offer his garland to those who had previously been senior wardens or who had twice served as wardens. When he had identified his successor and drunk to him, he stood aside at the high table. It was time for the Second Warden to 'compass' the hall, making a show of looking among the Assistants before he found the man upon whom he conferred his garland. The Third Warden sought his successor among members of the livery who had not yet been wardens. And, finally, the Fourth Warden 'essayed' his garland among the younger liverymen. These transfers of power were made official on the following morning, when the newly designated Master and Wardens convened in the parlor at Drapers' Hall. They took their oaths of office in the presence of the retiring officers, who then relinquished keys to the adjoining treasure house in which Company records were stored. The closing event was a private dinner in the parlor. Francis Barnham took part in these ceremonies each time he was elected to office, in 1558, 1566, 1569, and 1571, and each time he passed the keys on, in 1559, 1567, 1570, and 1572.

Year to year, there were variations. Some were intentional, as in 1575, when the sequence was altered to accommodate the presiding master's schedule. Some were unintentional, when a step in the routine was forgotten or misperformed. In that case, the custodian of Company protocol, the Clerk, might be reminded of his error. In 1558, Chester, who had already remarked absenteeism and neglect of duty, 'declared his advice to the Clerk that from henceforth no master of this Company should tender his garland to any but such as heretofore have been masters (guests, strangers, and gentlewomen only except) and likewise for the First Warden'.[67]

The admonition was a reminder that the honorific spine of the ritual was to be maintained and made legible no matter how festive the occasion. After all the eating and drinking, with the Master and Wardens acting as lords of misrule in feigning to offer the symbols of their offices to women and visitors, the mood turned riotous. In 1570, during Barnham's first mastership, a clerk kept count of the damages: the breakages included twenty out of

---

[67] In 1575 the dinner was held on Sunday because the new Master was away (Drapers' M.B.9, fo. 19^r). For Chester, M.B.5, fo. 94^r and M.B.7, p. 103. At the Cooks' Company William Stokes pulled the garland from the head of a warden 'very cruelly and despitefully'; for this 'lewd and evil behavior' he was 'discharged from the freedom and liberties of this city' and his shop windows were shut up (CLRO Rep. 17, fo. 257^r).

twenty-four pottle pots, thirty-four out of forty-two 'green' pots, four out of eight candlesticks, four out of six pans, and three out of six chafers. The revelry mandated security procedures, as well, with the man who brought bread from the pantry directed 'to see that it was carried nowhere else' but to the hall. 'Honesty and diligence' was required from the man designated to pour wine, to 'preserve that none was lacking'. On the kitchen stairs, a man ensured 'that the meat accordingly went to furnish the house and that nothing was purloined'. Two porters were stationed at the head of the stairs to the yard, two at their foot, and two at the great gate to 'write and take note of all pewter and napkins, etc., as went out of the house, that it might be called for again'.[68] Thus, good fellowship was continually in tension with the order enacted in parades to and from church, in pew placements during the sermon, in graduated seating at the feast, in menus varied according to status, in the collection of quarterage fees, and especially in the highly stylized behaviors, brief inversions, and secular relics associated with the transitions of office.

In both the communalizing and the hierarchizing aspects of Company rites, the spaces of Drapers' Hall played key roles. There was a lingering medievalism about most grand houses of the sixteenth and seventeenth centuries, which retained great halls as visible symbols of power and prestige despite their functional anachronism. In Drapers' Hall, the room may have ceased to shelter a participatory governance but, as at the colleges of Oxford and Cambridge, it continued to lead a purposeful life as the locus of institutional ceremony. Company events reinvigorated all the old spatial strategies for discriminating by rank and for entrenching status—with the dais end remote from the door, the high table anchored by its 'state', and fine graduations of proximity to authority. At the same time, the post-medieval processes of withdrawal and differentiation were enacted, as well. This was the significance of the parlor in the choreography of election. Each officer made a show of retiring to the place in which the leadership had privately appointed their initiates, pausing in this select space before bringing their secrets back with him to the hall and the rest of the fellowship, even there prolonging the revelations by feigning to honor guests such as Alice Barnham, whom the Assistants would never have admitted to the closed sessions they held in their chamber. For her, access even to the hall was contingent upon Francis's franchise of the parlor. She did service as an extra in the enactment of parody (and was perhaps as decorative as the 'comeliest and handsomest' Bachelors who waited the tables).

The Drapers' parlor was a hyper-intensive instance of the ways in which interiors could be imprinted by ideology in the early modern period. The room gave form to abstract ideas of order, segregation, specialization, power,

---

[68] Drapers' D.B.1, fos. 95^{v}, 87^{v}.

and privilege. It was an effect of the consolidation of power and an agent of further consolidation. Its disciplines were exerted by corporate numbers and group mentality, regularly renewed in homosocial bonding, performed in annual rituals, reinforced by oaths of secrecy, and fixed in the Company's documentary record. The Drapers evicted Roger Sadler for unpaid rents and because a newer man fancied his residence, but also because he thwarted their spatial imperatives, denying them access to a private meeting room. Before Martin Calthorp's lease of the head house was confirmed, he had first to pledge that he would cede use of the Ladies' Chamber for four days before and four days after each year's feast. The officers recognized the political capital concentrated in spatial control.

The codifications of the domestic arena were, by contrast, less completely evolved. The idea of the home as a refuge from public cares was already a familiar construct in early modern culture, but at least in London it was rarely a common experience. Even Sir William Chester, that rigorous defender of hierarchy and degree in Drapers' activities, had to admit that the private sphere was not as easily ordered. When he required seclusion 'to sit and write', for example, he knew that his 'dwelling house' was not the place for it. He secured permission from the Drapers to use a small lodge in their great garden. As was true for Francis Barnham and most early moderns, Chester's home was the center of his commercial activities. He also conducted significant business there, mediating Draper controversies (in 1560), convening St Thomas's board of governors (in 1569), and conducting an audit (in 1570).[69]

In addition, Chester may have been frustrated in his search for domestic solitude by the coterminous genderings of the private sphere. The Sadler case reflected the hydra-headedness of household political structures. Women could not be excluded from the domestic realm as they were from the livery company; it was, after all, their own seat of governance. Only in the Drapers' parlor could Mistress Sadler's concerns be set aside so unapologetically. It took a corporation to produce the level of privacy enjoyed by the Drapers' Assistants, which is some indication, to anticipate the themes of the next chapter, of how difficult it was to attain in daily life. In the field of spatial control, oligarchy was more effective than patriarchy.

---

[69] Drapers' M.B. 1/C, fo. 428^v (4 April 1547); twenty years later, Chester still had use of the lodge (W.A.5, 1568–9, fo. 7^r). For meetings at his home, M.B.7, p. 263; LMA H01/ST/A/001/003, fo. 22^r; H01/ST/A/024/001, fo. 136^r.

4

Boundaries

In 1599 Thomas Towne, a Kentish weaver, was presented at the Consistory Court of Canterbury for committing adultery with his maidservant, Elizabeth Preston.[1] Word had come to the court's officers that Tobias Robinson was an eyewitness to 'the act of incontinency'. Towne denied the charge and then went one step further, accusing Robinson of slandering him. When called, his neighbors impugned Robinson's character and credibility. Robinson was 'an alehouse haunter and an idle fellow', said one; 'outrageous', 'lewd', 'brutish', 'drunken', and 'unhonest', according to another. John Wisdom, a husbandman, testified that he had seen Robinson 'pull down his breeches and turn up his shirt and show his beastly parts' publicly. Wisdom also recalled an incident when Robinson had dropped a 'horseturd' into the breeches of a stranger. Sara Tripple, who worked in a victualling house, said that twice in the past year Robinson had 'much abused' her, grabbing her by 'the privy parts' and 'most beastly attempting her chastity'. He had suggested they play a game of 'nimbletrick', allegedly adding derisively that 'if he got her with child he would give her a halfpenny worth of pins towards the keeping of it'. Robinson exposed himself to her, too, at which she 'burned his breech with a firebrand'.

To make his case for slander, Towne had to be able to demonstrate that Robinson's allegations had circulated in his community and damaged his reputation. Thus he called also on Abraham Bucher, one of two men who heard the story as they sat at Towne's looms. Robinson was reported to have told the weavers that Towne and Preston 'were together in his the said Towne's kitchen after the said Towne's wife was gone to bed and then and there in the same evening through a chink or hole in the wall he said that he the said Robinson saw the said Towne and her the said Elizabeth Preston commit the act of incontinency. . . . He took [her] in his arms and laid a cushion upon the ground and . . . there took his carnal pleasure of the body of her.' Another

---

[1] CCAL X.11.3, fos. 133^r–136^r. This began as an office case (a disciplinary investigation into the alleged immorality of Thomas Towne by the ecclesiastical officers) and then continued as an instance case (a dispute between two parties), when Towne charged Robinson with slander.

worker confirmed that a 'fame of incontinency' had spread about Towne and Preston, thus giving testimony that Towne merited the damages he sought for his public disgrace.

Depositions in the *Towne* case show many of the hallmarks of statements taken in early modern church courts. They offer access to laboring-class and middling-sort voices which are otherwise unavailable to us—though it is mediated access. The court's recording clerks remade all testimonies formulaically, interpolating such legally significant terms as 'the said Towne' and 'the same evening'. Statements came in response to interrogatories, the questions shaping the answers. And some of the most arresting particulars were undoubtedly invented. Even though they testified under oath in ecclesiastical settings, witnesses would have been fully aware of the suasive power of detail. Credibility, the point on which judgment turned, was often lodged in reputation, so the court's receptiveness to a deponent's testimony not only followed from his public standing but also reflected on it. It can be frustrating that final determinations are often unrecoverable—as Bernard Capp says, many cases simply 'petered out', having importantly provided space for neighborhood disputes to be aired—but with multiple witnesses presenting competing accounts, what 'actually' happened on such occasions will almost always be a mystery.[2]

For the uses of cultural history, however, church-court depositions are avenues into common experiences as well as into specific events. Deponents may have told stories, but they were stories calculated by their tellers to seem plausible. The issue of record in Canterbury in 1599—whether or not Thomas Towne and Elizabeth Preston committed adultery—may ultimately be less interesting than the incidental information which enlivens its representation—the cushion laid on Towne's floor, Robinson's shameless invitation

---

[2] Bernard Capp, 'Life, Love and Litigation: Sileby in the 1630s', *Past and Present* 182 (2004), 77: 'Most instance causes in ecclesiastical courts never reached a verdict, simply petering out.' I am also indebted to F. G. Emmison on Essex records in *Elizabethan Life: Morals and the Church Courts* (Chelmsford: Essex County Council, 1973); Loreen L. Giese (ed.) on London records in *London Consistory Court Depositions, 1586–1611: List and Indexes*, London Record Society 32 (1995); Laura Gowing on London records in *Domestic Dangers: Women, Words, and Sex in Early Modern London* (Oxford: Clarendon, 1996); R. H. Helmholz in *Marriage Litigation in Medieval England* (Cambridge: Cambridge University Press, 1974) and *Roman Canon Law in Reformation England* (Cambridge: Cambridge University Press, 1990); Ralph Houlbrooke on Hampshire, Norwich, and Norfolk records in *Church Courts and the People during the English Reformation, 1520–1570* (Oxford: Oxford University Press, 1979); Martin Ingram on Wiltshire records in *Church Courts, Sex and Marriage in England, 1570–1640* (Cambridge: Cambridge University Press, 1987); and Diana O'Hara on Kent records in *Courtship and Constraint: Rethinking the Making of Marriage in Tudor England* (Manchester: Manchester University Press, 2000), though see also my review of O'Hara in *Huntington Library Quarterly* 64/1–2 (2001), 189–230. I am grateful for conversations with Loreen Giese, Elizabeth A. Hallam, and Catherine Richardson.

to a game of nimbletrick, and Tripple's spirited riposte with a firebrand. For the subject of privacy, the most intriguing detail of *Towne* v. *Robinson* is the chink through which Robinson claims to have peered.

Can there really have been so convenient a peephole in the kitchen wall, or was this a creation of Robinson's 'unhonest' invention? If so, it was less ingenious than the prank with a turd. According to Martin Ingram, '*any* series of church court records'—in London as well as the provinces—produces instances of witnesses looking 'through window panes or chinks in walls or doors' (emphasis added). Laura Gowing, who focuses on the city but who draws additionally on evidence from outside it (an approach also adopted here), confirms that 'most courts received testimonies like these'. Admitting that such a report may have been 'plausible', inasmuch as 'the early modern household was not built for privacy', Gowing finally finds it improbable that 'the real structures of city houses' could have allowed for as many peepholes as are described. Undoubtedly, most were 'legal fictions', 'legal formulas', or 'conventional motifs'. More emphatically, Ingram declares that because 'peering through a window or bringing witnesses to look too' were 'acceptable modes of proof' in canon law, their descriptions 'give a wholly misleading impression both of lack of privacy and the closeness of moral surveillance'. These were not spontaneous eyewitnessings but instead 'carefully planned, *legally purposeful* activity . . . the early modern equivalent of the private detective bursting into a hotel bedroom to secure photographic proof of adultery in divorce proceedings' (Ingram's emphasis).[3]

The problem with this analogy is that few early moderns had any incentive to be found to have committed fornication. Only in the rarest of cases was legal separation at issue; most often, a judgment of guilt resulted in punishment and public disgrace. Had Thomas Towne nonetheless wished to be condemned for adultery, he could have found a more credible complainant than Tobias Robinson. At his behest, the court examined witnesses on the subject of Robinson's character, not of the presence or absence of a chink in Towne's kitchen wall. Nor did its officers question the premise that Towne's personal affairs could have been betrayed to common knowledge in this way.

The gathering and circulation of private intelligence is the subject of this chapter. For the most part, archival peepholes look into early modern bedchambers, in the sense that they are occupied with sexual transgression. This is because the records that reliably preserve the fullest information about

---

[3] Ingram, *Church Courts*, 244–5; Gowing, *Domestic Dangers*, 56, 70–1, 190. Gowing also emphasizes the 'story-telling' element in depositions, ibid. 52–3. Ian W. Archer concurs with Ingram; see *The Pursuit of Stability: Social Relations in Elizabethan London* (Cambridge: Cambridge University Press, 1991), 77. Keith Thomas and G. R. Quaife, however, are more disposed to accept 'evidence of very close moral surveillance'; see Ingram, *Church Courts*, 244.

day-to-day domestic circumstances are those of the church courts, which were charged with moral discipline. Here, the substantive issue is not the nature of the transactions that were reported, however, but rather the ways in which their reporters came to learn about them. Sexual knowledge serves as a leading example for how much intimate information coursed through household and neighborhood cultures. Most went unrecorded, not being of interest to ecclesiastical officers. But a woman who knew that her neighbor was committing adultery with his maidservant also knew any number of other things about the routines, work habits, economic functions, sleeping arrangements, leisure activities, personal relationships, and everyday disputes of that household. In fact, conflicts of many nonsexual sorts seem to have been articulated in sexual terms precisely because that was what was actionable in Prerogative, Consistory, Archdeaconry, and Peculiar Courts. In 1596, John Harding admitted having called one 'Smith's wife' a 'whore', but he stated that these were nothing more than 'words uttered by him in his heat and rage' because he believed that William Smith had stolen 'certain poles of wood' from him. The terms of this neighborhood imbroglio shifted further from its origins, and escalated, when Mistress Smith claimed sexual slander.[4]

Even the reports with willfully obscured personal agendas, however, can be no more thoroughly desexualized than was their language: private knowledge of all sorts had erotic resonances, for there was pleasure to finding things out. In this respect, Tudor culture was highly eroticized. It can sometimes seem that there was nothing neighbors did not know about each other. Their lives appear porous in part because living conditions were so crowded. A certain amount of density resulted from population growth and housing shortages, both in London and elsewhere. But there were also powerful social conventions regarding shared bedchambers, communal beds, the personal security to be found in numbers, and the mutual regulation that was so much a feature of early modern culture. Consequently, illicit bed-work was often, of necessity, what *A Winter's Tale* calls 'some stair-work, some trunk-work, some behind-door-work' (3.3.70–1)—and sometimes also some open-field-work, some under-the-hedge work, and on occasion some church-porch work. Many extramarital liaisons were conducted in the house's most liminal spaces or, indeed, outside it. In the home's main chambers, privacy was scarce and serendipitous. The particular question for this chapter is how susceptible it was to the sorts of Peeping Tomism in which Tobias Robinson claimed to have engaged.

---

[4] GL Ms 9064/14 (London Commissary Court), fo. 113ᵛ. See Gowing, *Domestic Dangers*, for other instances, including a man who called a woman a whore 'because her apprentices had broken his wall' (p. 117). Capp also notes disputes between men who 'had chosen to pursue' their differences 'by making their wives' sexual reputations the main battleground' ('Life, Love and Litigation', 62).

PROXIMOUS LIVES

It has been estimated that London had 70,000 residents in 1550 and 400,000 by 1650. As the population neared 250,000, according to Roger Findlay, the average increase was over 3,000 persons annually which, because of offsetting mortality rates, meant that some 6,000 newcomers arrived in London each year. The effects of such rapid growth were exacerbated by those of the housing revolution. As Derek Keene has made clear, there should have been ample scope for expansion throughout the Tudor years. Not until 1600 was London again as populous as it had been in 1300, before plague deaths overtook birth rates. And yet, as Ian Archer has demonstrated, the sixteenth-century influx of immigrants from the provinces (who were known as 'foreigners') and from other countries (called 'strangers') was addressed mainly by sprawl in the suburbs rather than infill within the walls.[5] Throughout the late-medieval years, Londoners had been able to extend themselves in some structures and to abandon others in the depopulated city. Until about 1550, then, members of the upper and middling classes still had room to be receptive to the more ample material standards associated with the Great Rebuilding. From that point forward, however, a disarticulation of demographic patterns followed from the fact that persons of substance required expanded living space and, in the city's concentrated commercial culture, surplus storage capacity. For the ranks of the newly prosperous, like the Barnhams, the urban crisis of overcrowding was accelerated by their new spatial expectations and demands.

Plans drawn by the painter-stainer Ralph Treswell in the early seventeenth century show the less salubrious impact of increasing density on poorer housing.[6] In 1612, for example, Treswell surveyed a cluster of properties near Smithfield Market, owned by the Clothworkers' Company (see Fig. 4.1). One section had once been an inn called the Maidenhead, but by the time he mapped the area the old hostelry had been converted into residences now known collectively as Pheasant Court. In notes accompanying his sketchplan, Treswell

---

[5] Roger Finlay, *Population and Metropolis: The Demography of London, 1580–1650* (Cambridge: Cambridge University Press, 1981), 9. Derek Keene, 'A New Study of London before the Great Fire', *Urban History Yearbook* (1984), 11–21; see also Keene's 'Material London in Time and Space', in Lena Cowen Orlin (ed.), *Material London, ca. 1600* (Philadelphia: University of Pennsylvania Press, 2000), esp. 57–61. Robert Tittler notes that in the first half of the century, growth was 'still comfortably accommodated', *Townspeople and Nation: English Urban Experiences, 1540–1640* (Stanford: Stanford University Press, 2001), 6–7. Archer, *Pursuit*, 12–13.

[6] This section on London overcrowding is derived in part from my 'Boundary Disputes in Early Modern London', in *Material London, ca. 1600*, 344–76.

recorded that the principal tenant, Mistress Banckes, had nineteen subtenants.[7] Nicholas Ashley, one of ten men with court-level shops and accommodations, occupied a two-story building shoehorned into the courtyard itself. There were also two widows who had upper-level quarters. A partition wall in William Procter's chamber created a separate entry for the stairs to Mistress Howell's room, but Mistress Lee reached her own above-ground space only by passing through the lobby entrance of William Ashpoole's home. Two tenants lived in subterranean cellars originally built for storage; Treswell indicated that these had been made habitable by the addition of chimneys. With shops, kitchens, yards, outbuildings, and second, third, and fourth stories, most of the premises that adjoined Pheasant Court were less crowded, although they fronted onto the Smithfield pens. Even here, moreover, there were signs that property lines had migrated over time and under pressure of density. Edward Drewry and Christopher Askwith had negotiated an oddly angular partition, perhaps because, having added a stable, Drewry bartered for yard space for the wood and coal to stoke his oven. George Shelstone seems also to have annexed part of Askwith's yard for his shed. Robert Seger's house would once have had a configuration similar to the others, but his yard and rear buildings had earlier been subdivided to accommodate Tobias Harviste, Thomas Brettnor, John Showell, and, in the only off-street commercial building, William Haslome. Peter Clarke appears to have given ground as the Cow Lane shopkeepers crowded in behind him.[8] With a door onto Pheasant Court and its own chimney and privy, Clarke's free-standing 'back room' may have housed an unofficial twenty-fifth tenancy among the twenty-four of record in a complex roughly 90 ft square. The Smithfield families shared walls, fences, and gutters, as well as the sounds and smells of penned cows, sheep, pigs, and horses, nearby. Those in Pheasant Court also shared chimney-stacks, the narrow passage from Cow Lane, and three privies.

London's demographic crisis is often dated to 1580, because that is when the first of a series of royal proclamations against new building was issued.[9] In fact there were symptoms of stress much earlier, with municipal officers confronting the consequences of population explosion well before the Queen and her councillors did. The aldermen were intimately aware of strains on the

[7] Clothworkers' Plan Book. See also *London Surveys*, ed. Schofield, no. 46 (though his transcriptions are digested; he omits the tenancy of Mistress Banckes, for example). Information about the earlier history of the tract is from Schofield.

[8] Names are the available system of identification for the properties; these boundary negotiations could have been (and probably were) conducted with previous tenants.

[9] Paul L. Hughes and James F. Larkin (eds.), *Tudor Royal Proclamations*, ii. *The Later Tudors (1553–1587)* (New Haven: Yale University Press, 1969), 466–8. See for just two examples of the customary periodization of the housing crisis Ward, *Metropolitan Communities*, 17–18; and Lubbock, *Tyranny*, 25.

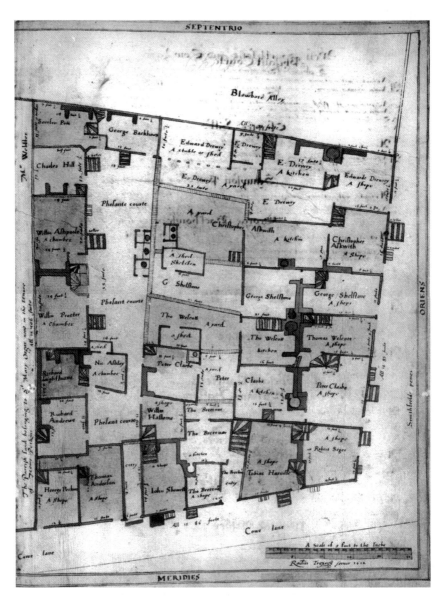

Figure 4.1 Plan of Smithfield properties bequeathed by woolmonger William Heron to the Clothworkers' Company. Drawn by Ralph Treswell, 1612.

city's infrastructures and services, increased demands for food supplies, and the threatened spread of disease, as well as of housing hastily erected in yards and alleys. They recognized that the old measures for population counts, like requiring parish officers to report the numbers of their communicants, failed to capture all the city's temporary residents and transients. In the 1560s they had already begun to institute new policies for identifying, disciplining, and, often, evicting 'inmates', as the impermanently housed were called.[10]

The aldermen also had to mediate the conflicts that arose from lives lived in close proximity. There were disputes over boundaries and fences, unwelcome drainage and blocked light, constricted passages and poor repair, shared chimney-stacks and common cesspits. Some of these controversies were adjudicated by the London Viewers, men recruited by the aldermen for their expert knowledge of carpentry, masonry, and tiling. The Viewers' determinations were recorded in written reports to the city officials. Tudor 'certificates' survive only to mid-sixteenth century (the last is from 1558), but already, decades before the first royal ban on new construction, they show the frequent collision of near neighbors.[11]

These were unlikely to have been nuisance suits. When they summoned the Viewers in 1577, the Drapers encumbered themselves with fees to the four adjudicators, the provision of food and drink, compensation of the Company beadle, and expenses for their own copy of the (lost) certificate—twenty-four shillings in all.[12] The principal historiographic virtue of the 423 surviving Tudor Viewers' certificates is their attachability as a discrete archive; their limitation, that they served persons and institutions of some substance. Of necessity, there were dozens of other mediating agents in London, as well. Policers of property lines included churchwardens, like those of St Bartholomew Exchange who reached an 'agreement of toleration' with a parishioner whose new-built foundations strayed four inches into their churchyard. Peacemakers among neighbors included the executive officers of the livery companies and other property-holding institutions, like the Drapers' Assistants who split

---

[10] By the early seventeenth century some parishes had ceased to rely on volunteers and hired 'searchers' for inmates. See Archer, *Pursuit*, esp. 67, 98, 184–5, 226, 242, 244; Jeremy Boulton, *Neighbourhood and Society: A London Suburb in the Seventeenth Century* (Cambridge: Cambridge University Press, 1987), esp. 16–18, 36 n. 68, 272–3; and my 'Temporary Lives in London Lodgings', forthcoming in the *Huntington Library Quarterly*, 2007.

[11] Janet Senderowitz Loengard (ed.), *London Viewers and their Certificates, 1508–1558: Certificates of the Sworn Viewers of the City of London*, London Record Society 26 (1989). Viewers were required to know building regulations and practices known as 'the custom of the city'. They also gathered information from property documents and the oral history of 'the oldest men and longest dwellers' nearby (no. 121). See no. 89 for a case dependent on local knowledge.

[12] Drapers' R.A.5, 1576–7, fo. 9^r. In 1558 they paid 13s. 4d. for a Viewer consultation (R.A.4, 1558–9, fo. 8^r). See also Drapers' R.A.5, 1565–6, fo. 9^v.

the costs for a party gutter between their old tenant and a Rebuilder, or the St Thomas's governors who ordered a man to remove the fence he had mislocated on another's land. Protectors of common ground included the Court of Aldermen and the Common Councillors, who required the church of St Peter Cornhill to reopen an alley, a mercer to tear down the brick wall he had constructed across a lane, a skinner to demolish an added story that obstructed the light of two nearby houses, a haberdasher to pay an annual fee for the cesspit he dug on city ground, and also Francis Barnham to pull back a cantilevered window projecting into St Clement's Lane. Any organization could call on specialists for ad hoc advice, as did the Drapers when paneling their parlor and the aldermen when commissioning carpenters to review the jetty of a building on Silver Street. Barnham took his turn as an inspector, ensuring that a new chimney was not a 'prejudice to the lights' of the city's clothselling center, Blackwell Hall, and arbitrating another, similar dispute between next-neighbors Humfrey Browne and Thomas Bylton. Light, which was necessary for work productivity, was an urgent subject of contention as buildings rose three, four, five, even six and seven stories.[13]

Among all the indicators of strain upon the city's systems and denizens, however, none makes a more eventful case study than that concerning the management of human waste. It was an old problem that was exacerbated as large buildings were subdivided and new ones were constructed.[14] In 1542, for example, the Viewers inspected a cesspit shared by two prosperous drapers, John Dymok and Henry Dolfyn. During a routine emptying, thirty tuns of accumulated waste were removed through Dolfyn's house. But Dolfyn had just one stool, in his own chamber, while Dymok had one stool for his chamber, one for his maidservants' chamber, and one for his menservants' chamber. Dolfyn told the aldermen that the procedure was 'a great nuisance'. The Viewers decided that since the three-stool man, Dymok, had suffered no trouble, he should bear all the costs. These were estimated by the Viewers at nearly £3 for fees, candles, food, and beer for the 'goldfinders', as well as materials to repair the damages to a median wall. There may also have been

[13] GL Ms 4384/1 (Vestry Minute Book of St Bartholomew Exchange), 246–7; Drapers' M.B.8, fos. 60ᵛ–61ʳ (1569); LMA H01/ST/A/001/003, fo. 101ᵛ (1573); CLRO Rep. 17, fo. 8ᵛ (1570); Rep. 16, fo. 498ʳ (1569); Rep. 17, fo. 204ᵛ (1571); Rep. 18, fo. 298ᵛ (1574); Rep. 16, fos. 420ᵛ–421ʳ (for this and for the Drapers' parlor, see Ch. 3); GL Ms 7784/1, no. 29 (Carpenters' Company records); CLRO Rep. 18, fo. 53ᵛ (1573); Rep. 18, fo. 239ʳ (1574). Treswell documents the height of London housing in the notes accompanying his plans.

[14] In the early fourteenth century, for example, containing walls were ordered when cesspits dug too near to neighbors' houses spilled sewage into their cellars and rotted their foundations. See Helena M. Chew and William Kellaway (eds.), *London Assize of Nuisance, 1301–1431*, London Record Society 10 (1973), nos. 2, 69, 110, 191, 219, 414, 426. By the sixteenth century, walls were generally in place but often needed rebuilding.

payments to an overseer for 'watching to see the tuns filled'. Thirty-six years later, the wall of the same vault had to be rebuilt again.[15]

It may be because cleansing was so expensive that John Balderstone, Robert Sharp, and the Widow Thomson, each living in a house furnished with a dedicated privy, had to be warned by the vestrymen of St Botolph Aldgate 'not to go to the common privy'; the privacy associated with use of their own facilities had to be forced upon them. In 1563, Mistress Twilles complained to the governors of St Thomas's Hospital that a man named William Cuer came frequently by her door to use a nearby privy; they agreed to close the privy down. A year and a half later Cuer made his own petition about excessive foot traffic and offensive odor, and they 'stopped and dammed up' the privy near his house. He promised to have a new privy built in the churchyard; this was but one 'amongst others'. But it seems not to have been in the nature of things for a privy to remain unused; in 1571 Cuer was back once more, asking that the old 'noisome' outhouse should be shut again. Learning of a tenant who sought to avoid the bother and expense of digging a cesspit by situating his privy over a ditch, the hospital's governors ruled that this, too, was too great an 'annoyance' to other inhabitants.[16]

Conditions were undoubtedly at their worst in situations to which the fee-based Viewers would not have been called, like those Treswell illustrated in Pheasant Court. Mapping another group of properties dominated by the bakers of 'Pie Corner', he identified a cluster of privies, one belonging to the household of William Parret, one to that of John Welles, and one a common privy for William Norris, Thomas Cobb, Margret Gryffin, Andrew Davy, Charles Bell, a man called only Dennis, their families, any servants, and guests or lodgers (no. 25). There was a single pit for three stools that served dozens of people, with accumulated waste presumably taken away through a shared yard. By 1560 the charges for cleansing a common privy had risen to £6, so it may not have been the case that an extra half-shilling was added for a load of loam to be spread over the path of removal. This was a courtesy the Drapers did two of their renters in 1568, so that 'the stench should not come through'.[17]

In early 1570, the Queen's central government signaled its own concern with the problem of waste disposal in the repopulating city. London's aldermen responded by delegating some of their members 'to search out, try, and

[15] Viewers no. 170 (the estimate was 56s. 8d.) and Drapers' R.A.5, 1576–7, fo. 20ʳ. For related Certificates, see nos. 202, 209, 267, 270, 288, 323, 333, 383.

[16] GL Ms 9234/2a, fo. 6ʳ (Balderstone, Sharp, and Thomson). LMA H01/ST/A/001/001, fo. 74ᵛ; H01/ST/A/001/002, fo. 3ʳ; H01/ST/A/001/003, fo. 65ᵛ (Cuer, 17 May 1563, 25 September 1564, and 22 October 1571). H01/ST/A/001/003, fo. 81ᵛ (ditch, 1572).

[17] £6 was budgeted for a common privy at St Thomas's Hospital, 11 November 1560 (LMA H01/ST/A/001/001, fo. 30ʳ. Drapers' R.A.5, 1567–8, fo. 11ʳ.

understand as nigh as they can what number of mansion houses are at this present surcharged or pestered with a greater or more number of people than they ought commonly or reasonably to be' and, in particular, to mark those 'not having convenient houses of easement'. A few months later, the Common Council took action against residents of all alleys with just 'one common house of office'. In mid-1571 the Court of Aldermen formally adopted the Council's decree that every dwelling place should have its own facilities. They directed one of their number, Sir Roger Martin, to survey the overcrowded tenements on the 'backside' of Fish Street and to commit to prison all those who had no 'houses of easement'. In answer to a complaint about the quantity of 'ordure and filth cast out' from chamberpots into Long Lane, they required a landlord to install privies for his renters. In 1574 they told another landlord that if he allowed his many impoverished tenants to continue in a building meant for just one occupant, he would have to add 'good and convenient houses with convenient easements'. They faced community pressure, as from the residents of St Botolph Aldgate who petitioned that their parish should be required to furnish privies. And they supervised individual arrangements. Simon Wallet, for example, appealed to them because he had no room for a 'house of easement' at the 'tenement which he lately erected nigh Bishopsgate where the cage stood'. The aldermen allowed him fourteen feet of ground to enclose a yard and install a privy, so long as he himself paid to move the lock-up during construction and then to return it afterwards.[18]

Meanwhile, there continued to be a need for common privies in public areas. In 1571, two aldermen were delegated to approach Sir Thomas Gresham about adding services at the Royal Exchange, 'some convenient place . . . to make water in for the ease of the people resorting to the same'. Otherwise there was the problem confronted by the Drapers, who in the early 1580s posted the walls of their garden with placards in which 'persuasion was used for men to pass by without making of water against the said walls'. The signs were protected from moisture of all sorts by a thin layer of horn. Finally, this brief overview of waste management would not be complete without mention of common drains. The Viewers told Richard Smythe that he had to accept the fact that Thomas Blunte's refuse water coursed through his bedchamber. The consequences for Smythe can be deduced from their warning to Blunte that he should not 'annoy' Smythe 'with no manner of corrupt water or any other thing'.[19] In the tense new living conditions of the city's explosive

---

[18] CLRO Rep. 16, fos. 530ᵛ–531ʳ; Journ. 19, fo. 255ʳ; Rep. 17, fo. 196ʳ; Rep. 17, fo. 215ᵛ; Rep. 18, fo. 54ʳ; Rep. 18, fo. 168ʳ; Archer, *Pursuit*, 81; Rep. 16, fo. 473ᵛ.

[19] CLRO Rep. 17, fo. 145ᵛ; Drapers' R.A.5, 1582–3, fo. 11ʳ; Viewers no. 293 (this reflects my own transcription from CLRO Misc Mss 91/93, which Loengard has modernized).

population growth, many Londoners shared not only drains and cesspits but also gutters, chimney-stacks, passages, entryways, yards, wells, and, perhaps most importantly of all for the history of privacy, walls.

SHARED SPACE

The plans drawn by Ralph Treswell correct any unthinking assumptions we may have cherished that London houses were generally independent, free-standing buildings.[20] Most residents lived in conditions of structural codependency resulting from the subdivision of space. Treswell himself appears to have tenanted a divided dwelling, if his map of properties on Aldersgate Street refers to his own home rather than that of his son (see Fig. 4.2). There, an old mansion house seems to have been twice partitioned. At first, two long and narrow buildings were created, running from the street front on the west to a garden on the east. Eventually, the northernmost of the two was shared out, with the Treswell family in the front rooms and a Master Percivall to the rear. What had been an interior yard was awkwardly split between them by means of a diagonal wall that allowed both Treswell and Percivall to draw well water and that also gave Percivall access to the street. Percivall's passageway was five feet across at streetside and just two-and-a half feet wide at its opening into the garden. Elsewhere, Treswell surveyed 'two tenements now divided into three', 'seven tenements sometimes but five', and 'two tenements sometimes but one'. In 1571 the vestrymen of St Michael Cornhill reviewed the five tenements located in their churchyard and decided they had twice too many occupants.[21]

---

[20] See Schofield: 'Treswell is describing individual tenancies rather than houses . . . Some of the plans and texts show the advanced nature of property subdivision in central London' (*London Surveys*, 17). Alan Dyer adds: 'documentary sources make clear that the sub-division of existing dwellings was very common, so that it is impossible to tell whether a given inventory represents a single house or a section of a larger one' ('Urban Housing: A Documentary Study of Four Midland Towns, 1530–1700', *Post-Medieval Archaeology* 15 (1981), 208). For resultant difficulties with conjectural reconstructions from inventories, see my 'Fictions of the Early Modern English Probate Inventory', in Henry S. Turner (ed.), *The Culture of Capital: Property, Cities, and Knowledge in Early Modern England* (New York: Routledge, 2002), 51–83.

[21] Christ's Hospital Evidence Book no. 10 (*London Surveys*, ed. Schofield, no. 1; henceforward, 'Schofield'). See also Clothworkers' Company Plan Book nos. 43 for Frauncis Wright (Schofield no. 47) and 17 for Masters Osborne and Heathersall (Schofield no. 18). In his transcription of the last, Schofield omits Treswell's header 'Seven tenements sometimes but five lying all together in Hart Street at Crutched Friars.' For St Michael Cornhill, GL Ms 4072/1, fo. 13^r. There were five new tenements housing two persons each; whenever the properties turned over, they should be 'henceforth let but to one man'.

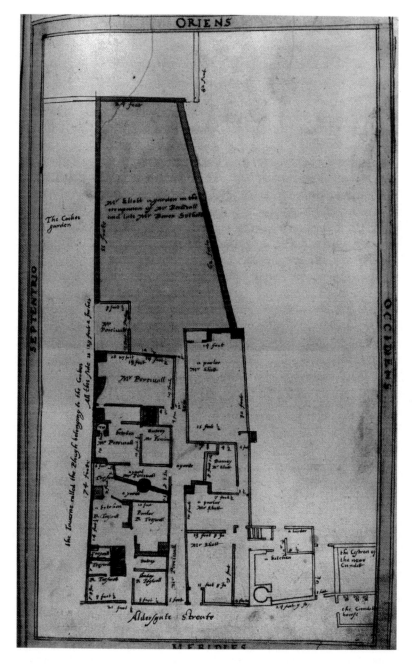

Figure 4.2 Plan of properties on Aldersgate Street bequeathed by Robert Mellish to Christ's Hospital. Drawn by Ralph Treswell, 1611.

An unavoidable occasion for subdivision was death. Then a man's property might be parceled out among his children, or the house might descend to a son with a parlor set aside for his widow. In the city, a widow who lost her husband's lease and who needed a new shop but not a whole house might look to share space. When she was able to stay in place, she might take in a tenant who would occupy any disused rooms and shop areas, his rent supplementing her reduced income. Because this sort of joint occupancy required the formal approval of the chief property holder, many requests to partition space were presented to the governing bodies of the parish churches, livery companies, and charitable institutions. For Francis Barnham, the oddest case probably involved John Jonson, who in 1560 admitted to the Bridewell governors that he was a bigamist. He was ordered 'to make a perfect and whole division between his said house and his said late supposed wife's house, and no more to resort into the company' of the second wife.[22]

Not knowing the negotiations that produced them, we can find the boundaries created by subdivision irrational. In a Barbican Street survey that Treswell left incomplete, for example, we note open space that has been parceled into three yards and three gardens for use by the three households headed by Richard Bewell, G. Graves, and H. Copcott (see Fig. 4.3).[23] For lack of full

---

[22] For authorizations to partition see e.g. LMA H01/ST/A/001/003, fos. 104[r], 116[v], 118[r] (1573–4); Drapers' M.B. 1/B, fo. 365[v] (1543), M.B. 8, fos. 9[v]–10[v] (1567); and M.B. 9, fos. 94[r–v] (1577). For Johnson, BCB-01, fo. 76[r]. Tudor population growth was not confined to London; in 1587, an Essex man split his property and directed his sons to 'leav[e] a space how they shall conclude for a way' between each part (*Essex Wills: The Archdeaconry Courts, 1583–1592*, ed. F. G. Emmison (Chelmsford: Essex Record Office, 1989), no. 771). In 1591 another man used language identical to Treswell's in bequeathing his wife the profits from 'both my tenements being sometime one tenement' (*Essex Wills: The Archdeaconry Courts, 1591–1597*, ed. F. G. Emmison (Chelmsford: Essex Record Office, 1991), no. 975). And see the 1569 will of John Seman: 'To [Edmund my eldest son] so much of my head house in Harwich as extends to the post of the door, which post adjoins the buttery and cellar of the house and to the outward post of the end of the towhouse; and it is to be noted that this part extends from the street door post adjoining the buttery and cellar to the end of that side of the street towards the market place . . . To Robert my son the other part of my head house; which part shall be divided and severed by him from Edmund's part; Robert's part doth contain a cellar, the buttery over it, a shop adjoining the buttery, a little room or chamber at the end of the shop, and the said towhouse at the end of the little room, also one sollar over the buttery, another over the shop, and a third sollar adjoining it over the little room, all to be divided by a line. Provided that the well at the end of the towhouse and on the ground given to Edmund remain in common between the two parts.' Seman designated another residence 'at the back gate of my head house' for his daughter Parnell (*Essex Wills: The Bishop of London's Commissary Court, 1558–1569*, ed. F. G. Emmison (Chelmsford: Essex Record Office, 1993), no. 1041). Even a provincial great house like East Riddlesden Hall could be subdivided, as indicated in the 1602 will of Robert Rishworth, giving part to his wife and part to his son. By 1662 there were two different families in residence in the two parts (National Trust guide to the house, 1993).

[23] Christ's Hospital Evidence Book no. 21 (Schofield no. 4).

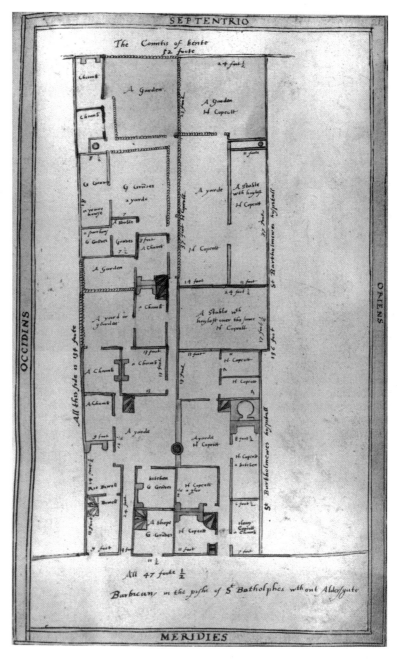

Figure 4.3 Plan of properties on Barbican Street bequeathed by Robert Mellish to Christ's Hospital. Drawn by Ralph Treswell, 1611.

labeling by Treswell, it is impossible to know who held tenure of one of the yards and two of the gardens. The rear chambers are tagged with the numbers 5 and 6, which might suggest that four of the five lower rooms were Graves's chambers 1, 2, 3, and 4, encircling the mid-property garden and yard. If that was the case, though—that is, if Graves's rooms enclosed that space—there would seem to have been no need for the fence that presumably demarcated Graves's ground from Bewell's. We require Treswell's usual method of identifying each space not only generically (a shop, a kitchen, a parlor) but also by means of the occupant's name in order to sort out the pieces in early modern London's patchwork of proprietorships.

For Bewell and Graves, subdivision meant that their rooms were decentered and scattered across the tract they occupied. Graves could not get from his streetside shop to his kitchen, or from either to his chambers, without going outdoors; his neighbors were in similar situations. In another Treswell plan (see Fig. 4.4), a man named West, subtenant to Thomas Alcoke, had a yard and two ground-floor rooms, one a shop, at the north end of a sprawling messuage that had once been a brewhouse called the White Hart.[24] West's upper-level chamber was located over Abraham Frithe's kitchen, across the yard. The chamber over his shop was occupied not by him but by Thomas Chilton, though West had the garret over Chilton's chamber. Even here, though, West had lost space to the building behind him, according to Treswell: 'at the northwest corner of one of these garrets is a corner five feet one way and seven feet another way being no part of this house but supposed to be of Jarret's Hall', a hostelry. There was scant spatial logic to the assortment of rooms West occupied; he had pieced his 'house' together out of the disparate elements that came available to him in this densely developed complex.

Treswell probably did not intend with the unfinished survey on Barbican Street (Fig. 4.3) to suggest another important aspect of city life, though in effect he does so: spatial assignments were never fully fixed. Boundaries changed as families grew, as nests emptied, as businesses expanded, or as they failed. At St Michael Cornhill, for instance, the vestrymen managed adjoining houses in the tenure of Goodman Hubbert and Doctor Willoughby. When Willoughby petitioned for more room, he was allowed to 'join' the two residences. Hubbert was relegated to the 'nether room which now the said Master Doctor useth for a kitchen'. Even outside London space-shifting was not uncommon. John Glover, a Durham weaver, lived in a house that he had split with his son Thomas. In his 1616 will, he reapportioned the property: his wife was to have

---

[24] Christ's Hospital Evidence Book no. 9 (Schofield no. 43). The plan refers to Jarret's Hall, mentioned by John Taylor (the Water Poet) in *The Carriers' Cosmography* as an inn on 'Basing Lane near Bread Street' (London: 1637).

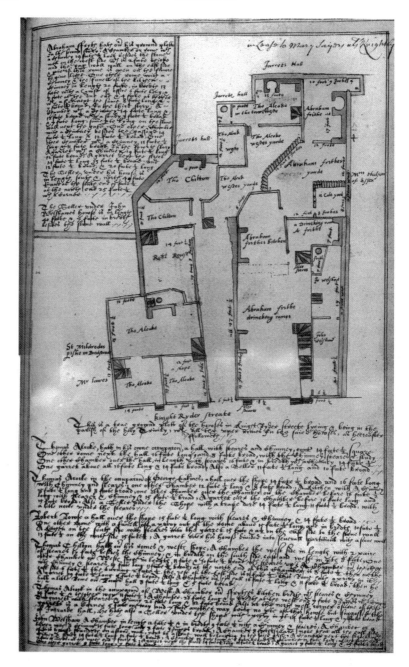

Figure 4.4 Plan of properties known as the White Hart, purchased by Christ's Hospital with the bequest of mercer William Mascall. Drawn by Ralph Treswell, 1611.

his own rooms for life; after her death, these would go to his son Thomas; the section occupied by Thomas would then descend to his grandson; and the kitchen and stables in Thomas's possession would first transfer to his wife, eventually to return to Thomas's control. Glover called each bequest from this movable collection of rooms a 'house'.[25]

One room could be a house, too, to its occupant. This was as true for Goodman Hubbert in St Michael Cornhill as for Essex singlewoman Anne Smithe, who spoke on her deathbed of the 'chamber . . . which she had to be her dwelling house'. John Brockall bequeathed Margaret Herryson the York 'house that Isabell Renton dwelleth in', which house, 'being underneath my chamber', was clearly a single room. In 1573 Mary Spakeman sold as an independent property 'one upper room, sollar, or coal house' in the London parish of St Martin Ludgate, 'in length sixteen foot seven inches and a half, and in breadth thirteen foot ten inches'.[26] For city dwellers, the most common source of supplemental income (and, because it was unregulated, the least visible) was the letting out of a room which became the primary residence for its tenant. The creation of rentable quarters was yet another occasion for partition.

In fact, 'rooms' could lack structural integrity entirely, to judge from such phrases as 'my chamber within the hall'. This presumably referred to appointed sleeping accommodations in a large open space. Eric Mercer is persuaded that 'free-standing furniture' came often to function 'as a partition wall'. Surviving evidence is unavoidably slight, though he is able to cite the use of settles in northern counties: 'the area divided off was essentially another room, and was thought of as such', as 'is shown by the almost invariable provision of a small "fire-window" in the external wall to light the enclosed space'. Mercer calls the strategic placement of beds, and of their head and foot boards, a fairly 'sophisticated' method of defining space, at least when compared to the use of curtains and hangings. A record from Chester describes joint inhabitants of one house, 'and nothing betwix them but a broken wall and a painted cloth'.[27]

[25] GL Ms 4072/1, fo. 7ʳ (Hubbert and Willoughby). Will of John Glover (1616), *Darlington Wills and Inventories, 1600–1625*, ed. J. A. Atkinson et al., Publications of the Surtees Society 201 (1993), no. 40.

[26] The term 'house' could refer not only to an independent physical structure but also to 'the portion of a building, consisting of one or more rooms, occupied by one tenant or family' (*OED*). Will of Anne Smithe (1570), *Essex Wills (England)*, ii. *1565–1571*, ed. F. G. Emmison (Boston: New England Historic Genealogical Society, 1983), no. 724. Will of John Brockall (1558), *Wills and Inventories from the . . . Archdeaconry of Richmond*, ed. James Raine, Publications of the Surtees Society 26 (1853), no. 98. Mary Spakeman, GL Ms 21096, 'Bargain and sale of an upper room in the parish of St Martin Ludgate, 1573'.

[27] F. G. Emmison reads this 1583 will to refer to a use for the hall, not to an inner room, in *Elizabethan Life: Home, Work and Land* (Chelmsford: Essex Record Office, 1991), 4. Eric Mercer, *Furniture, 700–1700*, The Social History of the Decorative Arts (New York: Meredith Press, 1969), 61. *Child-Marriages, Divorces, and Ratifications in the Diocese of Chester, 1561–6*, ed.

Even in chambers with architectural elements, enclosure was imperfect; John Schofield observes that 'internal walls were generally insubstantial'.[28] Some were screens, properly speaking, being not of full height. Subdivision was most often executed by means of timber partitions (see Fig. 4.5), as at Old Drapers' Hall, where in 1575 the Company hired carpenters to 'mak[e] up of a partition with boards in the same chamber' between two tenants. As specified in an Exchequer report from the 1520s, these were 'otherwise called paper walls'. They were no thicker than wainscotting, also known as 'sealing'; thus, such records as that 'for the sealing to divide the chamber of the middle room when Master Nicholls came to be lodged there'. Because of the value of oak, London property regulations, rental agreements, and wills were full of proscriptions against the removal of walls. The Drapers, for instance, directed that tenants be required not to 'take away any of the windows, doors, or partitions'—they were regarded, in other words, not as structural features but as fittings.[29] In the city's volatile living conditions, situational boundaries were only practical. The purpose of 'paper' walls was to demarcate territory, often temporarily and flexibly, rather than to effect privacy.

Meanwhile, beds were located in spaces of all sorts—not just bedchambers but halls, parlors, dining rooms, kitchens, pantries, butteries, shops, stables, even privies.[30] Many rooms had multiple beds, including those in which the

Frederick Furnivall, Early English Text Society os 108 (1897), 58; for cloth dividers in London, see Gowing, *Domestic Dangers*, 190.

[28] Schofield, *Medieval London Houses*, 149. He cites a record from 1390, though there is similar evidence for the sixteenth century, as documented below.

[29] Drapers' R.A.5, 1574–5, fo. 12[r]. L. F. Salzman excerpts the Exchequer report in *Building in England down to 1540: A Documentary History*, 2nd edn. (Oxford: Clarendon, 1967), 261. For Nicholls, *Plymouth Building Accounts of the Sixteenth and Seventeenth Centuries*, ed. Edwin Welch, Devon and Cornwall Record Society, ns 12 (1967), 100. Drapers' M.B.9, fo. 15[r]. Treswell describes partitioning in garrets in particular; e.g. a fifth-floor garret 'with diverse partitions in it' (Clothworkers' Plan Book nos. 10–11; Schofield no. 21, though this is not material Schofield transcribes), 'a chamber divided into diverse parcels wherein dwell diverse widows' (Clothworkers' Plan Book no. 31; Schofield no. 40); see also Schofield nos. 22, 43, 48.

[30] Frank E. Brown, 'Continuity and Change in the Urban House: Developments in Domestic Space Organisation in Seventeenth-Century London', *Comparative Studies in Society and History* 28 (1986), 580. Brown worked with probate inventories; wills are generally more reliable, being based in householders' own descriptions rather than in appraisers' observations. Will of Thomas Haywarde (1559), with 'two beds in the hall', *Essex Wills (England)*, i. *1558–1565*, ed. F. G. Emmison (Washington, DC: National Genealogical Society, 1982), no. 114; inventory of John Cuerden (1601), with 'the bed in the dining parlor', 'An Inventory of the Goods of John Cuerden of Cuerden, 1601', ed. R. Sharpe France, *Transactions of the Historic Society of Lancashire and Cheshire* 91 (1939), 202; will of Elizabeth Cooke (1589), with 'my joined bedstead in the kitchen', *Essex Wills: The Archdeaconry Courts, 1583–1592*, no. 1082; will of George Raimonde (1594), with 'my featherbed in the pantry', ibid. *1591–1597*, no. 1075; will of John Coker (1589), with 'the mattress in the buttery', *Essex Wills: The Bishop of London's Commissary Court, 1558–1569*, no. 301; will of Joan Whytinge (1589), with 'the bed in the buttery', *Essex Wills: The*

Figure 4.5 Partition wall of timber boards, separating a pantry from a corridor at Plas Mawr in Conwy, North Wales, *c.*1580.

Archdeaconry Courts, 1583–1592, no. 1081; will of Agnes Miller (1581), with 'my biggest posted bedstead in my shop', *Essex Wills: The Bishop of London's Commissary Court, 1578–1588*, ed. F. G. Emmison (Chelmsford: Essex Record Office, 1995), no. 427; inventory of Elizabeth Kirkhouse (1587), with 'in the little stable, one servant's bed', *Wills and Inventories from the Registry at Durham, Part II*, ed. William Greenwell, Publications of the Surtees Society 38 (1860), no. 137; inventory of Margerie Belassis (1577), with 'In the privy: a bedstead, a mattress, two blankets, a coverlet', *Wills and Inventories from the Registry at Durham, Part II*, no. 142.

householder and his wife slept. Shared occupancy was the norm even for gentry; the navigator Sir Martin Frobisher, for example, spoke of the bedroom occupied by his wife's daughter, waiting women, and chambermaids. There is plenty of evidence of shared beds, too. People were generally paired off by sex, status, and age (especially the young)—one bed for male servants, one for female servants, and one for children. But these were organizing principles that varied with occasion; when a husband was away, his wife might share with one of her maidservants, and space was often found for a short-stay lodger in the same bed as his landlord. In his report back from Russia in 1568, Thomas Randolph observed the oddity that the Muscovites 'eat together', but, unlike the English, 'they lie apart'.[31]

Early moderns shared their beds and their bedchambers for warmth, for companionship, and for personal security.[32] Not incidentally, conventional sleeping arrangements also allowed for a high level of mutual surveillance. It is undoubtedly for this reason that beds make relatively few appearances in bawdy-court testimonies as the sites of illicit liaisons—except when they are described in terms of the daily routines of housekeeping. Then, maidservants claim frequently to have been taken by surprise while engaged in their honest labor; there is no knowing how often they used their chores as pretexts for

---

[31] Will of Martin Frobisher (1594), *North Country Wills . . . 1558 to 1604*, ii, ed. J. W. Clay, Publications of the Surtees Society 121 (1912), no. 127. See also the will of Thomas Bowres (1569) for 'all the beds and bedsteads in the chamber that we [he and his wife] do use to lie in', *Essex Wills (England)*, ii. *1565–1571*, no. 284; will of Roger Nicholl (1594) for 'the bedstead wherein I lie . . . and a boarded bedstead in the same chamber', *Essex Wills: The Archdeaconry Courts, 1591–1597*, no. 848; will of George Mayer (1574) for 'one bed in which the maids lie', *Essex Wills (England)*, iii. *1571–1577*, ed. F. G. Emmison (Boston: New England Historic Genealogical Society, 1986), no. 737; will of Richard Marshall (1588) for 'the best bedstocks that my men lieth in', *Wills and Inventories from the Registry at Durham, Part II*, no. 143; will of William Freeman (1569), giving two daughters the 'bed they lie on', *Essex Wills: The Bishop of London's Commissary Court, 1569–1578*, ed. F. G. Emmison (Chelmsford: Essex Record Office, 1994), no. 298; will of William Hulke (1572) for 'the featherbed whereon the children lie', *Essex Wills (England)*, iii. *1571–1577*, no. 121. On mistress and maidservant, householder and lodger, see Joan Dils, 'Deposition Books and the Urban Historian', *The Local Historian* 17 (1987), 274. Shared beds make it 'difficult to assess household size from the number of beds listed', Ursula Priestley and P. J. Corfield, 'Rooms and Room Use in Norwich Housing, 1580–1730', *Post-Medieval Archaeology* 16 (1982), 123 n. 53. The history of same-sex partnerships is difficult to recover because shared beds were so common (perhaps it can be assumed for Devonshire bachelor Henry Marwood, who in 1547 referred to Peter Osborne not only as his 'bedfellow' but also as his 'special friend'; see *Devonshire Wills: A Collection of Annotated Testamentary Abstracts*, ed. Charles Worthy (London: Bemrose, 1896), 2–4). For Randolph, Hakluyt, *Principal Navigations*, iii. 102.

[32] In 1595, the Keeper of the Tower Gatehouse, Morris Pyckeryng, wrote to ask Cecil which security procedure to observe with a prisoner: should he 'put on hand bolts every night on his hands' or 'let my servant lie in his chamber'? *Calendar of the Manuscripts of . . . the Marquess of Salisbury . . . Preserved at Hatfield House*, 24 vols. (London: 1883–1976), v. 236.

assignations. Christian Ideley told the Bridewell that she was obeying her mistress's order to make the bed when one of their own governors, Thomas Aldersey, followed her upstairs (Aldersey heard her accusation while himself seated at the board). According to Ideley, Aldersey offered twenty pence 'to have the use of her body'. At her refusal, her mistress called her back down and sent up another woman instead; the implication is that Ideley declined to be recruited by an established provider of sexual services.[33]

More often, deponents testified to acts of incontinency committed in work spaces such as kitchens, garrets, and cellars, 'against the planches [boards] where the drink standeth' and 'against a tub', again during the working day. In another indication that bedchambers were comparatively well monitored, the liminal spaces of households are mentioned often. These include staircases and small, closet-like front porches. Ethellbarthe Thorne said that her master enforced her 'twice in his own entry within one week after she came to work with him'. In Canterbury, a servant named Crenche noticed that his fellow servant, Elizabeth Purfry, lingered at their master's door one evening with Peter Colbrand. Crenche 'heard them make a noise in the entry aforesaid rumbling against the walls'. He had occasion to confirm his suspicions when, locking up for the night, he 'saw where the said Colbrand's nature lay upon the ground' of the porch. Joan Walker alleged that her master impregnated her 'upon a pair of stairs in his own house'; Jane Squier maintained that her master 'many and sundry times' had sex with her 'upon his stairs leading from his hall to his chamber'; Humphrey Wilde reported of a man and woman presented at the Bridewell that he 'took them on his aunt's stairs in the night'; and Helen Hutchin said that Edward Francke 'did most filthily abuse her on the stair with a carrot root'.[34] The temporal dimension of early modern privacy was at least as important as its spatial aspect, and stories such as these give witness how often, because of its very rarity, it was a matter of serendipity.

For most Elizabethans, privacy was less a material condition than a consensual act. In Canterbury, a man named Conoway evicted a tenant from the 'part of the house' they shared because 'he was a bad neighbor and would ever be harkening and looking through holes in the walls to hear and see what he the

---

[33] BCB-02, fo. 201[r].

[34] BCB-02, fos. 113[v], 90[r] (planches and tubs). BCB-02, fo. 100[r] (Thorne). CCAL X.11.3, fos. 74[r]–76[r] (Crenche). BCB-02, fo. 103[r] (church porch). BCB-01, fo. 80[v] (Walker); BCB-01, fos. 195[v]–196[r] (Squier); BCB-02, fo. 98[v] (Wilde); GL MS 9064/14, fo. 44[r] (Francke; 'stair' is crossed out). For stairs see also BCB-01, fo. 80[v]; BCB-02, fos. 103[v], 149[v]–51[r], 204[r]; and Gowing, *Domestic Dangers*, 94. For corridors and stairways as the new 'common spaces' of Rebuilt houses which could 'compromise privacy' rather than advance it, see Subha Mukherji, 'Edmunds vs. Edmunds 1596', *Queens College Record* 16 (2004), 14–17. I am grateful to A. R. Braunmuller for sending me a photocopy of the essay.

said Conoway did in his house'.[35] Housemates expected certain conventions to be honored: when two people retired to a corner, they signaled their desire for a private conversation; when they drew their bed curtains, for private relations. But the built consequences of population growth and an expanding economy brought many into closer contiguities than had been the case in their recent past. In the new density of their physical circumstances, and amid all the tensions that followed from shared gutters and cesspits, civil protocols were strained, too. Londoners could not have presumed that their neighbors would respect their social boundaries, especially given the provocation that the structural boundaries between households were often as insubstantial as those between housemates.

Back at the White Hart (Fig. 4.4), for example, there is nothing more than a 'paper' wall between the homes of Thomas Alcocke and Robert Rowse. A chimney marks the logical border, but Alcocke evidently required a privy, and, even though it annexed what might have been thought to be Rowse's space, it was located, necessarily, directly under the privies on the two floors above (Treswell shows the two shafts behind Alcoke's stool, emptying into the same cesspit). Undoubtedly, the wall that enclosed the privy was a mere partition of boards. Bridget Upley described the even flimsier divider between her house in the parish of St Sepulchre and that of her 'next neighbor' Mary Wallys. She heard suspicious noises and, knowing that the bookbinder Richard Wallys was out of town, looked into his house by 'taking up a painted cloth' to discover Mary 'in naked bed' with a lover. Treswell remarks the many partitions added in garrets as they were converted for accommodations; clearly, there remained circumstances like that in Newcastle-upon-Tyne, where a merchant's widow had a shop and 'so much of the loft above it as doth directly upward answer to the same'.[36] The divisions of the loft were imaginary and approximate, created of the fragile ingredients of common sense and mutual concession.

London's civic institutions and church courts adjudicated the consequences when there was a failure of the collective understandings and social conventions that policed these domestic borders. Albert and Isabella Wells, sitting by their fire, heard Agnes Pope slandering Joan Bettes in the next house; Pope was presented at the Archdeacon's Court. Through her kitchen wall, Sara Flower discerned Anne Tayler calling her a whore; Tayler was charged in the Bishop's Consistory. While these instances were represented as innocent overhearings, there were also deliberate listenings-in by neighbors who acted on their curiosity or their malice (see Fig. 4.6). For the so-called 'nightwalkers' who

[35] CCAL X.11.6, fo. 106[r].

[36] BCB-01, fo. 32[r] (Upley). Will of Margret Lyddell (1604), *Wills and Inventories from the Registry at Durham, Part IV*, ed. Herbert Maxwell Wood, Publications of the Surtees Society 142 (1929), 1–2.

Figure 4.6 An eavesdropper witnessing the 'malice of a woman' in Thomas Trevelyon's pictorial commonplace book, *c*.1608. The image suggests the malice of neighborhood surveillance, as well.

loitered under others' windows in the dark, eavesdropping was a known leisure pursuit. Because of them, the Bishop of Coventry and Lichfield wrote in 1605, people 'can speak nothing in their beds, the man with his wife, or one man with another, but they [the nightwalkers] hear what they talk and make rhymes of it when they have done'.[37] The greater injury may have been subjection to sarcasm, not invasion of privacy.

Of the thousands of cases that came before them, the London Consistory's *Ampthill* v. *Legge and Skelton* is particularly interesting because its imputations of incontinency were argued almost exclusively in terms of the tangible circumstances of Samuel Skelton's lodging house.[38] William Legge rented a chamber and a garret room. Henry Smith, who had the chamber under the uppermost of Legge's two rooms, said that he heard noises that made him suspicious of Legge's nocturnal activities. Skelton's young daughter, the presumed object of Legge's interest, also slept on the upper level. To Smith's mind, nothing but libidinous intent could account for Legge's decision to bed down in an uncomfortable, unheated garret rather than in his lower chamber. Skelton's servant Thomas Hanwell countered staunchly that Legge's upper room was 'fit and convenient' even without a chimney; it was 'a private room to itself, and is severed with a wall and partition from any other room on the same floor or story, and the door thereof hath a latch and a bolt'. Anna Wade, another servant, also said that the garret room was 'fit and convenient' and 'private to itself, the door thereof being furnished with lock and key and a bolt on the inner side thereof, and there is two partitions betwixt that room and the other lodging rooms on the same story'. But Smith testified that Legge's garret chamber was 'very inconvenient and unfit for a lodging room, especially in the winter, it being on the highest story in the top of the said house which is very cold and naked'. The room was 'enclosed with old painted cloths and hath a thin door of deal board and only a latch upon it and that room is in the middest of the garrets'. In the microcosm of Samuel Skelton's lodging house, a breach of community manifested itself in conflicting reports of the

---

[37] GL Ms 9056, fos. 89ᵛ–90ᵛ (Pope, 1567); Gowing, *Domestic Dangers*, 98–9 (Flower, 1629). Nehemiah Wallington wrote his neighbor that 'I have heard you many times at prayer and sometimes a reading' (Paul S. Seaver, *Wallington's World: A Puritan Artisan in Seventeenth-Century London* (Stanford: Stanford University Press, 1985), 103). Diane Shaw's remarks for the medieval period are applicable to the early modern: 'the assumption is that a person could easily discover another's private habits and business, but that these should not be broadcast' ('The Construction of the Private in Medieval London', *Journal of Medieval and Early Modern Studies* 26 (1996), 460). Bishop quoted by Paul Griffiths, 'Meanings of Nightwalking in Early Modern England', *The Seventeenth Century* 13 (1998), 225. See also Marjorie Keniston McIntosh, *Controlling Misbehavior in England, 1370–1600* (Cambridge: Cambridge University Press, 1998), esp. 9, 57, 65–7, 198.

[38] GL Ms 9189/1, fos. 157ᵛ–63ʳ.

building's physical definitions: for one deponent, there were a structural wall and a partition; for another, two partitions; for the third, nothing more than cloth hangings.

London's overcrowding was undoubtedly the indirect cause of many strained relations; here, it may also have been the immediate occasion for complaint. Wade suggested that Smith wanted the garret room for his own use. This might explain why Smith took such care to depict his own disinterest.[39] Declining to represent himself as an eyewitness to the alleged indiscretions, he suggested merely that boundaries between the garret rooms in Skelton's house were flimsy and unenforceable. He was willing to say that Legge's chamber was created by painted cloths but not that he had lifted one; that Legge's door was of cheap fir or pine but not that he had looked through the gap between it and the hangings; that the door lacked a key and a bolt but not that he had applied his eye to the hole for the latch string; that the conditions were inherently suspicious but not that he had confirmed his suspicions. If Legge's room was as Smith described it, it was pocked with peepholes. Smith wanted it to be thought that he did not exploit the circumstances of the garret; others were willing to admit to less restraint.

FOUR SORTS OF PEEPHOLES

Margaret Browne reported on her next-neighbor, Clement Underhill, to the Lord Mayor and the Court of Aldermen.[40] Unlike Henry Smith, Browne took pains to demonstrate that she had not merely deduced an illicit liaison. Thus her report to London's chief executive officers was full of detail. On 13 May 1598, she had seen Underhill 'making merry' with a man named Michael Fludd. She knew that Underhill's husband was away, so she watched as Fludd waited in an upstairs chamber until six o'clock, when Underhill shut her shop windows and joined him. The two had 'carnal copulation'. Afterwards, Fludd rose, 'wiped his yard on her smock', and then went to 'a pail or a tub of water' further to 'wash' his penis. Over bread and butter, Underhill lifted a pot of beer and said to Fludd, 'Here, now I drink to thee.'

---

[39] A doctor of physic, Smith had reputation on his side and more autonomy than the two servants. A man named Ampthill—perhaps the 'friend' who reportedly advised Smith that this was a matter 'fit to be presented into the ecclesiastical court'—brought the complaint. By the time he gave testimony, Smith was also able to state that both he and a man named Radway had moved out of Skelton's house for 'dislike' of arrangements there.

[40] I am grateful to John A. W. Lock for referring me to <www.ucc.ie/chronicon/salkeld.htm>, accessed 4 May 2007; Duncan Salkeld includes a partial transcription of BCB-04, fo. 23^{r-v}.

Margaret Browne also had a supporting witness, her husband, and it was he who clarified that they looked 'through a great hole' into Underhill's bedchamber. Responding to his wife's urgent summons, Henry Browne had arrived at the viewing hole just in time to see Fludd leave the bed 'with his hose hanging about his legs'. Then Browne turned away. Either less interested than his wife or less willing to appear interested, he 'would see no more'. The aldermen would hear no more; they referred the matter to the Court of Bridewell. There, Michael Fludd escaped discipline by confessing. He was fined a pound, which the governors earmarked for 'the relief of the poor of this hospital'. Underhill, however, was 'punished', probably with a whipping. If no part of the Brownes' story was challenged—not even the hole—this may be because the mayor, aldermen, and governors of the Bridewell already knew of four sorts of peepholes in early modern housing.

First Sort: A Hole by Any Other Name

Some peepholes, clearly, were nothing more than key or latch holes. Syselie Sykman probably referred to a keyhole in saying that she 'looked through a hole in the door' and saw a man and woman 'on the bed together'. The same was undoubtedly true for Robert Davyson, testifying when Alice Atwell named John Stringer father of her illegitimate child. Recalling that Atwell had taken another man up to her bedchamber in the house of Stringer's father, Davyson reported that he 'went up and knocked at the chamber door to go in but he could not go in but looked through a hole in the door' (at the time, the two were 'not in any undecent order'). Alice Ryle spread the rumor that Constance Wade had committed adultery with Ryle's stepson. According to one deponent, Ryle gossiped that she had 'looked through a hole of a door at them into a chamber, and there the said Alice said she did see them as homely as ever her husband and she were'; others called it a 'privy hole' and a 'tote hole'. Dorothy Smith left nothing unspecified in testifying that she 'looked through a keyhole and saw one John Johnson being in the company of one Cysselie'. Smith confronted Johnson, who in reply 'broke the head of the same Dorothy with a candlestick'. At the Bridewell, Johnson had to answer to accusations not only about Cysselie but also about Johan Michell, John Fullam's wife, 'Jane the gardener's wife', and 'Mortimer's wife in Shoe Lane'.[41]

---

[41] BCB-02, fo. 137^v (Sykman); CCAL X.11.6, fos. 73^r–76^r (Davyson); *Child Marriages, Divorces, and Ratifications in . . . Chester*, 111–16 (Ryle); BCB-02, fos. 198^r, 200^v (Smith). In the rooms of women in childbirth, keyholes were stopped up (and curtains were drawn to

Early moderns may on occasion have described windows as 'holes'. Joan Clinton called the local watch to a Canterbury victualling house run by Joan Nowre: 'Yonder', she said, 'is a piece of work.' Roger Clinton was said to have explained that he had heard Nowre and the tapster William Harris 'blowing' (a frequent term for sexual panting). One deponent testified that Clinton stared 'in at a window into' Nowre's parlor; three witnesses reported instead that he 'put in his head at a hole'. A week later, Nowre discovered Joan Clinton outside her window and accused her of eavesdropping. Clinton said stoutly that she had every right to 'stand in her own ground and look into the house of the said Nowre, whereupon Joan Nowre called for a dish of water and flung into the face of the said Joan'. In another Canterbury case, Mary Philpott went to John Knoth's house because she knew William Atkin to be there. When no one answered her knock at Knoth's door, 'she thrust open the chamber window and when she had thrust open the window, she saw William Atkin . . . come from the bed of John Knoth's wife'. Henry Spoore had retired for the night when he overheard Robert Ogle promise to marry Margaret Milner; he 'rose out of his bed and looked in at a window at them, and heard their talk and saw their doings'.[42]

It is easy to appreciate that unglazed windows may have been called 'holes' when their shutters were open. There were also holes *in* windows. For glazed windows that were permanently fixed rather than fitted as casements, a quarry or two might be left empty in the leading, to permit ventilation. Margaret Jourdain suggests that some of these gaps were also deliberately introduced for their 'decorative effect against the light'.[43]

---

block all natural light); Adrian Wilson, 'The Ceremony of Childbirth and its Interpretation', in Valerie Fildes (ed.), *Women as Mothers in Pre-Industrial England: Essays in Memory of Dorothy McLaren* (London: Routledge, 1990), 73; I owe this reference to Susan Comilang. Privy-Council porter Robert Laneham was careful to prevent eavesdropping when the members met: 'If I take a listener, or a prier-in at the chinks or at the lockhole, I am by and by in the bones of him'; E. K. Chambers, *The Elizabethan Stage*, 4 vols. (Oxford: Clarendon, 1923), i. 69 n. 2. Of many references in stageplays to listening, peeping, and talking at keyholes, the most interesting appears as a stage direction in Ben Jonson's *The Alchemist*: Face 'speaks through the keyhole' (3.5). See also Christopher Marlowe's *Jew of Malta* (2.3), Ben Jonson's *The Case is Alter'd* (2.1, 4.7) and *Every Man Out of his Humour* (4.3), Philip Massinger's *The Bondman* (1.2), John Phillip's *Patient Grissell* (prologue), and James Shirley's *The Example* (1.1) and *The Traitor* (3.1).

[42] CCAL X.11.1, fos. 159ʳ–161ᵛ (Clinton, 1587). CCAL X.11.1, fos. 18ᵛ–19ᵛ (Philpot, 1585). *Depositions and Other Ecclesiastical Proceedings from the Courts of Durham Extending from 1311 to the Reign of Elizabeth*, ed. James Raine, Publications of the Surtees Society 21 (1845), no. 130 (Spoore, *c.*1570).

[43] Margaret Jourdain, *English Decoration and Furniture of the Early Renaissance (1500–1650)* (London: B. T. Batsford, 1924), 128.

Second Sort: Accidental Holes

Because glass was notoriously fragile, moreover, property surveys are full of orders to replace broken and missing quarries. At St Michael Cornhill, for example, the glazier was paid for 'mending of sixty-six holes in fifteen windows' in 1562 and then for sixty-seven more in 1570. There were myriad other repair problems that were hole-producing. St Thomas's Hospital was unable to keep pace with the maintenance requirements in its tenanted properties; in 1571 the governors disallowed any 'reparations' except those to make a building 'wind tight and water tight or to keep or uphold any house from falling down'. This was not an idle concern; Henry Machyn made note of a house in St Clement's Lane that was in such bad condition that it collapsed without warning. The 'good man' of the house was killed and his wife and maid 'sore hurt'. The Drapers hired a carpenter to replace the foundational timber under a partition wall at one of their rental properties; the 'plate' was so rotten that it 'was like to shoot into the next neighbor's house'. At another, they paid a joiner to patch a floor with 'a piece of deal board'. Other upper-level floors sagged over time and under great weights, sinking away from partition walls to create breaches between adjacent rooms, or causing gaps in the boarding which made openings to rooms below. The subject of supposed satanic possession, Sara Williams, said in the course of her examination that 'a bird came suddenly flying in . . . and that the bird did afterwards (being a robin red-breast) escape out, being on the floor at a hole in the boards, there being light to be seen, and wide lathes underneath unmortared, so as the bird might easily escape'. Doors, too, came to be 'sagged down and thereby would not open and shut'.[44]

Some walls were wattle-and-daub, built of slender poles through which flexible lathes were woven, the whole then caulked with a thick mixture of mud and straw. Because a 'pale' was a stake like that used in a fence, it was probably damaged wattle-and-daub that Elizabeth Page described when she said that she had 'seen through a little crevice of a wall or a pale out' in her master's home; in the next house, Sara Bonivall sat in a chair, John Crosbie

---

[44] GL Ms 4071/1, fos. 68ᵛ, 93ᵛ (St Michael Cornhill). LMA H01/ST/A/001/003 (1571), fo. 55ʳ. *The Diary of Henry Machyn: Citizen and Merchant-Taylor of London, from A.D. 1550 to A.D. 1563*, ed. John Gough Nichols, Camden Society 42 (1848), 34. Drapers' R.A.5 1567–8, fos. 12ʳ, 13ʳ (plate). Drapers' R.A.5 1566–7, fo. 19ʳ (floor). Samuel Harsnett, *A Declaration of Egregious Popish Impostures, to Withdraw the Hearts of her Majesty's Subjects from their Allegiance and from the Truth of the Christian Religion Professed in England, under the Pretense of Casting Out Devils* (London: 1603), 178 (Williams). See also a 1550 Viewers' report regarding a 'decayed' floor in St Clement Eastcheap (no. 272); damage caused by 'weighty gear' on a gallery floor in 1551, Drapers' M.B.1/C, fo. 517ᵛ; doors (1557), GL Ms 4071/1, fo. 52ʳ.

'kneeling before her' to 'grope' her beneath her skirts. John Davis described a half-timbered building from which 'some of the clay of the wall was fallen', making possible an escape from incarceration. Wattle-and-daub, brick, and stone walls were also highly vulnerable to the kinds of stress described in a Viewers' report, which concluded that the 'new decays and cracks' in an 'old and rotten' wall followed from the digging out of a vault beneath it. The reclamation of underground space through the construction of cellars was arguably the most common building project in early modern London; it made for the undermining of many walls.⁴⁵

Board partitions were particularly vulnerable to cracks and were weakened by knotholes. The timbers of these 'paper' walls warped and withdrew from the loadbearing walls and chimneys they were butted up against. When the Drapers repanelled their parlor, the officers took 'good regard' of the oak; it should 'be thoroughly seasoned before the setting up thereof, lest after that the same shall be set up it might happen to shrink, which would be a great displeasure and disgrace to the work. And that rather than the thing should not be well, they would protract the setting up thereof till this time twelve months. In which time the wainscot being sawn shall have good time of seasoning.' But it was the rare builder who could let cut oak dry for a year. The principal alternative to wood that was green was wood that was salvaged for reuse and that came to its new purpose with all its old peg and nail holes. In either case, partition planks were deliberately fitted loosely into their grooves, in order to allow for continued expansion and contraction. It often happened, as William Horman wrote, that 'the joining of these boards gapeth'. Walls were also damaged by the addition and removal of doors, wainscotting, shelves, benches, counters, cupboards, and other built-in furnishings and fittings.⁴⁶

As attic subdivisions were usually created by wooden walls, this is probably what Joan Whitehead referred to when she said that she 'had a hole in her garret in the said house (being the next house adjoining unto the house wherein the

---

⁴⁵ I am grateful to Loreen L. Giese for the reference to Page (1597) in LMA DL/C/215, fos. 43ᵛ–44ʳ and to John A. W. Lock for the reference to Davis (1546) in 'The Imprisonment of John Davis, a Boy of Worcester, Written by Himself in After Life', *Narratives of the Days of the Reformation*, ed. John Gough Nichols, Camden Society 77 (1859), 66. Nichols thinks this report, found among Foxe's papers, is by Davis himself. GL Ms 7971 includes a rare survival of a Viewers' report from 1617, copied into the records of the Company for the Propagation of the Gospel in New England. For cellars, see the records of the Carpenters' Company, e.g. GL Ms 7784.

⁴⁶ Drapers' M.B.9, fo. 11ʳ. Horman (1519) quoted by John McCann, 'Dissatisfaction with Builders in the Sixteenth Century', *Historic Buildings in Essex* 4 (November 1988), 9. For the removal of shelves, counter boards, settles, wainscot, doors, and floorboards, see Drapers' M.B.6, fos. 22ʳ, 26ʳ (1554); LMA H01/ST/A/001/001, fo. 8ʳ (1557). For the reuse of old boards, LMA H01/ST/A/001/002, fo. 63ʳ (1567); Drapers' R.A.5, 1575–6, fo. 18ʳ; Drapers' M.B.9, fo. 32ʳ (1575).

said Dorothy Bucke did and doth lodge) and that she saw a man and her the said Dorothy Bucke naught together on her bed when her husband was out of town'. There were also deponents who took the problematic condition of walls so much for granted that they felt no need to specify the circumstances of their supervision. Three Southampton women told the watch that they had 'looked through a hole in the wall' and seen Catherine Vallet entertaining John Chawke while her husband was away at sea.[47]

Poor construction was as pervasive a problem as were poor materials. The records of the London Carpenters' Company demonstrate, as Joseph P. Ward says mildly, that 'not all builders who practiced in the metropolis had mastered their crafts'. One complainant found he could 'not lie dry in his bed'. The Company's officers inspected a house made a story-and-a-half taller that had 'sundry defects', including posts too narrow and rafters too slight to carry the raised roof. In the city's close quarters, work on one building often resulted in damage to its neighbor. The Viewers observed the side of a building stripped off, a bay window carried away, and holes broken in a stone wall for the insertion of timber support beams. The search book of the Tilers' and Bricklayers' Company recorded work 'very insufficiently done to the discredit of the Company, which was scoffed at by the plasterers'. In addition, there were projects undertaken by home handymen. Nehemiah Wallington tried to remove some of the crumbling bricks in his chimney himself. When the chimney collapsed it brought down one whole end of his house, rafters and all. He recorded his survival among instances of God's mercy.[48]

Chimneys, like stairs, doors, and other fixtures and fittings, were often associated with structural breaches. Walls were not always built flush to the brick of the stacks, for fear they would catch fire. Thus, Jehanne Guyffine, a Southampton servant, described a 'great hole in the wall by the chimney' between her master's house and that of a neighbor. It was 'covered with a painted cloth so big as this examinate might easily creep in at it'. In London, Madelon Plonkett had a 'chimney which is so made that one may easily see all the other chamber where her sister lay'. Through that hole she witnessed her sister-in-law in bed with a manservant. Nehemiah Wallington described a cold winter when 'we kept a fire continually in the chamber, but the fire burnt down under the hearth and burnt the beam whereon the chimney stood'.

---

[47] GL Ms 9189/2, fo. 84ʳ (Whitehead, 1629). *Book of Examinations and Depositions, 1570–1594*, ed. Gertrude H. Hamilton, Publications of the Southampton Record Society 16 (1914), 30–1 (Vallet, 1577).

[48] Ward, *Metropolitan Communities*, 47–8, 80. *Viewers' Certificates*, nos. 175 (1542); and 286 (1550). GL Ms 3047/1 for 9 October 1606. For Wallington (1626), Seaver, *Wallington's World*, 58–9.

His coals fell through the hole that was created, 'down in the next neighbor's house'.[49]

In his shop, Edmund Alden 'made a partition with painted cloths and so within the said painted cloth set a bedstead and bed'. The greater threat to his privacy, as it happened, was that George Mathew's stairs were 'almost right over' the bed, and Mathew could look 'through a hole' to see Alden with another man's wife. The stairs were probably not boxed in and may have been little more than a fixed ladder with open treads. Like all other fittings, stairs were movable. When they were relocated, though, the old site was not always completely closed. It might appear like 'an well hole or trap door now shut up which hath been cut through the same floor as it seemeth into the rooms over the same'.[50]

Doors were problematic not only for their key and latch holes but also because they were frequently recycled and often ill-fitting. In the hasty construction associated with subdivision, they might be inserted without door-frames. Many were shorter than the openings into which they were roughly fixed. When William Pegden saw two men accompany Elizabeth Busshe up to her chamber, he had little difficulty breaking in even though Elizabeth 'held the door'. He merely 'threw the door on the floor'. In Somerset, an elderly woman watched a girl named Dorothy enter John Morris's house, making his back door 'fast'. Then Morris returned home, locking the front door behind him. The suspicious neighbor 'looked in between the durns and the door'—that is, between the doorframe and the door—in order to observe the two 'enclose themselves together', Dorothy 'put[ting] one of her hands about his neck and the other in his codpiece'.[51] Morris evidently had privacy in mind when he closed his house up, but he needed more than locks and bolts to achieve it.

Third Sort: Built Holes

For those with walls not built against their chimney stacks, fear of fire was a more urgent concern than the protection of privacy. Other types of holes were deliberately introduced in early modern construction, as well. In great houses, for example, platforms were often built atop the screens passages in

[49] See the *Assize of Nuisance*, no. 77, for a chimney built 'too near' a 'party wall, causing danger of fire' in 1305. *Book of Examinations and Depositions* (Southampton), 14–15 (Guyffine, 1576). LMA DL/C/214, fos. 53–8 (Plonkett, 1591); I owe this reference to Gowing, *Domestic Dangers*, 258–61. For Wallington (1628), see GL Ms 204, p. 419.

[50] LMA DL/C/211/1, fo. 191^{r-v} (Mathew, 1573); I owe this reference to Gowing, *Domestic Dangers*, 189. GL Ms 7971 (Viewers' Report of 1598) for the trap door.

[51] BCB-02, fo. 166^{r-v} (Pegden, 1575). G. R. Quaife, *Wanton Wenches and Wayward Wives: Peasants and Illicit Sex in Early Seventeenth-Century England* (London: Croom Helm, 1979), 51–2 (Morris, from Somerset Quarter Sessions records).

Figure 4.7 Squint into the great hall of Cotehele, near Saltash in Cornwall, built *c*.1540.

tall halls. When they were open they were known as 'minstrels' galleries'; when closed, they might be outfitted with a 'squint' into the hall (see Fig. 4.7). Archbishop William Parker welcomed Elizabeth I to 'come in through my gallery, and see the disposition of the hall at dinner-time, at a window opening thereunto'. In 1632 Donald Lupton described squints as 'peeping windows for the ladies to view what doings there are in the hall'. At Drapers' Hall the window in a chamber overlooking the hall was latticed for easy viewing. Below, some great-hall screens were also built with another type of opening, which permitted platters to be passed through. T. F. Hunt describes a door off the passage at Haddon Hall in Derbyshire, 'with a little wicket in the middle, just big enough to put a trencher in or out'. At Tretower Court in Wales, there was a sliding panel for the opening between kitchen and hall.[52]

The new sixteenth-century fashion for symmetrical façades, which were designed independently of interior floorplans, could produce odd mismatches

---

[52] For great-hall squints, see Cooper, *Houses of the Gentry*, 275; Cooper also cites Lupton. Drapers' M.B.1/C, fo. 377ᵛ. T. F. Hunt quotes Parker in *Exemplars of Tudor Architecture* (London: Longman, 1830), 97; on Haddon, 96. Royals and nobles often had small closets near their household chapels, with what Andrew Boorde called a 'prospect' into the chapel. The Drapers' head house had a latticed prospect (M.B.1/C, fo. 377ʳ), and Sir John Petre constructed an opening so members of his family could hear services at some remove from servants, below (Emmison, *Tudor Secretary*, 33; Emmison also quotes Boorde).

between form and function. At Breamore House in Hampshire, for example, upper-level space was divided in such a way that a chamber wall was required inside at the midpoint of a window sited for aesthetic balance outside. From the window sill down, interior and exterior walls met flush, at right angles. But above the window sill, the interior wall stopped short of the exterior wall by about a foot, so that it would not be visible from outside and so that the casement could remain operative. Inside, this created a waist-high opening between the two chambers that was large enough to afford credibility even to such reports as those describing holes a witness could 'thrust' his entire head through.[53]

In London, it was probably the case that new partitions were built with similar disregard for the location of old windows. There, and perhaps even at Breamore as well, neither aesthetics nor privacy was finally as urgent an object as the provision of natural light to both rooms. Dark chambers were a particular hazard of subdivision. Ralph Treswell describes part of an upper-level room in a London tavern left 'open on the floor to give light' to the ground-floor below; in another, 'there wanteth a piece over the entry to give light to the under rooms'. This is also the reason that doors and partition walls were not always built to full height, so that light could pass from the outer chamber, with its window, to an inner one. When Oxfordshire baker Nicholas Hill installed a buttery in one corner of his hall, the two boarded buttery walls were 'each of them latticed' for this purpose, in the 'overpart'.[54]

The practice was common enough to have been itemized as a construction specialization during a proprietary dispute between two London livery companies, the Carpenters and the Joiners. A committee empaneled by the Corporation of London in 1629 spent three years distinguishing the matters 'belonging' to each company. They finally confirmed that the more ancient Carpenters were, in effect, victims of the Great Rebuilding; status work had gravitated away from them. The Joiners were assigned furniture made with mortises and tenons; presses for wearing apparel; wainscotting and paneled doors; church pews and coffins; shop windows requiring glue in construction; and more. The Carpenters were allocated tavern and work tables and stools; flooring, partitioning, and shelving; and various other items that were boarded and nailed, not wainscotted, carved, or glued. On the Carpenters' list was the note: 'we conceive fit that the setting up of all pillars or balusters for lights in a partition of what wood soever if the partition be made by the Carpenters do belong to them but if the partition be of the Joiners making then do belong to

---

[53] Description of Breamore (as also of Tretower Court, above) is from personal observation.

[54] Christ's Hospital Evidence Book no. 9 (Schofield no. 43) and no. 6 (Schofield no. 50). Inventory of Nicholas Hill (1590), M. A. Havinden, *Household and Farm Inventories in Oxfordshire, 1550–1590* (London: HMSO, 1965), no. 247.

them'. In other words, holes were deliberately introduced in partition walls by open rails, to permit the passage of light. Some nonspecific testimonies—like the report of Anne Aylwarde, John Westcote, and John Kevell that they saw Johan Sutton in bed with an unnamed laborer 'through a wall'—may refer to these purpose-built apertures.[55]

Gutter 'windows' were often encountered in the city. These were the openings for drains carrying refuse water through a building, sometimes among multiple tenants, to the outside. The holes were big enough that they were known to permit the entrance of thieves and the egress of runaway apprentices. Francis Barnham was present when a constable presented Agnes Browne at the Bridewell for rendezvousing with Peter Temple. She was 'taken creeping through a gutter window in a single petticoat and her smock' and 'bare-legged'. The Drapers employed a carpenter in their rental property at St Swithins' Lane 'for making of a grate of wood to the gutter window to keep out folks for coming in to the same house as heretofore they have done'. Others tried to secure the holes with special 'doors'; Nehemiah Wallington, in one of his many failed suicide attempts, thought to open his 'gutter door' in order to 'leap out of the gutter into Pudding Lane'. There were obvious alternative uses for openings which were large enough to admit persons; Jone Homffrey employed a 'hole in a wall' to pass an accomplice a carpet, two dozen napkins, two pillowberes, and 'two handfuls of new money and gold' that belonged to her master.[56]

Fourth Sort: Vandalized Holes

John Pedder could count on the known incidence of weakened walls when answering charges in the Kent Quarter Sessions in 1602. He said that he went to Thomas Myllenden's house 'to borrow a kettle and, finding nobody in the said house, he did set his hand against a hole in the wall and the said wall fell down'. There may well have been a hole, although the collapse was undoubtedly less spontaneous than he tried to suggest; he went on to help

[55] CLRO Rep. 46, fos. 361[r]–382[v] (Carpenters). See also Edward Basil Jupp, *An Historical Account of the Worshipful Company of Carpenters of the City of London* (London: William Pickering & Chatto, 1887), Appendix B, pp. 295–9; B. W. E. Alford and T. C. Barker, *A History of the Carpenters' Company* (London: George Allen & Unwin, 1968), 78–81; and Jasper Ridley, *A History of the Carpenters' Company* (London: Carpenters' Hall, 1995), 61–2. On the place of the Turners in this division of the woodworking kingdoms, see Seaver, *Wallington's World*, 114. BCB-02, fo. 103[r] (Sutton).

[56] BCB-01, fo. 97[r] (Browne, 1560); see also BCB-02, fo. 93[v], for an escaping apprentice. Drapers' R.A.5. 1578–9, fo. 12[r]. Seaver, *Wallington's World*, 23 (Wallington). BCB-01, fos. 136[r]–137[r] (Homffrey, 1561). See also BCB-01, fo. 120[r], for a thief 'creeping through a hole' into Thomas Cressy's house; BCB-02, fos. 134[v]–135[r], for a woman escaping a constable by going 'out at a hole in the wall'; BCB-02, fo. 65[v] for a woman escaping the watch 'out at the hole, in her petticoat'.

himself to a kettle, a bowl, two gallons of honey, a pair of sheets, a black hat, two table napkins, and a pound of yarn. In London, the Bridewell governors took testimony about a suspicious house owned by a man named Taylor. He had devised an escape outlet so that 'when any search should be made' any 'suspect persons' could be 'convey[ed] . . . through that hole'. More common motives for such sabotage, though, were probably curiosity and scopophilia. Jehanne Guyffine, the Southampton servant who reported a great hole beside Ralph Robins' chimney, stated also that one day she 'pulled open a painted cloth that was hanged before a hole made between the guest chamber' in Robins's house and the bedchamber of his neighbor's wife. The hole was 'as big as a man's fist'. When Robins saw the cloth pulled back, he demanded to know who had discovered the hole, and was relieved to learn that it was Guyffine and not his wife. He ordered Guyffine to 'go her ways and say nothing', but later he charged her with theft and dismissed her, presumably in order to keep his secret about the peephole.[57]

There was a dense physical reality behind such pornographic literatures as Painter's *Palace of Pleasure*, where multiple stories turn on the device of the hole in the wall: a thief named Ricciardo drugs a Venetian duke's guards, looks through 'a hole of the door' to assure himself that the sleeping potion has taken effect, and then steals some veal; a womanizer named Philenio is locked by an honest wife into a small closet, steps on an unnailed board, falls through to a dark storehouse, but there discovers 'certain vents in the wall which gave some light', and picks at them until he has 'made so great a hole' that he can escape; a servant breaks 'a board between his mistress's chamber and his' own, 'enter[s] in at the hole which he had broken', stabs her repeatedly, and rapes her before she dies. In one of the Friar Bacon stories, the monk's man famously gains secret knowledge of adultery by 'peep[ing] through a chink of the partition' in his hostess's wall. This episode probably inspired Robert Davenport, whose Friar Bernard and Friar John similarly discover a 'cranny' through which they can 'spy' on the doings of a household in the stageplay *A New Trick to Cheat the Devil*. Thomas Nashe describes his alter ego Jack Wilton looking 'through a cranny of my upper chamber unsealed' in order to see a 'sad spectacle' in *The Unfortunate Traveller*. Forobosco, in Fletcher's *Fair Maid of the Inn*, plots to steal a 'mass of gold and jewels' he has seen 'through a chink of wainscot that divides my lodging'.[58]

---

[57] CKS Q/M/SI/1603/3/11, Q/M/SRc/1602/210, Q/M/SB/489 (Pedder, 1602). BCB-02, fo. 142ᵛ (Taylor, 1575). *Book of Examinations and Depositions* (Southampton), 14–15 (Guyffine, 1576).

[58] William Painter, *The Palace of Pleasure*, ed. Joseph Jacobs, 4th edn., 3 vols. (London: David Nutt, 1890): novel 48 (ii. 15); novel 49 (ii. 21–2); novel 50 (ii. 29–31). *The Famous Historie of Fryar Bacon* (London: T. Bensley, 1816), 91–5. Robert Davenport, *A New Trick to Cheat the*

Peepholes provided the grounds for narrative, dramatic, and probably also legal fictions without themselves being necessarily fictional. Such skeptics as Martin Ingram would make much of the imaginary hole described by Susan Makenas, who was presented in the London Bridewell in 1578 for having been 'lately delivered of a child in whoredom'. Her master, Henry Wynborne, was the first to 'examine' her when her pregnancy made itself apparent. She confessed to him that the father of her unborn child was Edward Waynman, servant to Sir Christopher Hatton, and she suggested that she might petition Hatton for relief. But Wynborne told her that there was little purpose to naming Waynman; 'he is able to do nothing for thee'. He then asked in a leading fashion if the prosperous Sir John Smyth 'had not to deal with her'. 'Yea', she said obligingly, subsequently telling the Bridewell governors that she intended thereby 'to please her master and mistress'. Wynborne had already dismissed her from his service, and 'put her away out of doors', and she thought in her 'misery' that if she fell in with his plans he would 'receive her again, and do somewhat for her'. She also alleged that Wynborne then volunteered to corroborate the false paternity claim against Smyth: 'I will say I saw him myself, through a hole.'[59]

Wynborne did not see Smyth with Makenas, but this does not mean that he did not, like so many Londoners, have chinks and crevices in his walls. The mass of evidence suggests that there were indeed holes that were not what Laura Gowing calls 'conventional motifs' or 'legal fictions'. When Thomas Howard's man Charles Bailly was incarcerated in connection with the Ridolfi plot, he suggested a way for others of the conspirators to maintain contact: 'My chamber where I am prisoner doth open upon the street, and under the window there is a little house of some poor man. Almost in the top of the house inward, there is a hole that cometh to my chamber, wherein I may easily thrust my hand.' Bailly would have had no reason to advertise a nonexistent hole as a depository for letters from his fellow conspirators.

Nor did the canny merchants of the Drapers' Company pay out real money for legal fictions when they hired workers for the 'stopping of crevices and joints', for 'daubing up the partition in the Clerk's counting house', for 'mending' floors with deal board, or for building a grate 'to keep out folks for

---

Devil, 3.1. Thomas Nashe, *The Unfortunate Traveller*, in *Thomas Nashe: Selected Writings*, ed. Stanley Wells (Cambridge, Mass.: Harvard University Press, 1965), 254. John Fletcher, *The Fair Maid of the Inn*, 5.1.

[59] BCB-03, fos. 369^v–372^v. Makenas went on to charge that Wynborne himself had been the first to 'abuse' her body. One Mistress Blunte reportedly instructed Makenas to abandon her child at Smythe's door (and urged women in Smythe's neighborhood to conceal her identity from authorities).

coming in to the same house' through a 'gutter window'.[60] For these purposes, financial accounts are disinterested records, offering incontrovertible evidence of myriad occasions for structural breaches and potential peepholes.

WHAT THE SALTERS SAW

The ecclesiastical courts, the Bridewell, and quarter sessions gathered information from witnesses; they did not dispatch agents to authenticate chinks and crevices. Either there was broad acceptance that there were holes in early modern walls, windows, floors, and doors, as is argued here, or, as Martin Ingram believes, there was collusion among all the parties involved, including litigants, defendants, and officers of the courts. Especially in such bitterly disputed cases as those involving fornication, illegitimate pregnancy, broken marital contracts, and sexual slander, this is on the face of it difficult to believe.

In the absence of interrogatories, we cannot know how hard the courts pressed their witnesses for details about the peepholes they employed, though depositions are generally so nonspecific that they seem not to have done so often. Thus, the particular interest of *Reading* v. *Church*. First, from this Archdeacon's Court case in 1630s Leicestershire, the interrogatories are preserved, along with a clerk's notes. Second, more than sixty depositions were taken, so many that, Bernard Capp says, we are able to 'construct a microhistory that illuminates the social dynamics of an entire community'.[61] Third, the central figure, who was accused of committing adultery, did not participate in the sort of cultural fiction that Ingram imagines. Bridget Church took it for granted that her accusers would claim the use of some sort of peephole, but proceedings were so protracted that she was able both to solicit precise information about conditions at the sites of her alleged indiscretions and also to call deponents who would challenge these reports. Her witnesses provided detailed information about the peepholes through which Church's antagonists claimed to have peered.

---

[60] *A Collection of State Papers Relating to Affairs in the Reign of Queen Elizabeth from . . . 1571 to 1596*, ed. William Murdin (London: William Bowyer, 1759), 3–5 (Bailly, 1571). Drapers' R.A.5 1575–6, fo. 18ᵛ; R.A.5 1588–9, fo. 11ᵛ; R.A.5. 1566–7, fo. 19ʳ; R.A.5 1578–9, fo. 12ʳ.

[61] Bernard Capp discusses *Reading* v. *Church* in 'Life, Love and Litigation' (quoting p. 55). I am grateful to him for telling me, in private conversation, that gaps and holes featured so largely in this case. Documents are catalogued as LRO ID 41/4 Box 23, Files 42–54, Files 55–73, and Files 74–81; Box 26, Files 22–6 and File 27; and Box 27, Files 35–6. Interrogatories are from Box 23, File 59; testimonies of the Salters from Box 26, File 22 (and court summary, Box 23, File 74); and testimonies of Oswin, Wilde, Gardiner, Brettle, and Thorpe, from Box 23, File 76.

Church, a grocer's wife, was presented for fornication with Amos Crosley, a clergyman's son; John Morton, a leading local gentleman; and Thomas Thorpe, her own father. She was also said to have flirted provocatively with a chapman. The most significant charges were the first two, because for these there were eyewitnesses John and Isabel Salter. When the liaisons were said to have taken place, Isabel was a maidservant in the Thorpe household and John was her frequent visitor. By the time of the trial, Isabel had been dismissed for pilfering and suspected premarital pregnancy, the Salters had married, and they were dependent on parish charity for housing. In other words, their personal circumstances were sufficiently precarious that they were seen as susceptible to bribery by Thomas Reading, who brought the complaint. Reading had a long history of bad blood with Bridget's husband Thomas Church. He had accused Church of keeping improper accounts as a churchwarden; Church had charged Reading with slander; Reading had sued Church for trespass when a horse strayed; and each man denounced the other's wife for unchastity. Finally, Reading initiated the Archdeaconry allegation.

In consultation with the Churches, the court compiled more than two dozen questions for the Salters. 'To depose to any of the crimes,' one interrogatory opens, 'let him, her, or such witness specify in what manner were such crimes done. Was the party ministrant at such pretended time or times in a bed or upon a bed? Was there any curtains to such bed, and what color were they of?' Further, 'In which house, what room of such house, what place in such room, what year, what month, and week, whether in the day time or the night time, what day or night, what hour of the day or night was the pretended crimes committed or any of them?' Then:

Was the door or window open? Or did he or she see such acts through any *hole* or *open place* of the wall? How many *open places* or *holes* were there in the wall? How big was such place where he or she peeped or looked into the pretended room where such pretended crimes were committed? Did any other person besides this witness look through the said wall or at the door, window, or other pretended place of seeing the said crimes done at one and the same time with this witness, or one after another, or at some other *hole* or *crink* or *chink* in the door, wall, or window?   [emphasis added]

In response to these questions, John Salter deposed that he came to the Thorpe house and searched in vain for Isabel. Upstairs, hearing whispers, he 'peeped (or looked) in over the door thereof (being too short for the doorcase)' and saw Bridget Church and Amos Crosley in bed. Downstairs again, he found Isabel and urged her to creep back up with him. The couple watched Crosley rise on his knees over Bridget, holding his 'privy member' in one hand. Bridget urged Crosley to hurry because she expected both Isabel and her mother home soon. 'Cannot you hit it?' Bridget demanded. 'Yes, straightaways', Crosley replied. 'Immediately' after, Bridget said, 'Why, now you are in.' They were, attested Salter, 'in the very act of generation'. Although Isabel gave substantially the same report, there was sufficient variation to suggest that the two had not been over-coached. Isabel, for example, remembered Crosley as saying, 'Now I am in.' She called the chamber door 'a low one, of about a yard and half high'. She also deposed that Crosley left surreptitiously, 'going out of the said room into the next, and out of that down into the kitchen (by a hole where as seemeth a falling door was formerly) and thence away through the backside'.

A few weeks later, Isabel allegedly beckoned John back into the Thorpe house. The door of the street-level parlor was 'at the jar', 'being about half a foot opened', and the Salters saw Bridget in bed with Morton. In this instance, their testimony was more persuasive for the fact that it was so sketchy. The bed was against the far wall, and the Salters evidently did not hear or see with the clarity they claimed on the earlier occasion. But they appear not to have been tempted to invent further particulars. In fact, it would be easy to conclude that the Salters fell on hard times when Isabel was dismissed not for pilfering but, like the Southampton maidservant who discovered her master's secret peephole behind the painted cloth, for inconvenient knowledge. The Salters were two socially marginal witnesses against the army of more substantial allies produced by the Churches, the Thorpes, and, especially, the wealthy Morton.

Nicholas Oswin, for example, deposed that there was no seeing over the chamber door 'without it be a little glimmering of one of the posts thereof' (he referred to bedposts). Richard Wilde said that the door was hung in such a way that 'there is very little space left'; it was 'hardly an inch's breadth to look in at', and 'two parties would hardly see and look over the door in the upper chamber at one and the same time'. Elizabeth Gardiner maintained that she had personally 'made trial of the chamber door' and 'could not see or perceive any party upon the bed'. According to Wilde, meanwhile, the parlor door would stand open only three inches if not latched, but Gardiner stated that 'the door of the lower parlor will not stand upon the jar without it be forced', and William Brettle agreed that it 'will not stand upon the jar but will full close of itself'. Wilde knew of no changes that had been made in the Thorpe house since the alleged incidents, and William Thorpe attested that 'the doors both of the chamber and parlor do hang in that manner and form as they have for these twenty years last past and have not been altered'.

In the end, Bridget Church was cleared of all charges. As always, there is no knowing if she committed the alleged offenses, whether there were any honest motives in this case or any true declarations, what the Salters actually saw, and how substantial were the gaps at the chamber and parlor. If the doors were as the Salters deposed, though, then privacy in the Thorpe household was yet again a matter of unspoken consensus, a convention which was easily betrayed with sufficient motivation. Ingram makes the important connection between the degree of privacy in early modern life and 'evidence of very close moral surveillance'.[62] On this subject, and for the sake of argument, it is worth supposing that events occurred as the Salters described them. If so, Bridget Church had no illusions about her circumstances; she expected her housemates to monitor her. She seized what she believed to be an unusual opportunity in the briefly unattended house, though she miscalculated with respect to the Salters' activities. But *Reading* v. *Church*, like all these cases, presents us only with negative evidence. We cannot know, to speak locally, how many other men Bridget Church entertained without being caught. She may have successfully maintained her privacy on a greater number of occasions than we can ever recover.

Perhaps, then, it is helpful to think of peepholes from an entirely different perspective. The Reformation opened a public dialogue about private and personal accountability for the spiritual state. Meanwhile, as London repopulated, its residents feared it was becoming more anonymous (a topic of further concern in the next chapter). These were epochal changes and, like all such transitions, were not universally welcomed. To many, in fact, privacy seemed a menace to public well-being. It threatened to deprive people of knowledge to which they thought they were entitled and about which they felt a sense of social responsibility. From this point of view, peepholes are significant not only as evidence of failed construction techniques, poor materials, bad repair, or accidental effects, but also as instruments of resistance. They restored the old communal conventions of shared knowledge and mutual surveillance. Any newly erected boundary could be breached by a defiant chink or cranny.

---

[62] Ingram, *Church Courts*, 244. He refers to Keith Thomas and G. R. Quaife.

5

The Chronicles of Francis Barnham

LET US imagine entries in the minute books of the Drapers' Company and the Court of Aldermen as peepholes in the great temporal wall that separates us from the personalities, transactions, and transgressions that made up everyday life in Tudor London. As administrative accounts, they are generally less biased to the domestically dysfunctional and locally scandalous than are the records of ecclesiastical courts. They are also less forthcoming, rarely including witness depositions or narrative detail. Many of the early Bridewell reports similarly offer terse summaries rather than testimonial evidence. Even at their least informative, however, these London archives demonstrate that through his executive appointments Francis Barnham had an authorized point of access to intimate particulars about the relationships, activities, work products, and living conditions of hundreds of men, women, and children. His various courts were the end destinations for much of the personal information that circulated in Tudor culture, places where shared knowledge and communal surveillance found a social purpose. Municipal institutions legitimated and incited native curiosity as a necessary ingredient for both social order and economic expansion—with the latter, this chapter suggests, being the more urgent objective of Francis Barnham and other leading Londoners. Privacy had less commodity value than did vigilance and the knowledge it produced.

The argument made here concerns powerful instruments of deprivatization in sixteenth-century England. These operated in a time more commonly known to us for its cultivation of interiority, self-examination, and personal responsibility for spiritual health. Alan Sinfield is characteristically astute on reformed religion as an impetus for heightened self-awareness in the period. English Protestants, he remarks, wanted an observance less defined in mediatory agents than was the Roman church, with its sacramental rituals, confessional priests, Latin liturgy, and intercessory saints. They valued direct and immediate experience, which was facilitated by Bible translations that made scriptures accessible to lay readers and by devotional texts published for household consumption. Early moderns 'wished religion to be more *inward*',

Sinfield emphasizes. But, writing also of the 'incoherence' of power which produced the Protestant subject, Sinfield would presumably be the first to acknowledge the cracks that have lately appeared in our governing paradigms about the Reformation and its effects. Ramie Targoff, for example, points out that when the celebrant turned his back on the nave during the Catholic mass, or recited publicly inaudible prayers, he created space for the free play of introspection among his parishioners. The Protestant service was more collective, more directive, and more monitory.[1]

R. H. Helmholz identifies another post-Reformation source of deprivatization in the church's new regulatory functions. Offenses that had once been confided into the ear of a confessor were now aired among the churchwardens, apparitors, summoners, recording clerks, and presiding ecclesiasts of Prerogative, Consistory, Archdeaconry, and Peculiar Courts. The small dark closet of the parish confessional was supplanted by a large liminal space—semi-sacred, quasi-judicial—which was fitted out for its many participants with long benches and a great table (see Fig. 5.1). Even the church-courtrooms themselves did not contain the secrets that were shared there, because the principal parties to their disputes were given copies of witness depositions which, as is known to have happened in *Reading* v. *Church*, might then circulate widely.[2] Through proceedings based in the gathering and reporting of community intelligence, these ecclesiastical arenas encouraged a promiscuous spread of intimate information.

Their more public pieties were also more officious, as vices for which priests had imposed private penance were entered into a forum with powers not only of discipline but also of public punishment. Casual slander, drunkenness, non-observance of the sabbath, swearing, and dice-playing were added to the roster of community concern. In this climate social scrutiny was so thoroughly naturalized that an Essex man who left his wife three farm animals in 1569, to descend to his children after her death, authorized her to sell the cattle only '*if it shall be thought by her honest neighbors* that she be in poverty' (emphasis added). It could seem that the church courts had an army of allies. Alice Pyckeringe was able to charge Anne Parry with slander in the

---

[1] Alan Sinfield, *Faultlines: Cultural Materialism and the Politics of Dissident Reading* (Berkeley: University of California Press, 1992), 152–80 (quoting 154, 174). Ramie Targoff, *Common Prayer: The Language of Public Devotion in Early Modern England* (Chicago: University of Chicago Press, 2001), ch. 1.

[2] R. H. Helmholz, *Roman Canon Law in Reformation England* (Cambridge: Cambridge University Press, 1990), 104–17, esp. 113. Martin Ingram says that depositions were made 'available for scrutiny by both parties' to a dispute in *Church Courts, Sex and Marriage in England, 1570–1640* (Cambridge: Cambridge University Press, 1987), 48; Bernard Capp notes that this happened with *Reading* v. *Church* in 'Life, Love and Litigation: Sileby in the 1630s', *Past and Present* 182 (2004), 75.

Figure 5.1 Consistory Court Room at Chester Cathedral, a gated corral with a large square table, spaces reserved for the officers of the court (including a canopied seat for the presiding judge), and benches to accommodate witnesses, proctors, and apparitors.

London Archdeaconry in part because Edward Godfrey sat in Pyckering's window taking notes as Parry railed against her neighbor. 'Neighbor Parry,' said Elizabeth Roberte, 'take heed what you say, for there is one in Pyckeringe's window that writeth all that you speak.'[3]

As the setting that might conceivably have had the highest resistance to deprivatization, London makes an important test case for this way of understanding the post-Reformation period. The metropolis should have been the most anonymous of places, because its population was so large and transient. Provincial gentry as well as subsistence migrants rotated in and out of its bounds. Many people lived on temporary terms in inns, lodging houses, and leased rooms. Intent nonetheless on maintaining accountability in this volatile urban setting, Francis Barnham and his colleagues placed a high premium on the accumulation of information. Unique to London

---

[3] Helmholz, *Roman Canon Law*, notes the 'wider range of human behaviour . . . subjected to regulation by the ecclesiastical courts after the Reformation', 109–17 (quoting 109). Will of Richard Burne (1569), *Essex Wills (England)*, ii. *1565–1571*, ed. F. G. Emmison (Boston: New England Historic Genealogical Society, 1983), no. 681. GL Ms 9056, fo. 87[r–v] (Roberte, 1566).

was the Bridewell, which instantiated the project to criminalize vice. It was the 'most controversial' of the city's Edwardian charitable and disciplinary foundations, according to Paul Griffiths, because it represented 'an overmighty intrusion into everyday life, running an eye over the most intimate personal matters'.[4]

The Bridewell was also one site of designedly redundant structures of control in the capital: the parish, the ward, the livery companies, the city offices, Parliament, the royal court, and various judiciaries. As has already been seen, some building infractions were reviewed personally by the London Aldermen, some by their Viewers, some by senior members of livery companies, and some by corporate property owners with governing boards, such as that of St Thomas's Hospital. So, too, sexual misconduct was penalized not only by London's Bishop and Archdeacon but also by the city fathers at Christ's Hospital and St Thomas's, as well as the Bridewell; in 1582, John Howes had already observed that 'Bridewell did somewhat abridge the ecclesiastical court of their jurisdiction.' Thus, Jane Squier told the Bridewell governors that her master, a farthingale maker named Gunstone, had fathered her illegitimate child. Gunstone advised her to go to the gate of Alderman Martin Bowes to 'make an outcry' accusing another, wealthier man, and 'if Sir Martin Bowes do refuse to hear thee, go to the Bishop of London'.[5] The point is not the false paternity claim but rather Gunstone's awareness of the overlapping dispensations of the civic and ecclesiastical authorities.

Against this known jeopardy, though, there were presumed benefits—of necessity, for the city's officers were busy men. In an ordinary week Francis Barnham spent Mondays at St Thomas's Hospital or the Bridewell, Tuesdays and Thursdays at the Guildhall, and Wednesdays at Drapers' Hall. His various courts convened in the mornings but could continue into the afternoons, and meanwhile he had also to manage his merchant ventures, his procurements and resales, and his property speculations. For the corporate executives of their time, the reduplicativeness of London governance would have been an unthinkable luxury were it not for their shared convictions about keeping as comprehensive a watch as possible.

This chapter focuses on some of Barnham's more important interventions in the private affairs of other Londoners. They help establish the texture of life in the sixteenth-century city. Because of the nature of the evidence, the selected episodes also represent London's textual life. Carol Kazmierczak Manzione notes with regret that the minute books of Christ's Hospital 'detail facts and

---

[4] Paul Griffiths, 'Contesting London Bridewell, 1576–1580', *Journal of British Studies* 42 (2003), 285.
[5] Howes, *Brief Note*, 72. BCB-01, fos. 195ᵛ–196ʳ (Squier, 1562). See also on this subject Archer, *Pursuit*, 239–40.

decisions, not motivations or interpretations'. And Ian Archer observes that 'the historian can be easily seduced by the formality of the minutes of the proceedings of the aldermen and common councillors into an acceptance of the myth of civic harmony they were designed to perpetuate'.[6] It is true that the aldermen's repertories are often unrevealing; for instance, we know nothing about the petition of a man named John Leake except that one day it was read aloud in the Guildhall, 'and thereupon it was ordered that Sir Rowland Heyward, Master Barnham, and Master Woodroffe, Aldermen, shall consider thereof and make report unto this Court'. There are hundreds of such assignments for which the issues and determinations remain unknown. But there are also more divulgent records, like the Drapers' reports of 1543, which acknowledged heated dissent surrounding the purchase of the Cromwell estate.[7] As will be shown, the governors of the Bridewell allowed their clerk to document their own procedural misgivings. Even in the Repertories we can observe aldermen in the process of inventing certain of their procedures.

Some of these archival peepholes were closed down, it is argued here, by Francis Barnham. He was the first of the Drapers to attempt to shape institutional culture through self-censorship. The minute books of the 1580s and later, so much less rich than those of the 1560s and 1570s, are the end products of lessons he learned in Star Chamber about the double agencies of which social knowledge was capable. It was an instrument that could turn on its managers. Subsequent archival silences are, again, a privacy initiated in the public sphere—the documentary equivalent of closing the parlor door in the Company Hall.

The textual acts of Francis Barnham were dispersed into multiple institutional archives and overwritten with the rhetorical strategies of anonymity, collectivity, amanuensis, and administrative formula. For anyone focused on the *idea* of an author, his are irredeemably corrupt texts. They are also, nonetheless, more sedimented with personality than is much so-called life-writing of the sixteenth century. In the course of mediating other Londoners' personal concerns and disputes, Francis Barnham left behind something approaching a journal of his own life. They show not only what he saw about other people's affairs through his official peepholes but also how he saw and why he looked. In the end, his life was no more anonymous than was that of his fellow Londoners. While Francis Barnham embodied his culture's commitment to shared knowledge and communal surveillance, the very accounts

---

[6] Carol Kazmierczak Manzione, *Christ's Hospital of London, 1552–1598: 'A Passing Deed of Pity'* (Selinsgrove, Pa: Susquehanna University Press, 1995), 39. Archer, *Pursuit*, 40.
[7] CLRO Rep. 18, fol. 249ᵛ (22 July 1574). For the Cromwell estate, see Ch. 3.

that show him to have been in possession of so much private information about others also betray a great deal about his own life and personality.

THE COURTS OF PUBLIC OPINION

John Burton and Alice Clerk were household servants who 'did not only lecherously and filthily abuse themselves but also practiced the spoil and robbery of their master and mistress'. They escaped execution because the poison they put in the family's frumenty, or wheat pudding, did not achieve its purpose. On a scaffold at Cheapside, their two right ears were nailed to the pillory and, after three hours, cut off. The next market day, the same was done with their left ears. Burton and Clerk spent three more days on the pillory and then were stripped, tied to a cart's tail, and 'openly' whipped 'through all the notable streets of London'. Papers were prominently displayed that described 'the effect of their devilish doings'; the 'intent' of this signage was that 'these their wicked doings may be *apparent and known* to the world' (emphasis added).[8] Auricular mutilation communicated the same message for life.

London's chief officers used public punishments strategically, both for their deterrent effects and to lastingly prejudice the 'fame' of transgressors. Exposure was especially important for those charged with bad business practices and consumer fraud. Robert Cockes's potential customers were given fair warning when he was placed on 'a little poor and homely horseback', a basket hanging down behind, with a label reading 'For using this false measure as a bushel and selling diverse things thereby to the great loss of the buyers of the same.' Thomas Allen was set backwards on a horse with a paper announcing that he had wrongly marked various billets. Katheryn Hogson and Agnes Palmer spent an hour on the scaffold for marketing coals rolled in sand, 'not being wholesome'. Cardsharps were pilloried for cheating a husbandman of all his money; one of them was given an extra hour 'for that he blasphemously abused the name of God in denying the evil and detestable fact'. During Francis Barnham's tenure as an alderman, few cases were prosecuted as thoroughly as that of Peter Stone, an 'unlearned' man who pretended to practice physic and who distributed abortifacients 'to the destructions either of the children or of the maidens or of both'. Stone was set backwards on a horse. 'Naked from the middle downwards', he was 'well' whipped by two men, one on each side of the horse, and was then led 'from Bridewell round about the Conduit in Fleet Street, and so down from Fleet

---

[8] CLRO Journ. 17, fo. 129^r.

Street through Cheapside to the stocks and round about the little conduit there and so to the compter in the Poultry'. His tag read 'MINISTERING OF MEDICINES TO THE DESTRUCTION OF MANKIND.'[9]

Punishment was as colorful and propagandistic an element of London's street theater as were royal entries, mayors' processions and pageants, and funerals for the great and powerful. The slogans that were nailed over malefactors' heads or pinned to their clothes defined each infraction for popular understanding: 'FOR PULLING DOWN OF PAPERS SET UP FOR THE ESCHEWING OF THE PLAGUE'; 'FOR COMMITTING OF WILLFUL PERJURY'; 'FOR CONVEYING A WOMAN BY WATER AGAINST HER WILL'; 'FOR DEVISING AND PRACTICING BY COZENS AND WITCHES TO DESTROY AND MURDER HER HUSBAND' (and, for the intended mariticide's accomplices: 'FOR DEVISING AND PRACTICING WITH ALICE LAMBARD BY WITCHCRAFT AND COZENING TO DESTROY THE SAID ALICE'S HUSBAND'). Signs were written in 'great letters' for all to see.[10] As the city's officers enlisted all London residents to monitor the behaviors of their neighbors, so, too, they encouraged them to take an active part in shaming rituals and physical torment. Making evildoers known in the court of public opinion was itself a disciplinary strategy.

Francis Barnham was co-author of these ways of scripting the city. One of the most surprising things about the correctional records of his time is how little routinization they reveal. No punishment was ever described in exactly the same way and no descriptor was ever used twice. Some historians of London emphasize the long-term stability achieved by its leaders; others, the city's unmanageable anarchic energy. For the latter, the aldermen's endlessly inventive sloganeering may seem to betray an extemporizing and reactive governance. It can as easily be seen, however, to demonstrate that the Aldermen were micro-managers to an astonishing degree. They devoted meticulous attention to the business of keeping the city small, personal, and responsive, and they evaluated each case with an eye not only to the transgressor before them but also to the larger purposes of social order.[11]

---

[9] CLRO Rep. 16, fos. 540ᵛ–541ʳ (Cockes, 9 March 1570); Rep. 17, fo. 22ᵛ (Allen, 13 June 1570); Rep. 18, fo. 396ʳ (Hogson and Palmer, 23 June 1575); Rep. 17, fo. 195ʳ (cardsharps, 28 August 1571); Rep. 17, fo. 296ʳ (Stone, 2 April 1572).

[10] CLRO Rep. 17, fo. 1ᵛ (plague, 1 April 1570); Rep. 17, fo. 158ʳ (perjury, 29 May 1571); Rep. 17, fos. 316ʳ–317ʳ (hired kidnappers whose ears were nailed to the pillory—they were 'suffered to pull out the nails with their own hand'—20 May 1572); Rep. 17, fo. 465ʳ⁻ᵛ (Lambard, 14 April 1573). Frank Foster says, 'The purpose was public humiliation' (*Politics*, 90).

[11] Griffiths has emphasized that in criminalizing begging, vagrancy, and prostitution, the Bridewell functioned to 'defin[e] deviance' for the period. Innovation is not surprising in an institution that, as he points out, was both new to London and unique to it, a prison, hospital, shelter, and workhouse; see 'Meanings of Nightwalking in Early Modern England', *The*

The city fathers knew that public knowledge was not always biddable; in particular, they were aware that their decisions redounded to their own prestige. They were willing to pillory a servingman named Glascock 'FOR SPEAKING OF VERY HEINOUS AND SEDITIOUS WORDS AND FOR SPEAKING AGAINST THE QUEEN'S MAJESTY'S CITY of LONDON', as also Gryffyn Ap Ryce 'FOR SLANDERING OF THE LORD MAYOR and COURT of ALDERMEN.' But they sent Elizabeth Bradley to the Bridewell to be whipped. They may not have wanted to provide a more public platform for her 'wish' to see the Lord Mayor 'in hell'; 'he was the cause that bread and coals was so dear that she could get none'.[12] Confronted with other provocative accusations, or with a culprit of substance, they could discreetly impose an especially private punishment, a fine, rather than feed the beast that was early modern 'fame'.

As shown in a 1560s case involving Giles Lambert, institutions had contingent reputations, too. Lambert's complaint had begun in an uneasy relationship between master and apprentice, turned into a conflict between an under-age heir and his designated trustee, and then exploded into open accusations against the Drapers which, in effect, put their own credit on trial. The story has been told by Retha Warnicke in terms of the defiance Lambert showed a London livery company and without any mention of Francis Barnham.[13] In fact, Barnham kept a low profile in the matter, but he may have played the most important role of all when the Company emerged not only undamaged in the court of Star Chamber but also that of public opinion.

Barnham was six years a member of the Assistants in 1564, when it became known that Lambert had a grievance against his former master John Calthorp (brother to Martin Calthorp and uncle to Judith Calthorp, who was later to be Martin Barnham's second wife). Lambert's father John was a past Master of the Drapers, an alderman, erstwhile Sheriff of London, and wealthy merchant. At

---

Seventeenth Century 13 (1998), 214–15; 'Contesting London Bridewell', 286–7. But from within the more venerable institution of London's executive branch, the aldermen were engaged in their own ongoing attempts to devise effective responses to urban disorder. Steve Rappaport remarks their 'extraordinary attention to detail' in such other matters as 'repairing walls and gates, paving streets, mending conduits, cleaning ditches and privies', paying workers, 'organising fire brigades, provisioning the city with grain, providing some support for those who could not care for themselves' (*Worlds*, 179, 181).

[12] CLRO Rep. 16, fo. 508ᵛ (Glascock, 14 October 1569); Rep. 19, fo. 3ᵛ (Ap Ryce, 8 November 1575); Rep. 18, fo. 90ᵛ (Bradley, 15 October 1573).

[13] The following narrative draws upon Drapers' M.B.8, fos. 9ʳ⁻ᵛ, 19ʳ, 20ᵛ, 48ᵛ, 249ʳ; PRO STAC 5/L3/30, STAC 5/L7/21, STAC 5/L8/28, STAC 5/L11/27, STAC 5/L16/29, STAC 5/L26/27, STAC 5/L32/29, STAC 5/L40/5, STAC 5/L47/4, STAC 7/13/26. And see Retha M. Warnicke, 'A Dispute among the Freemen of the Drapers' Company in Elizabethan London', *Guildhall Studies in London History* 1 (1974), 59–67.

John Lambert's death in 1554,[14] he named Calthorp to oversee his properties until his two minor sons achieved their majorities, and both came to suspect mismanagement of the estate. Giles, the younger, turned 21 in 1559 but was not made free until 1564. This was a long incubation period for rancor and resentment. Because Calthorp was a former warden who enjoyed the privileges of the Drapers' parlor, Lambert believed he could not get a fair hearing there.[15] He prepared to take his charges to the Lord Mayor of London. But the officers of the Company had a known prerogative to put their own house in order, especially so as to disburden other courts of their internal disputes, and John Calthorp seized the advantage by himself preemptively seeking to be heard by his colleagues on the Court of Assistants.[16]

The officers asked each complainant to agree on pain of £500 that he would accept the ruling of William Beswicke, John Broke, Nicholas Wheeler, and Matthew Colclough, four of the Assistants who were appointed 'arbitrators'. If mediation failed, then John Quarles, Sir William Chester, and John Minor would stand as 'umpires'. Lambert accepted these conditions, which, as was explained in another Drapers' case, obligated complainants to 'bear and behave themselves friendly and brotherly to the other' after mediation.[17] But Lambert soon developed a fierce animosity towards the first of the umpires. For one thing, Quarles encountered Lambert on the street shortly after the officers agreed to intervene, and he 'admonished' Lambert in what he termed a 'friendly' manner to 'consider of the matter to the end he might be able to answer the said John Calthorp truly and substantially'. For another, when Calthorp was later awarded £50, moneys were exchanged in Quarles's own house. Quarles insisted that there were innocuous explanations for both events: for the first, he cut through corporate bureaucracy to, he joked, play the beadle himself; for the second, his residence in one of the Cromwell properties that adjoined the Company Hall made for a convenient and prudent alternative to the open street. To Lambert, however, the advice was arrogant and patronizing; the exchange, secretive and collusive. Common as it was for business to be conducted outside such dedicated places as shops

---

[14] Death noted by Henry Machyn, *The Diary of Henry Machyn, Citizen and Merchant-Taylor of London, from A.D. 1550 to A.D. 1563*, ed. John Gough Nichols, Camden Society 42 (1848), 67.

[15] John Calthorp was elected Second Warden on 7 October 1556, to replace Richard Champion in that office, when Champion was elected Alderman (Drapers' M.B.5, fo. 98^r).

[16] A. H. Johnson cites from Drapers' M.B.8: 'If any brother find him grieved with another that they first complain to Master Wardens before any other place' (*History*, ii. 286). Foster recognizes the advantage that Courts of Assistants tended to work more quickly than did courts of common law, and at less expense to the complainants (*Politics*, 48). But Joseph P. Ward points out that appeals to the Crown (and, implicitly, other courts) worked to 'restrain' the oligarchic tendencies of livery-company officers (*Metropolitan Communities*, 74).

[17] Dispute between Bate and Pryor, Drapers' M.B.8, fos. 80^v–82^v.

and livery halls, the monetary transfer seemed from Lambert's perspective to have been contaminated with conspiracy by its sojourn in the private sphere.

At issue was Lambert's allegation that Calthorp owed him £150 in maintenance money from his minority. Calthorp countered that Lambert had borrowed—and not returned—£237. Lambert insisted that this was not a loan but instead income due him from rents on the property he had inherited. As Lambert had feared, however, the arbitrators decided so easily for Calthorp that they made no recourse to the umpires. They voided the orphanage money of £150, required Lambert to repay Calthorp £200 (of the £237), and then, when Lambert's reaction was fiery enough to see him committed to ward, declared his £500 bond forfeit. Although he secured his release by giving them a pot worth £10 to hold in pawn, Lambert remained indignant. He continued to complain both about Calthorp's stewardship of his estate and about the Drapers' complicity with Calthorp. In 1567 he slandered one of the mediators, William Beswicke; wardens Francis Barnham and John Thoroughgood assessed a fine of £5. When Lambert refused to pay the penalty, he was returned to prison. He offered up another pawn and was freed again.

Lambert then made good his original threat to go outside the Company by appealing to the Lord Mayor of London, Sir Roger Martin. On 17 November 1567 the four wardens of the Drapers' Company reported to Martin's house, where Lambert's charges were 'very long disputed and debated there on both sides'. The Drapers presented written testimony from Barnham and Thoroughgood regarding the 'just causes' for the outstanding £5 fine; Martin upheld their decision. But finally he 'prayed' the Wardens 'that they would be good to the young man, the plaintiff, and give him leave to sue for his right'. Over the Drapers' fierce objections to this impeachment of their entitlement, he ruled that the Court of Aldermen would hear Lambert's complaint. Martin imposed as a condition, however, that Lambert should make peace with the Drapers by, first, paying the outstanding £5 fine that Barnham and Thoroughgood had assessed and, second, offering a written 'submission' that he would from henceforth behave 'as a good, obedient, and loving brother should do, and that unfeignedly'.

Lambert presented the Drapers with the required statement. The Assistants declined to accept it. Rather than confining himself to what they considered to be the issue at hand, his impudence, he had insisted on 'mingling' in his own grievances 'very intricately', stubbornly charging the officers of the Company with 'unequal dealing', and asking still for 'due remedy' of the 'wrong' done him.

May it please your worships, I am come according to the request of my Lord Mayor and mine own duty to submit myself to the laws and ordinances of this house and to your worships (which for the time have the execution of the same credited unto you) as I have oftentimes heretofore done, beseeching you to pardon whatsoever in heat of speech or otherwise hath passed me, and praying you forasmuch as this whole unquietness hath grown by the unequal dealing of some of this brotherhood that with your favors I may prosecute against them before my Lord Mayor in the Court of Aldermen for due remedy of my wrong in that part sustained. Hereof, if it shall please you to have consideration, I doubt not but in the whole sequel of my conversation amongst you to show myself as I have always sought to be, a conformable and obedient member of this company.[18]

Lambert made a second submission that was similarly rejected. His only success with the Board of Aldermen was to involve this submission, which Sir Roger Martin believed the Drapers should have accepted.

'It must have seemed', writes Warnicke, 'that the livery company and its system were on trial and in a sense that was the case. . . . Neither [the Drapers] nor, indeed, the officialdom of the other livery companies, with whom they shared power in the City, could afford for them to lose in this challenge to their authority.'[19] The Corporation of London relied on the livery companies in countless ways. The Aldermen could not have answered the Crown's call for soldiers and subsidies, or set watches in times of unrest, or provisioned the city with grain, or maintained its infrastructures, had they not been able to delegate to and rely upon the companies.[20] While from this point of view the Aldermen's determination seems foreordained, the Drapers nonetheless took the trial seriously. They could count on the interests and values they shared with the other merchants on the Court of Aldermen, but they knew also to exploit the advantage of their records. Barnham was one of those who searched the Drapers' treasure house for 'copies of all the whole acts and process in our Hall from the beginning of this matter until this present day'. The documents they compiled included Giles Lambert's complaint, John Lambert's will, a letter from the absent John Calthorp, the allegedly unhumble submissions, 'and also' the 'attestation . . . of Master Barnham and Master Thoroughgood' about the slandering of William Beswicke.

For Lambert, the court of next resort was Star Chamber. There, his long hostility to the Company elite finally came to the forefront. It was not a venue for the recovery of debts, nor indeed for censure of Calthorp; instead, Lambert

---

[18] Drapers' M.B.8, fo. 9ᵛ. PRO STAC 5/L8/28. Submissions were intended to indicate humility; one apprentice, for example, was described in 1560 as making his submission 'upon his knees' before the Assistants and livery (Drapers' M.B.7, p. 221).

[19] Warnicke, 'Dispute', 64.   [20] Rappaport, *Worlds*, 191.

alleged conspiracy on the part of the arbitrators and umpires.[21] Implicitly, he asked Elizabeth's Privy Councillors and her two Chief Justices to open the door to the parlor at Drapers' Hall. John Calthorp was bankrupt, Lambert attested (in fact Calthorp was at the time in debtors' prison), and Calthorp's brother Martin, an Assistant since 1562, would have been liable for the £150 orphanage money had his fellow officers not voided it. The £200 he was forced to repay John Calthorp, Lambert charged further, was distributed among the arbitrators in bribes. And, finally, the £500 bond he forfeited was awarded to Quarles, because Calthorp also owed Quarles money.[22] In an investigation that continued for two full years and called upon thirty-five deponents, there were also many collateral tales and charges. Calthorp, for example, refused to give an accounting for £40 disbursed on repairs to the Lambert properties 'in secret manner'; he 'beseeched the court not to urge him to disclose the same'. One witness remembered a dispute that dated back to Lambert's apprenticeship, when he was Calthorp's factor in France.[23] But the central allegation, as Quarles summarized, was that the Drapers were 'corrupt persons' who had 'spoiled the complainant of his goods and divided the same amongst them as a spoil, booty, or share'. Quarles countered forcefully that 'nothing of this shall be found true'. The prediction was accurate.

Among the last of the men deposed, on 23 January 1570, was Francis Barnham.[24] Unlike those who were formally named in the indictment and who took pains to appear forthcoming, he was cagey. Of twelve interrogatories, Barnham answered just four. Lambert was committed to ward, he said, in consequence of his own disobedience, 'not by the procurement of anyone otherwise'. When asked why Lambert was so often called to Drapers' Hall for discipline 'and yet no end made' despite 'four years continually in trouble', Barnham repeated that Lambert was 'the only cause, by his disorder'. To a third question, Barnham admitted that Lambert had 'no voice' in the Company, but again this was because he refused to 'show himself a conformable brother'. Barnham depicted the Drapers as always ready to see signs of amendment, and he denied that Lambert had been dismissed from the fellowship. Regarding

[21] Star Chamber was 'a court open to private litigants—indeed, a pawn to the demands of the private litigant', according to Thomas G. Barnes ('The Archives and Archival Problems of the Elizabethan and Early Stuart Star Chamber', in *Prisca Munimenta: Studies in Archival and Administrative History Presented to A.E.J. Hollaender*, ed. Felicity Ranger (London: University of London Press, 1973), 144).

[22] There were reports that Calthorp had borrowed money from the City of London on the estate of orphans named Watson, and that Quarles had married one of the Watson orphans; see below for more on the Aldermen's Court of Orphans.

[23] T. S. Willan reports the tendency to use apprentices as factors in foreign countries (*Studies in Elizabethan Foreign Trade* (Manchester: Manchester University Press, 1959), 4, 12).

[24] PRO STAC 5/L40/5; Warnicke seems not to have known the collection of interrogations and examinations in which Barnham's examination is to be found.

the Company's authority and policies, Barnham said finally, it was customary that any two drapers 'in question' should bring their dispute to the Assistants. 'If either of them shall refuse their order and so prosecute the law court', then a fine might be imposed 'to the intent that example may be given to others to be conformable' to the officers' determinations. Thus Barnham answered only the interrogatories that allowed him to deliver a consistent message about Lambert's bad behavior and the Drapers' good governance. Otherwise, he three times claimed a failure of memory and three times stated that he could 'say nothing' responsive. Twice, he 'referr[ed] himself to the order of their Register Book of their Court [of Assistants] made for this and like causes'.

In May 1571 Lambert's suit in Star Chamber was finally dismissed. No damages were awarded. Because the decision was taken 'without prejudice', says Warnicke, Lambert was free to pursue the estate issues at yet another of the many judicial venues, the common law.[25] He appears not to have done so; instead the 'little man' with the 'red beard', as he was described by one witness, disappeared from public view. His older brother, by contrast, was to develop some early modern celebrity. William, who testified in Star Chamber on Giles's behalf, had produced his father's receipt books to prove a loss in rent, deposing that he himself had been forced to seek redress from the Court of Requests for his inheritance, and saying also that he had assisted Giles by authoring the complaint to the Aldermen as well as the much-debated submissions to the Drapers. William Lambert had considerable legal acumen, having in 1567 been called to the bar at Lincoln's Inn. As author of the first county study, *The Perambulation of Kent* (1576), and of the foundational textbook on the duties of Justices of the Peace, *Eirenarcha* (1582), he is best known by an alternate spelling of his name, William Lambarde.[26]

Retha Warnicke assumes that Lambarde did not share his brother's conspiracy theories, but she has no more particular way of accounting for the fact that, in the 1570s, Lambarde endowed an almshouse in Kent and entrusted its governance to the Drapers' Company.[27] John Quarles was Master when the agreement was executed, in November 1574, but it was certainly not

[25] Warnicke, 'Dispute', 65.

[26] See Retha M. Warnicke, *William Lambarde, Elizabethan Antiquary, 1536–1601* (London: Phillimore, 1973); and the Oxford *DNB* entry for William Lambarde. It was to Lambarde that Elizabeth I reportedly remarked in 1601, 'I am Richard II, know ye not that?' He died fifteen days later.

[27] Lambarde entrusted the almshouse to the Upper Wardens specifically. The building of Queen Elizabeth College was begun in 1575; residents were first admitted on 18 October 1576. A. K. Sierz, former archivist to the Drapers' Company, calendars materials relating to the founding and governance of the house in 'Drapers' Company Records: List of Trust Documents', Part III. For the college's ordinances and statutes, see Johnson, *History*, i. 181; ii. 158–9. See also

Quarles who effected the rapprochement between Company and benefactor. Lambarde moved in the same Kentish circles as did Francis Barnham; in 1590, he was to serve as executor for Robert Rudston, father of Martin Barnham's first wife. Thus it happened that on 3 February 1574 Barnham addressed an assembly of Drapers, reading a list of 'certain requests [to] which Master William Lambarde desired to have answer'. Francis arranged for two wardens to 'repair' to Lambarde the next day, not only to 'satisfy him in the things he required' and thus finally to put to rest any lingering suspicions Lambarde may have held about the Company, but also, further, 'to declare unto him the good opinion that the Company here assembled had of him'.[28]

It was in Lambarde's interest to find an organization willing to take on the administrative burdens of the almshouse, but it was also to the Drapers' benefit to receive this highly visible affirmation of confidence in their governance. When the younger Lambert insisted on lodging his accusations outside the Drapers' parlor, he made the decision to take a private matter—or so the Assistants would have preferred to think of it—public. Like so many other events in the small world of London's civic culture, his complaint became a commodity in the market of common knowledge. But Francis Barnham, who knew that fame was as much a matter for institutions as for individuals, had his own way of courting popular opinion. The enlargement of the Drapers' charitable portfolio was a wildly improbable end to the case of Giles Lambert, transforming a short-term scandal into long-term validation and protecting the Drapers' image as good public citizens.

THE COURT OF ORPHANS

Francis Barnham can also be glimpsed, though dimly, on the fringes of another, more notorious event in London's sixteenth-century history.[29] He was an alderman when Anne Saunders conspired to kill her merchant-taylor

---

M. A. Greenwood, *The Ancient Plate of the Drapers' Company* (London: Humphrey Milford, Oxford University Press, 1930), 15–16.

[28] Drapers' M.B.8, fo. 249[r].

[29] The principal sources on the Saunders murder are John Roche Dasent (ed.), *Acts of the Privy Council of England*, 32 vols. (London: HMSO, 1890–), viii. *1571–75*, 91, 92, 94, 96, 105, 121, 142; and Arthur Golding, *A Brief Discourse of the Late Murder of Master G. Saunders* (London: 1573). Golding is reprinted by Charles Dale Cannon in his edition of *A Warning for Fair Women* (The Hague: Mouton, 1975), Appendix D; subsequent references are to this edition. See also E. St John Brooks, 'A Pamphlet by Arthur Golding: The Murder of George Saunders', *N&Q* 174 (12 March 1938), 182–4; and Joseph H. Marshburn, ' "A Cruell Murder Donne in Kent" and its Literary Manifestations', *Studies in Philology* 46 (1949), 131–40.

husband. Anne's lover George Browne was arraigned for the murder of George Saunders at the King's Bench on 17 April 1573. He was hanged in chains at Smithfield three days later. Her own trial was delayed due to her advanced pregnancy; she was delivered and churched before she was condemned at the Guildhall on 6 May. Executed with her on 13 May were her co-conspirators Anne Drury (a neighbor) and Roger Clement (Drury's manservant). George Mell, a minister who tried to bribe Drury to accept all blame, watched the hangings from a nearby pillory. The 'paper pinned upon [Mell's] breast' read 'For practicing to color the detestable facts of George Saunders' wife.' As Arthur Golding was to report in one of the first English murder pamphlets, 'almost the whole field and all the way from Newgate was as full of folk as could well stand one by another. And besides that, great companies were placed both in the chambers near abouts (whose windows and walls were in many places beaten down to look out at) and also upon the gutters, sides, and tops of the houses and upon the battlements and steeple of St Bartholomew's.' The Earls of Bedford and Derby were in attendance, and so surely were the officials of the Guildhall, the London Aldermen. The homicide brought the four Saunders children into their fiscal custody as 'orphans of the city'.

In public culture, the sensation of 1573 had a long afterlife. Golding's *Brief Discourse of the Late Murder of Master George Sanders, a Worshipful Citizen of London* was published immediately that year and reprinted in 1577. The story was retold in Holinshed's *Chronicles* (1577 and 1587), Stow's *Annals* (first issued in 1592), an undated ballad ('The Woeful Lamentation of Mistress Anne Saunders'), and the crime omnibuses *A View of Sundry Examples Reporting . . . All Memorable Murders Since the Murder of Master Sanders by George Browne* (1580) and *A World of Wonders, A Mass of Murders* (1595). Most famously, the murder was staged in the domestic tragedy *A Warning for Fair Women* (published in 1599 but probably performed by the Lord Chamberlain's Men some years earlier).[30] If the Aldermen shared the popular fascination with infamous crime, disordered households, and the moral meanings of private lives, however, this does not surface in their records. For them, the fallout was financial.

Walter, Thomas, Elizabeth, and George Saunders appear among many hundreds of children whose estates were supervised in the city's Court of Orphans.[31] When any man who was free of the city died with children in their

---

[30] Cannon also excerpts and reprints Stow (Appendix E) and Holinshed (Appendix F).

[31] In the following discussion, I am indebted to Charles Carlton, *The Court of Orphans* (Leicester: Leicester University Press, 1974); and to P. E. Jones, 'Orphanage', CLRO Research Paper number 7.33.

minorities, even if their mother was still alive, the mayor and Aldermen became guardians to his heirs. They required the deceased's executors to produce men who were willing to stand surety that inheritances would be forthcoming when the orphans came of age (four men for every £300). Thus, Alice Barnham appeared before the Court of Orphans in 1577, seconded by her son Steven, Thomas Herdson, William Gilborne, Nicholas Wheeler, and George Utley, and presenting inventories and sureties on the 17-year-old Benedict's behalf (these do not survive).[32]

Alternately, the Aldermen could take the freeman's assets into the Chamber of London until his heirs achieved their majority. Funds held by the Chamber were put to use, lent out to merchants like Roger Sadler. For the borrowers, these were low-interest loans that fueled economic expansion. For the orphans, the earned interest constituted 'finding money', funds for their feeding, housing, clothing, and education. In this way, when orphans came of age they received their inheritances intact, undiminished by daily expenditures in the interim. Estate administration expanded significantly during Francis Barnham's aldermanship; the number of cases in the 1560s was four-and-a-half times that of the 1540s. It was not so much in consequence of population growth, according to Charles Carlton, as of the increasing wealth of London's freemen.[33] And the cultivation of wealth in its varied biographies and projects—as made by an individual merchant, as sheltered for the long-term benefit of his heirs, as invested to the short-term profit of other freemen, and as aggregated to promote London's economic growth—was the principal business of the Court of Orphans.

London's inheritance law called for a man's estate to be divided in thirds, with one-third for the widow, one-third to be shared among his children, and one-third to be distributed at his discretion (as indicated in his will or in deathbed directions). Where the City of London played a custodial role, the Common Sergeant was responsible for sorting out the thirds. In the Saunders case, one of London's sheriffs jumped to claim the widow's share for the city, 'by reason of the felony committed by her'—this was the crime's sole citation in the Aldermen's records.[34] However, George Saunders's brother Francis was unpersuaded that murder should so alter custom as to cause family moneys to be redirected to city coffers. He agreed to place the mariticide's forfeited 'third' in arbitration with the Court of Aldermen.

---

[32] CLRO Rep. 19, fo. 183[r] (14 March 1577).   [33] Carlton, *Court of Orphans*, 23.
[34] For the Saunders orphans, see CLRO Rep. 18, fos. 33[r] (25 June 1573), 94[r] (22 October 1573), 108[r] (24 November 1573), 123[r] (14 December 1573), 134[r]–135[v] (14 January 1574), 144[r] (28 January 1574), 144[v] (4 February 1574), 159[v]–160[r] (18 February 1574), 217[v] (27 May 1574), 334[v] (27 January 1575); Rep. 19, fos. 35[v]–36[r] (31 January 1576), 92[v] (3 July 1576), 104[r] (24 July 1576), 177[v] (5 March 1577), 186[v] (26 March 1577), 189[v] (28 March 1577). Quoting from Rep. 18, fo. 33[r].

As is so often the case in these records, the determination was not explicitly recorded, but Francis Barnham and his fellows seem to have decided for Saunders.[35] On 14 January 1574, the homicide's brother gave 'his' third part of George Saunders's goods to the orphans, declaring that he did so 'of his own mere and voluntary good will'. Francis Saunders would have had title to this portion of the estate under only two conditions. The first possibility was that the murder victim had made his brother heir to the entire third that was his to allocate. Unexpected as his death was, it is not surprising that George Saunders seems not to have made a will. The second possibility was that Francis Saunders had won the widow's third against the claim of the sheriff. He delivered £600 to the executors of the Saunders estate, on condition that the moneys would revert to him if all the orphans should die in their minorities and childless ('as God forbid'). There were further negotiations regarding the amount of child support the estate would provide.[36]

The Aldermen were also concerned to recover debts owed the estate. In 1577, the city Chamberlain received £100 from Richard Tottell. Because Tottell was identified as a stationer, there is small doubt that he was the printer who is now best remembered as the compiler of the most important verse anthology in Tudor England, the 1557 'songs and sonnets' by Surrey and Wyatt which is otherwise known as *Tottell's Miscellany*. Blase Saunders, a London grocer and importer of Spanish goods, also had evidence that nearly £460 from George Saunders's estate had been withheld by a former factor in Spain, Anthony Totto.[37] When Totto returned to England, Blase Saunders took the initiative to have him imprisoned in Ludgate for the amount still due, nearly £255. But Totto's allies appealed to Francis Saunders, arguing that Totto, 'a very poor man', could not begin to repay the estate as long as he was incarcerated and 'miserably like to die in prison'. 'If the case were mine own', Saunders wrote to the Aldermen, he would 'consent to this enlargement'. Because

---

[35] The Saunders family was a substantial and influential one; Francis and George were first cousins to both Edward Saunders, Chief Baron of the Exchequer, and Alice Saunders, mother of Sir Christopher Hatton.

[36] In his will of 1584 (PROB 11/68), Francis Saunders confirmed that he had fulfilled his part of the bargain, paying £600 into the Chamber of London as well as goods worth an additional £600. He also made bequests of £54 to each of the three orphans who were still minors at the time of his death.

[37] CLRO Rep. 18, fo. 186[v]. Barnham crossed paths with Tottell on at least two other occasions; see Rep. 18, fos. 275[v] (7 October 1574) and 378[v] (26 April 1575). He was also an alderman when Blase Saunders was commissioned to procure winter food stores for 1573, Rep. 18, fos. 59[v]–60[r]; see Ch. 1 (n. 32). For Blase, see also T. S. Willan, *The Muscovy Merchants of 1555* (Manchester: Manchester University Press, 1953), 121–2. In 1570 Blase was made Garbler of Spices in London. When he died in 1581 with his term unexpired, Walsingham intervened to protect the interests of his widow.

the debt was owed to the orphans, not to him, Saunders again deferred to the city, requesting only that he not be held liable should the estate not be made whole. On 24 July 1576 the Court liberated Totto, requiring him to sign a bond for the moneys, to be repaid over fourteen years.[38] Of necessity, the Aldermen took a long view, considering the limits on Totto's earning potential and also the extreme youth of the Saunders orphans. It would be nearly eighteen years before the last-born would come of age. Francis Barnham saw the claim of the sheriff settled and the controversy with Totto broached, but he died in May 1576, long before any Saunders orphan achieved majority.

If the murder of George Saunders represented a disruption of the compacts and hierarchies that were believed to stabilize the order of the cosmos, and if his wife's active complicity reinvigorated always-latent fears of the power of women, none of this surfaces in the Aldermen's accounts. The homicide achieves notice only as an unusual source of economic opportunity—one finally forborne as the Aldermen honored prevailing codes of merchant solidarity. The social and political meanings of *A Warning for Fair Women* are similarly emptied out of other archives. In the vestry minute book for his parish of St Dunstan in the East, the death of Saunders was noticed merely because he was unable to complete his term as Collector for the Poor; one of the previous year's collectors was pressed back into service.[39] Execution of the homicides was postponed from a Saturday till the following Monday not for any legal reason but for an economic one: 'the book of Master Saunders' accompts and reckonings, whereupon depended the knowledge of his whole state, was missing', and it was 'desired and sought for to the behoof of Master Saunders' children'. The insistence of real-world concerns surfaces in the subplot of George Mell's infatuation with Saunders's widow, too. Mell promised to fund a marriage portion for Anne Drury's daughter if Drury would falsely exonerate Anne Saunders.[40]

The difference between the received history of the admonitory playtext and the fiscal concerns of city figures demonstrates how reductive each was in its own way. *A Warning* embraced sensation as a vehicle for delivering the moral messages of prescriptive literature, and the Repertories ignored it as irrelevant to the balance sheets and payouts of a very complicated estate. The city fathers went about their public business which, at base, was business.

[38] The agreement was for Totto to pay £4. 10s. 4d. on 6 August 1578; £10 on 6 August 1579; and then £20 on each 6 August for the next twelve years.

[39] GL Ms 4888, 22 June 1572 and 21 June 1573; Saunders had also leased property from the church, 30 November 1571 and 5 December 1571.

[40] Golding, *Brief Discourse*, 220–1.

DISENTANGLING ELIZABETH HYNDE

Children with inheritances had commodity value in Tudor England. The Barnhams themselves fostered two orphans, but neither was the foundling Charity of God. Francis and Alice were builders of wealth and enactors of an emergent class consciousness, not sentimentalists. Thus, they took in the daughters of merchants who came with their own means of support, such as Helen Kettle.[41] Helen's clothworker father died in March 1574. Her mother was already well known to the city fathers for a dispute with a grocer's wife in which she displayed such 'unwomanly usage and behavior' that she was consigned to Newgate. When a servant made fresh complaints against the widow Kettle and her new husband, Francis was one of four aldermen who decided to remove from her custody both Kettle's personal papers and his two under-age daughters. In January 1575, Helen was placed with the Barnhams for a month. Nearly two years later she was still in the house on St Clement's Lane and Alice, herself recently widowed, made her second appearance before the Court of Aldermen in as many months. She claimed unpaid 'finding money'. The Aldermen ruled that, indeed, 'she the said Mistress Barnham hath by all the said time at her proper costs and charges maintained and kept' the daughter of William Kettle.[42]

The earlier and shorter stay of Elizabeth Hynde was more dramatic. On 1 August 1572, Hynde was lodged in the Barnham household with an unusual proviso, that 'none shall have access unto her in the mean time as a suitor in marriage without the license of this Court first had and obtained'.[43] By 28 August this prohibition was modified when Randall Hurleston, 'cousin german' to Hynde's father, was given visitation rights. Even Hurleston, though, was never to be alone with the girl. One or two aldermen were detailed to 'hear

---

[41] For Helen Kettle, see CLRO Rep. 18, fos. 27[r] (16 June 1573), 172[r] (9 March 1574), 225[r] (15 June 1574), 235[r] (1 July 1574), 237[v]–238[r] (12 July 1574), 250[v] (27 July 1574), 330[v] (20 January 1575), 354[v] (8 March 1575), 362[v] (22 March 1575), 364[r] (26 March 1575), 381[v] (3 May 1575), 407[r] (21 July 1575); Rep. 19, fo. 6[v] (15 November 1575), 56[v] (15 March 1576), 135[v] (6 November 1576), 138[r] (13 November 1576).

[42] CLRO, Rep. 19, fos. 135[v] (6 November 1576), 138[r] (13 November 1576).

[43] For Elizabeth Hynde (daughter of Clothworker and alderman Augustine Hynde), see CLRO Rep. 17, fos. 355[v] (1 August 1572), 358[r–v] (26 August 1572), 359[v] (28 August 1572), 361[r]–362[v] (2 September 1572), 363[r] (4 September 1572), 364[v]–365[r] (9 September 1572), 366[r] (11 September 1572), 367[r] (16 September 1572), 370[v] (23 September 1572), 375[r] (7 October 1572), 376[v] (9 October 1572), 398[r] (18 November 1572), 400[r] (20 November 1572), 403[r] (25 November 1572), 405[v] (27 November 1572), 416[v] (11 December 1572), 427[r] (20 January 1573), 464[r] (14 April 1573). On Augustine Hynde, see Alfred B. Beaven, *The Aldermen of the City of London*, 2 vols. (London: E. Fisher for the Corporation of the City of London, 1908–13), i. 131, 156; ii. 32, 215. His burial was noted by Machyn, *Diary*, 67.

what communication shall be had betwixt' them. Hurleston soon petitioned 'to talk and confer with' Elizabeth more freely and more frequently. His request was granted on 9 September, but the Court insisted that he take a 'corporal oath' that he 'shall not persuade the said Elizabeth to marry with any man nor shall go about to dissuade her from any lawful contract as shall appear to him to be already made between her and any person or persons'. The proscription against persuading was not uncommon, but that against dissuading was. An investigation into multiple claims of precontract was already underway. On 2 September the Aldermen had taken depositions regarding a betrothal to Samuel Knowles. A week later, they received information concerning a 'pretended cause' of marriage with 'one Appleby'. A man named Crowley also petitioned, in vain, to see Hynde.

Although Francis Barnham was keeper of record, Alice bore the responsibility for supervising the young heiress and her visitors. On 16 September, when Francis was out of town, the City's Common Sergeant was told to go 'to Master Alderman Barnham and advertise his wife that there hath been some practice with Elizabeth Hynde to entangle her'. He reminded Alice that 'the order of this court is that no man shall repair to her nor have any conference with her but only Master Hurleston'. On 7 October, Hurleston petitioned to remove Hynde from the Barnhams' custody. The Aldermen, who had received information that Hurleston had committed 'disorder' by 'persuading' Elizabeth, 'contrary to his oath taken in this Court', refused the request. Alice would certainly have been the source of the report, as well as the cause of Hurleston's frustration.

The most serious suitor seems to have been Knowles. On 25 November, when the sequestration orders were repeated, he was mentioned by name as someone to be denied access to Hynde. Two days later, Hynde was called to the Guildhall to be examined by the Lord Mayor and those aldermen who were knights, the highest ranking of the city oligarchs. The subjects were certain 'slanderous reports' she was said to have made against Knowles. Soon after, Knowles was paid £100 out of the city accounts. On 20 January 1573, the Court of Orphans finally eased the restrictions on Hynde, granting Knowles's request for 'leave and license' to visit her. Their only requirement was that he be bound in the amount of £200 that he would not marry her 'within this two years'. Knowles observed the Aldermen's condition for no more than four months. On 14 April 1573, he and Hynde appeared before the Court as husband and wife.[44] Insulated by so many supervisors, regulations, and interrogations,

---

[44] Samuel Knowles and Elizabeth Hynde obtained a 'general license for marriage' on 28 January 1573 (*London Marriage Licenses, 1521–1869*, ed. Joseph Foster (London: Bernard Quaritch, 1887), 806).

she would have had every defense against Knowles had she desired it. Even the Archbishop of Canterbury, whose ecclesiastical courts customarily held jurisdiction in causes of matrimonial enforcement, had intervened. He had summoned the Aldermen to his London headquarters on 4 September 1572 to review the case of Elizabeth Hynde. Undoubtedly, thus, this orphan of the city made the match she preferred.

With four sons, Alice may have wished privately for a daughter, but the surrogates she found satisfied that desire in class-conscious and fiscally advantageous ways. She shared the values of her merchant husband. Most of the disciplinary activities of London's civic leaders had at base an economic mainspring. The city fathers did not scruple to use political ideology and corporal punishment to achieve their ends, but as cases in the Court of Orphans so suggestively indicate, their overriding concern was the making, moving, and managing of money. Wealth qualified men for membership on the Court of Aldermen and, so too, wealth motivated them.

SPINNING THE ARCHIVES

Francis Barnham was an archival activist. One small entry in the Drapers' minute books is interesting only in so far as it goes to establish the fact: 'This day Master Francis Barnham uppermost Master Warden this last year past delivered to the foresaid Master Parker one bunch of keys late in his custody.'[45] These annual transfers were rarely acknowledged; clearly, Francis demanded that the record show he was discharged of all accountability for the keys. It must also have been the case that he called personally for the meticulous detail with which the protocols of his shrieval inauguration were recorded on the last leaves of a minute book, a special appendix to be consulted on any future occasions; this had not been done for other Draper sheriffs, or even for Draper mayors. The survival of correspondence about the Drapers' 'head house', with Barnham the lead signatory on letters addressed to Roger Sadler, may also be attributable to his concern for paper trails. Records aggregated around him in an unusual number.

Few Drapers were more intimately familiar with the contents of the documents closet or 'treasure house' than he. In 1560, Francis was one of six men appointed to review Company by-laws. A further consequence of the hierarchized partition of the fellowship was that two sets of ordinances were broken out, one for the livery and one for the Bachelors. Then the disjoined

---

[45] Drapers' M.B.8, fo. 1[r].

regulations had to be 'reformed', 'augmented', 'abbreviated', and 'diminished', in some cases 'for avoiding of prolixity and tediousness of reading of the same', in others because 'some acts for one self matter are twice written in either book'. Barnham also helped search the archives for papers implicated in the Lambert case.[46]

Had Giles Lambert had access to the Drapers' Company minute books in the 1560s, he would have found some confirmation for his conspiracy theories in the preferential treatment that was accorded John Calthorp in 1559. Calthorp had quarreled with another draper named Poynter. The bad blood between them may have gone back to the Wyatt Rebellion, when both men served on the jury that failed to convict Sir Nicholas Throckmorton of treason. Most of the jurors were jailed, including Calthorp, but Poynter was unaccountably spared a term in the Fleet. On 18 May 1558, Calthorp was required to file his own humble submission with the Drapers, presumably for personal attacks on Poynter. In a changed political climate after Mary I died, however, the Assistants revisited the case and, on 12 June 1559, found it not 'meet, decent, nor convenient that this foresaid submission . . . should stand, wherefore they all willed the Clerk to cross it out'. Calthorp's statement had been copied into the minute book. In an otherwise unexampled instance of afterthought, the passage is now illegible under heavily inked scorings, with only its first line dimly decipherable ('Which day Master John Calthorp appearing before . . .'). There is little evidence that the Assistants worked by taking formal votes; even for the election of officers, no counts are logged. Here, however, the Clerk listed all sixteen names of those colluding in the rewriting of their own history, with 'Master Barnham' named as the most junior member. This loss of archival innocence was then endorsed by the full fellowship on 23 June 'for the good maintenance of brotherly love between brother and brother of this house, all malice ceasing and Master Poynter thereto consenting'.[47]

It was the Lambert case that led Francis Barnham to see the records in a new way, to understand the commodity value not only of the Drapers' reputation, but also of their information. He had himself referred agents of the Crown to Company 'register books'. Then, just three weeks after his Star Chamber

[46] Drapers' M.B.7, pp. 220, 244, 247, 248. Four others on the review team were John Calthorp, William Beswicke, John Quarles, and John Broke. Revised policies were read out at a gathering of all liverymen and yeomen, formally approved, and copied into two volumes purchased for the purpose. In 1574, Barnham was one of three aldermen undertaking a curatorial project for the Court, 'to examine all the records as well for the enrollments of deeds and testaments as recoveries and to make report to this court whether the same be well and truly done' (CLRO Rep. 18, fo. 191[r]).

[47] Drapers' M.B.7, pp. 90, 159, 164.

testimony, on 13 February 1570, he presided (as Master of the Company) over the decision to revise transcription practices:

From henceforth all acts and orders established and made at any Court of Assistants and commanded to be penned down, the same shall at the next Court of Assistants after the penning down thereof be read again to the whole Board to see if they be entered and penned down in the Repertory according to their meaning, to the intent the same may be reformed if they be not done in such sort as they ought to be. And this to be put among the Ordinances.[48]

The minute books had never been fully transparent: the Company clerk was excused from the parlor for the most confidential conversations and, when present, was given direction as to the matters requiring documentation. This new policy, however, represented an even higher level of control over the official record, formalizing an editorial role for the Assistants between rough minutes and fair copy. Among other things, it enlisted the Drapers in creating that 'myth of civic harmony' that Ian Archer describes for the Aldermen.[49] By adding Barnham's provision to the Company ordinances, the Assistants also made it binding on all future Courts.

The careful supervision of the Drapers' minutes—more than the commission of a great chair of state, more than the renewing of the officers' garlands, more even than the preservation of the annual election dinner—was Francis Barnham's administrative legacy to the Company. He recognized that the authority of the Drapers' parlor was as much a function of the data it secured within its treasure house as of its rituals, disciplines, and perquisites. His archival policies implicitly testify to how difficult it was to maintain institutional privacy in early modern London; there were too many venues for complaint and redress. In the Lambert controversy Barnham discovered a material need for the Drapers' Company to manage its image even in its internal documents, with the consequence that these corporate registers were subsequently compiled as if for a public readership. This was the second wave of a new information age, in which recordation was known to carry risks as well as rewards.

PROFIT AND POWER

It is a principal argument of this book that early modern London was a surveillant society. Ever since Foucault linked the terms *surveiller* and

---

[48] Drapers' M.B.8, fo. 90[r].
[49] Archer, *Pursuit*, 40. For more on anxieties that Clerks might not keep 'all things secret', see Ward, *Metropolitan Communities*, 87.

punir—and even though he himself suggested that the infinitive *surveiller* might best be translated into 'discipline' (rather than to 'supervise', 'inspect', or 'observe')—the critical orthodoxy has been that surveillance and punishment were joint instruments through which state power importantly exerted, maintained, and celebrated itself. Steven Mullaney influentially localized this political paradigm in London, arguing that the popular theater was established in geographically liminal areas because parishes within the walls were more tightly regulated by men for whom ideological control was essential to social stability. Ian Archer has determined that six of the ten early governors of the Bridewell had Puritan leanings and that others 'showed signs of that stern moralism' associated with authoritarian oversight.[50] But for Francis Barnham and many of his fellows, it is asserted here, godliness was not incompatible with economic aspiration, and power was often less an object of desire for its own sake than one more instrument in their toolkit for achieving personal wealth.

Admittedly, this sense of their motivation can be difficult to extricate from the ways in which it was expressed. Francis, for example, was frequently involved in matters of discipline. His presence at one Bridewell whipping is explicitly recorded. At Drapers' Hall he helped deal with the troublesome Simon Horsepoole, who would not be 'reformable'; with John Fabian, sent to ward as 'a rebel'; with William Keltrydge, who struck Fabian; with William Tenche, also guilty of violent assault; and with Anthony Pryor, said to have spread 'certain evil and slanderous reports' about his own apprentice.[51] Some of these men made more than one appearance in the Company's minute books.

Barnham was Master of the Drapers' Company during one particularly thorny case, when William Hobbes appealed for help with his wayward apprentice Francis Langley. It may again be due to Francis's archivizing instincts that there survives a letter written by Langley himself.[52] Hobbes seems

---

[50] Alan Sheridan, 'Translator's Note', in Michel Foucault, *Discipline and Punish: The Birth of the Prison* (New York: Vintage, 1979). Steven Mullaney, *The Place of the Stage: License, Play, and Power in Renaissance England* (Chicago: University of Chicago Press, 1988), chs. 1 and 2. Archer, *Pursuit*, 253–4.

[51] BCB-01, fo. 71^r (whipping of Elizabeth Dickson, 1560). Drapers' M.B.8, fos. 2^r, 5^v (Horsepoole); M.B.8, fos. 15^{r-v}, 16^r–17^r, 59^r, 72^v, 241^r (Fabian); M.B.8, fo. 2^r (Keltrydge); M.B.7, pp. 132–3, 145 (Tenche); M.B.8, fos. 80^v, 82^v (Pryor). Some apprentices and servants were also corrected at Bridewell (e.g. BCB-02, fo. 177^r and below, n. 55).

[52] We know Hobbes's concerns only as represented in Langley's letter (Drapers' A.III.151). This corrects the record for the biography by William Ingram, who found 'no surviving correspondence' and who notes the record of Langley's punishment while regretting that 'Though we might wish to know more precisely what the offences were, the records will not tell us' (*A London Life in the Brazen Age: Francis Langley, 1548–1602* (Cambridge, Mass.: Harvard University Press, 1978), 6, 18). The 'typical apprenticeship indenture' specified that the apprentice should 'not haunt taverns nor playhouses, nor absent himself from the master's

to have charged Langley with stealing his own indenture papers (presumably preparing to break his contract), with being a 'tavern hunter' (*sic* for 'tavern haunter'), with absenting himself from church on 27 December 1569, and with once having run away. Those, in any case, are the complaints against which Langley chose to defend himself in his letter of 15 January 1570. First, he wrote, Hobbes had himself surrendered the apprenticeship papers 'instead of an obligation'. Second, Langley claimed that he had dispatched all manner of errands for master and mistress, and 'at no time hath he neither found me in ale house nor tavern'. Third, Langley could name witnesses that 'I was present all the sermon while' on the specified sabbath. Fourth, he had fled his master in self-preservation. On the disputed Sunday, Hobbes 'did beat and pummel me about the head more like a boy than otherways', and the next day Hobbes rose 'about five o'clock and called me up and against I came down he had provided a staff to beat me with'. Langley protested that 'if I had not escaped his cruel hands I had surely repented it all the days of my life'. He petitioned the Assistants either to let him depart his master, 'seeing that my service will not please him', or to require Hobbes to 'use me hereafter as a servant ought to be used'.

As Steve Rappaport has emphasized, most apprentices were nearly 20 when bound, 'hardly the boys of textbook fame'. And yet they were, as Langley resentfully put it, too often treated 'more like' children. The situation may have been especially strained in draper establishments, for the Assistants had ruled in 1557 that any apprentice bound under the age of 18 would be required to serve nine years, rather than the usual seven. Thus, all apprentice-drapers remained in service into their late twenties. The system was intended to provide mutual economic benefit—a training program for apprentices and a workforce for masters—but Rappaport also recognizes the ways in which these purposes could diverge. An apprentice learned most in the early years of his term; especially if he planned to set up shop in the provinces, he had small incentive to work out his full indenture. A master realized his advantage from the arrangement only in the last years, when his apprentice was capable of providing real assistance, and so he had an interest in prolonging the association well into his man's maturity.[53] In addition to the political tensions surrounding hierarchy, authority, and mutual dependence, there were varied and complicated financial arrangements, as well—as Langley hints in his somewhat improbable report about the displaced indenture papers and an

service day or night unlawfully' and should not marry, 'commit fornication', nor play cards, dice, or tables. He should 'his said master faithfully serve, his secrets keep, his lawful commands everywhere gladly do' (Rappaport, *Worlds*, 234).

[53] Rappaport, *Worlds*, 295, 297, 315. See also Paul Griffiths, *Youth and Authority: Formative Experiences in England, 1560–1640* (Oxford: Clarendon, 1996).

unknown obligation. Tradesmen often mentioned debts to their apprentices in their wills, for unpaid wages, for goods purchased on their behalfs, and even for moneys borrowed. Detailed as was Francis Langley's letter, it would not have exhausted the matters that lay between him and William Hobbes.

It might seem predictable that the Assistants would side with the master rather than the servant, but they had not done so with Anthony Pryor. And it may also be that Francis Langley, who is now best known for having built the Swan Theatre in the mid-1590s, was already as ruthlessly ambitious and as arrogant as William Ingram believes him to have been in later life. Langley felt aggrieved that Hobbes had 'procured my friends' displeasure against me', but it is difficult not to suspect that his loss of their good will proceeded from his own behavior. On the day appointed, 18 January 1570, 'the correction of this house was ministered to Francis Langley' for 'diverse his offenses against his Master'. He was whipped with birch rods by two anonymous, disguised drapers, 'whereat were present Master Aldermen Barnham our Master'. With other Assistants, Francis stood for the decision his court had taken. He probably spoke the disciplinary envoi that was inscribed in the Company minute book, as well: 'I pray God this small and charitable correction may be to him such a warning as thereby he may avoid a greater.'[54]

Even in voicing the conventional platitudes, however, Francis had every reason to be skeptical about the effectiveness of disciplinary initiatives. And indeed, in the spring of 1571 Langley ran away again. The Drapers authorized William Hobbes to end the apprenticeship if he so chose. Recidivism was another reason for multiple layers of governance in the city: when one disciplinary venue failed another could be essayed. The Bridewell was especially useful as a correctional catch-all. A man named Watson brought his renegade apprentice there, for instance, rather than to the officers of the Carpenters' Company. A woman called 'Mistress Luson' paid a fee to have her servant 'broken under the governance of the matron of this house'. And Christopher Meryng reimbursed the governors for the daily expenses of his daughter, whom he consigned 'for the amendment of her life and lewdness'.[55]

It is impossible to follow the parade of Bridewell presentments without wondering also about the effect upon its governors of witnessing so much human tragedy: a girl aged 6, sodomized; another, 10, assaulted repeatedly by a man who brandished a knife and threatened 'that if she either told or cried he would stick her'; a boy, 10, taken into a 'blind alley' to be abused 'by the

---

[54] Drapers' M.B.8, fo. 88^v.

[55] BCB-01, fo. 194^v (1 February 1562; in the event, Watson was referred back to the Carpenters' Company for correction); BCB-01, fo. 82^v (Luson, 31 May 1560); BCB-01, fo. 79^v (Meryng, 14 May 1560). See also BCB-01, fo. 57^r, for a man the governors sent back to his parish to ask forgiveness and promise never to offend again.

way of buggery'; a child, 7, raped by her father both vaginally and anally and told that if she complained 'he would stop her breath', or her mother's, or that of a neighbor. Another father ordered his 12-year-old daughter and his 11-year-old son 'to be both naughty together'; a man and his wife beat their 12-year-old maidservant brutally and then 'powdered' her wounds with salt; a cobbler tied his wife to the bedstocks for six weeks before committing her to Bedlam, all so that he might freely cohabit with his 'harlot'.[56]

From its founding in 1553 the bawdy court attracted controversy. On Francis Barnham's first day on the board of Governors, 8 December 1559, Agnes Lorde accused him and his fellows of putting their inmates to work in the sex trade, for their own profit. In August 1560, Margaret Grenewood was punished for spreading the report that she had been so severely whipped in their custody that 'she might turn her fingers in her flesh'. Barnham also took part in a January 1560 decision to cart a woman because the 'Governors have considered how slanderous it will be to suffer for a notorious person to pass unpunished and namely for that it is said the beggarly harlots are punished and the riches escape'.[57]

There was some truth to accusations of partiality. In December 1559 the governors questioned the suggestively named and frequently presented Ellyn Remnaunt. She admitted that 'immediately after her last departure out of this house' she had reported to the notorious madam, Long Meg of Westminster. She spent a full night and a day with a man she called a foreign 'prince' and then allowed herself to be 'abused' by two men identified only as 'MM' and 'Master A'. In a subsequent entry the clerk noted that the man now referred to as 'MMM' was summoned to the court and confessed his vice, 'but, for as much as this was the first time of his detection and also that he is a man of calling in a company of most worship and hath a good wife and great family, it was considered by the Governors of this house upon his most humble submission that after exhortation and admonition given for the amendment of his life' he should be discharged. The name of Remnaunt's 'abuser' was not made public, nor was it confided to the court minute book. He was discreetly fined, as much in deference to his citizenship as to his family connections.[58]

---

[56] BCB-01, fo. 125^v (6-year-old girl, 1561); BCB-02, fo. 153^r (10-year-old girl, 1575); BCB-01, fo. 106^v (10-year-old boy, 1560); BCB-02, fos. 110^r–111^r (7-year-old girl, 1575, who was found to be 'hurt by man both before and behind'); BCB-01, fo. 62^r (12-year-old girl and 11-year-old boy, 1560); BCB-01, fo. 75^r (12-year-old maidservant, 1560); BCB-02, fo. 72^r (cobbler's wife, 1574).

[57] BCB-01, fo. 38^r (Lorde); BCB-01, fo. 95^r (Grenewood); BCB-01, fo. 51^v (punishment).

[58] BCB-01, fos. 42^r, 54^v. Like some other offenders, MMM was required to contribute to the building of Bridewell's wharf, in his case by paying for 25 ft of it.

Some of the Bridewell's administrative problems were imputed to the incompetence and dishonesty of the staff. Francis Barnham was one of the signatories to a formal censure of the resident matron, who had developed a profitable sideline by providing some prisoners with better food than the 'common diet', for a price, and by putting them to work in occupations other than the 'common works of this house' (if she trafficked the women, this is not specified). But the Governors were also themselves subjects of controversy. In 1560 they persuaded Edward Smyth to take into his service a woman who had been lodged in the Bridewell not for correction but 'for relief of necessity'. Nonetheless, Smith complained, while in residence she had been 'unreasonably beaten by the motion of this house'. The Governors dictated into the record that they 'were ashamed to behold the same'. With decisions presented as judgments rather than statements of fact—'it plainly appeared unto us' that a woman was guilty of training a boy to beg as if 'deaf and dumb'—they also conceded that they could not be sure their verdicts were sound.[59]

More than any other court on which Barnham sat, Bridewell was an instrument of social order rather than economic advancement. It cannot have been a coincidence that he was an unenthusiastic governor at the bawdy court (unlike William Boxe, his Under Sheriff in 1570). His record of attendance was uncharacteristically spotty, and in surviving documents he makes not a single presentment. The pattern suggested by his performance at the Bridewell is filled out by other derelictions of disciplinary duty. He was absent from a Drapers' search of yards in 1567. During his Mastership in 1569 a search was entirely 'forgotten' until nearly too late. It 'should have been done before St Thomas's Day', on 21 December, and was generally conducted in August or September, but on his watch it was neglected until the very last day of the year. In January 1570 he was heavily preoccupied with the Lambert and Langley cases; the next month an aldermanic admonition required him to 'take some good order . . . for the reformation of all the alleys and misorder' in his unruly ward. It is impossible not to wonder whether he was able to tolerate so long a tenure in Farringdon Without because he neglected to intervene as often as a more diligent officer would have done.[60]

To impute his social inactivism to a progressive politics, to moral distaste, or to sentiment would be untrue to his times or his interests. For Barnham, who seems generally to have acted with economic purpose, there was undoubtedly value to be realized in suburban disorder. Joseph P. Ward has recognized

---

[59] BCB-01, fo. 137ᵛ (matron); BCB-01, fo. 91ᵛ (Smyth); BCB-01, fo. 89ʳ (beggar).

[60] Drapers' M.B.8, fo. 2ᵛ (absent from search); M.B.8, fo. 88ʳ (forgotten search); CLRO Rep. 16, fo. 529ᵛ (unruly ward). See also Ch. 1, n. 34.

the many ways in which income was generated by populous and turbulent conditions. Landlords earned extra rent as they crowded strangers and foreigners into their buildings. Construction workers were kept busy erecting new houses and subdividing old ones. Suppliers profited from increased demand for timber, tile, stone, gravel, guttering, and glass. Those living without the walls tended more often to work outside the livery system and its regulations for manufactury, producing notoriously poor and counterfeit products.[61] Barnham can be associated with nearly all these enterprises.

For example, he was accused of trading in shoddy textiles in 1574 (as is shown in Chapter Seven). He also had a profitable sideline in building supplies, judging from the 'two racks of iron' (worth £43) he delivered to St Thomas's Hospital in 1563 and the load of stone and chalk he sold the Drapers' Company in 1570. These may have been materials salvaged from his property purchases. Throughout the country, new landowners were stripping the lead off monastic roofs, using old stone for rebuilding projects, and recycling other architectural spoil. Especially notorious in London, according to John Stow, was the Second Marquess of Winchester. After inheriting the former house of the Augustine Friars, Winchester 'sold the monuments of noble men there buried in great number'. The story may suggest the best way of reading an otherwise mysterious record that Francis Barnham procured not only two racks of iron for St Thomas's Hospital, for 7s. 2d., but also a 'gravestone which lyeth before the surgeon's door', for 13s. 4d. Stow was not unhappy that some of Winchester's plunder 'proved not so profitable as he looked for', and the same was true in this instance for Barnham. Eleven years later, apparently unremunerated in a culture that famously ran on protracted debts, Francis was forced to 'put the masters in mind of a gravestone which he bought long time since, and the same stone lyeth at the surgery house door in the yard'—still.[62] A public opinion such as Stow's was of no more concern to Francis Barnham than was discipline for its own sake. He trafficked in commodity and knew the uses of disorder.

AN ACCIDENTAL AUTOBIOGRAPHY

Francis Barnham was a merchant of many accomplishments who, because he was at the material center of everyday life in early modern London, had

---

[61] Ward, *Metropolitan Communities*, 19.
[62] LMA H01/ST/A/001/001, fo. 72ʳ (iron and gravestone, 5 April 1563); Drapers' R.A.5, 1569–70, fo. 8ᵛ (stone and chalk); LMA H01/ST/A/001/003, fo. 132ᵛ (gravestone, 25 October 1574). Stow, *Survey*, 159 (Winchester).

direct influence upon the private lives of hundreds of its residents—as well as knowledge of their intimate affairs. This was yet another means to the end of his wealth. He was among the city's fifteen richest merchants as a lender of funds to the Crown. He laid the foundations for his two older sons to become country gentlemen and the youngest to amass a celebrated London fortune.

As Alice observed in the memorial she commissioned in her parish church, he was one of London's worthies. Freedom records are lost for 1541, when Francis became a citizen, but a copy of those between 1551 and 1553 survives, and it shows that out of more than five hundred men who achieved citizenship in those years just fourteen were to become masters of their companies. Francis leapfrogged the offices of the Drapers' Bachelors to join the livery's Court of Assistants as one of its youngest but most prosperous members, and he then had a long and demonstrably influential tenure among the Company's elite. He was the Common Councillor chosen to represent the city in negotiations with the Merchant Taylors over the location of the great enterprise that was to be known as the Royal Exchange. As an alderman, Francis was one of the twenty-six most influential men in London between 1568 and 1576. He was tapped for the most notoriously difficult aldermanic assignment, Farringdon Without. As Upper Sheriff, he was London's principal Justice of the Peace.

It was a far from anonymous life. Francis Barnham was undoubtedly known by name to the woman who left Charity of God at his gate. And in 1570 he suffered an early modern version of identity fraud that similarly proceeded from a high public profile. Thomas Garroune, a baker, confessed 'openly' before the Court of Aldermen that 'he had counterfeited the handwriting of Sir William Chester, Knight, and Master Francis Barnham, Alderman, to a counterfeit passport'. Garroune probably had access to a legitimate passport for copying; as officers of St Thomas's, both Chester and Barnham would frequently have signed documents for patients released from the 'bawdy' hospital. The forged paper undoubtedly emulated a template that survives in the St Thomas's records as 'The form and order of the making of such passports as be made for the discharging of the poor':

To all mayors, bailiffs, and constables and all other the King's officers, greetings. Know ye that ＿＿＿＿＿＿＿ was discharged out of the hospital of Saint Thomas the Apostle within the borough of Southwark by the Governors of the same. And by them assigned to depart unto the *T* of *L* in the county of *S* within ＿＿ days next ensuing the date of these presents and there to exhibit this present passport unto the head officer or officers in that place appointed, that they may take further order for ＿＿＿＿＿＿ demeanor.

Garroune was judged to 'stand tomorrow next the space of three hours during the market time with his head in the pillory in Cheapside with a paper upon his head with these words in great letters: "FOR COUNTERFEITING OF A FALSE PASSPORT." '[63] Barnham's forged signature is another form of testimony to his local celebrity.

By 1582, though, he was forgotten. In his *Brief Note of the Order and Manner of the . . . Three Royal Hospitals*, John Howes paid tribute to Christ's major benefactors without mentioning Barnham's 1576 grant of lands in Southwark.[64] This is just the sort of citizen philanthropy that the *Survey of London* celebrated. But while John Stow noted the presence of a Barnham monument in the church of St Clement Eastcheap, and while Anthony Munday in his 1613 revision of the *Survey* recognized Alice's charitable legacies to young scholars, neither cited Francis as a philanthropist. His biography seems not to have been sufficiently compelling to have captured the historical attention even of his near contemporaries.

Those who today tell the tales of Francis Langley, Giles Lambert, the Saunders murder, the building of the Royal Exchange, or (a subject of the next chapter) the Ridolfi Plot have had no reason to mention the now-forgotten name of Francis Barnham. And yet he played a role in all these stories. Frank Freeman Foster separates the Elizabethan 'elite' of London, sixty-four men who were mayors between 1558 and 1603, from the ninety-one who were mere 'notables', and Barnham falls into the latter category. The standard reference on London's executive officers is Alfred B. Beaven's *Aldermen of the City of London*, which charts Francis's election to represent the ward of Farringdon Without and then his translation to Tower ward but which otherwise takes small note of a career of so much less interest than those of, for example, Sir Rowland Heyward or Sir Thomas Ramsey. F. G. Parson's three-volume *History of St Thomas's Hospital* purports to name all the hospital's treasurers, but it overlooks Barnham's two-year term in that office. In his exhaustive five-volume *History of the Worshipful Company of the Drapers of London*, A. H. Johnson first neglects Francis (omitting him from a list of drapers who were also Merchant Adventurers and members of the Russia Company) and then confuses him with his son Benedict.[65] Johnson recognizes none of Francis's achievements in preserving the election feast, acquiring the Lambert almshouses, and repurposing the Company archives.

---

[63] CLRO Rep. 17, fo. 10ʳ. Sample passport is from LMA H01/ST/A/001/001, fo. 1a. Counterfeit passports and licenses were frequent subjects of concern; see e.g. CLRO Rep. 16, fo. 462ʳ; Rep. 17, fo. 71ʳ; Rep. 17, fo. 234ᵛ; Rep. 17, fo. 321ʳ; Rep. 17, fo. 338ʳ; Rep. 18, fo. 2ᵛ.

[64] Howes, *Brief Note*, appended list of donors.

[65] Johnson associates the Benedict Barnham trust with Francis Barnham's date of death (*History*, iii. 69 n. 1); he omits Francis Barnham from ii. app. XXXb, which purports to list all drapers who were also members of the Merchant Adventurers' and Russia Companies.

The key to Francis Barnham's inner life may be found, as seems so often to have been the case in this period, in an act of resistance, when he slighted the assignment of reconciling Lady Barbara Champion and her daughter by a first marriage, Abigail Herdson. Francis must have been known to his fellow aldermen as a master negotiator. In his first year on the Court, for example, he was a delegate to the Earl of Leicester; generally, notes Foster, more senior members were chosen to meet with central-government representatives and other important personages. He would have been thought more than a match even for the redoubtable Champion, whose title derived from her husband's term as mayor. And, as Sir Richard Champion's erstwhile apprentice, Francis must have seemed particularly well equipped to resolve a dispute involving his widow.[66]

Herdson was an 'orphan of the city' who had made a controversial match, wedding Charles Dixwell without either the Aldermen's 'license, assent, or consent' (as was their 'ancient right and custom time out of mind') or her mother's 'will, knowledge, or assent'. Among other things, this meant that no one had protected Herdson's fiscal interests in the matter. For the pragmatists on the Court of Aldermen there was now no room for negotiation, but Lady Champion would not be reconciled. Despite his long history of mediating thornier and more momentous conflicts, however, Francis was unable to 'move' Lady Champion to accept the marriage.

Perhaps at base he was unwilling to do so. Instead, he brought in a recommendation that Herdson's entire portion should be forfeited and redistributed among others of Lady Champion's children. Barnham and Champion shared a values system as well as a personal history, and he had already demonstrated a profound loyalty to the memory of his mentor. On the occasion of his first election as Master of the Drapers, he led the Company's most prominent members on a viewing of Champion's tomb, in what Caroline Barron calls a remarkable act of 'filial piety'.[67] Thus, in the matter of Abigail Herdson's unauthorized marriage, he broke with aldermanic ranks. When a second delegation to Lady Champion was required—Francis Saunders's kinsman, the Baron of the Exchequer, had intervened on behalf of Dixwell—Barnham's name was conspicuously omitted. Others would carry the arbitration forward.

---

[66] CLRO Rep. 16, fo. 458^r (Leicester, 22 March 1569); Rep. 16, fo. 539^r (assignment of 6 March 1570); Rep. 16, fo. 542^v (Barnham's report of 9 March 1570 recommending that Herdson's portion should be entirely forfeited); Rep. 17, fo. 6^r (new delegation of 13 April 1570); Rep. 17, fos. 12^v, 13^r, 14^{r-v} (resolution of the controversy, with Dixwell and Herdson receiving her full orphanage 'to their own proper uses').

[67] Drapers' D.B.1, fo. 106^v (1571); see also GL Ms 4887, p. 189. Caroline Barron, in private conversation. The Champions remembered the Barnhams in their wills, PROB 11/50, fo. 169^{r-v} (22 November 1568); PROB 11/58, fos. 200^r–202^r (15 October 1576).

This is one instance in which Francis Barnham's personality emerges from the public records in sharp definition.

'The Character of Sir Martin Barnham, Knight' gives evidence that Francis Barnham's ambitions for his family were realized. Personal chronicles were a fashionable product of the gentry and nobility of the seventeenth century. There, Sir Francis describes his father as a writer, too, compiler of 'a true collection by way of an historical narration'. As was more characteristic of Martin's earlier era, this lost account was apparently a catalogue of providential events, the 'divine punishment' visited upon men who challenged Martin's title to his principal inheritance. His antagonists experienced 'remarkable misfortune' following their 'unlawful and dishonorable' suits to seize the manor of Bilsington, says Sir Francis. Martin, meanwhile, was confident that his father's purchases had been 'as good as law and equity could make it'—and thus as well-authenticated as his grandfather's deeds and compacts could witness.[68] From this evidence, Francis Barnham appears to have been a textual activist and archivist in his private life as in his professional career. In one aspect, then, Sir Francis's family history traces a lineal concern for self-documentation across three generations. For each, the genre of personal expression that was conceptually available differed: memoir, for Sir Francis; providential narrative, for Martin; and property evidences, for Francis. Sir Francis does not ascribe acts of authorship to his grandfather, but then he did not have access to those records in which Francis more fully revealed himself. Francis's interventions in the private lives of other Londoners constitute a deconstructed diary in their own right, a portrait of a merchant ethos that governed Tudor London.

[68] Sir Francis Barnham, 'The Character of Sir Martin Barnham, Knight, by his Son Sir Francis Barnham', ed. Lena Cowen Orlin, in Ann Lake Prescott and James Dutcher (eds.), *Renaissance Historicisms* (Newark: University of Delaware Press, 2008).

6

Galleries

PRIVACY WAS a scarce commodity in Tudor England. First, the built environment was inhospitable. Even the Rebuilt environment of conscious design and high investment made fewer advances than has often been thought. To the contrary, old barriers between the principal family and service workers—represented in tall halls, courtyard lodgings, and occasional stairs—were dissolved in new building. The motives for reinventing housing arrangements may more often have been accumulation and display than withdrawal and solitude. Second, most private homes were centers of production and consumption, harboring populations with diverse and sometimes conflicting needs and objectives. They were explosively uncontainable by the strictures of abstract ideology; in everyday life, political hierarchy was rarely as sustained a concern as was economic purpose. Third, social density was a convention of long standing. The universal practice of shared beds and bedchambers alone created a vast store of shared knowledge, and there was resistance to any impeachment of the traditional circulations of personal information. Fourth, mutual surveillance was a public mandate. The officers of church and state encouraged all early moderns to monitor their fellows in the interest of civil order. In their redundant, over-busy courts, local intelligence was solicited for wider exposure. The unspoken principles of rights in these matters went not to privacy protections but instead to the need to know.

These are the arguments of the previous four chapters. Together, they suggest that in the early modern household conditions for privacy were adverse, whether the issue was sexual intimacy, bodily functions, or personal interiority. Here, however, the subject is a different form of privacy, a particularly urgent one in the period: how, in these circumstances, was it possible to have a private conversation? To the extent that the household

Earlier versions of this chapter have been published as 'The Tudor Long Gallery in the History of Privacy', in *InForm: The Journal of Architecture, Design, and Material Culture* 2 (2001), 84–98; and as 'Spaces of Treason in Tudor England', in Lena Cowen Orlin (ed.), *Center or Margin: Revisions of the English Renaissance in Honor of Leeds Barroll* (Selinsgrove: Susquehanna University Press, 2006), 158–95. These essays include illustrations not reproduced here.

parlor fulfilled the function implied by its French-cognate name, it was a chamber for *social* conversation, not for the speaking of secrets. But there was another domestic space that achieved an accidental capacity for enabling confidences and that thus played a key role in the history of privacy. The irony is that it was not, as W. G. Hoskins and others would have assumed, a *small* room. Instead it was the largest, most extravagant, and also the most distinctive architectural innovation of Tudor and Stuart building, the long gallery.[1]

As the great hall dominated the medieval castle, so the long gallery was the quintessential room of the early modern stately home (see Fig. 6.1). Its declared purpose was to shelter recreational walking in the heat of the day and during inclement weather. At the outset, this was a luxury for royal houses, incorporated at Richmond by 1504, Bridewell by 1515, and Greenwich in 1518. Henry VIII famously disassembled one of Thomas Wolsey's galleries at Esher in order to re-erect it at Whitehall; by the end of the sixteenth century this riverside palace was 'a complex of galleries', according to H. M. Colvin and John Summerson. Thanks to works projects at Hampton Court and the Tower, among other places, Henry VIII earned an encomium in his funeral oration as himself the creator of 'galleries of great pleasure'. The oldest surviving gallery in a private home, at the Vyne, was erected by Sir William Sandys in 1531 in preparation to receive Henry, and from there the form was more widely popularized. Elizabeth, who was not otherwise a builder, added galleries at Windsor and Woking.[2]

---

[1] This chapter developed out of my experience of walking in surviving long galleries; I am grateful to the National Trust, private and municipal owners, and the staffs at Astley Hall (Lancashire), Aston Hall (West Midlands), Audley End (Essex), Blakesley Hall (West Midlands), Burghley House (Lincolnshire), Burton Agnes Hall (Yorkshire), Chastleton House (Oxfordshire), Gosfield Hall (Essex), Haddon Hall (Derbyshire), Hardwick Hall (Derbyshire), Hatfield House (Hertfordshire), Knole (Kent), Little Moreton Hall (Cheshire), Lyme Park (Cheshire), Montacute House (Somerset), Parham House (Sussex), Penshurst Place (Kent), and The Vyne (Hampshire). The definitive work on the long gallery is that of Rosalys Coope in 'The "Long Gallery": Its Origins, Development, Use, and Decoration', *Architectural History* 29 (1986), 43–72. In this splendid study she has preceded me in many conclusions, including that the long gallery was 'an excellent place in which to conduct difficult diplomatic interviews' (p. 60). See also Howard, *Early Tudor Country House*, who suggests 'the long gallery's usefulness as a place for private conversation' (p. 116). And see Coope's 'The Gallery in England: Names and Meanings', in *Design and Practice in British Architecture: Studies in Architectural History Presented to Howard Colvin*, a special issue of *Architectural History* 27 (1984), 446–55. In understanding the meanings of the long gallery, a complicating factor is that the documentary trail is not always clear; the term 'gallery' could also signify lobbies or anterooms, corridors, and what we would call 'minstrels' galleries'. When associated with recreational walking, however, the space indicated is usually that which is the subject of this chapter.

[2] *The History of the King's Works*, iv. *1485–1660 (Part II)*, ed. H. M. Colvin, John Summerson, et al. (London: HMSO, 1982), 224, 55, 101, 89, 18–19, 30. Bishop Fisher's funeral oration cited by Coope, 'The "Long Gallery": Its Origins', 46.

Figure 6.1 The long gallery at Albyns House, near Stapleford Abbots in Essex.

The room defied conventional spatial wisdoms. We tend to have clear expectations for the signifying capacity of elevation, for example, because we assume that public or shared areas will be encountered at ground level and that private bedchambers require vertical separation from them. We also suppose that we can recognize a room by its place in a floorplan, associating such presentational spaces as foyers and lounges with the front of the house and imagining workrooms such as kitchens and laundries tucked inconspicuously behind them. And, perhaps most importantly, we divine a room's meaning from its contents. Furnishings are the primary mechanisms for communicating to us the behavior that is appropriately engaged in a given space, whether this is to gather with others to eat, to lie down to sleep, or to sit in seclusion to read or think. Long galleries, however, demonstrate how anachronistic all these assumptions can be. These were public rooms located at the tops of houses and often at the back, to afford views over gardens and orchards. Uniquely in the Renaissance home, they were not given definition by objects. Meant to provide walking space, they were kept more or less bare of any obstacles. They were recognizable solely by their dimensions. The length of the gallery at Buckhurst was 254 ft; at Ampthill, 245 ft; at Worksop, 212 ft; at Audley End, 190 ft; at Montacute, 170 ft; at Parham, 166 ft; at Hardwick, 160 ft; at Aston, Holdenby, and Copt Hall, 140 ft; at Rufford Abbey, 114 ft; at Haddon and Littlecote, 110 ft; at Ingatestone, 95 ft. Even in a small house such as Chastleton, the long gallery was impressive at 72 ft.[3]

Although the gallery is usually associated with spatial prodigality in stately homes, there is some evidence that it was imitated in lesser establishments, as well. One tenement near Whitehall had a room that was 55 ft long and just under 12 ft wide; it was described in a contemporary document as a 'large and spacious gallery'. At Blakesley Hall in Birmingham a 35-ft-long open area on the upper level occupies the main front of the house (see Fig. 6.2). Built in 1590 by the merchant Richard Smalbroke, the space gives every evidence of aspiration to be considered a long gallery, especially because it is lit by two bay windows.[4] And some long galleries descended into middling-sort hands with the redistribution of church properties following the Dissolution of the monasteries. It appears to have been the case that the house on St Clement's Lane which had once belonged to the Abbot of Stratford Langthorne had a gallery to go with its garden—Benedict Barnham refers to it in his will.[5]

Francis Barnham, meanwhile, himself had a point of connection with a high-politics story that can rightly be told only in terms of its long galleries. He played a minor role in events associated with the Rebellion of the Northern Earls and the Ridolfi Plot. The latter constitutes one of the more curious episodes in the history of privacy. Investigations into treasonous activities of the 1560s and 1570s had a strong spatial dynamic. They showed both the ways in which some of the alleged conspirators managed to secure conversational privacy and also how their very attempts to do so were in themselves incriminatory. This was the continuing stigma of privacy; it seemed that no one who sought to be private could be believed to have done so with an innocent intent.

---

[3] Long gallery measurements come from Coope, 'The "Long Gallery": Its Origins', 51.

[4] *The Survey of London*, xiii. *The Parish of St Margaret, Westminster, Part II (Neighbourhood of Whitehall*, i), gen. eds. Montagu H. Cox and Philip Norman (London: B. T. Batsford for London County Council, 1930), 232–3 (Whitehall tenement). The Blakesley space is termed a 'long gallery' in Department of Local History Information Sheet 15, by the Birmingham Museum and Art Gallery. Ralph Treswell mentions many London galleries in his early seventeenth-century surveys (*London Surveys*), but these were most often raised passageways along the sides of yards, providing work space above the dust and traffic below.

[5] Will of Benedict Barnham (29 May 1598), PROB 11/91, fos. 304[r]–309[r]. The family owned more than one house on St Clement's Lane, and it is possible that Alice moved house in widowhood.

Figure 6.2 A merchant's long gallery, at Blakesley Hall in Yardley in West Midlands. Built by Richard Smalbroke *c.*1590.

THE WALLS HAVE EARS

When it was rumored that Elizabeth I was having an affair with Robert Dudley, she told one diplomat that 'My life is in the open, and I have so many witnesses that I cannot understand how so bad a judgment can have been formed of me.' At the other end of the social scale, trial depositions taken from private citizens exposed all manner of intimate details about the behavior, possessions, housekeeping practices, sleeping arrangements, dangerous liaisons, and secret conversations of near neighbors.[6] Because it was usually assumed that household walls had ears, it was also generally accepted that the domestic interior could not be trusted for what was called 'private conference'. Seekers of intimate exchange found the obvious solution: to go outdoors.

In the diplomatic correspondence of the period, one has the sense of an operative, now lost code, a shorthand language of place. It meant one thing when an envoy was received in chambers, always crowded with courtiers, but something else again when he was invited into the royal garden for a private hearing. Ambassadors made a point of informing their superiors when they were favored with such privileged communication. In December 1558, the Count de Feria complained to the Spanish king that his two meetings with the English queen had been 'in the presence chamber crammed with people'. The following March, however, he was pleased to report that the Treasurer of her Household, Sir Thomas Parry, had relayed the message that he should go to an outdoor area 'near the execution place, so that the Earl of Pembroke and other gentlemen who were walking in St James' Park should not see' him with Elizabeth, much less overhear them. 'I say this to show how suspicious and distrustful they are', wrote the Count. Similarly, in order to emphasize the confidentiality of a conversation with Sir Thomas More, More's son-in-law William Roper specified its outdoor setting. The occasion was More's return home to Chelsea after having been brought before Parliament on a charge of misprision of treason in 1534. 'Then walked we twain alone into his garden together', Roper described. In the garden, Roper was able to put questions more directly than he might have dared had he been in an enclosed space within hearing of More's wife and daughters.[7]

---

[6] See Carole Levin, *The Heart and Stomach of a King: Elizabeth I and the Politics of Sex and Power* (Philadelphia: University of Pennsylvania Press, 1994), 77. For church-court reports, see Loreen L. Giese, *Courtships, Marriage Customs, and Shakespeare's Comedies* (New York: Palgrave Macmillan, 2006); Gowing, *Domestic Dangers*; and Ingram, *Church Courts*.

[7] *CSP Spanish*, i. nos. 4 (14 December 1558) and 18 (19 March 1559). See also the first reports of Sir Thomas Smith as junior ambassador to France in 1571, reprinted in Sir Dudley Digges, *The*

While private conversation was an occasion for concern among those who feared that they could not speak without being overheard, it was also a source of anxiety for those who feared that there might be speech they were not overhearing. Elizabeth Tudor learned this lesson when she was imprisoned during the reign of her sister Mary.[8] As John Foxe recounts at length, a 4-year-old boy made daily visits to Elizabeth's Tower lodgings to bring her flowers. Because the child was known to have regular contact with a past participant in Wyatt's Rebellion against Mary, the Earl of Devonshire, it was feared that he was conveying messages between the two.

Elizabeth's interior accommodations surrendered fully to the surveillance of Mary's Privy Councillors when 'the child's father was commanded to permit the boy no more to come up into [her] chambers'. But the Queen's men were less effective with respect to the 'little garden' in which, after a month's repeated requests, Elizabeth had been given leave to walk for the sake of her health. There, Tower keepers were charged with monitoring other prisoners for the duration of her recreation, specifically to ensure that no one spoke to her. Elizabeth herself was always accompanied by two officials of the court and three of her own gentlewomen, a party of six to prevent any collusion of two—that is, to preclude private exchange. Nonetheless, it was in the garden that the boy managed one last covert exchange with the imprisoned princess. 'The next day', as Elizabeth 'was walking' in the Tower garden, 'the child, peeping in at a hole in the door, cried unto her, saying, "Mistress, I can bring you no more flowers." Whereat she smiled, but said nothing, understanding thereby what they had done.' On the face of it, this incident seems an unlikely subject for Foxe's project to heroize the Protestant princess. But Elizabeth's access to the outdoors, like the boy's semiotic identification with flowers, established a plausible context for resistant private knowledge in a period of persecution. The anecdote developed from and depended upon cultural conditions in which surreptitious communication was rarely associated with interior spaces.

It may seem self-evident that the best strategy for the pursuit of private conversation was to step into the garden, the area immediately beyond

---

Compleat Ambassador: or Two Treaties of the Intended Marriage of Qu: Elizabeth . . . Comprised in Letters of Negotiation (London: 1655). For an audience in the King's Chamber, Smith listed the presence of the Duke of Alençon and other nobles; in the Queen Mother's Chamber, there were a 'great number' of ladies (Thomas Smith and Francis Walsingham to Elizabeth (1 March 1571), 169–70). But in the King's Garden the conference included only Smith; his senior, Francis Walsingham; the Queen Mother; and her man Malvosire (Thomas Smith to Burleigh (22 March 1571), 196–7). William Roper, *The Life of Sir Thomas More*, in Richard S. Sylvester and Davis P. Harding (eds.), *Two Early Tudor Lives* (New Haven: Yale University Press, 1962), 235.

[8] John Foxe, *Foxe's Book of Martyrs Variorum Edition Online*, Version 1.1 <www.hrionline. ac.uk/johnfoxe>, accessed 4 May 2007: 1570 edition, Book 12, p. 2291.

betraying internal walls. What must additionally be emphasized, however, is that the place was inseparably associated with a behavior, which was walking. Paths were essential to the strict geometry of Renaissance garden design. In his 1625 essay on gardens, Francis Bacon called for 'alleys, spacious and fair...enough for four to walk a breast'. Even in describing the scents of flowers, Bacon specified that they were to be planted so 'you may walk by a whole row of them'. The significance of the activity in this context can be indicated by the companion proverb to 'the walls have ears': 'hedges have ears'.[9] If any structure of sufficient size could conceal eavesdroppers, then what was reassuring about the garden was not only its acoustical inefficiency, as sound dissipated in open air, but also its spatial range, so that confidences could be exchanged elusively, in motion, rather than captured in stasis.

The construct was so prevalent as to have been thoroughly internalized. In his notorious dream of 1597, Simon Forman imagines jesting to the aging Elizabeth, 'I mean to wait *upon* you and not under you, that I might make this belly a little bigger to carry up this smock and coats out of the dirt.' His fantasy takes him not into a palace chamber, as might seem at once more appropriate and more titillating to us, but instead to the countryside. He remembers having delivered his scurrilous remarks as 'she and I walked up and down through lanes and closes'. Even in his unconscious imagination, the outdoors was more intimate than the bedroom, and the license of space and motion were required for clandestine speech. As late as 1663, Roger Lowe described his courtship of Mary Naylor in similar terms: 'we went into a narrow lane and spoke our minds walking to and fro, and engaged to be faithful till death'.[10]

Walking was a highly popular form of exercise in the sixteenth century, especially after dining, when it served, as the educator Richard Mulcaster wrote, to 'settle [meat] better in the bottom of [the] stomach'. A familiar proverb recommended: 'After dinner, talk a while; after supper, walk a mile.' Elizabeth preferred the mornings, and she took her constitutional at a sufficient pace 'to get up a heat'. She was 69 in September 1602, when the visiting Duke of Stettin saw her walking 'as briskly as though she were eighteen years old'. Mulcaster analyzed in detail the differing health benefits of walking swiftly or slowly, uphill or downhill, on even or uneven ground, over long distances or

---

[9] Francis Bacon, 'Of Gardens', in *Sir Francis Bacon: The Essayes or Counsels, Civill and Morall*, ed. Michael Kiernan (Cambridge, Mass.: Harvard University Press, 1985), 142, 140. See Morris Palmer Tilley, *A Dictionary of the Proverbs in England in the Sixteenth and Seventeenth Centuries* (Ann Arbor: University of Michigan Press, 1950), for proverb W19: 'Walls (Hedges) have ears (eyes).'

[10] Paul Johnson, *Elizabeth I* (New York: Holt, Rinehart & Winston, 1974), 117; Louis Montrose, 'Shaping Fantasies: Figurations of Gender and Power in Elizabethan Culture', *Representations* 2 (Spring 1983), 61–94. For Lowe, *English Family Life, 1576–1716: An Anthology from Diaries*, ed. Ralph Houlbrooke (Oxford: Basil Blackwell, 1988), 19.

short, in sun or in shade, before midday or in the evening. He concluded that the benefits of walking were no respecter of person, age, or gender. It was 'not only the most excellent exercise', he wrote, 'but almost alone worthy to bear the name of an exercise'.[11]

This was the excellency to which the long gallery was explicitly dedicated. George Cavendish characterized Wolsey's galleries as 'large and long and good to walk in'. In Massinger's *A New Way to Pay Old Debts* a character describes 'walking, for health sake, in the gallery'. The 1620 will of John Wilson specified that his widow was to be permitted to 'walk and recreate herself at all times in the gallery' at Charlton House in Kent. The gallery also made space for related leisure activities. For example, that at the More in Hertfordshire had a butt for Henry VIII to practice his crossbow, and, in Kent, Knole still retains a pulley contraption so that those stretching their legs can also strengthen their arms.[12] But it was the known physical benefit of walking that gave the makers of long galleries an irreproachable pretext for their spatial profligacy. At Burton Constable in Yorkshire the room was measured out so that anyone walking up and back twenty-four times would travel precisely a mile.

GARDENS AND GALLERIES

Walking was the behavior practiced in both gardens and galleries. The two had always shared other sorts of material and conceptual space, as well. Most

---

[11] Richard Mulcaster, 'Of Walking', ch. 20 in *Positions* (London: 1581), sigs. L1^r–L4^v. For the proverb: in his *Heptameron of Civic Discourses*, George Whetstone depicts a party who 'pause[d] a little after their dinner, observing therein an old health rule: "After dinner, talk a while, After supper, walk a mile."' (*A Critical Edition of George Whetstone's 1582 An Heptameron of Civill Discourses*, ed. Diana Shklanka, The Renaissance Imagination 35 (New York: Garland, 1987), sig. E4^r). Johnson, *Elizabeth I*, 432. Mulcaster adds that 'walking in a close gallery is not so good, because the air there is not so fresh . . . unless the gallery be in the uppermost buildings of the house' (sig. L3^v).

[12] Cavendish quoted by Coope, 'The Gallery in England', 448. Philip Massinger, *A New Way to Pay Old Debts*, ed. T. W. Craik, New Mermaids (London: Ernest Benn, 1964), 4.1.166. Will of John Wilson cited by M. Jourdain, *English Decoration and Furniture of the Early Renaissance* (London: B. T. Batsford, 1924), 5. *The History of the King's Works*, 168 (More). In 1698, Roger North said 'This is a room for no other use but pastime and health' (quoted by Platt, *Great Rebuildings*, 78). Galleries were also used for musical entertainments and as safe places for children to play (when Jane Seymour was pregnant, a gallery was built connecting her lodging with the nursery; see Simon Thurley, *Hampton Court: A Social and Architectural History* (New Haven: Yale University Press for the Paul Mellon Centre for Studies in British Art, 2003), 66–8). They were frequently sites for shovelboard tables (as at Ingatestone, where the table was 4$^3/_4$ yd long; see Emmison, *Tudor Secretary*, 220).

of the very earliest galleries were described as 'going into the garden', and they continued throughout their history to be built in intimate relationship to gardens, either running alongside them, providing private entrance to them, or offering overviews of them. At Richmond, Spanish visitors who accompanied Catherine of Aragon to her marriage with Prince Arthur in 1501 were shown through 'goodly gardens' to the 'gallery upon the walls', and this sheltered viewing area was eventually extended to make a complete enclosure of the tended grounds. The first known reference to a private long gallery is from 1509, when Edmund Dudley's London house was described as having a 'long gallery against the garden'. And a Venetian visitor to Whitehall in 1531 referred to 'three so-called galleries which are long porticos or halls without chambers, with windows on each side looking on rivers and gardens'. The standard definition of the space remains that of H. M. Colvin and John Summerson: 'a long room which leads nowhere'—that is, it is not a corridor—'but exists in its own right as a place of recreation overlooking the garden'.[13]

The paucity of goods and furnishings in a long gallery further exaggerated its kinship with the garden because, while within the dominion of the householder, it was nonetheless less marked by personality and possession than other enclosed spaces. As was also contributory to its conversational virtues, it was thus comparatively neutral territory. In the earliest long galleries, the principal decorations were painted cloths which brought nature scenes indoors. Through their close associations and shared activities, therefore, at least one difference between interior and exterior was deconstructed in the early modern period, until there occurred a sort of conceptual merge. In 1549 Edward VI complained that Windsor had 'no galleries nor no gardens to walk in' (Elizabeth was not to add one until the early 1580s). Henry Peacham reported that in Europe the 'gardens and galleries of great men are beautified and set forth to admiration' with antiquities. By the time Francis Bacon wrote 'Of Gardens' in 1625, the chief aspect of the long gallery was so thoroughly established that he could read it back into the garden: there, he said, 'You are to form [alleys] likewise for shelter, that when the wind blows sharp, you may walk, as in a gallery.'[14]

No interior structure could seem more unnatural on first acquaintance, more transformational, more a flight from what we suppose to be rational

[13] *History of the King's Works*, 17. Coope, 'The Gallery in England', 448, 446–7 (Dudley and Whitehall). *History of the King's Works*, 17–18 (quoting 17). The *OED* cites Bartholomew Yong's *Diana* (1598): 'The Lady is in the gallery over her garden, taking the fresh air of the cool night.'

[14] *History of the King's Works*, 18 (Edward VI). Henry Peacham, The *Complete Gentleman, The Truth of Our Times, and the Art of Living in London*, ed. Virgil B. Heltzel (Ithaca, NY: Cornell University Press for the Folger Shakespeare Library, 1962), 117. Bacon, 'Of Gardens', 144.

architectural organization. This was space thinly interiorized, wrapped to the extent possible in sheets of glass, often tethered to the house merely by one long shared wall, sometimes only by an end wall. Frequently, the gallery went 'without chambers', that is, without the proximity to other spaces adjoining it or beyond it that characterized all other architectural experience. Its main connection with the rest of the house was not a room but a staircase, which through its own vertical shaft also worked its way free of the horizontal map of interrelated household spaces.

The near-perfect autonomy of some long galleries was part of their almost magical affiliation with the outside world, with gardens. Hardwick was designed from the first to culminate in its long gallery, but many houses had to be retrofitted to accommodate the Tudor craze for the space. It was easy enough to create new parlors and private dining chambers in old buildings, for these rooms were boxy, interchangeable, and adaptable. But at The Vyne, for example, a whole new wing had to be constructed. Little Moreton Hall in Cheshire was a rambling fifteenth-century house of two stories throughout until 1570 or so, when a third floor was superimposed on a gatehouse wing for a gallery with ornamental plasterwork and with windows on both long sides. At Penshurst in Kent, a new two-storied wing was constructed in 1599, linking one section of the house with a free-standing tower, the long gallery on the upper level and a 'nether gallery' below letting out into the garden. At Burton Agnes, in Humberside, frontal symmetry was ingeniously executed. But the mounting of a third story along the entrance façade, only for the sake of a long gallery running the entire width of the building, rendered the side façades oddly asymmetrical. Astley Hall in Lancashire was significantly remodeled as late as 1656, but it was a curious throwback, thoroughly Elizabethan in design, with another third story added only across the front to allow for a glass-walled long gallery. In imperfectly integrated spaces such as these, the free-floating autonomy of the long gallery realized its purest form. As came increasingly to be understood, its nature was to be hospitable to private conversation.

The network of associations between garden, gallery, walking, and intimacy can be traced in an investigation conducted by Elizabeth's Privy Council in December 1580. Edward de Vere, seventeenth Earl of Oxford, had accused Charles Arundel, Henry Howard, and Francis Southwell of treason. Arundel counter-claimed that he had incurred Oxford's anger by refusing to falsely name the two others 'papists'. The attempted solicitation was made, according to Arundel, 'On Sunday last, being Christmas Day', when Oxford 'desired secret conference with me'. Their appointed rendezvous was outside 'the Maids' chamber door' at Whitehall Palace, where Anne Vavasor, then six months pregnant by Oxford, 'was the mean of our meeting'. Together, the two men 'departed thence to have gone to the garden. But the door being double locked or bolted, we could not get in. Then we returned to the terrace and there, in the farther part of the low gallery', the private conversation that was in search of a secure location finally took place.

Oxford and Arundel had moved uneasily from the eavesdropping household out toward a garden but, finding it inaccessible, had sought its domestic cognate. The 'low gallery' at Whitehall ran along the east side of the Privy Garden and may have been named for its proximity to the Thames.[15] If Arundel's anecdote goes to confirm the related uses of gardens and galleries, another report from Guzman de Silva suggests that on some occasions the gallery could be even more facilitative of private conversation. In July 1564, the Spanish ambassador wrote to Philip II that he had called on Elizabeth where she visited in a courtier's house. She was walking in a garden at the time with her noblemen and ladies, and de Silva was shown into a room while his arrival was announced. She then honored him by sending for him to join her, and bid him 'forget that the Queen was there and look upon her as a private lady'. He indicated his awareness of others about her, and 'answered that wherever monarchs were there was their regal state, as I perceived in this case'. Elizabeth rose to the implicit challenge. 'We then went into a very large gallery, where she took me aside for nearly an hour.'[16] In the long gallery, Elizabeth was able to be as 'private' a lady as was possible for her.

Walking is mentioned so often in these accounts that it must have come to serve as a sort of mnemonic device, a conditioned response to the stimulus of the site. The behavior, walking, was itself capable of inciting the state of being, privacy. But in some cases walking seemed to be no more than a necessary prologue to private conversation. It actively reassured discussants that they were taking themselves out of the overhearing range of others, especially as they reached the 'farther part' of a gallery. With their conversational intents established, however, they might then step 'aside' into one or another of the bay windows that were invariably an adjunct of the space. Sometimes the size of a small room, these alcoves typically contained such meager furnishings as the gallery might have.

---

[15] I am grateful to Alan H. Nelson for introducing me to this episode and for sharing his facsimiles of PRO SP15/27A[/46], fos. 81–2. I rely also upon Nelson's since-published version of the episode, in *Monstrous Adversary: The Life of Edward de Vere, 17th Earl of Oxford* (Liverpool: Liverpool University Press, 2003), 249–58. For more on accusations against Oxford, see also Conyers Read, *Lord Burghley and Queen Elizabeth* (New York: Alfred A. Knopf, 1960), ch. 9, 'Theobalds and the Oxford Marriage', and esp. 129–30. On the 'low gallery' (and other Whitehall galleries), see *The History of the King's Works*, *The Survey of London*, and Simon Thurley, *Whitehall Palace: An Architectural History of the Royal Apartments 1240–1698* (New Haven: Yale University Press in association with Historic Royal Palaces, 1999).

[16] *CSP Spanish*, i. no. 256: Guzman de Silva to the King (10 July 1564), 367–8.

The bay represented a distinct advance over the garden in nurturing conversational privacy. It was a structural paradox: a defined, interior space that had no interior walls at all. It projected out into empty air at the second or third story, was sheathed in glass on three sides, and for a fourth opened into the long gallery, itself nearly free-floating. A space without walls was a space miraculously incapable of sustaining the proverbial listening 'ears' of the treacherous house. The sound of private conversation was contained in the bay and protected, for no other walker could approach unnoticed. Francis Bacon called 'inbowed windows' 'pretty retiring places for conferences', and that was precisely how Sir Peter Legh used his long gallery bay at Lyme Park in the late sixteenth century. Seated there, he met with members of his household, gave them their wages, and heard their complaints. In the bay, each could be assured that these discussions took place in confidence. It was a strategy that had been adopted far earlier by Thomas Wolsey, known to have used the bays of his dining and presence chambers for conversation. He was also to be one of the great builders of long galleries, with their even more secretive effects.[17]

WHAT THOMAS WOLSEY KNEW

At Richmond in 1501, gallery windows looked into the royal garden on one side and out to the river on the other. The way in which old corridors were converted into galleries at Knole and at Croyden was through the addition of windows. Because these fittings were essential to the form, long galleries played a more significant role in architectural history than their eccentric proportions alone suggest. They were key to the process by which great houses reoriented themselves, no longer turning exclusively in upon themselves but instead opening out and interacting with their gardens, their orchards, and their surroundings. The moment of transformation is captured perfectly at Gosfield Hall in Essex. The lower level presents a blank brick wall broken by a single arched entrance into its medieval courtyard. On the upper level,

---

[17] Bacon, 'Of Building', 137. Coope also cites Sir Roger North, who wrote in the late seventeenth century that 'these recesses are for select companies to converse in' ('The "Long Gallery": Its Origins', 59). Lady E. Newton, *The House of Lyme from its Foundation to the End of the Eighteenth Century* (London: William Heinemann, 1917), 58 (Sir Piers Legh). George Cavendish, *The Life and Death of Cardinal Wolsey*, in Sylvester and Harding (eds.), *Two Early Tudor Lives*, 168, 175 (conversations in long gallery bays), 99 (conversation in presence chamber bay), 143 (conversation in dining chamber bay). My argument is that the bays associated with galleries were doubly private.

however, sun glints off the glass that pierces the wall of the Elizabethan long gallery.

From the perspective of the viewer within, the change could be less social and interactive than imperial. Renaissance Rebuildings changed the 'way of being related to the world', according to Terry Comito, making the setting of a house not only 'a positive presence' but also 'a medium to be shaped and given form'. The walker in the gallery believed himself to inhabit an architecture known previously to the ancients, and any apprehension of an 'achievement of classical greatness' was 'felt as a conquest and transformation of space, of the natural world'.[18] The visual command afforded by the gallery was an important aspect of the power it seemed to confer upon its owner. Thus, status competitions arose around long galleries. François I, for example, inquired jealously after the length of Henry VIII's gallery. The builder of Berwick vowed that 'Worksop gallery was but a garret in respect of the gallery that would there be' (that is, at Berwick).[19]

Inside, the intuition of supremacy that the gallery inspired found expression in the most ambitious decorative programs of the age. The long gallery at York Place (later to be known as Whitehall) overlooked the Thames, with fourteen windows on both sides. Still there was room for intricately carved wainscoting 'representing a thousand beautiful figures', and, above, twenty-one tapestries illustrating the stories of Jacob and Joseph. In another of his galleries Wolsey hung cloth of gold, cloth of silver, and finely embroidered ecclesiastical vestments. Henry VIII hired Henry Blankston to create 'antic work' on the walls of his gallery at Hampton Court, with gilded images of mermaids and naked children. This, François I disdained; he told the English ambassador Sir John Wallop that he preferred 'divers colors of natural wood such as ebony, brazil, and others'. Theobalds had both a 'Green Gallery', which showed painted trees laden with the arms of all the noble and gentle families of England, and a 'Great Gallery', with a magnificent display of world emperors, the knights of the Golden Fleece, and 'the most splendid cities in the world and their garments and fashions'. A carved overmantel in the gallery at Audley End illustrated the labors of Hercules. The plasterwork ceiling of the Blickling long gallery had emblems based on Peacham's *Minerva Britannia*, including the five senses and the virtues; that at Lanhydrock featured Old Testament scenes interspersed with various birds and beasts. A pretext for this proliferation of ornament was the visual entertainment of the walker, but at

[18] Terry Comito, *The Idea of the Garden in the Renaissance* (New Brunswick, NJ: Rutgers University Press, 1978), 8, 152–3.

[19] *History of the King's Works*, 20–1. George Chaworth quoted on Berwick (1607) by Girouard, *Robert Smythson*, 113.

Oatlands, with wall paintings of eight royal houses, a 'leaning place' was also provided for more leisurely viewing.[20]

In mid-sixteenth century, tastes changed. Rather than commissioning wall paintings, many great owners began to collect easel paintings. A gallery at Hampton Court already had twenty by 1547, each hung from a nail by means of a red ribbon, and each provided with its own curtain. The famous perspective portrait of Edward VI was mounted in the long gallery at Whitehall. As early as 1546, the third Duke of Norfolk had twenty-eight 'physiognomies of divers noble persons' in his gallery at Kenninghall. In 1577, William Lovelace owned a show of Roman emperors. The collection of the Dean of St Paul's, in Thomas Heywood's *If You Know Not Me, You Know Nobody, Part Two*, was presumably based in fact; there, his Doctor Nowell explains to visitors that 'I have drawn you to this walk, | A gallery, wherein I keep the pictures | Of many charitable citizens.' The point, says Nowell, is that 'having fully satisfied your bodies, | You may by them learn to refresh your souls.'[21]

Leicester House, Beddington, and Old Thorndon Hall were all known for their portrait groups. Viscount Howard of Bindon wrote to Robert Cecil about 'the gallery I lately made for the pictures of sundry of my honored friends, whose presentation thereby to behold will greatly delight me to walk often in that place where I may see so comfortable a sight'. The gallery at Wollaton Hall was one of many in which maps were hung. Thomas and Aletheia Howard, Earl and Countess of Arundel, so prized their marble antiquities that for their companion portraits they posed at the entrance to the gallery in which were displayed their Greek and Roman statuary, busts, monumental inscriptions, and sarcophagi. Paintings, portraits, and sculpture were eventually to become inextricably associated with the field of their exhibition; by the late seventeenth century the 'gallery' had accrued its modern connotation as an exhibition area.[22]

---

[20] For Whitehall, *History of the King's Works*, 304. Wolsey's gallery is described by Cavendish, *Life . . . of Wolsey*, 102–3. *History of the King's Works*, 21, 133, 216 (Hampton Court and Oatlands). John Summerson, 'The Building of Theobalds, 1564–1585', *Archaeologia* 97 (1959), 116–17, 124 (Theobalds). See also Frederic Gerschow, 'Diary of the Journey of Philip Julius, Duke of Stettin-Pomerania, through England in the Year 1602', ed. Gottfried von Bülow, *Transactions of the Royal Historical Society* NS 6 (1892), 31.

[21] Coope, 'The "Long Gallery": Its Origins', 62. Thomas Heywood, *If You Know Not Me, You Know Nobody, Part II*, ed. Madeleine Doran, Malone Society Reprints (Oxford: Oxford University Press, 1935), ll. 759–63.

[22] Coope, 'The "Long Gallery": Its Origins', 62 (Leicester House); Roy Strong, 'Sir Francis Carew's Garden at Beddington', in Edward Chaney and Peter Mack (eds.), *England and the Continental Renaissance: Essays in Honour of J. B. Trapp* (Woodbridge: Boydell, 1990), 233; Jennifer C. Ward, 'The History of Old Thorndon Hall', in *Old Thorndon Hall* (n.p.: Essex County Council, 1972), 8. Howard quoted by Coope, 'The Gallery in England', 449–50. D. E. L. Haynes, 'The Arundel Marbles' (Oxford: Ashmolean Museum, 1975). Arundel was the grandson of the

The earlier history of the long gallery as a space of status was inextricably bound up with that of Thomas Wolsey. All evidences are that the room was a French invention, and it was in that country that Wolsey evidently developed the taste he was to bring back to England. George Cavendish describes a diplomatic mission in which the English cardinal met with the French king at a castle in Compiègne. Making a subtle testimony to Wolsey's standing, Cavendish says that the lodging space at Compiègne was split into equal parts. Even the long gallery was 'divided between them, wherein was made in the middest thereof a strong wall with a door and window'. According to Cavendish, 'the King and my lord would many times meet at the same window and secretly talk together'.[23] In the bay windows of his dining room and presence chamber Wolsey had already demonstrated a shrewd sense of the political uses of private exchange. The long gallery allowed him to create yet more sophisticated and coercive effects. Wolsey understood the gallery's powers of intimidation, that its authority was exerted not only in terms of vast size and material display, but also of conspicuously discrepant awarenesses. Knowledge was as susceptible to gradations of privilege as were buildings and furnishing—as the long gallery was uniquely capable of making manifest.

At York Place, for example, Wolsey placed a form (or bench) at one end of his long gallery. There, his men could 'take their ease' as he conducted negotiations further along, out of overhearing range. Wolsey had strategic uses for this entourage as for the space. When Henry VIII confided his 'secret affection' and 'secret intendment' for Anne Boleyn, it was because the king required Wolsey's intervention in the matter of a competing 'secret love', the private understanding between Boleyn and Henry Percy. To end the affair, Wolsey ordered Percy to appear in his long gallery. It would have been obvious to all that he could have dealt with Percy delicately. Instead he spoke within earshot of the assembled 'servants of his chamber': 'I marvel not a little . . . of thy peevish folly that thou wouldst tangle and insure thyself with a foolish girl.' Wolsey also summoned Percy's formidable father, the Earl of Northumberland, to London. His attendants watched as the two men had 'secret communication' at the far end of the gallery. Northumberland then replicated Wolsey's strategy, walking to the bench-sitters to say distinctly, 'Son . . . thou hast always been a proud, presumptuous, disdainful, and a very unthrift waster.' To take this private matter into a private space but then

---

fourth Duke of Norfolk; she, the daughter of the Earl of Shrewsbury. While conversational privacy dominates most sixteenth-century associations with the long gallery, and while the exhibition of paintings and maps features most strongly in the seventeenth century, both functions were current in both centuries, as Coope and Howard make clear.

[23] Cavendish, *Life . . . of Wolsey*, 61.

to expose it in a publicly humiliating way was a brute demonstration of prerogative. Percy broke off with Anne Boleyn.[24]

What Wolsey had also crucially recognized was that if the achievement of privacy was a rare event, then the public exhibition of that achievement was an act of power. Amid the backdrop of all the pressures to be public that have been the subjects of earlier chapters in this book, here at last was a privacy with commodity value—though its value lay in its public performance.

SPATIAL KNOWLEDGE

Soon enough, the peculiar effects of the long gallery were matters of common awareness. In 1573, they were foregrounded in George Gascoigne's notoriously pornographic *Adventures of Master F.J.*, where the conversational intimacy of the long gallery, its ambulatory range, its structural autonomy, its spatial neutrality, and its outdoor analogies took on a sexual charge.[25] The fictional F.J.'s infatuation for the married Dame Elinor is represented as having first been encouraged in a garden (p. 146). Their relationship advances, however, when 'his chance was to meet her alone in a gallery of the same house', where 'they walked and talked traversing divers ways' and where, as he offers to kiss her hand, she instead kisses his lips (pp. 148–9). The intimacy of this scene is set in high relief by subsequent action in Elinor's bedchamber, which is always shown to be crowded with a 'company' of other gentlemen and women (pp. 151–2). F.J. then 'counsel[s] his Mistress by little and little to walk abroad, saying that the gallery near adjoining was so pleasant, as if he were half dead he thought that by walking therein he might be half and more revived' (p. 156). The next night, 'taking him apart from the rest' who clutter the chamber-landscape, Elinor suggests that 'she would talk with him more at large in the gallery' (p. 167). F.J. waits until the servant sharing his own chamber is safely asleep. Then, with his nightgown concealing his 'naked sword', he steals 'to the gallery, where he [finds] his good Mistress walking in her night gown'. There follows a vivid depiction of their lovemaking on the 'hard floor' (pp. 167–8).

C. T. Prouty, long Gascoigne's chief editor, calls these markers of 'the physical environment' 'added details which have no direct connection with

---

[24] Ibid. 31–6. Wolsey's palace at York was to be renamed 'Whitehall' by Henry VIII.
[25] Although references below are to *A Hundreth Sundrie Flowers*, ed. G. W. Pigman III (Oxford: Clarendon, 2000), I have modernized more fully. For an excellent review of the criticism, especially regarding genre and textual revision, see 548–55.

the action of the love story'.[26] This, of course, goes against the grain of all this chapter would argue regarding material structures and how they shaped early modern social and secret relations. In fact, nearly every stage of F.J.'s love story has a totemic point of intersection with the long gallery, including its unhappy conclusion. The affair is made known to Elinor's sister, and F.J. thereafter grows suspicious that Elinor has lost interest in him. He haunts 'the gallery near adjoining' her chamber, wishing that it might work its magic yet one more time (p. 167). But, walking there, he overhears Dame Elinor and her 'secretary' exchanging ominously 'kind words'. With the secretary wielding the phallic pen, F.J. becomes all ears, listening surreptitiously near the threshold (p. 214).[27] The long gallery is not implicated in the sister's discovery of the affair; other spaces are, and now the easily eavesdropped bedchamber betrays Elinor's newer secrets and dashes F.J.'s forlorn hopes. *The Adventures of Master F.J.* was a symptom of spatial knowledge in Elizabethan England.

Thus, when Sir Henry Brounker was invited up to the long gallery of Hardwick Hall in 1603 he knew exactly how to orchestrate events.[28] Positioned at the uppermost level of the house, the gallery was 162 ft long, as wide as 40 ft at some points, and 26 ft high (see Fig. 6.3). It was hung with tapestries depicting the story of Gideon and featured two chimney pieces incorporating alabaster statues of Justice and Mercy.[29] Clearly, Bess of Hardwick considered this to be the most impressive of her presentational spaces, and so when she learned that an emissary of Elizabeth I had called upon her, she elected to receive him there. Brounker subsequently reported to the Queen that Hardwick 'sent for me into her gallery'. She had obliged him to cross the full length of the great

[26] C. T. Prouty (ed.), *George Gascoigne's A Hundreth Sundrie Flowers* (Columbia: University of Missouri Press, 1942), 199.

[27] Gascoigne describes a long gallery that did not go 'without chambers'; instead, Elinor's room opens off it.

[28] The incident recounted below has become familiar in recent years through work on women writers. See especially Sara Jayne Steen (ed.), *The Letters of Lady Arbella Stuart*, Women Writers in English, 1350–1850 (New York: Oxford University Press, 1994), 28–44, 120–76; and Barbara Kiefer Lewalski, 'Writing Resistance in Letters: Arbella Stuart and the Rhetoric of Disguise and Defiance', in *Writing Women in Jacobean England* (Cambridge, Mass.: Harvard University Press, 1993), 71–7. For this spatial analysis of the story, I have also consulted the *Calendar of the Manuscripts of . . . the Marquess of Salisbury . . . Preserved at Hatfield House*, 24 vols. (London: 1883–1976), xii. 593–7, 681–96 (Series of letters from or connected with Lady Arbella Stuart); David N. Durant, *Bess of Hardwick: Portrait of an Elizabethan Dynast* (New York: Atheneum, 1978), 202–13; id., *Arbella Stuart, a Rival to the Queen* (London: Weidenfeld & Nicolson, 1978); Sarah Gristwood, *Arbella: England's Lost Queen* (London: Bantam, 2003); and Oxford *DNB* entries for Elizabeth Talbot (by Elizabeth Goldring) and Arbella Stuart (by Rosalind K. Marshall).

[29] Mark Girouard, *Robert Smythson*, 143–60; id., National Trust guidebook to *Hardwick Hall* (1976 and revised edn., 1989).

Figure 6.3 The long gallery at Hardwick Hall, near Mansfield in Derbyshire. Photographed in the late nineteenth century.

hall and climb two tall flights of stairs to reach her as, in a feigned show of unconcern, 'she was walking with [her granddaughter] the Lady Arbella and her son William Cavendish'.

As the great-great-granddaughter of Henry VII, Lady Arbella Stuart had been instilled since birth with the very highest ambitions, and Hardwick had built her long gallery as a fit setting not only for herself as countess but also for her granddaughter as possible heir to the throne.[30] At the age of 27, recognizing that Elizabeth I was in failing health, and knowing also that no successor had been named, Stuart had finally grown impatient with nearly three decades of royal hopes and strict supervision. Unbeknownst to Hardwick, Stuart had dispatched a servant, John Dodderidge, to make an offer of matrimony to

[30] Henry VII's daughter Margaret Tudor had three husbands. Mary of Scotland was Margaret's granddaughter by her first marriage to James IV of Scotland. Arbella Stuart was Margaret's great-granddaughter by her second marriage to Archibald Douglas. The Hardwick connection came with the marriage Bess of Hardwick negotiated between her daughter (by her second marriage) Elizabeth Cavendish and Margaret's grandson Charles Stuart; Charles Stuart and Elizabeth Cavendish were Arbella Stuart's parents.

Edward Seymour, who was kin to the third wife of Henry VIII.[31] A statute of 1536 prohibited any person of royal blood from marrying without the reigning monarch's approval, and, to compound this intended act of treason, Stuart also sought to strengthen her own princely status by joining two formidable pedigrees. The proposal was brought to the attention of the Queen.

Seymour, then just 16, lived in Hampshire with his grandfather, the Earl of Hertford. In 1560 Hertford had secretly wed Katherine Grey, herself a great-granddaughter of Henry VII and tenth in the line of succession established by the dying Henry VIII.[32] For lack of proof, the marriage was invalidated; even so, Hertford and Grey were punished for having attempted a match without Elizabeth's permission. They were confined to the Tower for two years (and conceived their second child there) before being transferred to house arrests which kept them separate until Grey's death in 1568. Only then was Hertford allowed to return to Court, but he was assessed heavy fines and, forty years on, still had not succeeded in legitimating his descendants, including the young Edward Seymour. In 1595 he had been reminded of the royal will in these matters when it was discovered that his second son had sought to have the marriage reinstated; Hertford was returned to the Tower for several months. Stuart may have imagined that this personal history would dispose Hertford to fall in with her dangerous scheme, but in fact the opposite was true. He sought immediately to disassociate himself from it.[33] Dodderidge brought Stuart's proposal to Hertford's house on 30 December 1602; Hertford immediately sent him to Robert Cecil for questioning; Cecil referred Dodderidge to the Privy Council for further interrogation on 2 January; and Elizabeth personally commissioned Sir Henry Brounker to investigate the affair on 3 January. By 7 January, Brounker had traveled 145 miles from London to Derbyshire to examine Arbella Stuart.

In the long gallery at Hardwick Hall, Brounker made certain that Stuart knew from whence he had come and on whose authority: 'I told her Ladyship [that is, Hardwick], in the hearing of her grandchild, that your Highness . . . commanded me to see her.' Next, he expressed the Queen's

---

[31] Steen, *Letters*, is skeptical that the throne was Arbella's principal goal, noting that Stuart's 'consistently stated objectives were freedom from her grandmother's domination, the right to live where she chose, and the opportunity to marry' (p. 30). Brounker's view was that she sought mainly to draw attention to a situation she found intolerable.

[32] Henry VIII's will established the succession on his three children and their heirs, then the descendants of his younger sister Mary (with Catherine Grey preceded by her older sister Jane). He excluded the descendants of his older sister Margaret (including James V, Mary of Scotland, and their heirs).

[33] Steen, *Letters*, suggests that Hertford refused to see Dodderidge without witnesses and that, once Dodderidge's mission was made public, Hertford had no choice but to 'exonerate himself' (p. 31).

'gracious favor', at which point, he observed wryly, Hardwick was so relieved that 'I could hardly keep her from kneeling.' Then, Brounker led Hardwick aside: 'drawing her on with other compliments towards the further end of the gallery to free her from the young lady, I delivered your Majesty's letter'. With Stuart out of earshot, Brounker told Hardwick that it was Elizabeth's 'pleasure' that 'I might speak privately with the Lady Arbella'. Finally, 'leaving her there', recounted Brounker, 'I led the Lady Arbella to the other end of the long gallery'. Stuart at first 'denied all' but, under questioning, eventually offered to 'deal plainly and sincerely so as I would promise to conceal it from her grandmother'—this as Hardwick watched helplessly, out of hearing range, from the other end of the gallery.

While Stuart's scheme was not to succeed, she had the fleeting pleasures of having outfoxed the older woman in sending Dodderidge to Hampshire and now for the length of this private conference. She did not have many such opportunities, for she not only lived in her grandmother's house, she was required to sleep in her grandmother's bedchamber. It is difficult to determine whether Bess of Hardwick simply observed general custom in her household organization or whether she was more personally motivated by the suspicion that, in the interest of Stuart's royal prospects, her granddaughter could not be trusted ever to be private. In 1602 Hardwick wrote to Cecil and Sir John Stanhope that 'I have ancient gentlewomen in my house which are much with her, and gentlemen and others of good sufficiency.'

Brounker was finally persuaded that Hardwick, Seymour, and Hertford were guiltless in the matter, and he wrote to Elizabeth from Derbyshire that he 'found the house without any strange company'—that is, without any sign of political conspiracy or armed rebellion. There was only Stuart's secretly conceived plot. Hardwick, who forty years earlier had herself spent thirty-one weeks in the Tower for having been Katherine Grey's confidante in the matter of the unauthorized marriage to Hertford, wrote to Elizabeth at once. 'I did in my heart most humbly thank your Majesty for commanding that course to be taken', she said, referring to Brounker's disposition of events in her long gallery. At first, she admits, his strategy 'did make me doubtful that your Majesty had some suspicion in me', because of 'his preciseness at his first coming to keep the offense from me till he had privately talked with Arbell'.

Given what was revealed in the long gallery at Hardwick Hall, it was clear that Hardwick's hopes for her granddaughter would not be realized; in 1603, Bess disinherited the unfortunate 'Arbell'. In 1610, with James VI of Scotland fully secured as Elizabeth's successor on the English throne, Stuart finally made a clandestine marriage with Edward Seymour's younger brother, William. The union was even then so politically fraught that Hertford was summoned for interrogation by the Privy Council and Stuart was imprisoned. She died in the Tower in 1615. The room that Hardwick had designed as a fit setting for a royal aspirant had not achieved its end. Moreover, in the matter of the Brounker investigation, it had betrayed its designer. Its size and its acoustics had had the unintended consequence of making Hardwick a distant witness to, not an active participant in, the examination in which Stuart's potentially treasonous ambition was so momentously confessed.

The accidental aspects of the long gallery were not, moreover, the last of its effects. Associated in the first instance with ostentation, it surprised its earliest makers by affording them a new form of conversational privacy. When this by-product of status building was generally known, the long gallery also became a marker for the wish to achieve privacy. Elizabethans were keenly observant of those behaviors which demonstrated an *intent* to be secretive, because it was almost always a dangerous desire. Thus the index of material keys to recognizing private intents was lengthened in the 1560s to include resort to the long gallery. Just as, at the routine level of sexual liaison, deponents in the church courts reported that their suspicions were raised when two people retired behind a locked door during daylight hours, when a door was bolted on the inside, or when windows were shut, so, too, at the elevated level of political intrigue, witnesses to the central government confirmed official fears when they said that two alleged conspirators talked in a long gallery. This was the signifying capacity of the space for William Cecil, when he undertook an investigation into the so-called Ridolfi Plot against Elizabeth I. For him, the central questions seem to have been, 'What did you know and *where* did you know it?'

THE STIGMA OF PRIVACY

The events of 1568 through 1571 included various opposition schemes to free Mary Queen of Scots from virtual imprisonment in England, to raise funds for her in Catholic countries in Europe, to place her on the English throne (if necessary with the aid of Spanish forces in the Netherlands), and to restore the old religion. The man who was most famously judged guilty of the conspiracy that was to become known as the 'Ridolfi Plot' was Thomas Howard, fourth Duke of Norfolk.[34]

---

[34] For the following discussion of the Ridolfi plot, principal sources include: *A Collection of State Papers Relating to Affairs in the Reigns of King Henry VIII, King Edward VI, Queen Mary, and Queen Elizabeth from . . . 1542 to 1570*, ed. Samuel Haynes (London: William Bowyer, 1740) (hereafter, 'Haynes'); *A Collection of State Papers Relating to Affairs in the Reign of Queen*

When the fourth Duke succeeded his grandfather on 25 August 1554, he became the only living possessor of an English dukedom and, as such, 'the second person in this realm'. In the long gallery at his country seat, Kenninghall, he was accustomed to walking amidst the collected 'physiognomies' of twenty-eight world leaders, including Louis XI, François I, Charles IX, Richard III, and the Queen of Hungary. Norfolk himself added a long gallery to his London residence. This was known as the Charterhouse even after the Dissolution of the monasteries, when it was granted to Sir Edward North, but in Norfolk's possession it was proudly renamed Howard House. Norfolk was England's greatest landowner and richest man, heir to fifty-six manors, thirty-seven advowsons, and property incomes of some £4,500 annually.[35] He had a long personal history with Elizabeth, being kin to her through her Boleyn connections, and a significant public involvement with Scotland, having served the Queen as Lieutenant General of the North from 1559. In this role he became an ally of Cecil's, and in 1562 he was made a member of the Privy Council.

In 1564, thus, Norfolk joined in anxious discussions of 'the Mary problem'. At the time, Mary Stewart represented trouble primarily within Scotland, to which she had returned following the death of her first husband, François II, in 1560. Having come of age, she assumed a personal rule in her birth country despite the opposition of powerful Scottish lords. Her principal allies included William Maitland of Lethington and her illegitimate half-brother, Lord James Stewart, whom she created first Earl of Moray. Within two months of her arrival

Elizabeth from . . . 1571 to 1596, ed. William Murdin (London: William Bowyer, 1759) (hereafter, 'Murdin'); *The Trial of Thomas Duke of Norfolk by his Peers, for High Treason against the Queen*, ed. Joseph Brown (London: J. Morphew, 1709) (hereafter, *Trial*); CSPD; and *A Compleat Collection of State-Tryals . . . From the Reign of King Henry the Fourth, to the End of the Reign of Queen Anne*, 4 vols. (London: Timothy Goodwin et al., 1719) (hereafter, '*State Tryals*'). Especially helpful in establishing a chronology for the examinations is Neville Williams, *Thomas Howard, Fourth Duke of Norfolk* (London: Barrie & Rockliff, 1964) (hereafter, 'Williams'). I am also indebted to Francis Edwards, *The Marvellous Chance: Thomas Howard, Fourth Duke of Norfolk and the Ridolfi Plot, 1570–1572* (London: Rupert Hart-Davis, 1968) and the following entries in the *Oxford DNB*: Charles Baillie (by Peter Holmes), William Barker (by Kenneth R. Bartlett), William Brooke, tenth Baron Cobham (by Julian Lock), William Cecil, first Baron Burghley (by Wallace T. MacCaffrey), Henry Fitzalan, twelfth Earl of Arundel (by Julian Lock), William Herle (by David Lewis Jones), Thomas Howard, fourth Duke of Norfolk (by Michael A. R. Graves), John Lesley, Bishop of Ross (by Rosalind K. Marshall), Sir Richard Lowther (by C. H. H. Owen), John Lumley, first Baron Lumley (by Kathryn Barron), William Maitland of Lethington (by Mark Loughlin), Thomas Morgan (by Alison Plowden), Charles Neville, sixth Earl of Westmoreland (by Roger N. McDermott), Thomas Percy, seventh Earl of Northumberland (by Julian Lock), Roberto di Ridolfi (by L. E. Hunt), Sir Ralph Sadler (by Gervase Phillips), James Stewart, first Earl of Moray (by Mark Loughlin), Mary Stewart, Queen of Scots (by Julian Goodare), and John Story (by Julian Lock).

[35] John Martin Robinson, *The Dukes of Norfolk: A Quincentennial History* (Oxford: Oxford University Press, 1982), 54–6.

in Scotland, Mary had commissioned Maitland to represent her to Elizabeth in requesting that she be named next in line of succession to the English throne. This, Elizabeth declined to do; instead, in 1564, Elizabeth suggested that Mary might be matched with Robert Dudley, recently made a more suitable partner through his elevation to Earl of Leicester. The idea was that 'the Mary problem' would be best contained were she married not to a Catholic foreign prince but instead to a Protestant English nobleman. Later, with the Leicester match tabled, both Henry Fitzalan, twelfth Earl of Arundel, and also the newly widowed Norfolk were put forward as possible husbands, but Mary made the independent decision to wed her cousin Henry Stewart, Lord Darnley. Though his own initiatives were betrayed by this marriage, Maitland remained loyal to Mary. But Moray was sufficiently opposed to the Darnley match that he broke with his sister irrevocably. Following the ignominious failure of his rebellion, the so-called 'Chase-about Raid', Moray retreated to England, then France. In 1567, however, he was called back to Scotland. That year, Darnley was murdered; Mary was abducted by James Hepburn, fourth Earl of Bothwell, and then married him; Mary relinquished the throne to her infant son; and Moray, a committed Protestant, became regent of Scotland during the minority of James VI. Mary escaped imprisonment in 1568 and fled to England, where the succession issue was again urgently pressed. At this point, Norfolk favored Katherine Grey to be named next in line to the throne and not, as Leicester did, Mary Stewart. The pieces were soon to come together differently.

In May 1568, Elizabeth authorized an October commission on the future of the dethroned Queen. Mary agreed to the summit on the understanding that the subject in arbitration should be the conditions for her return to power in Scotland. She was herself unable to attend the negotiations in York, being forcibly domiciled at Bolton; Maitland represented her interests, as did John Leslie, Bishop of Ross. Moray appeared as her adversary. Elizabeth appointed as mediators Thomas Radcliffe, third Earl of Sussex; Sir Ralph Sadler; and, as chief commissioner, Norfolk. Although Norfolk seems not to have been enthusiastic, he accepted a charge that was to prove so fateful that his apologists subsequently suggested that his enemies had intended to entrap him by means of his assignment to the Lord Presidency of the Council in the North. In York, he went hawking privately with Maitland on 16 October. Outdoors, alone, and face-to-face, Maitland raised the subject of a match with Mary. The alliance would advance Maitland's own goals to secure Mary's position as chief claimant for the English crown and to unite the two kingdoms. The proposal now achieved a more favorable reception from Norfolk. With some prospects for Elizabeth's marriage newly abandoned, with Katherine Grey recently dead, and with Mary auspiciously furnished with a son, Mary's position in the English succession suddenly appeared significantly stronger. Norfolk could anticipate that the normal course of events, which at some point would include Elizabeth's natural death, would bring him and his heirs to the throne of England.

Thus encouraged, Maitland advised Moray and Ross to undertake 'familiar conference' with Norfolk, each to 'speak with the Duke secretly alone, without the [other] commissioners'. At seven o'clock in the morning Ross and Norfolk talked 'alone in a gallery', cautiously acknowledging common interests. And Moray, who by this point regarded Maitland as a 'necessary evil', also agreed to meet Norfolk at a 'time and place convenient in the gallery of the house where the Duke was lodged'. In the private exchange that the long gallery admitted, the two men concluded that they themselves, each so powerful and so esteemed in his own country, represented the best hope for amity between England and Scotland.[36] At Norfolk's later trial for treason, his accusers traced the origins of his misplaced ambition and suspicious behavior back to York: 'If you meant directly, then needed you not to have dealt so secretly in conference with Lethington [Maitland] without the rest of the commissioners.' Both Ross and Moray, declared Sergeant Nicholas Barham, had confirmed 'your practicing with them to the same intent'.[37]

Norfolk and his fellows were abruptly summoned south for a new commission, the Westminster Conference. The climate had changed, and Mary's reinstatement in Scotland was no longer at issue. Instead, Moray, who had been promised that Mary would not be restored were she proved guilty of murder, displayed the 'Casket Letters'. They had the sensational effect of seeming to show that Mary had committed adultery with Bothwell and had conspired with him to kill Darnley. Before Mary's allies adjourned the commission, admitting defeat, Moray and Norfolk again met independently. In the park at Hampton Court, Norfolk scrupulously deplored the events of Mary's recent past, but he said that he might nonetheless 'find in [his] heart to love her' if she repented her ill-advised behavior and divorced Bothwell. When questioned subsequently, Norfolk neglected to mention where these early interviews took place. The eventual charges against him emphasized not the substance of the discussion with Moray, for example, but the fact that the two men 'secretly confer[red] thereof in the park'.[38]

The next spring, at Easter time 1569, Norfolk tested the idea of marriage with Mary on his man Lawrence Bannister, this time in the garden at Howard

---

[36] For Ross, see Murdin, 'Letter from the Bishop of Ross' (6 November 1571), 53; *State Tryals*, 73–4; Williams, 139. For Moray, *State Tryals*, 75–6.

[37] *Trial*, 49.

[38] Haynes, 'A Summary of Matters wherewith the Duke of Norfolk hath been charged for the Attempt to Marry with the Scots Queen' (20 January 1569), 574. For Moray, *State Tryals*, 76.

House.[39] Cecil, who may originally have approved the notion, withdrew his support after quarreling with Norfolk in mid-May.[40] Leicester and William Herbert, first Earl of Pembroke, rallied to the proposed union; their motives included opposition to the man whose increasing power had not long before been celebrated in his creation as Lord Burghley. Other supporters of the marriage included strange bedfellows Moray and Maitland, the English agent Sir Nicholas Throckmorton, and the Scottish go-between Ross.

In June 1569 Mary agreed to wed Norfolk. On 1 July, Norfolk wrote to Moray in cipher regarding his own 'secret determination'. With respect to the proposed marriage he had 'proceeded so far therein as I with conscience can neither revoke that that I have done, nor never mean to go back from it'.[41] This was a language of betrothal; in the church courts, witnesses to a disputed promise might remember the dissenting party having once claimed to have 'gone so far he could never go back'. However, Mary had raised the crucial question of how Elizabeth's approval was to be obtained. It was one thing for Elizabeth herself to have matched one of her noblemen with her Scottish 'sister', but, as the Earl of Hertford knew, it was another thing entirely for plans to go forward without the English Queen's knowledge and consent. Norfolk had already taken the initiative of discussing the issue with Leicester as Leicester sat fishing at Thamesside near Kew. Leicester insisted that he should broach the subject with Elizabeth himself, though it was nearly a year before he contrived an occasion.

Feigning illness, Leicester begged the Queen to visit him at the Earl of Southampton's house in Titchfield. On 6 September 1569, immediately after talking with Leicester, Elizabeth summoned Norfolk to Southampton's gallery for a private confrontation. She 'commanded and charged him that he should not deal any further therein with the Queen of Scots, nor any other person in that matter'. Later, she said she had charged him 'upon his allegiance', which meant that to defy her was treason. Norfolk professed at first not to remember this stricture. He may have been emboldened in his denial by the knowledge that the long gallery would yield up no third parties to contradict him. If so, this was another mark of the arrogance he is said to have displayed throughout, because the principal witness against him was an incontrovertible one. Sergeant Barham subsequently asked sarcastically if he could name a single occasion on which he had in fact honored his Titchfield pledge: 'I

[39] For Bannister, see Murdin, 'Banister's [*sic*] Declaration' (29 September 1571), 134; Williams, 222.

[40] See the 15 May 1569 letter from Sussex to Cecil regretting his falling-out with Norfolk (*Hatfield*, i. no. 1301) and the 9 June 1569 letter from Sussex to Cecil 'heartily glad' for their reconciliation (ibid. i. no. 1307).

[41] Ibid. i. no. 1312; see also Haynes, 520.

pray you, at what time . . . *did* you forbear to deal with the Scottish queen?' (emphasis added). Under the duress of his trial, Norfolk finally admitted that Elizabeth had indeed engaged his allegiance.[42]

Three days later Cecil wrote to Sir William Drury in the Queen's name, requiring him to investigate Moray's activities and advising him that Elizabeth would never be 'so weak in this great cause as to suffer this to proceed'. Another week passed and then Norfolk angrily left Titchfield without Elizabeth's permission to do so. He traveled to London to meet with Pembroke. It could be argued that at this point Norfolk still imagined only a politic marriage and an orderly succession, and that he did not countenance the plots of others to secure the help of Spain, to rally a force to free Mary from her current captivity, and to revolt against Elizabeth. But it also seems increasingly unlikely that he was entirely ignorant of these plans. Hugh Owen, a servant of Norfolk's former father-in-law the Earl of Arundel, later reported that he joined Norfolk on the road to London and there told him of a scheme to seize the Tower of London. Its treasures were to be used to fund Mary's cause. Ross subsequently confirmed that the 'device' of the Tower had been concocted in the 'low gallery at Arundel House', where he, Arundel, Norfolk's man Liggons, and also Roberto Ridolfi met. At Norfolk's trial much was made of the fact that his knowledge of the device proved an 'intention to pursue the marriage with force'.[43]

Norfolk was in London for less than a week in the fall of 1569, but in that time Ross was secretly smuggled into Howard House. Liggons met Ross at about seven o'clock in the evening at Norfolk's great gate, showed him to the Back Court, and led him into 'the gallery next the churchyard'. The secretary William Barker did not see or hear the meeting, but he observed that Ross came 'privily' and 'closely', through the 'backside', rather than 'openly' as in the past. He later remembered speculating with his fellows as to why Norfolk and Ross 'dare[d] not be seen in their business'—in other words, why the meeting and their conversation were so private.[44]

Said to be 'always upon the watch', Cecil received intelligence from all directions about Norfolk's ambitions. On 23 September it was reported to him that even in Strasburg it was rumored that 'England is in a ferment on account of the Duke of Norfolk seeking the Scottish Queen in marriage.' A

---

[42] *State Tryals*, 80; Williams, 159; *Trial*, 69, 57.

[43] For Cecil to Drury, see *Hatfield*, i. no. 1325. For Owen, Williams, 160. For Arundel, Murdin, 'The Bishop of Ross's Examination touching Sir Henry Percy and Diverse Others' (26 October 1571), 23; *Hatfield*, i. no. 1456; *Trial*, 59.

[44] For Ross, see Murdin, 'The Examination of the Bishop of Ross' (6 November 1571), 50. For Barker, see Murdin, 'The Examination of William Barker' (7 November 1571), 125–6. On 3 November 1571, putting together the pieces, Cecil made a note that 'the Bishop of Ross was at Howard House three days before the Duke fled from thence into Norfolk' (*Hatfield*, i. no. 1710).

week later, Lord Wentworth wrote Cecil that 'it is concluded by astronomy that the Scottish damsel shall be queen, and the Duke her husband'. Thus provoked, Cecil 'bent his mind diligently to sift out the matter' of Norfolk's 'secret conferences'. He ordered a series of examinations, beginning with the Earl of Pembroke and continuing throughout the month of October with Sir Nicholas Throckmorton, the Earl of Arundel, Lord Lumley, Edward Herbert, John Farnham, William Cantrell, Robert Wiseman, John Parsons, Sir Thomas Cornwallis, Edward Clere, Thomas Kytson, Michael Hare, and others. Cecil also sought out the Earl of Moray, receiving his account of the York and Westminster conferences before Moray was assassinated in January 1570. After his own questioning, the Bishop of Ross warned an ally that 'in case we were demanded severally upon our meeting and conference . . . both should say it was upon the sudden and not of purpose'.[45]

Meanwhile, warned by Leicester that there was talk of his imprisonment, Norfolk had hastily left London for Kenninghall. On 24 September he wrote to the Queen that he 'thought no way so good as privily to withdraw' to his 'private house'. Her overnight reply summoned him 'upon his allegiance' to appear at Windsor. Clearly, there was at this time still hope of containing the situation; the Lieutenants of the Shires were advised by the Privy Council that Norfolk's presence was demanded in deference to his nobility, not in censure, to protect him from the 'abuse' of 'untrue reports'. But Norfolk himself was not reassured; he told Edward Clere that, having been warned that his 'life was in peril', he had just three options: to obey the Queen's command; to flee England and live 'privately' abroad; or 'to stand upon his guard'. In the event, he hit on a fourth, pretending himself too ill to travel. Elizabeth refused this excuse and repeated her demand that he come to court. That same day, Cecil wrote to Norfolk, too, promising him that the Queen was not 'offended' with him. If Norfolk was skeptical, this may be because, in an indication of the level of central government concern, only three days had passed since he had first notified Elizabeth of his departure. Within a week he was placed under house arrest. Keeper Sir Henry Neville was advised that the Duke was to be held 'without conference with any person without [your] knowledge'.[46]

[45] *Hatfield*, i. no. 1336 (Strasburg); ibid. i. no. 1353 (Wentworth). For examinations, see ibid. i. nos. 1356, 1366–72, 1374–8, 1383–4, 1388–90, 1392, 1394–6, 1398. Murdin, 39 (Letter of the Bishop of Ross, 2 November 1571).

[46] *Hatfield*, i. no. 1338 (letter from Norfolk to the Queen, 24 September 1569); ibid. i. no. 1339 (letter from the Queen to Norfolk, 25 September 1569); Haynes, 529; *Hatfield*, i. no. 1342 (letter from the Council to the Lieutenants of the Shire, 26 September 1569); Haynes, 531; *Hatfield*, i. no. 1395 (testimony of Edward Clere); ibid. i. nos. 1344 (letter of Queen to Norfolk) and 1345 (Cecil to Norfolk, 28 September 1569); Haynes, 533; *Hatfield*, i. no. 1361 (instructions to Neville, 3 October 1569).

On 8 October 1569 Norfolk was returned to London, interrogated, and confined in the Tower room that had once been occupied by his grandfather. Again, he was strictly supervised so that 'no conference [could] be had' with him. Except for one reported discussion between Norfolk and his secretary Robert Higford on the leads of the Tower roof, Norfolk's part in the Ridolfi plot temporarily ceased to operate by means of secret conversations in walking spaces.[47] The correspondence of the conspirators continued actively, however. Norfolk himself wrote to Mary in cipher and sent her tokens of courtship.[48]

When Ridolfi's encrypted reports from the Continent were intercepted, Sir Henry Cobham, Lord Warden of the Cinque Ports, was persuaded to protect his friends by substituting innocent letters in the packet sent on to Cecil. In subsequent months, Cobham required multiple meetings in his Blackfriars long gallery, demanding reassurance that his part in the plot would not be revealed.[49] Meanwhile, Ross met with the Earl of Shrewsbury's man, John Hall, in Ross's gallery in Islington. Shrewsbury, fourth husband to Bess of Hardwick, was now Mary's jailor in his houses at Tutbury and Sheffield. Ross persuaded Hall to smuggle out letters from Mary to her followers; Hall was to be intercepted with the incriminating documents. Called in, Ridolfi was held in Sir Francis Walsingham's house rather than the Tower. For this reason, some have speculated that there may have been an attempt to 'turn' him into a double agent, and even that the attempt may have been successful; from the course of subsequent events, this seems unlikely.[50]

Governmental concern mounted with the launch of the Northern Rising on 14 November 1569. This was also known as the Rebellion of the Northern Earls, so named when Northumberland and Westmoreland, refusing a royal summons to answer to the parts they may have played in the marriage scheme,

[47] Williams, 161–2, 165, 190. For the Tower, CSPD (October 1569), 345; Hatfield, i. no. 1373. After little more than a week in the Tower, Norfolk petitioned for liberty to walk on the walls or in the gallery, because his health was suffering. Permission was granted to him to be moved to lodgings near the long gallery, so that he could walk there, so long as one of his jailers was always in his company. Later, a man at the Tower was disciplined because his 7-year-old daughter came almost daily to bring Norfolk flowers. The similarity of this story to that of the imprisoned Elizabeth is striking and suggests the workings of cultural construct. Notably, what was a garden in Elizabeth's story is a gallery in Norfolk's.

[48] Higford detailed how communications among the conspirators continued even with Norfolk in the Tower: letters were put into wine bottles with crosses marked on their corks; signs were held up in the window of an adjoining house; voice messages were exchanged through a shared privy shaft; and Lawrence Bannister left letters wrapped in black paper in a dark privy (Murdin, 'The Most Humble and True Answer of me Robert Higford' (1 October 1571), 79–80).

[49] Williams, 202–3, 205–6, 221; Murdin, 78–9, 85 (Answers of Robert Higford, 1 October 1571 and 13 October 1571).

[50] The principal source for this speculation, as also for such other suggestions as that Cecil sought to entrap Norfolk by assigning him to the York Conference and releasing him from his first imprisonment in the Tower, is Edwards.

instead plotted insurrection. While walking in Gray's Inn Fields, Thomas Bishop was alerted to the revolt by the Earl of Northumberland's servant. He was one of those who traveled to a close called Balterby Brome to rendezvous with the Earl. Also present were Richard Norton, Francis Norton, William Norton, and Oswald Wilkinson. Ordering their servants to 'stand afar off', the conspirators conferred for two hours; a subsequent meeting took place in the gallery of one 'Tancred's house'.[51] The rebels' first action was forcibly to restore Catholic services in Durham Cathedral. On 20 November Elizabeth appointed the Lord Admiral, Lord Clinton, and Ambrose Dudley, Earl of Warwick to be her 'Lieutenants General of the forces that are presently to be assembled against the said rebels'. Her instructions included an inventory of the soldiers, horses, armor, and weapons that would be dispatched to Leicestershire by early December. She also promised 'some treasure' for the troops' provisions: 'We have already given order for £1,500 to be with all expedition sent unto you by one Barnham.'[52] This appears to have been yet another of Francis's royal loans.

Norfolk knew that the Northern Rising would endanger him by seeming to implicate him. On 15 December he wrote to Cecil that his only purpose in considering marriage to Mary was that 'by that means no papist prince should obtain the Scottish Queen'.[53] Still, it was two months before Elizabeth accepted his letter denying any part in or sympathy with the insurgency. Many more months passed before Norfolk wrote a humble letter of 'submission', promising 'upon his faith and allegiance' never again 'to deal with that marriage nor with any other matter touching the Scottish Queen'. Cecil's papers include his 'analysis' of this submission.[54] Implicitly, Norfolk admitted that he had violated the pledge already made at Titchfield; he also, duplicitously, sent a copy of the letter to Mary by way of Ross.

Norfolk was permitted to leave the Tower on 3 August 1570 for fear of plague, though he continued under supervision at Howard House. Ridolfi nonetheless met with him there less than a week after his release, and Ross made a clandestine visit in December. Norfolk's man Bannister testified that 'he left the door open of his own lodging, which hath a back-door in the Duke's house . . . for the Bishop of Ross to come to the Duke secretly'.[55] Ross's servant

---

[51] *Hatfield*, i. no. 1489 (Examination of John Hamelyn, 10 May 1570); ibid. no. 1490 (Letter of Thomas Bishop to the Council, 22 May 1570).

[52] Haynes, 561 (Minute from the Queen's Majesty to the Lord Admiral, November 1569). *Hatfield*, i. no. 1414 (Queen to Lord Admiral, 24 November 1569); ibid. i. no. 1427 (Queen to Earl of Warwick, 1 December 1569).

[53] Ibid. i. no. 1444 (15 December 1569).

[54] Ibid. i. no. 1497 (Norfolk's first submission, 23 June 1570); Haynes, 597–8; *Hatfield*, i. no. 1504 (Norfolk to Privy Council, 15 July 1570). 'Analysis of submission' (2 August 1570), CSPD Add., pp. 304, 315–16.

[55] Murdin, 'Banester's [*sic*] Examination' (18 and 19 September 1571), 133.

Charles Bailly specified that the covert meeting was held in the long gallery. As Barker later deposed, Ridolfi talked with Norfolk in the gallery at Howard House twice more in the spring of 1571, each time around eight or nine o'clock, after Norfolk's keeper Neville was safely in bed. Barker was so specific, describing the differing surreptitious routes used on each occasion, that it was prejudicial to Norfolk when, at his trial, he disputed the report of a second assignation. With respect to the first, he claimed to have summoned Ridolfi only to negotiate a personal loan. The queen's Solicitor General, Thomas Bromley, asked rhetorically, 'What needeth that secret coming in the night time about a private cause?' [56]

Norfolk subsequently consulted again with Bannister. Mary was restless and eager to flee to the Continent, and a plan had been evolved for her escape from a window in Shrewsbury's long gallery. Ross had measured the casement in preparation. But Norfolk dispatched Bannister to persuade Ross that England was the safest place for her. By this time, Ross was lodging near Paul's Wharf. The meeting between Bannister and Ross took place 'in the gallery alone'. Bannister reported back to Norfolk 'in the gallery over the gate' at Howard House, carrying three letters that Ross had prepared for Norfolk's signature. The plot now centered more certainly on the removal of Elizabeth and restoration of the Roman church, and the conspirators sought monetary and military support from Pope Pius V, Philip II of Spain, and Philip's governor in the Netherlands, the Duke of Alva. Norfolk refused to sign the letters, however: 'if I should set my hand to this, I shall commit treason'. In a second meeting between Ross and Bannister, a compromise was reached. Norfolk's name would appear on the documents, if not his autograph. Norfolk's man Barker would personally 'affirm' the Duke's support of the letters to the Spanish ambassador in London. And Barker would travel to

---

[56] Murdin, 'William Barker's last Confession' (19 September 1571): 'Upon this, I brought him [Ridolfi] to my Lord in Lent last, between eight and nine of the clock (Sir Henry Neville being in bed) and he talked with my Lord about three quarters of an hour and I brought him out of the gate' (p. 99). Murdin, 'Answer of William Barker to the Interrogatories' (10 October 1571): 'and so this Examinate, about eight or nine of the clock the night in Lent last, did bring Ridolfi secretly to the Duke; where Ridolfi did talk with the Duke in his Gallery half an hour and more' (p. 111). Murdin, 'Barker's Last Answer upon Interrogatories' (11 October 1571): 'Ridolfi came to the Duke of Norfolk the second time, and about nine of the clock at night, and this examinate did bring him thither; and in the Gallery they talked together about half an hour' (p. 115). Barker described how the gate was left open for Ridolfi and how 'The first time I brought him up on the back side, by the long workhouse, at the further end of the Laundry Court, and so up a new pair of stairs that goeth up to the old Wardrobe, and so through the Chamber where my Lady Lestrange used to dine and sup. The second time I brought him up at the stairs of the entry that goeth to Sir Henry Nevill's Chamber, and down again that way' (pp. 120–1). See also Murdin, 'The Duke of Norfolk's Answers' (13 October 1571): 'that Night Barker brought Ridolfi to this Examinate into the long Gallery, next the Duke's Bed-chamber, where the Duke walked with Ridolfi, and Barker stood in the Window' (p. 161); *Trial*, 95–6, 106.

Europe with Ridolfi, as Norfolk's public surrogate in the fundraising efforts. In the long gallery at Howard House, Norfolk gave instructions to Barker privately.[57]

Charles Bailly was taken with damaging letters in April 1571. Within a few months more, other aspects of the scheme were fully exposed. In Italy, Ridolfi had confided too much to Cosimo de Medici, who promptly sent a warning to Elizabeth. In England, according to the Queen's Attorney General, the plot 'was opened by God himself'.[58] The authentic originals of the letters switched by Cobham found their way into Cecil's hands. And a draper named Thomas Browne came to Cecil with a suspicious package. Barker and Higford had asked Browne to carry a bag to Bannister, then in the north; they told him it contained £50 in silver. Instead, Cecil discovered £600 in gold meant for Mary, along with some letters written in cipher. He had Howard House searched, and the key to the cipher was found there. Cecil continued his interrogations, some under torture. Lawrence Bannister was examined ten times; the confidential secretary and cryptographer Robert Higford, twelve times; the junior secretary William Barker, twenty-one times.

Cecil ordered Norfolk returned to the Tower on 7 September 1571. The city of London was put on alert as it became clear that he would be accused of treason. On 16 October the aldermen appointed two persons to stand at each gate to watch for invaders, and the sheriffs' attorneys were required to take the Oath of Supremacy. On 17 October Francis Barnham assembled the principal members of the Drapers' Company to hear the Lord Mayor's directives regarding 'the horrible and heinous conspiracy pretended against the Queen's Majesty and the whole realm and namely the city of London by the Scottish queen, the Duke of Alva, and the Pope, with other their adherents'. All were enlisted to report the names of any who 'mislike in any wise the Queen's proceedings in imprisoning the Duke of Norfolk and others'. On 22 October the watch at the city's gates was upgraded, Barnham appointing the Assistants themselves to stand guard. Sir William Chester, for example, was assigned to one of the postern gates, presumably that at the Tower.[59]

---

[57] For Bannister at Paul's Wharf, see Murdin, 'Confession of Lawrence Banester [*sic*]' (11 October 1571), 142. For the letters to Alva, see Murdin, 'The Examination of the Bishop of Ross' (6 November 1571), 46. For Norfolk's desire to help Mary, see Murdin, 'Examination of William Barker' (31 October 1571), 123. For Norfolk refusing treason, see Murdin, 'Laurence Banester [*sic*]' (13 October 1571), 144.

[58] *Trial*, 84 (quoting Gilbert Gerrard, the Attorney General).

[59] For 16 October, CLRO Rep. 17, fos. 213[v]–214[r]. For 17 October, Drapers' M.B.8, fo. 167[v]; and Girtin, *Triple Crowns*, 159–60. For 22 October, M.B.8, fo. 169[v]. Schofield says the 'two most important postern or minor gates built in the medieval period' were the Tower postern and Moorgate (*Medieval London Houses* (New Haven: Yale University Press for the Paul Mellon Centre for Studies in British Art, 1995), 11).

Exactly a month later, a preliminary hearing on Norfolk's case was held. On 16 January 1572 his trial opened. That night he was found to have committed treason by seeking to deprive Elizabeth of her crown and her life, by giving aid to the rebels of the Northern Rising, and by assisting others of the Queen's enemies in Scotland. Those who ruled him guilty included the Earls of Leicester, Hertford, Pembroke, and Sussex. There were attempts to cause uprisings in the north as a distraction, so that Norfolk might be broken out of the Tower by loyal Londoners, but these came to nothing. The day of his execution, 2 June 1572, the Tower warders locked the postern gate and took the keys with them, a strategy never previously employed. Francis Barnham was one of three city leaders delegated to remonstrate with the Lieutenant of the Tower that the charge of the gate historically and rightly belonged to the citizenry.[60]

Cecil, largely silent during the trial, had interrupted at one point to ask why Norfolk produced no witnesses in his own behalf and brought forward no evidence of his innocence. This was to suggest that the case against him was so strong that it was incontestable, but the question went also to the continuing mystery of Norfolk's motivation in the matter of the Ridolfi plot. Though he had fallen in with the conspiracy against Elizabeth and had withheld information about it from her and from her government, he seems not to have been sufficiently moved to devise any aspect of it himself. He vehemently denied that his objective was to restore the Roman church, claiming always to have been a loyal Protestant, insisting in his last letters to his children that they should give no credence to false rumors of his papistry, and declaring his religious conformity on the scaffold, too. His prosecutors suggested an overreaching ambition. In consequence of the Casket Letters, they said, he must necessarily have had 'an evil opinion' of Mary Stewart. Thus, it was impossible to believe that he might 'seek the marriage in respect of her person'—that is, for love. It must have been 'in respect of her false title, and that not to the kingdom of Scotland, which she had not, and which [he] despised, but to the Crown of England'.

Only one witness claimed to understand Norfolk rather than to interpret him, and that was Higford. On the leads of the Tower, he said, Norfolk had confided that his chief motivation was grievance, because he was not in the Queen's favor. In fact, his behavior at trial seemed consistent with Higford's image of a man full of self-importance and resentment. As Cecil remarked, Norfolk mounted no defense. He confined himself to what the Solicitor General called 'a bare denying'. He leaned heavily on his stature. He derogated the standing of those whose depositions were read into the record:

[60] CLRO Rep. 17, fo. 333ᵛ.

Ridolfi, whom he described as a money lender, was away in Europe; Ross was a foreigner and a Scot; Barker was an admitted traitor himself. Others, Norfolk dismissed contemptuously as men whose spending money amounted to fewer than five marks a year. He spoke more often to the alleged illegitimacy of the investigation and trial than to the matter of the charges, demanding legal counsel, asking to see his accusers face-to-face, and raising challenges to the Crown's readings of the applicable statutes.[61]

These were, in fact, legitimate. Henry VIII had lengthened the list of forbidden activities with the Treason Act of 1534, but Elizabeth's Second Treasons Act of 1571 went further yet again, adding that it was seditious 'to move or to stir any foreigners or strangers with force to invade this realm'. Also proscribed were support for any person who 'hereafter shall make claim to the crown' and any impeachment of the Queen's right to determine the succession. The offenses with which Norfolk was charged were committed between 23 September 1569 and 16 July 1571, all but one predating the expanded statute. Although his prosecutors claimed to try him by the terms of the old act, in fact they returned repeatedly to offenses set out by the new one.[62]

Norfolk's most cogent complaint may have been that 'the indictment containeth sundry points and matters to touch me by circumstance and so to draw me into matter of treason, which are not treasons themselves'. Indeed, Cecil and his agents had set out to prove 'how the design was continued by secret conferences and messages . . . and by other indirect means of dissimulation and falsehood on the part of the Duke'.[63] The circumstantial evidence to which Norfolk referred was the long roster of clandestine meetings that included encounters held safely out of doors, while hawking at York, in a park at Hampton Court, in the garden at Howard House, while fishing in the Thames, on the road to London, in Gray's Inn Fields, at a close called Balterby Brome, or on the leads of the Tower. There was also the string of secret conferences in the long galleries at York, at Titchfield, at Arundel House, at Cobham's house, in Ross's residences in Islington and near Paul's Wharf, at Tancred's house, and, over and over again, at Howard House.

All information about the consultations held in these long galleries proceeded from witnessings by the principals, not overhearings by observers. There were no reports of eavesdropping in these vast and curiously configured Tudor

---

[61] For Cecil, see *Trial*, 69; for Norfolk's motivation, 62; for his denying, 110.

[62] See John Bellamy, *The Tudor Law of Treason: An Introduction* (London: Routledge & Kegan Paul, 1979), 65. *The Tudor Constitution: Documents and Commentary*, ed. Geoffrey Elton (Cambridge: Cambridge University Press, 1962), 72–6.

[63] *Trial*, 15; David Jardine, *Criminal Trials: Supplying Copious Illustrations of the Important Periods of English History during the Reigns of Queen Elizabeth and James I* (London: M. A. Nattali, 1847), 150.

spaces. By contrast, the bedchambers of the Ridolfi plot again revealed their unreliable nature. In the early spring of 1571, for example, William Barker was summoned to Ross's lodgings one morning. Ross had not yet risen, and Barker 'sat by him on the further side of his bed next the wall. . . . Whiles we were talking, one of his men came to him, and told him there was one would speak with him.' It was Hugh Owen. Ross advised Barker he would 'hear more of the matter'. Ross drew the bed curtain 'so that [Barker] was not seen' behind it. At Ross's bedside and in Barker's hearing, Owen reported that Sir Henry Percy had enlisted in their cause. A related spatial dynamic is operative in the deposition of a go-between named Edmund Powell. Powell would visit Ross secretly in the night and then convey news to Sir Thomas Stanley. After one session with Ross, Powell went to Stanley's 'own chamber at Cannon Row'. Powell deposed that 'Sir Edward Stanley was by in the chamber, but heard no part of our talk. There was none else present with me, nor heard anything.'[64]

No one describing a conference in a gallery needed to say, 'There was none else present, nor heard anything.' As had already been documented in *The Adventures of Master F.J.*, a powerful cultural construct was at work: the deponent who testified that he had witnessed a meeting that took place in a gallery was in effect declaring that it was aurally inaccessible. The gallery seems to have provided a legitimate way for some on the fringes of the Ridolfi plot to state, 'I could not overhear; I cannot testify.' This was a proposition in which the government's investigators were apparently willing to collude, because finally the gallery's chief virtues were less auditory than visual. It allowed no eavesdroppers to approach unseen or listen at a nearby threshold unknown. The rooms may have been quite 'live' acoustically; in later years some would earn the name 'whispering galleries' for the fact that words spoken at one end could be heard at the other. Thus, when Henry Brounker conducted his investigation at Hardwick Hall, he probably relied on age-related impairment to Bess of Hardwick's hearing rather than on the material capacities of her gallery. *Leicester's Commonwealth*, an extended attack on Robert Dudley written in 1584, sustained the cultural myth. It pretends to report verbatim a lengthy conversation in a long gallery, and closes as a lawyer begins 'to shrink and be appalled . . . doubting lest something had been discovered of our conference'. 'But indeed', the long gallery preserves its privacies: 'it was not so'.[65]

The textual record in the Ridolfi matter is far from trustworthy. Inevitably, Cecil's witnesses would have introduced self-serving lies, evasions, omissions,

---

[64] For Owen, Murdin, 'William Barker's Answer to Articles' (14 October 1571), 119, and *Hatfield*, i. no. 1664. For Powell, ibid. i. no. 1680.

[65] *Leicester's Commonwealth: The Copy of a Letter Written by a Master of Art of Cambridge (1584)*, ed. D. C. Peck (Athens, Ohio: Ohio University Press, 1985), 195.

and exaggerations, their descriptions of the long gallery's inhibiting effects perhaps among them. But whether or not all the secret meetings of the Ridolfi plot took place as reported, or had the agendas described, is not at issue here. The primary significance of the spatial history that Cecil compiled was what it revealed to him about the intent of those who resorted to their long galleries. They sought to exploit its accidental effects to traitorous ends. Norfolk could not be accused of a literal act of treason: Elizabeth was still alive and on the throne, he was not married to Mary Stewart, the Scottish queen remained in custody, Spanish troops had not invaded from the Netherlands, the country was not in liege to Rome. But the man who had sworn as the Queen's privy councillor to 'keep secret all manner of counsels and conferences without disclosing any part thereof to any manner of person' had unforgivably employed the strategies of secrecy not in her interest but in his own.[66] Norfolk was condemned largely for having demonstrated in historically specific ways a suspicious intent to control his own privacy rather than to subordinate it to that of the national interest. It is no accident that later legislation in these matters was to be known as 'the Statute of Silence'.

[66] Stephen Alford locates Norfolk's crime in indiscretion: 'As a privy councilor, Norfolk had sworn to "furder kepe secrett all maner of counselles and Conferencees without disclosing any part thereof to any manner of person". This is exactly what he did not do at York when he discussed the future of Mary and his own interest in it beyond the limit of his instructions' (*The Early Elizabethan Polity: William Cecil and the British Succession Crisis, 1558–1569* (Cambridge: Cambridge University Press, 1998), 202. This is another way of putting conversation and secrecy at the center of the Ridolfi Plot.

7

The Barnhams' Business Secrets

FRANCIS BARNHAM participated in uncounted controversies of personality, politics, and property. Most he adjudicated in his public roles: churchwarden in the parish of St Mildred Poultry, member of the Drapers' Court of Assistants, governor of the Bridewell and St Thomas's Hospital, alderman of the City of London, and Sheriff. But, as seems to have been impossible to avoid in the Tudor and Stuart years, he also had extensive private experience of 'variances', disputes, and allegations. There were the 1554 quarrel with William Beswicke over a jeweled pendant, a 1556 argument with former apprentice John Kydd, a 1560 complaint filed against clothworker Henry Broune, and the 1568 petition of Robert Collet about the 'round compassed window' in St Clement's Lane.[1] To none of these was as much jeopardy attached as a 1574 accusation that he had violated the Statute against Usury. As Alderman, Barnham was one of the Queen's agents for the governance of the city; he had been installed as Sheriff before others of her delegates for order in the country, the Barons of the Exchequer; now, he came before the Exchequer charged with malfeasance, and his private business practices were opened to public scrutiny.

In his study of usury in early modern England, Norman Jones writes that the crime was constituted in 'false shifts and chevisaunces' like a feigned exchange of merchandise to camouflage a loan of money, in the specification of a fixed schedule for repayment of loaned funds, in an exchange in which the lender seemed determined to protect himself from risk, in the lender's stratagems to realize interest higher than 10 per cent, and, above all, in the appearance of 'corrupt' design.[2] As was true for the treason investigations taken up in the previous chapter, in this arena, too, agents of the Crown sought to identify the material keys which would allow them to divine private intent. Suspected

---

[1] Drapers' M.B.5, fo. 25^{r-v} (Beswicke); Drapers' M.B.5, fo. 79^v (Kydd); CLRO Rep. 14, fo. 510^r (Broune); CLRO Rep. 16, fos. 388^v, 392^r, 413^v, 419^v–420^r, 420^v–421^r (Collett). Only Collett's complaint is fully detailed; see Ch. 3. The controversy with Beswyck involved funds for which Barnham, Beswicke, and Robert Fryor stood surety in the Court of Orphans.

[2] Norman Jones, *God and the Moneylenders: Usury and Law in Early Modern England* (Oxford: Basil Blackwell, 1989), 120–1. I am indebted to Jones for much of this discussion of usury.

cases of usury had been prosecuted exclusively in the church courts until 1545, when a Tudor statute made infractions indictable at the Queen's Bench, the Court of Common Pleas, and the Court of Requests, as well as at the Court of Exchequer. In 1571, a revised Statute against Usury was accompanied by calls for stricter enforcement; Francis Barnham was one of those caught up in the wave of arraignments that followed.

'It began', Jones says, 'on 15 January 1573, when Sir Walter Waller sent his servant to a broker named Wilkinson to borrow £600'; Wilkinson replied that 'Alderman Barnham would "serve his turn".' For Jones, *Queen v. Barnham* offers a classic illustration of the 'double stoccado' or 'double stab', one of the usurious tricks recorded by Thomas Wilson in 1572. It is unfortunate, Jones adds, that 'we do not know how the case came out in the end'. If Jones omits a detailed profile for any individual lender, borrower, or prosecution, this is because his larger purpose is a 'biography' of the 1571 act itself. As constituted, Jones emphasizes, 'the statute has no effect. An enforcement mechanism is necessary. . . . Moreover, the statute takes effect not as written but as *interpreted* in the courts' (Ingram's emphasis). To trace the act's life in Elizabethan culture, Jones surveys cases brought before that court of the royal treasury which pursued revenues owed to the Crown. He prefers Exchequer records to those of the Queen's Bench, Common Pleas, and Requests 'because its cases are easily found. Indexing them by term, the Clerks of the Exchequer usually grouped all cases of the same kind together in their lists.'[3] His argument regarding the organizational disciplines of the Exchequer suggests not that he has taken the easier route of research but instead that he has chosen the archive that makes itself knowable in a comprehensive way. The less categorical protocols of other offices might be expected to allow accidents of omission. Thus Jones validates his practice in an ability to be exhaustive.

Queen v. Barnham was, however, less straightforward than Jones recognizes. A more classic instance of the double stab can be found in *Queen v. Slanye*; *Queen v. Barnham* actually began not with Sir Walter Waller but instead with *Slanye*; and the outcome of *Barnham* is indeed knowable—from sources outside the Exchequer. This chapter represents a process of detection into the activities of Francis Barnham but also, and more importantly, a demonstration that it is not in the nature of any single archive to be whole. Like most collections of witness depositions, the Exchequer papers are dense with material detail. When assembled, the interrogatories and responses for *Queen v. Barnham* can be reshaped into a narrative that gives off its own deceptive sense of fullness. This is one of the illusions performed by archives: the reader's credulity

---

[3] Ibid. 122–3, 1, 4.

is engaged by his own complicity in making them productive. In this case study, however, a range of other, seemingly unrelated entries in the registers of the Drapers' Company and the Court of Aldermen clarify how much the Exchequer accounts neglect. Some of the gaps represent things undiscovered by the Barons; Francis Barnham, after all, relied upon a level of public ignorance about his private affairs. But much of the missing information follows from an absence of curiosity rather than a lack of knowledge. The more we wed ourselves to a methodological myth of completeness, the more tempted we are to imagine documentary lacunae as having been grounded in something more meaningful than, say, institutional custom and convenience. To presume that things not knowable now were things not known then is wrongly to imagine each obscurity as a symptom of privacy in early modern culture.

The Crown's inquiry into Francis's financial dealings eventually incriminated Alice, too, in his alleged wrongdoing. This is one point of access to the working life of a Tudor wife: information that the Exchequer had received against her was prejudicial to her husband, because she was automatically assumed to be his partner in a business that was, like nearly all others in the period, household-based. There was more to Alice Barnham's professional career than this, but it was not a matter with which the officers of the Exchequer had cause to occupy themselves. Evidence for her economic authority must be pieced together from the documents of male-dominated institutions that had no reason to address those latter-day questions to which we seek answers. She is an unintended casualty of the recordation process.

Topically, the chapter is about what can be deduced from *Queen* v. *Barnham* about the joint and separate business careers of Francis and Alice Barnham. Historiographically, however, it is less about the privacy that they might willingly have preserved than the gaps that history and its textual mechanisms have accidentally created. Most privacies display intent, which is a form of interest. These artificial privacies reflect not interest but its absence.

QUEEN V. SLANYE

Francis Barnham's name entered the Exchequer accounts in the matter of *Queen* v. *Slanye*. *Slanye* concerned a loan made by Stephen Slanye, a skinner of London, to Sir Warham Sentleger, a Kentish knight and Irish colonist.[4]

---

[4] For *Queen* v. *Slanye*: PRO E 123/5, fo. 101[r] for the initial decree of 12 February 1574; E 133/1/188 and E 133/1/190 for depositions from Sentleger, Brett, and Wilford; E 123/6, fos. 45[v] and 61[v] for orders regarding Slanye's sentence; *CPR: Elizabeth I*, vi. *1572–1575*, no. 3093, for his penalty. See Ch. 3 for Slanye's move when elected Sheriff in 1584.

Sentleger and his friend Jerome Brett were deposed on 24 November 1573. Three years earlier, they testified, Sentleger had found himself in need of funds—though, in a fine show of relative nonchalance, he declared (and Brett loyally repeated) that he sought merely to consolidate his debts into the hands of two or three men, as if to simplify his life. At his London home in Southwark, Sentleger interviewed two brokers. The first, John Bowland, reported that Alderman Francis Barnham was prepared to sell Sentleger merchandise said to be worth £2,000 which, when resold, would actually bring £1,700 in ready money. The professed market value of the goods was, in other words, a fiction. Sentleger would immediately receive £1,700 cash by selling the wares and at the end of one year would owe Barnham £2,000 for them. Barnham's gain of £300, fifteen pound for every hundred, would constitute his interest on a loan prudently disguised as a transfer of goods. But Sentleger indicated that he had hoped, perhaps naively, to receive cash directly, and so he 'paused' rather than move forward, and sent Bowland away.

He then met with the second broker, John Wilford, who recommended Stephen Slanye as a lender with similar cash reserves and identical terms of interest at fifteen pound per hundred. Sentleger had just one question: would the loan be made in wares or currency? Not surprisingly, Slanye offered merchandise. Wilford said smoothly that he had seen the goods himself: they 'would make ready money in an hour'. Sentleger acquiesced and agreed to meet with Slanye. In a gratuitous (and probably exaggerated) reference to Sentleger's reputation, Brett said that Slanye found Sentleger 'a meet person for him to join withal for the good report he heard of him'. Brett also explained, more clearly than did Sentleger or the broker Wilford (who was himself deposed on 1 February 1574), how complicated the arrangement then became.

Slanye first asked the amount of Sentleger's debts, so that he could determine how much would be required to cover both the old obligations and the new interest charge. When Sentleger said he owed £2,150, Slanye recommended a loan of £2,600. With interest at fifteen pounds per hundred, or £390, this would give Sentleger £2,210 outright, and the 'overplus' of £60 would cover such collateral expenses as the paperwork that would finalize the loan. Then Sentleger asked how long Slanye would 'forbear' repayment. Slanye had assumed the usual year, but Sentleger asked for three. He was due to travel to Ireland—on the Queen's business, he threw in grandly—and he preferred not to come back 'in haste'.[5] Slanye was willing to extend the loan, at fifteen

---

[5] According to David Edwards in the *Oxford DNB*, Sentleger (there given as St Leger and also known as Sellenger) was disappointed: in 1566, Elizabeth refused to confirm his appointment to head a provincial government in Munster, and his repeated requests for a commission went unanswered until 1581, when he was finally designated commander of the royal forces

pounds per hundred per year, but he required additional assurances. 'Be your own carver', said Sentleger with bravado, 'You shall have my book of revenue and take what lands you will so much as shall double worth your money.' Slanye settled on a guarantee of rental incomes due at midsummer from five of Sentleger's manors that would return the fifteen pounds per hundred per year. Brett protested that together, the rents and the expected loss from the sale of Slanye's goods would total thirty pounds per hundred in the next months, rather than fifteen. Sentleger exclaimed that this was 'abominable', and he said pointedly that Alderman Barnham had promised more reasonable rates. According to Sentleger, Slanye was 'loathe that Alderman Barnham should prevent him of the bargain'; Brett called Slanye 'very greedy to go through' with the deal. With 'the shameful loss so plainly proved', Slanye agreed to just two years' worth of rent from the 'false mortgages', with the third year's interest paid through the transfer of merchandise. Sentleger found these 'conclusions' to be so 'friendly' that he magnanimously offered Slanye an annual gift of two deer, as well—or so he deposed.

In the end, according to continued testimony from Sentleger and Brett, Sentleger borrowed £2,600 from Slanye but received only £1,700 in cash, not the promised £2,200. To the Barons, Sentleger repudiated an acquittance he had himself signed for full receipt of the goods, claiming instead that some £800 worth had been withheld. Those that were conveyed were 'paltry wares', he said, and it was five months before Wilford, who had the job of selling them, could find a buyer willing to offer even £1,700. Wilford produced a book of accounts to demonstrate that he had done his best to sell 'at most advantage'. When the rents were added, Sentleger was reportedly obligated in the amount of £1,600 interest on Slanye's £1,700 loan, more than 30 per cent per year for the three years. Slanye was 'condemned for lending of money to usury', although only for a profit of £390—the amount originally set, not that alleged by Sentleger. Even this, however, was £130 over 'the ten per centum allowed by statute'.

There are many reasons to be skeptical about Sentleger's testimony—not least because he disavowed his own acquittance. Almost certainly his debts were more serious than he suggested in claiming merely to tidy his accounts. The story of his initial preference for cash over goods was undoubtedly designed to imply that he was a novice in these matters, when he may well not have been. He overplayed his knightly condescension with respect to the gift

---

there. Edwards attributes his failure to secure patronage to debt, and remarks Sentleger's 'chronic insolvency'. For a petition to Cecil that is roughly proximate to the time of the loan from Slanye (5 July 1569), see *Calendar of the Manuscripts of . . . the Marquess of Salisbury . . . Preserved at Hatfield House*, 24 vols. (London: 1883–1976), i. no. 1313.

of venison, as also the degree of royal favor he enjoyed. Most dubious of all was his alacrity. Sentleger would have had all the usual reasons to have wished for this story to have been kept quiet: not that he required a loan but that he had so depreciated his credit and exhausted his friends that he resorted to London brokers, not that he cared to protect the standing of Slanye but that he might have wished to preserve his own credibility with future lenders. Instead, he hit every possible note of incrimination against Slanye. There was what Thomas Wilson had called the 'double stoccado', a 'first stab' in providing goods rather than money and a 'second stab' in a loss of over 30 per cent, rather than 15, at the resale of those goods.[6] There was the fixed program for repayment and Slanye's unwillingness to engage risk. With their report of the 'abominable' proposal regarding Sentleger's rents, Sentleger and Brett also worked assiduously to amplify the evidence of usurious intent. They could not document this discussion, which had, by their own account, fallen out in the negotiations. But, like Brett's use of the characterization 'greedy', it went to insinuate that Slanye's private purposes were, as the Barons had charged, 'colorable or deceitful'.

Although Sentleger was 'examined concerning an information' provided by a yeoman named John Midleton, it is thoroughly conceivable that he had himself initiated the action in the Exchequer, with Midleton as his mouthpiece. A decision against Slanye would, after all, cancel Sentleger's debt. The statute of 1571 mandated not only that Sentleger's bargain was defaulted, leaving him free to pocket whatever portion of the £2,600 loan he had realized, but also that Slanye was charged a further penalty amounting to triple the principle, or £7,800, with half payable to the Queen and half to the informant of record, Midleton.[7] If Sentleger really had been Midleton's secret source, then presumably he took a share of the fine, as well.

Norman Jones discusses *Queen v. Slanye* not for its employment of the 'double stoccado' but instead because the full penalty was not, in the end, exacted. At the request of Court officers Robert Colshill and Henry Mackwilliam, Slanye received a pardon for the £3,900 fine he owed the Queen. 'One wonders', speculates Jones, 'how much Slanye had to pay' those officials. He seems not to know that Slanye brought forward a 'writ of error'.[8] Although

---

[6] Thomas Wilson, *A Discourse upon Usury* (1572), cited by Jones, *God and the Moneylenders*, 122.

[7] Jones notes that 'A charge of usury could help one escape one's debts', ibid. 99. He instances a borrower lodging an information against his own lender and also two borrowers reciprocally charging each other's lenders. Informers, billed for 'every step' in the process, took the financial risks (p. 94); if usury was proved, their reward was half the fine (p. 92, and see below). All speculations about Sentleger are my own.

[8] In his discussion of *Queen v. Slanye*, Jones confines himself to the determination from *CPR: Elizabeth I*, vi. *1572–1575*, no. 3093. Presumably because he was unaware of the 'writ of error'

the grounds of Slanye's appeal are not specified in the Exchequer's books of Orders and Decrees, on balance it seems likely that, whether or not a bribe was paid, his protest had some merit.

QUEEN V. BARNHAM

If *Queen* v. *Slanye* demonstrates precisely what the Barons of the Exchequer were looking for in prosecuting such cases, *Queen* v. *Barnham* was not as clear-cut.[9] The Court of Exchequer began by gathering information from Thomas Pennington, who deposed on 20 May 1574 that about two years earlier Rowland Searle had sold him three tenements in Billingsgate for £300. Pennington paid down £240, and Searle, according to Pennington, immediately took that £240 to Francis Barnham's house in St Clement's Lane and there was received by a family servant. On 22 May 1574 Searle was himself deposed. He admitted that he had been indebted to Barnham, but he declared that the moneys owed were for goods purchased, and he testified that Barnham's merchandise was fully worth £240. Unlike Sentleger, Searle had no wish to incriminate his lender. He said strenuously that he 'borrowed no money', 'did not desire to borrow any money', 'absolutely did desire to buy certain wares', and regarded the transaction as 'a very plain and absolute bargain' involving 'no interest, usury, profit, or any other commodity'.

Searle maintained that he had mortgaged the three tenements in Billingsgate strictly as collateral. If he defaulted on the debt for the goods then the properties would be 'lost' for ever, alienated to Barnham. But Searle, not Barnham, continued to receive the rents from those tenements 'during the whole time of the mortgage and more'; Searle sold the buildings and himself realized the difference between their value and the amount owed Barnham;

(PRO E 123/6, fo. 45ᵛ), he speculates that Slanye may have bribed the Court to secure the pardon of half his fine (ibid. 97). Elsewhere, Jones describes writs of error as most often 'technical arguments' (p. 102). Slanye evidently narrowly avoided a prison term. When the case was finally settled, it was mandated that the Warden of the Fleet should not be cheated of his expected fees, and Slanye was required to pay them (PRO E 123/6, fo. 61ᵛ).

[9] What I call '*Queen* v. *Barnham*' is a collection of interrogatories and depositions that pertain to loans to Rowland Searle and Sir Walter Waller but that have been catalogued in the National Archives under various other case names. Jones uses *Queen* v. *Barnham* to illustrate the 'double stoccado' (ibid. 122–3), having consulted only PRO E 133/2/269. In fact, proceedings against Barnham began with PRO E 133/1/205 (Pennington) and E 133/1/210 (Searle) and led to continued examinations and actions documented in E 133/2/221, E 133/2/230, E 133/2/233, E 133/2/234, E 133/2/238, E/133/2/269, E 133/10/1591, E 123/6, fo. 96ᵛ.

and the mortgage was 'discharged' when payment for the goods was made. The wares, 'certain silks', were consigned to a grocer, Robert Savage; Searle claimed not to remember what they returned. Unlike the broker in the *Slanye* case, he presented no book of account to show 'what was lost or gained in the sale of the same wares'. Deposed on 27 May, Savage confirmed that Searle had given him some silks to sell, but he, too, professed not to recall what they had been worth. He remembered Searle 'thank[ing] God he had discharged Master Barnham', but as far as he knew this 'was a bargain as is amongst merchants simply'. Then, in response to the penultimate interrogatory put by John Birche for the Crown, Savage finally suggested that Searle's original desire may have been for £200 in ready money, not £240 worth of silk. Judging from the Court's leading questions about a loan of £200 on 29 May 1571, this confirmed their own information. A repayment of £240 would put Barnham's interest within the usurious range of 20 per cent.

Thus the investigation continued, based as before in highly specific intelligence. The interrogators next asked about a loan of £600 made on 10 January 1573 by Barnham to Sir Walter Waller.[10] They also knew the mediums of exchange: from Barnham, a quantity of ferret silk, a kind of coarse silk ribbon or tape; from Waller, a supply of iron. On 15 July and 22 November 1574, they asked witnesses William Martin and Francis Ardes what term of forbearance was arranged, whether any of Barnham's goods were 'false and naughty', how much Waller had 'lost' in the exchange, and whether Barnham had bought back the ferret silk from the merchant to whom it had been transferred. If he had done—if, after all the disbursing of funds and sealing of bonds, the silks had returned in the end to Barnham's own inventories—then the exchange was the more transparently fraudulent.

Both Martin and Ardes testified that, far from being 'greedy' for the transaction, Barnham hesitated at critical junctures. Martin said Barnham was concerned that the exchange would fall afoul of regulations regarding the buying and selling of foreign goods. Less plausibly, Ardes suggested that Barnham delayed while seeking advice on how to avoid 'the danger of the statute' against usury, receiving counsel 'not to deal with any gentleman' but instead to create the illusion of a bargain between merchants. Even though Ardes's testimony was thick with particulars about Barnham dispatching his apprentice Henry Swynerton to consult scrivener John Turner, it is highly unlikely that Barnham would have required any such guidance.[11] If he

---

[10] PRO E 133/2/221, E 133/2/230, and E 133/2/269.

[11] Scriveners were understood to have specialist knowledge because of their experience drawing up contracts. See Jones, *God and the Moneylenders*, 63, and Craig Muldrew, *The Economy of Obligation: The Culture of Credit and Social Relations in Early Modern England* (Houndmills: Macmillan, 1998), 112, on scriveners as brokers for large loans in the 1590s.

balked—if, that is, this was not mere strategy on his part—it may have been because he was worried about Waller's ability to repay. He demanded that the bonds be executed not in Waller's name but in those of three Sussex landholders who were willing to stand surety for Waller.[12] A concurrent Exchequer investigation involved a possible loan of £500 from which Barnham reportedly withdrew when the borrower, Sir John Sentleger, was unable to provide sufficient guarantees. Francis's instincts in the matter were correct. At the eventual death of the inveterately indebted knight, the west-country Sentlegers 'disappeared as a landed Devon family'.[13]

In the transaction with Waller, thus, and as had undoubtedly been the case with Sir Warham Sentleger as well, it was the lender who was wary and the borrower who was 'greedy'. At one point Waller stormed Barnham's house 'in great anger that he might not have his bargain', and told one of Barnham's sons that he would not hesitate to spend £100 to sue Barnham for default if the deal did not go forward. He vowed to base the claim on £5 earnest money he had paid at the outset. Such a scenario, if true, amplifies Lawrence Stone's representation of the overwhelming pressures of the period both upon those aristocrats who were in 'crisis' and also upon the merchants who accepted financial entanglements with them, lured by the twin promises of privileged patronage and handsome profits. Stone summarizes that between 1580 and 1620 at least forty aldermen in London's 'tight little oligarchy' were 'drawn into money-lending'.[14] *Queen* v. *Barnham* gives evidence that the pattern was evident earlier and obtained for knightly debtors as well as for peers.

Ardes and Martin deposed that Waller and Barnham had never met directly; negotiations were conducted through the broker, William Wilkinson, with Ardes sometimes carrying messages. Ardes, Waller's man, was the only deponent who stated that he had talked with Barnham directly and the only one anxious to impugn Barnham. His declaration that Barnham 'did use

[12] Marjorie K. McIntosh says that many Elizabethan yeomen from the close-in provinces 'had no connection with agriculture apart from an occasional investment in land for speculative purposes. Instead they . . . loaned money on a large scale' ('Money Lending on the Periphery of London, 1400–1600', *Albion* 20 (1988), 569).

[13] PRO E 133/2/238. The west-country knight Sir John must be distinguished from the Kentish knight Sir Warham. In the 1570s and 1580s Sir John sold most of his lands and in the 1590s was involved in multiple lawsuits for debt (see *The House of Commons, 1558–1603*). Barnham also met Sir John at the Court of Aldermen, when Sentleger was one of three men who brought a complaint against Richard Paramor (regarding a 'bargain' for cloth worth £580). Sentleger then took his grievance to the Exchequer instead. With their 'aid' thus rejected, the aldermen encouraged Paramor to 'help himself' against Sentleger (CLRO Rep. 17, fo. 43ʳ).

[14] Lawrence Stone, *The Crisis of the Aristocracy, 1558–1641* (Oxford: Clarendon, 1965), 532–3. He cites Sir Thomas Culpeper's *Tract against Usury* (1621): 'generally all merchants, when they have gotten any great wealth, leave trading and fall to usury'.

sleights and practices in the said bargain to defeat the statute', though freely offered 'upon his oath', was based in the improbable story that Barnham required tutelage from the scrivener John Turner. Ardes alleged also that some of Barnham's wares were 'not right' and that they eventually sold at a loss of twenty pound in the hundred. In what looks like a confession to extortion, Ardes further claimed to have promised Swynerton that he would flee to Ireland 'if that the merchant'—that is, Barnham—'would give him anything to live in another country'. Swynerton reportedly replied that Barnham would consult other merchants about relocation money. Barnham regarded the Waller transaction as 'a plain bargain', Swynerton was said to have explained, 'but he would not have his name come in question for £100'.[15]

Sir Walter Waller was finally called to the Court on 20 June 1575. He answered fully but minimally, with none of the rancor displayed by Sir Warham Sentleger in *Queen* v. *Slanye*. Waller denied acquaintance with Barnham and refused to accuse him of any intention to circumvent the statute. He indicated that he had himself 'procured' the merchant John Chapman to resell Barnham's goods. He admitted that he wanted money, not wares. He said that he owed Barnham £600. 10s. for the silks and that they sold for £435.[16] He had paid his earnest money on the broker's promise that he would not lose more than twelve pounds in the hundred; when, he said delicately, it 'fell out otherwise', the £5 was returned by Swynerton in a prudential display of apparent good faith. Waller also clarified a subject on which Ardes had been muddled, which was that the terms of the loan had been renegotiated sometime before midsummer 1574. Waller's mother and others came on board to insure repayment in the form of regular deliveries of iron to men named Pullyson, Kirby, Gilborne, and Ashbornham, as well as to Barnham.

These names were not new to the Exchequer. Its officers were already sufficiently well informed to have taken depositions regarding loans to Waller of £110 from Phillip Cursine (Barnham's neighbor on St Clement's Lane), £200 from Richard Blunte, £300 from John Kirby (who also preferred to be paid in iron 'to avoid the danger of the statute'), £360 from William Gilborne (again with the assistance of merchant John Chapman), £500

---

[15] On the economic value of reputation, see Muldrew, *Economy*, esp. ch. 6. Bonds extended on credit were increasingly more popular than cash loaned directly; he says that in King's Bench and Common Pleas there were five times as many bond suits in 1606 as in 1560 (pp. 111–12).

[16] Jones emphasizes that Waller protected Barnham from the charge of false chevisaunce by insisting that he did not know if Barnham bought back the silks. Giving £500. 10s. as the amount of the loan, rather than £600. 10s., Jones miscalculates the interest at 15 per cent (*God and the Moneylenders*, 122).

from Robert Taylor (himself an officer of the Exchequer), and £500 from Thomas Pullyson (another draper and alderman of London).[17] Waller's financial difficulties would seem to have been chronic ones. In subsequent decades, Herman Langerman charged that Waller made a practice of defrauding his creditors by 'subtle means', and, from the Compter, Thomas Pratt complained that he suffered for Waller's bad debts. The legal jeopardy attached always to the lenders, and Burghley himself took Waller's part against Pratt.[18] But it may have been with a pragmatic eye to future financial requirements that Waller was so reticent and nonrecriminatory in 1575.

In the archives of the Court of Exchequer, the outcome of *Queen* v. *Barnham* is obscure. On 3 November 1574, in another record not noticed by Jones, Barnham was required to 'amend his plea' in a manner unspecified.[19] While this last, nebulous notation in one of the Exchequer books of Orders and Decrees suggests that some sort of discipline may have been exacted, it does not contravene a prevailing sense that the Court had hit repeated dead ends in the prosecution of this case. There were Pennington's and Searle's unwillingness to incriminate Barnham, Barnham's refusal to loan money to Sir John Sentleger, and Waller's reluctance to confirm shifts and chevisaunces. The blackmailer Ardes was more than cooperative, but no one else seems to have been motivated to assist the Crown in its inquiries.

Still, it cannot be assumed that Francis Barnham was innocent of usury as it was defined by the statute of 1571. As is further detailed below, there are too many signs of his thorough engagement with the persons and practices prosecuted by the Exchequer. Even to think in terms of guilt or innocence, however, is to re-enact the sixteenth-century disconnect between legislative action and economic reality. Before 1545 no interest was legally permitted; from 1545 to 1552 10 per cent was acceptable; from 1552 to 1571 all interest was again forbidden; after 1571, interest was officially disallowed but, with market rates running between 12 and 15 per cent, the courts overlooked amounts under 10 per cent.[20] Nothing in the switchback course of English statutory law kept pace with the true value of ready money to cash-poor

---

[17] PRO E 133/2/233 and E 133/2/234. In 1576 Steven Barnham partnered with William Gilborne for a loan in the Court of Orphans (see Mark Benbow, *Index of London Citizens Involved in City Government, 1558–1603*, deposited in CLRO, for Steven Barnham). See also Ch. 8 for more on Gilborne as kin to the Barnhams.

[18] PRO SP 46/32, fo. 137; SP 46/33, fo. 205; and SP 46/37, fo. 104. In PRO SP 46/38, fo. 39, Burghley sided with Waller against Pratt (23 March 1590).

[19] PRO E 123/6 (Exchequer Orders and Decrees), fo. 96ᵛ.

[20] Jones outlines the statutory history, *God and the Moneylenders*, 47–9, 63, 121 (in 1571, all interest was disallowed, but convicted violators lost only the principal for interest under 10 per cent, and triple the principal for more). See also Stone, *Crisis*, 529–30; Benjamin Nelson, *The*

gentry. Some sought capital for investments in the explosive land market. Others, among them the wealthiest of men, experienced cash-flow problems that impelled them to borrow to 'bridge the gap' till rents were payable (as Stone describes it).[21] Then there were those who had more long-term financial difficulties. The Exchequer accounts give ample justification for public interest in these private transactions; Elizabeth's aristocrats could so easily become mired in debt. Of course, for every gentleman who declined there were merchants who rose; Francis Barnham was himself a model for the threat that the new financial adventurism posed to the old social order.[22]

Stone thought it inevitable that the few men who practiced usury would 'demand a high return to compensate them for being generally regarded as moral lepers'.[23] But Stephen Slanye, in counterexample, suffered no disgrace following the judgment against him in *Queen* v. *Slanye*. By 1584, he was sufficiently recovered financially to be elected Alderman of Portsoken Ward; that same year he was named Sheriff (and moved to a suitably great house) and then, in 1595, Lord Mayor of London. He was Master of the Company of Skinners four times and served as President of the great civic institutions, Bethlem, Bridewell, and Christ's Hospitals. Following his mayoralty he was knighted.[24] In Slanye's city circles and elsewhere, wealth commanded respect if not affection, and for most Londoners market pressures were more urgent than ethical ones. Ready cash found its own material value, while moral value was debased into a convenient language for articulating the pecuniary anxieties of a new monetary economy. Homilists continued to inveigh against usury and its practitioners, but their preachments had small effect on arrangements that were vital for personal consumption and financial expansion. More to the point is the later remark of Francis Bacon, who had himself embraced the profits of a moneylending operation when he married Francis Barnham's 14-year-old-granddaughter: 'to speak of the abolishing of usury is idle'. It is difficult to know how much—or how little—Richard Porder exaggerated

Idea of Usury: From Tribal Brotherhood to Universal Otherhood, 2nd edn. (Chicago: University of Chicago Press, 1969), 83.

[21] Stone, *Crisis*, 506. Ann Rosalind Jones and Peter Stallybrass have also described the occasional cash-poverty of the very rich. Even Lionel Cranfield, 'one of the wealthiest men in England', raised funds by pawning his goods (*Renaissance Clothing and the Materials of Memory* (Cambridge: Cambridge University Press, 2000), 28).

[22] Muldrew notes that 'By 1641 the total indebtedness of the 121 members of the peerage stood at a staggering £1,500,000, or over £12,000 each' (*Economy*, 97). See also Jones, *God and the Moneylenders*, 43–4.

[23] Stone, *Crisis*, 529; see also Jonathan Gil Harris, *Sick Economies: Drama, Mercantilism, and Disease in Shakespeare's England* (Philadelphia: University of Pennsylvania Press, 2004), esp. 56.

[24] Alfred Beaven, *The Aldermen of the City of London*, 2 vols. (London: E. Fisher, 1908–13), ii. 42.

when he complained earlier, in 1570, that 'Not only money men, merchant men, and citizens be usurers, but also noblemen, courtiers, gentlemen, graziers, farmers, plowmen, and artificers—yea, I would the clergy were free.'[25]

Because affluence was a prerequisite for office, the city fathers were almost invariably 'money men'. Speaking more epigrammatically than rhetorically, Portia was to ask, 'Which is the merchant here, and which the Jew?' As a merchant, Francis Barnham was expected to extend credit to purchasers; from this point of view any 'first stab' involving a transaction based in goods was mere routine.[26] As an alderman, he also engaged the special affinity between municipal governance and lending, borne out of the policies of the Court of Orphans. Holding the funds of a fatherless child in trust, responsible too for the orphan's upbringing, the Aldermen were able to preserve the principal of an estate only by putting it to use. Interest provided (and dictated the amount of) a minor child's 'finding money', or living expenses. Needless to say, the Aldermen were not altruists—'they would', says Charles Carlton, 'as soon let their apprentices as their money lie idly around'—but this was a win–win policy. The circulation of orphans' legacies fueled the growth of English trade in general and the advancement of individual merchant borrowers in particular. Loans in the Court of Orphans were well under the working threshold, with interest of between 1 and 4 per cent, but they were nonetheless usurious in the sense that the Aldermen took no risks. For this case of a competing interest that could be described as charitable, therefore, the statute made explicit provision. It also insisted, however, that exceptions for orphans should not constitute precedents in other spheres.[27] The Crown's faith in the efficacy of such warnings may be judged from the prosecutorial provocation it gave its Barons of the Exchequer. It was Francis Barnham's bad luck that indictments under the new statute were at their most aggressive between 1571 and 1575, the very years he was at his peak as a civic leader and wealthy lender. He may have recognized the irony that in 1571 the Queen's

---

[25] Sir Francis Bacon, 'Of Usurie', in *The Essayes or Counsels, Civill and Morall*, ed. Michael Kiernan (Cambridge, Mass.: Harvard University Press, 1985), 126. See also Harris, *Sick Economies*, 54–6. Porder's *Sermon of God's Fearful Threatenings for Idolatry* is quoted by Jones, *God and the Moneylenders*, 67 (here silently modernized).

[26] On merchant credits, see Muldrew, *Economy*, 96.

[27] For the London Court of Orphans, see Ch. 5 and also Carlton, *Court of Orphans*, 83. Jones notes that even the Court's low interest rate was illegal in periods of zero tolerance like that which followed the Act of 1552, though there were attempts to gain legal exemptions (*God and the Moneylenders*, 50). The London livery companies also lent and borrowed. As an Assistant, Barnham was involved in the Company's loans to the city for the purchase of corn, which carried interest of 12 per cent (e.g. Drapers' M.B.8, fos. 243[r], 246[r]; Drapers' W.A.5, 1573–4, fo. 4[r]). The Drapers also acted as pawnbrokers and suretors for their members (see Girtin, *Triple Crowns*, 88–9, 148).

government had both enacted the new Statute against Usury and borrowed £1,432 from him.[28]

THE CAPCASE IN DRAPERS' HALL

Despite all the information that the Court of Exchequer compiled for *Queen v. Barnham*, its archives are incomplete and unreliable. To begin, it must be emphasized that they are far less coherent than this narrative, pieced together from multiple interrogatories and depositions, suggests. Then there is the matter of the outcome. What was the ruling? How did Barnham amend his plea? Did he suffer the applicable penalties? And these are only the most obvious of questions about the case. We must also make interpretive room for all the other impairments to the evidentiary status of documents produced in courts of inquiry, including facts obscured by deliberate misrepresentations, faulty memories, and evasive strategies—perhaps even more so here, as the Exchequer did not require defendants to testify under oath. Nor do the Court's transcriptions always acknowledge arrangements that were made behind the scenes. In other cases, Norman Jones instances informants either securing protection fees by threatening to bring suits or accepting payments to abort them, lenders attempting to inoculate themselves against big penalties by paying informants to charge them with small violations, and the Court's own officers negotiating settlements, as encouraged by the Crown, to avoid the trouble and expense of trial.[29] There are myriad occasions for doubt about any legal proceeding based in information, examinations, and depositions.

The special significance of *Queen v. Barnham* is that it is possible to demonstrate at least some of the gaps in the Exchequer's records. There is, for example, the matter of Waller's testimony that he personally recruited John Chapman to receive Barnham's merchandise. This may reveal nothing so much as the fact that Waller, with an eye to future loans if for no other reason, went as far as he dared to thwart the Exchequer, for the odds are that

[28] Henry Mackwilliam and Richard Colshill were especially encouraged to search out and try offenders between July 1571 and April 1575; their reward was half the Queen's share of the fine, plus 10 per cent (Jones, *God and the Moneylenders*, 94–5). Royal debt amounted to £900,000 by 1618 (Muldrew, *Economy*, 97). For Barnham's royal loans, see Chs. 1 and 6 (it is unclear whether the loan of £1,432 is part of the £1,500 he couriered to those suppressing the Northern Earls). Frank Foster, *Politics*, 138. In 1561 the Queen licensed Sir William Chester, among others, to earn 10 per cent on moneys loaned her 'without incurring the penalties of the statute against usury'.

[29] Jones, *God and the Moneylenders*, 98–100.

Barnham, not Waller, made this connection. While there were more than one John Chapman in London in 1573, it would be difficult not to suspect that the John Chapman of this exchange was Francis's brother-in-law of the same name, husband to his sister Dorothy and his associate for a 1569 property transaction.[30] In his will, Barnham bequeathed three gowns to the Chapmans and their son Thomas. There, we also encounter Barnham's 'cousin'—that all-encompassing term for kinship by marriage as well as blood—Stephen Slanye, the defendant of *Queen* v. *Slanye*. Slanye, too, was Barnham's quondam partner in land speculation; together, they bought and immediately resold the manor of Chatham in Kent. Slanye was also appointed an administrator of Barnham's estate. More than twenty years later, first Benedict and then Alice Barnham remembered Slanye and his wife in their own testaments.[31]

Francis Barnham seems to have been at the center of an active network of Londoners who made money from money in what Craig Muldrew has called an 'economy of obligation'. As early as 1558 Barnham lent £30 to fellow draper Jasper Umpton. In 1572, fletcher Thomas Deane died with moneys due him amounting to nearly £436 and with his own modest debts of 9s. 9d. in rent, 45s. to a tailor, and £5 to Francis Barnham. As was customary for merchants and shopkeepers, Deane would have carried debts for his own customers, but the roundness of the amount owed to Barnham suggests a bridge loan rather than another trade transaction. In 1565, Sir Ralph Bagnall wrote Sir Nicholas Throckmorton, asking him to 'send for Master Francis Barnham, a merchant whom I do owe a thousand pound unto, and to will him the rather for your sake to bear with me for somewhat longer time than he did this time twelve months, when I did owe him and pay him £700, and to promise him that he shall be paid and so considered for the time in the forbearing of his money as he himself shall be satisfied with the same'.[32] These are scattered hints of what

---

[30] *The Visitations of Kent*, ed. W. Bruce Bannerman, Publications of the Harleian Society 74, 75 (1923, 1924) lists Francis Barnham's sister as married to 'Chapman of London, gent' (1592). Benbow lists four John Chapmans in Elizabethan London, including a Collector for the Poor in St Lawrence Jewry in 1559, a governor of Christ's Hospital for 1564–6, and a father and son who paid subsidies in St Olave, Southwark.

[31] Will of Francis Barnham (25 April 1575 and 12 May 1576), PROB 11/58, fos. 76^v–78^r and *CPR: Elizabeth*, vii. *1575–1578*, no. 123. Will of Alice Barnham (7 December 1598), PROB 11/104, fos. 53^r–54^r. Will of Benedict Barnham (29 May 1598), PROB 11/91, fos. 304^r–309^r and *Abstracts of Inquisitions Post Mortem Relating to the City of London, Part III: 19–45 Elizabeth, 1577–1603*, ed. Edward Alexander Fry for the Index Library (London: British Record Society, 1908), 257–63. *CPR: Elizabeth*, vi. *1572–1575*, no. 2653 (Chapman and rents in Gorhambury). Francis and Slanye purchased Chatham from Thomas Wentworth and sold it to John Hart and Michael Barker; see Hasted, *History*, ii. 67.

[32] Umpton owed the Drapers £30; Barnham advanced the money to the Company 'so that he [himself] be repaid again by Umpton' (Drapers' M.B.7, p. 124). Kay Staniland suspects that Dean had 'unstable fluctuating finances', as he died with £20 in ready money but a gown out at pawn ('Thomas Deane's Shop in the Royal Exchange', in Ann Saunders (ed.), *The Royal*

was undoubtedly an extensive moneylending operation. In reality, Francis Barnham's low profile as an importer of merchandise may follow from the fact that his primary focus was on lending and land speculation.[33]

In iron he procured for St Thomas's Hospital (in 1563) and gravel he sold to the Drapers (in 1569–70), we may recognize wares that came to Barnham, as did Waller's own 1573 iron, in repayment of loans. Others of Barnham's loans were undoubtedly acquitted by property transfers, as may have been the case for the Horselydown tract that had once belonged to the deeply indebted Lewis Stoddard, or for the lands Francis came to 'co-own' with James Blount, Lord Mountjoy. When the Mountjoy property reverted to the Crown, the Barnhams achieved a twenty-one-year grant of rents and tithes that provided an enormous new influx of cash and materials for further loans, ventures, and acquisitions.[34]

Such an interpretation of Francis Barnham's career may also cast new light on the 1573 testimony of Sir Warham Sentleger in *Queen v. Slanye*. About six years earlier, Sir Warham, William, and Nicholas Sentleger had together alienated the manor of Bilsington Priory to Francis. This was the estate by means of which Martin Barnham was to cast off his merchant heritage and achieve country gentility.[35] It is unclear whether the Bilsington conveyance was an outright sale or whether it, too, was an exchange that began as a loan for which property that served as collateral was then forfeited when the loan defaulted. Whatever its configuration, the transaction may have informed Sentleger's 1570 decision to borrow from Slanye rather than Barnham. He may merely have feigned reluctance about an exchange through merchandise—thus disingenuously representing himself to the Exchequer as a neophyte borrower—while in truth he sought to avoid dealing with a man who had capitalized on his own need for cash to take possession of lands once granted his family by the Crown.

Sentleger may also have preferred to bargain with someone he believed he could intimidate with his talk of large holdings in Kent and royal service in Ireland. Slanye was to become a powerful man in London, but at the time of his loan to Sentleger he was still nearly fifteen years away from election as

---

Exchange, London Topographical Society 152 (1997), 60). See also Muldrew on a girdler who had loaned out £118 (to 110 different people), while he owed £306 to others (*Economy*, 96). Bagnall probably suffered steadily worsening circumstances, having retired one debt of £700 only to take out another for £1,000 (PRO SP 15/12, fo. 94).

[33] The cloth trade between England and the Low Countries declined in the 1550s and led also to a search for new markets like Russia. See Eric H. Ash, ' "A Note and a Caveat for the Merchant": Mercantile Advisors in Elizabethan England', *Sixteenth-Century Journal* 33 (2002), 1–31.

[34] LMA H01/ST/A/001/001, fo. 72^r (5 April 1563); Drapers' R.A.5, 1569–70, fo. 8^v. CLRO Rep. 19, fos. 189^v–191^r; *CPR: Elizabeth I*, iv. *1566–1569*, no. 2638.

[35] *CPR: Elizabeth I*, ibid. no. 1831.

alderman and twenty-five years from his term as Lord Mayor. He more than Barnham was likely to have been overawed by Sentleger's superior status and affect. If Francis Barnham's civic standing, large liquidity, and hard-nosed trafficking could discomfit a country knight, this is a modest example of the unsettling effect of an increasingly cash-based economy on the old social order. Equally, Sentleger may never have entertained a proposal from the broker Bowland in the first place. He may have tried to turn his world of landed privilege right side up again when to the Barons of the Exchequer he gratuitously and repeatedly dropped the name of the man who now owned the manor of Bilsington Priory.

In the records of the Court of Aldermen we find evidence of how municipal power worked to Barnham's advantage in his private transactions. He was one of a small group appointed to adjudicate 'the supplication of the sworn brokers of this city', for example, approving such requests as those of John Bowland, John Wilford, and William Wilkinson, who sought careers as brokers. He also had specific leverage over Rowland Searle. Searle borrowed money from the Chamber of London as well as from Barnham, in the former case through the Court of Orphans. He seems to have used his properties in Billingsgate as collateral for both. In March 1575 it came to the attention of the Court that the Billingsgate houses had been sold to Thomas Pennington. If Barnham was the source of this information, he had waited to see his own loan safely repaid. And when Searle was found by the city to be 'decayed and broken', Barnham was in place to manage the damage personally. With William Boxe (a fellow governor at Bridewell and his Under Sheriff in 1570), he was assigned to examine Searle's circumstances and to devise recommendations for further action. In June 1575 Barnham and Boxe ordered that Searle should make restitution of the orphans' legacies and 'finding moneys' and void his accounts with the city. They then arranged that the loan Searle had held should be extended instead to Pennington—that other deponent from the first phase of *Queen* v. *Barnham* who was unwilling to testify against Francis Barnham.[36] Barnham seems to have known how to reward, which undoubtedly means that he was known also to punish. He fully exploited the peepholes into others' private lives that his administrative posts provided.

Can it really be that the Court Barons were unaware of the betraying connections and transactions between Barnham and Chapman, Barnham and Slanye, Barnham and Sentleger, Barnham and Searle, Barnham and

---

[36] Brokers were appointed exclusively by the mayor and aldermen of the city; for one example see CLRO Rep. 16, fo. 466ʳ. For a petition from brokers heard by Barnham and others, see Rep. 18, fo. 266ʳ. For the assignment of Barnham and Boxe to the Searle inquiry, Rep. 18, fo. 363ᵛ; for their lengthy report, Rep. 18, fo. 392ʳ⁻ᵛ. Searle still owed the Court money on 17 January 1576, when it was noted that he had died, Rep. 19, fo. 26ᵛ.

Pennington? They did not press Waller on how he came to approach John Chapman, and, with Francis as their object, they would have had little reason to interest themselves in other financial dealings by Sentleger, Searle, and Pennington. What is least likely is that they were ignorant of his kinship to Slanye, but again it is impossible to be sure which were facts not known and which were facts not recorded. Into the latter category, presumably, fell what must have been the probative information of *Queen* v. *Barnham*. This had to do with those 'other merchants' who were involved in the renegotiation of the terms for Waller's repayment, who were consulted about Ardes's proposed flight to Ireland, and who were co-owners of a mysterious capcase in Drapers' Hall.

On 8 November 1574, a box was placed in the custody of the Drapers' Clerk. Originally designed to store caps, it now contained twenty-eight 'obligations'. The Clerk recorded that these documents were held 'to the use of' Francis Barnham, draper Thomas Pullyson, and grocer John Kirby, and the case was sealed with their three signets. Each obligation pledged the delivery of twelve-and-a-half tons of iron on a calendrical quarter. Three months later, when a load of iron was received, the capcase was opened in the presence of witnesses, the first obligation was removed and canceled, the twenty-seven papers still in force were counted and replaced, and the case was resealed with the three signets. Although Waller's name is not mentioned in the Drapers' court minutes, these were unquestionably the vouchers drawn up to settle his debt. In June 1575, Waller was to depose in the Exchequer that he had 'entered into several obligations' with Barnham, Pullyson, Kirby, Gilborne, and Ashbornham for 400 tons of iron to be furnished on a quarterly schedule. Already at the time of his interrogation, Waller said, they had received a first installment of twelve-and-a-half tons.[37]

The capcase did not involve Company business, because Kirby was a grocer. But it was not uncommon for private persons temporarily to secure safe storage in public and corporate strong rooms.[38] And, just as there was a tradition that institutional chests and treasure houses should have multiple keys held by various officers representing a larger population, so, too, Barnham, Pullyson, and Kirby were probably lead men for the larger group investigated by the

---

[37] Drapers' M.B.9, fos. 4^r, 10^r, 30^r; PRO E 133/2/269. Jones misunderstands Waller's deposition to refer to 400 tons quarterly rather than 400 tons total (*God and the Moneylenders*, 123). This is not surprising from the wording of the deposition; it is in the Drapers' Company records that the meaning becomes clear.

[38] Executors for Lady Askew persuaded the Drapers to hold a chest until her linens could be divided among her heirs (Drapers' M.B.5, fo. 118^v); the Aldermen held document chests for the widow of Sir Thomas Pope and the children of John Saunderson (CLRO Rep. 17, fos. 15^v, 18^r; Rep. 18, fo. 100^r).

Exchequer. This, far more dramatically than the depositional reticence of Pennington and Searle or the aborted loan to Sir John Sentleger, would have short-circuited the deliberations of the Exchequer. The unspecified change of plea that Barnham was required to make must in fact have acknowledged that what was investigated as *Queen* v. *Barnham* was not after all a transaction between two private individuals but instead a conglomerated bargain difficult to prosecute under the terms of the Statute against Usury. Immediately after Barnham was required to 'amend his plea', the Barons called in Cursine, Blunte, Kirby, Gilborne, Taylor, and Pullyson. Presumably these men confirmed that Barnham had assembled a syndicate for the Waller loan.[39]

When Barnham died before Waller's debt was retired, the capcase passed into the primary custody of Kirby. On 10 July 1576 Martin Barnham brought his father's signet to Drapers' Hall, 'authorized from his mother Mistress Alice Barnham executrix to her late husband Master Alderman Barnham deceased', so that Barnham's seal could be broken once again and Kirby could recover the twenty-three obligations that then remained.[40] The Drapers' Clerk noted the event because it absolved him from further responsibility for the case and its contents. In this accidental way the Clerk tells us what the Exchequer did not. First, the loan investigated as *Queen* v. *Barnham* involved as principals more men than Waller and Barnham, because the obligations did not transfer to Alice Barnham for probate with her husband's estate. Second, the loan had not been voided by the Exchequer in 1575, because its repayment was still in force in 1576. The Barons must have known the contents of the capcase, which played so important a role in the final frustration of their long investigation. But there was small reason for their Clerk to expend more effort on a closed prosecution by explaining for the historical record why Francis Barnham had not been found guilty of violating the Statute against Usury.

A GREAT ESTATE

A leading indicator for a charge of usury was that the lender took no risk. From his reluctance to deal with Sir John Sentleger and Sir Walter Waller and from his use of a serviceable influence over Rowland Searle and Thomas

---

[39] Again, Barnham had models for this business arrangement from civic life. The Drapers' Company, forced to provide military loans to the Crown and food subsidies to the City, did not spend down a corporate reserve. Instead, funds were collected from individual members.

[40] Drapers' M.B.9, fo. 47r.

Pennington, Francis Barnham seems to have been fairly risk-averse.[41] But no one in his position could avoid all hazard. The prospects of borrowers could be as uncertain as those of special pleader Sir Ralph Bagnall, who repaid £700 only to borrow £1,000, and who then required an extension for that £1,000. There were also the jeopardies of his merchant ventures. Francis Barnham accumulated 'a great personal estate', according to his grandson, 'which yet by some ill fortunes at sea and bad debtors was a good deal lessened some years before his death'. The statement cannot be accepted simply at face value. Elsewhere in his memoir, Sir Francis understates Martin's privilege in order to valorize him, and this same impulse may have moved Sir Francis to overstate his grandfather's latter-day losses.[42] Lacking Francis's business accounts, however, we can only parse such public hints as remain regarding the financial reverses he may have suffered before his death, whether like Shylock from desperate debts or like Antonio from miscarried ships.

There was a third site of peril, which was the expense of office. A 1562 mayoral term had ruined Sir Thomas Lodge, for example. Though he was confined to the Fleet with debts amounting to £2,500, Lodge was frequently in the public eye in the late 1560s through appeals made on his behalf by city officials and agents of the Crown. The Drapers lent Lodge £100 but refused to do more, even when the Queen's Remembrancer of the Exchequer, John Osborne, and her Customer, Thomas Smith, called on the Assistants 'personally'. The Court of Aldermen, meanwhile, reached an agreement that each of their members—Barnham among them—should 'lovingly' loan Lodge £20. Lodge's second son and namesake was to have a middling literary career as the author of the prose romance *Rosalynde* (1590). He also published *An Alarum against Usurers* (1584), which includes a quasi-autobiographical complaint about the financial difficulties of his youth.[43] Barnham did not live long enough to face the fiscal challenge of the mayoralty, but even his election as alderman required him to be worth at least 2,000 marks (£1,333) in annual rental income and to be willing to expend between £1,200 and £1,500 yearly on the charges of his office. His shrieval year's costs, scarcely abated by a 1535 petition to reduce these expenses because so many 'have been reduced to

---

[41] Barnham did not purchase a ticket for the national lottery held by the Crown in 1567 (Drapers' M.B.8, fo. 13[r–v]; and see Girtin, *Triple Crowns*, 155–6).

[42] Sir Francis Barnham, 'The Character of Sir Martin Barnham, Knight', by his son Sir Francis Barnham', ed. Lena Cowen Orlin, in James Dutcher and Anne Lake Prescott (eds.), *Renaissance Historicisms: Essays in Honor of Arthur F. Kinney* (Newark: University of Delaware Press, 2008).

[43] Drapers' M.B.8, fos. 5[r], 49[v], 70[r], 79[r–v]; CLRO Rep. 16, fo. 461[v]. Lodge's son complained bitterly that merchants 'eat our English gentry out of house and home' (quoted by T. S. Willan, *The Muscovy Merchants of 1555* (Manchester: Manchester University Press, 1953), 2).

extreme poverty', amounted to £2,500. In addition, many of his posts made him responsible for rents and fines which could be difficult to gather, and he was answerable for any shortfalls. Referring to collections of as much as £2,000, Sir William Wentworth was to advise his son that 'by the sheriffic . . . there comes great loss and danger'.[44]

In the public records, it becomes clear how fantastical a fiction is *The Shoemaker's Holiday*, with its happy celebrations of Simon Eyre's ascendancy to be Lord Mayor of London. The financial demands of municipal office not only mandated a privileged elite, they also ensured a reluctant candidate pool. Stow exaggerated only a little in reporting that 'every man rather shunneth than seeketh the mayoralty'. Ian Archer finds that in the twenty years between 1559 and 1579, fifteen men refused the city's shrievalty; indeed, William Boxe, named Under Sheriff with Francis Barnham, 'by word and gesture utter[ed] himself unwilling to supply the office' (though he was finally persuaded to accept). Benedict Barnham was elected at the premature age of 32 because thirteen men more senior than he declined to serve in 1591. Archer observes further that the Queen's 'rare' interventions in City elections were 'usually motivated by the desire to spare her servants from office'. John Branch, for example, procured a royal letter requesting the Aldermen to discharge him from executive duties; the exemption lasted a year until he yielded to civic pressure. Inducements to accept the call could also include punitive fines: five hundred marks, charged to John Quarles for avoiding all city offices; two hundred pounds, for an unwilling sheriff; forty pounds ('without any forgiveness'), for any draper refusing a wardenship. Such penalties became so common, it has been argued, that they were relied upon as revenue enhancements for the underfunded city. But more was at issue than a pretext for fines; one man spent a full year in Newgate before finally agreeing to serve his ward as constable. John Lowen consented to be elected Master of the Drapers only on condition 'that he should no more hereafter be chosen warden, but be dispensed therewith for ever'.[45]

---

[44] See Frank Foster, *Politics*, 148, and William Smythe, 'A Brief Description of the Royal City of London' (1575), GL Ms 2463, sigs. 8ᵛ–10ʳ. Beaven, noting the petition, lists two mayors and ten sheriffs who were ruined (ii. pp. xxxvi–xxxvii). 'Sir William Wentworth's Advice to his Son', in *Wentworth Papers, 1597–1628*, ed. J. P. Cooper, Camden Society, 4th ser., 12 (London: Royal Historical Society, 1973), 12–13.

[45] Archer, *Pursuit*, 21, 33. Richard M. Wunderli quotes Stow in 'Evasion of the Office of Alderman in London, 1532–1672', *London Journal* 15 (1990), 14. 'These were rational, indeed bourgeois decisions that consciously weighed profit and loss', he argues. For Boxe (1 August 1570), see Drapers' M.B.8, fo. 112ᵛ; for Benedict, Foster, *Politics*, 61; for Branch (22 March 1570 and 17 August 1571), CLRO Rep. 17, fos. 1ᵛ, 192ʳ⁻ᵛ; for Quarles (20 October 1569), CLRO Rep. 16, fo. 509ʳ; for sheriff Thomas Kighley (10 and 14 August 1571), CLRO Rep. 17, fo. 191ʳ⁻ᵛ; for the Drapers' regulations (31 July 1568), Drapers' M.B.8, fo. 39ʳ; for constable George Brathwait

Francis Barnham, by contrast, chose to serve the city and seems to have successfully weathered his highest office. In 1571 he remained sufficiently prosperous to be elected to a second financially demanding term as Master of the Drapers' Company. A year later he was still making plans for significant economic expansion. In November 1572, Richard Rennoldes put the Drapers' Company on notice that he was interested in assuming the lease of a storeyard they owned on Bearbinders' Lane. The storeyard was to become available in July 1575. Francis Barnham immediately expressed his own, competing interest. A year later, facing a City assessment of £375 for the corn subsidy of 1573, the Drapers found themselves with something under £115 in cash reserves. Barnham offered to lend the Company the remaining funds, over £260, on condition that he would be preferred to the lease of the storeyard. The terms would otherwise be routine; he would pay the 'accustomed' Bearbinders' rent of £2 annually. Barnham delivered the subsidy money on 19 December 1573.[46]

Just eleven days later, on 30 December 1573, he suddenly terminated the agreement. 'Upon considerations him moving', Barnham 'surrendered and released again all his whole right, title, and interest' in the storeyard, on condition that his subsidy money be returned by 6 January 1574. With the help of John Quarles, who made up the loan at 10 per cent interest, the Drapers were able to meet Barnham's deadline.[47] Barnham may simply have identified another, more promising investment for his funds. But in this context the mid-1574 renegotiation of the bargain with Sir Walter Waller, which brought other merchants on board, might have represented a strategy for shared risk, could have resulted from Waller's wish to borrow more, but may as easily have followed from Barnham's own need to recall some portion of his cash assets.

There was another scaling-back of plans between 1575, when Barnham wrote his will, and 1576, when he amended it. His bequests were made in two parts, one for moneys and tokens and one for lands and properties. As composed on 25 April 1575, the first section included a remembrance of £60 to his brother Thomas and an endowment of £100 to the Drapers'

(8 and 10 January 1572), CLRO Rep. 17, fos. 247[r], 248[v]; for Lowen (7 August 1548), Drapers' M.B.1/C, fo. 456[r]. Wunderli notes that the fines helped the city meet Crown demands for war funds, pp. 7–8. See also Ward, *Metropolitan Communities*, 85–6.

[46] Drapers' M.B.8, fos. 209[r], 241[r], 246[r]; W.A.5, 1573–4, fo. 4[r].

[47] Drapers' M.B.8, fos. 246[v]–247[v], W.A.5, 1573–4, fos. 4[r], 5[v]. The Drapers repaid Barnham on 4 January 1574. Losses included 24[d]. paid to the Company Clerk to make two sets of obligations, one for Barnham and then one for Quarles. The Drapers borrowed £200 from Quarles for six months and repeatedly extended the loan, at the end of each six-month period paying him £10 interest (M.B.8, fo. 247[v]; M.B.9, fos. 5[r], 12[v]). In July 1575 the Bearbinder lease went to a merchant taylor, William Handforth (M.B.9, fos. 15[v], 17[v]).

Company to provide start-up loans to young merchants. In a codicil of 1 April 1576, Barnham revoked both gifts without reallocating those funds (Thomas had since died, but the lost legacy to the Drapers' was not redistributed).[48] The second section, written on 26 April 1575, granted a building on Friday Street in London to Christ's Hospital as well as properties in Horselydown in Southwark to Benedict Barnham. In the codicil to this part of the will, also dated 1 April 1576, Francis gave the Horselydown lands to Christ's Hospital rather than to his youngest son. The Friday Street house had been sold.

With holdings in London, Middlesex, Kent, Surrey, Essex, Dorset, and Wales, and with goods worth more than £2,200, Francis Barnham died a wealthy man. His sons Martin and Steven were already solidly established as a landowner in Kent and a merchant in London, respectively. But the financial retrenchments of December 1573, midsummer 1574, and April 1576 seem to support Sir Francis's contention that Alice Barnham and her children inherited a somewhat reduced estate. Its spectacular recovery falls outside Sir Francis's scope, being best demonstrated not in his father Martin's life story but instead in his uncle Benedict's. Despite an untimely death, Benedict left behind one of the great London merchant fortunes, with vast lands and their rental incomes and, in addition, personal property worth £14,614.[49] He was just 17 when his father died, still under-age, and the business partner with whom Benedict launched a brilliant career was his widowed mother.

Even during her marriage, when prescription would have had it that her husband's duty was to 'get goods' and hers just to 'keep them', Alice Barnham had her own economic role as a senior partner in the family firm. As Judith M. Bennett has summarized, England was 'a society where work was structured more around households than individuals', but, she adds, 'our public records focus so often on house*holders* as the persons legally responsible for domestic employment that they obfuscate the realities' of production (emphasis added).[50] Alice's work was not necessary to the Barnham family in the way that other women's was to those living at subsistence level, but it was essential to the creation of the 'great estate' that her grandson attributed to her husband alone.

Barnham's business activities were less home-based than most. Like the gentlewomen who managed country houses and large lands when their husbands were away, Alice had significant responsibilities in consequence of Francis's frequent absences. For the administrative courts of the Drapers'

---

[48] Will of Francis Barnham, PROB 11/58, fos. 76ᵛ–78ʳ. The legacy to the Drapers was revoked 'for certain considerations me moving'; these were not specified.

[49] For Benedict's personal estate at probate, see Willan, *Muscovy Merchants*, 79.

[50] Bennett refers specifically to brewers in *Ale, Beer, and Brewsters in England: Women's Work in a Changing World, 1300–1600* (Oxford: Oxford University Press, 1996), 60–1.

Company, Bridewell and St Thomas's Hospital, and the London Aldermen, he attended meetings in the mornings—and sometimes into the afternoons—as often as five or six days a week. His absences from the various boards tended to come in short sequences that suggest travel or ill-health rather than truancy. In addition to these sessions, for which rosters have survived, there were his unrecorded conferences, as alderman, with the deputy and constables of his ward; his attendance of the irregularly documented assemblies of London's Common Council; and his lost history of sitting in the Sheriff's Court.[51] For the four corporate bodies with which he was associated he conducted searches for proper business practices, participated in views of institutional property, was named to various delegations, undertook multiple arbitrations, acted as purchasing agent, gathered fees and subsidies, appointed and supervised staff, and audited accounts. He was involved in the Company of Merchant Adventurers and the Russia Company. His work with St Thomas's Hospital required trips to survey a farm in Hackney in 1563 and a woods in Crofton in 1565; to hold courts in Denam in 1565, in Cambridgeshire in 1567 and 1568, in Kent (twice) and Essex in 1568, and in Cambridgeshire and Essex in 1569. Inevitably, there were scheduling conflicts; in June 1572, the Drapers 'enacted and established' a decision only 'so far forth as Master Alderman Barnham our Master being now absent from this assembly shall at his coming hither to dinner allow'.[52]

Given the demands of Francis Barnham's public schedule, it was inevitable not only that Alice Barnham was his working partner, but also that her active role would be widely assumed. This is indicated in an interrogatory prepared for *Queen v. Barnham*, as the Barons of the Exchequer followed the apparent trail of Francis Barnham's ferret silks. To disguise a loan of money as a sale of goods, Francis allegedly gave Sir Walter Waller a quantity of ribbons, Waller consigned them to John Chapman, Chapman sought buyers for them, and Chapman returned to Waller whatever cash they realized (less his own commission). But the officers of the Exchequer suspected, first, that the ribbons

---

[51] Drapers' Assistants met on Mondays and Wednesdays, Aldermen on Tuesdays and Thursdays; Governors of St Thomas's Hospital on Mondays; auditors of St Thomas's accounts on Saturdays. Fines were chargeable for absences. Attendance is infrequently recorded for Common Council meetings, but Barnham's presence is mentioned on 13 June 1570, 1 August 1570, 3 May 1571, 22 May 1571, 1 August 1571, 1 August 1572, 6 November 1572, 16 November 1572, 15 June 1574, 26 October 1574, 6 December 1574, and 1 March 1575. Benbow notes that Barnham attended 84 out of 98 sessions of the Court of Aldermen in 1569–70, 94 out of 102 in 1570–1, 75 out of 96 in 1571–2, 63 out of 83 in 1573–4, and 54 out of 99 in 1574–5.

[52] LMA H01/ST/D/01/001, fo. 126^v; H01/ST/A/001/002, fos. 8^r, 24^v, 69^v, 89^r; H01/ST/A/001/003, fo. 20^v. On 13 August 1571, the Drapers noted that Barnham was 'absent out of town', M.B.8, fo. 159^r; on 3 June 1572, the day Martin Barnham received his freedom by patrimony, Francis was elsewhere, M.B.8, fo. 194^v. M.B.8, fos. 106^r, 176^v and M.B.9, fo. 4^v give other absences, including a conflict with his schedule at Guildhall.

had never been placed on the open market; second and consequently, that they had not found their best value; and third, that the entire scheme allowed Barnham to fix a price that ensured him a risk-free return of something like 27 per cent interest on his loan. 'Do you not think', they asked Francis Ardes, 'or have you not heard say that the wife of the said Barnham bought the same or some part thereof?' The implication was that the only cash involved in the transaction was Francis's own, passed directly or indirectly to Waller, while the goods meanwhile moved in a meaningless charade. For the last leg of their diversionary travels Alice was understood to have been responsible.

Ardes replied that Waller had told him 'that the wife of the said Francis Barnham bought some part of the wares when they were in Master Chapman's hands (but how much nor at what prices he knoweth not)'. To a similar interrogatory, William Martin said the same.[53] Waller himself refused to confirm this report, as he had so many others. To the question 'do you not think that the said Barnham or his wife did buy some of the said wares again?' he answered that he could not depose.[54] Thus he refused to give evidence of false chevisaunce. While the Barons of the Exchequer may not have been able to convert their knowledge into a conviction, that does not mean that they did not have this part of the transaction, as so many others, substantially right. About one crucial aspect of the arrangement, however, they were again wrong—or, to put it more precisely, they allowed their records to leave us with the wrong impression, coming to them as we do with our own preconceptions about Tudor women and work. Alice Barnham may not have played a supporting role in Francis Barnham's moneylending business. Instead, her commerce and his seem to have stood in a reciprocal relationship, he dealing in hard currency and she in such goods as the notorious ferret silks.

ALICE BARNHAM, SILKWOMAN

This study of Alice Barnham began as a search for the private lives of the middling sorts in public documents. For the Tudor and Stuart period, such personal instruments as diaries, correspondence, and memoirs were ineluctably skewed to the gentle and the literate, as well as the godly. The Barnhams were of the middling sort, but their story is nonetheless an imperfect

---

[53] Substantially the same question and answer appear in PRO E133/2/221 (Martin) and E133/2/230 (Ardes). I quote from the latter (the twelfth interrogatory).
[54] PRO E133/2/269.

one for the seeker of the everyday. Alice's grandson may have described her husband as self-created, and in important respects that was the case, but for the larger portion of the early modern population Sir Francis's perspective was unarguably elitist. Francis Barnham went from a position of relative privilege to become one of the wealthiest and most powerful merchants in Elizabethan London. Still, his new-man biography is sufficiently obscure to be historiographically interesting, requiring as it does assembly out of dispersed records in institutional archives.

For his wife, as for all underdocumented early modern women, the patchwork pieces are even more difficult to reassemble. Alice Barnham owns business secrets, too, though hers are of a different order from her husband's. She did not, like Francis, have an immediate purpose in obscuring her professional profile, except perhaps as his confederate. The loans to Rowland Searle and Sir Walter Waller may have been common ventures in Tudor society, and necessary to economic growth, but they were nonetheless legally dubious. Her grandson suppressed this aspect of his family's success story. That which interposes itself between Alice's principal career and our understanding is not, by contrast, shame or circumspection. Instead it is history—that is, history as we have known it, so often oblivious to women's work and women's lives. The archives have no reason to confirm the argument that is made here, that Alice Barnham was one of the last of the London silkwomen.

A first hint at her commercial identity is that sometime between September 1560 and September 1561 the wardens of the Drapers' Company paid 'Mistress Barnham' £4. 19s. for 'silk fringe yellow and blue', which they used to trim their new blue taffeta banners and streamers. These ceremonial devices were renewed for the inauguration of a Lord Mayor. The Drapers' Clerk recorded the purchase in terms of weight, as silk was customarily sold, at 54 ounces, and then added that this amounted to 119 yards of fringe. At the same time the Drapers purchased from 'Mistress Barnham' seven dozen 'black silken points' or fastening cords, used by the trumpeters and waits (or singers) on the occasion. At 2d. the dozen, they totaled 14d. The next year, the wardens bought three new green carpets. They remodeled them with red buckram linings purchased from a man named William Keltredge but turned again to 'Mistress Barnham' for green silk fringe. In this case, only the weight was recorded, 24 ounces, and the price, 26s.[55] Although Company Clerks rarely noted the names of purveyors as well as items purchased, information is unexpectedly full during the 1560s, when the Drapers also bought silk fringe from Richard Buckfold (1562–3), Bryan

---

[55] Drapers' W.A.4, 1560–1, fo. 7[r–v]; R.A.5, 1562–3, fo. 11[r]. For the banners, see also M.B.7, pp. 287–8.

Calverley (1564–5), Mistress Thoroughgood (1565–6), and Mistress Trott (1569–70).[56]

The fact that Alice keeps archival company with Rose Trott is the principal clue to her occupation. After the death of her draper spouse, John, in 1551, Trott bound at least six apprentices as an independent businesswoman. Judging from various city assessments and subsidies (including £20 to the Bridewell project in 1556 and £40 for wheat in 1560 and 1561), she was highly successful. By long tradition, a woman who was married to a freeman and living with him at the time of his death could herself be made free of the city, so long as she did not remarry. In this fashion Trott operated autonomously under the auspices of the Drapers; she left the Company a standing silver-gilt cup when she died in 1575. Francis Barnham was among those who attended her funeral and afterwards enjoyed her bequest of cakes, buns, and spiced wine.[57] However, our best insight into the nature of her occupation comes not in the Drapers' archives but instead from a record in the Aldermen's Repertories from August 1560: 'Master John White and Master Martin, Aldermen, were this day appointed by the Court here to travail with Mistress Trott and other the silkwomen of this City to learn of them the cause why they are not contented to weigh their silk at the common silk beam.'[58] Though details of the controversy are lost, the note is significant for its characterization of Mistress Trott and her cohort. In furnishing fringe to the Drapers, she was no occasional craftswoman or hobbyist wife. By a reasonable process of association, Alice Barnham, too, was a professional silkwoman.

As Maryanne Kowaleski and Judith M. Bennett have emphasized, silkworking was 'not a mere sideline to domestic duties'; it was 'a true "mystery"', with 'secrets of production and trade passed only from mistress to apprentice'.[59] Even having grown up in the clothworking household of her mercer father, Alice Barnham would have observed a term in training that prohibited her

---

[56] Drapers' W.A.5, 1562–3, fo. 9ᵛ (Buckfold); W.A.5, 1564–5, fo. 6ᵛ (Calverley); W.A.5, 1565–6, fo. 5ᵛ (Thoroughgood); W.A.5, 1569–70, fo. 9ᵛ (Trott). And see the Assistants' resolution that 'the Company shall at all assemblies prefer such as be brethren of this fellowship afore a stranger in all manner of things for the which they shall disburse any money, be it for wares, workmanship, victuals, or any other things necessary, provided always that they may be served as well and as good cheap of our said brethren as of a stranger' (cited by Johnson, *History*, ii. 76). The regulation may also have applied to 'sisters' of the Company.

[57] For Trott's apprentices I am indebted to the manuscript register compiled by Percival Boyd, kindly transcribed by Penelope Fussell. Drapers' M.B.9, fo. 6ᵛ (her funeral and gift). On a widow's freedom, see especially Caroline M. Barron, 'The "Golden Age" of Women in Medieval London', *Reading Medieval Studies* 15 (1989), 44; Maryanne Kowaleski and Judith M. Bennett, 'Crafts, Gilds, and Women in the Middle Ages: Fifty Years after Marian K. Dale', *Signs* 14 (1989), 478; Rappaport, *Worlds*, 40; and Robert Tittler, *Townspeople and Nation: English Urban Experiences, 1540–1640* (Stanford: Stanford University Press, 2001), 24.

[58] CLRO Rep. 14, fo. 518ʳ.   [59] Kowaleski and Bennett, 'Crafts', 480.

marriage before its completion in her early to mid-twenties. She would then have required substantial start-up funds for stock and supplies, and over time would have invested also in trading ventures. We have seen the signs of her husband's ambition in his early history; this career choice displays Alice's corresponding sense of her own standing, for it was the preferred occupation for wives and daughters of aldermen. Status followed from silk's associations with significant capital, global exchange, and exclusive custom. Silkwomen purchased raw silks from mercers and turned them into yarn, imported fine finished silk and metal threads (especially from Italy), supervised the production of various luxury goods and ornaments, and catered to an elite clientele. They dealt in ribbons, laces, fringes, tassels, points, knotted buttons, fancy gloves, and finely worked personal and table linens. Queen Elizabeth's silkwomen were sufficiently diversified to supply her with blackwork embroidery as well as the so-called 'narrow ware'.[60]

Thus, Alice was the retailer in the Barnham household. As the wife of a freeman, she was authorized to share in her husband's privileges, even to the extent of operating *sole*, meaning not only that she could bind her own apprentices and maintain her own shop but also that she was responsible for her own debts. So, too, were Rose Trott, Barbara Champion, and Mistress Sadler; in fact, we should understand that it was more the rule than the exception that merchants' wives were businesswomen. Undoubtedly, Alice had it both ways, and was her husband's partner as well as an independent agent. Caroline Barron has pointed out the 'financial advantages in being able to shift goods, or cash, from one partner to another', and shifting was a practice in which the Barnhams were demonstrably expert.[61] After Francis's death, the titles to family property moved between Alice and her sons in ways that unquestionably had economic purpose and value, even if we will never be able to decode them.[62]

---

[60] On silkwork, see Kowaleski and Bennett, ibid., esp. for the business aspects of the trade. For the goods in which silkwomen traded, see also Alice Clark, *Working Life of Women in the Seventeenth Century* (London: Routledge & Kegan Paul, 1919), 138–45; Marian K. Dale, 'The London Silkwomen of the Fifteenth Century', *Economic History Review*, 1st ser., 4 (1933), 324–35 (and repr. in Kowaleski and Bennett, 'Crafts'); Kay Lacey, 'The Production of "Narrow Ware" by Silkwomen in Fourteenth- and Fifteenth-Century England', *Textile History* 18 (1987), 187–204 (I am grateful to Judith Bennett for sending me a copy of this essay); and Anne F. Sutton, 'Alice Claver, Silkwoman (d. 1489)', in Caroline M. Barron and Anne F. Sutton (eds.), *Medieval London Widows, 1300–1500* (London: Hambledon, 1994), 129–42. Study of the trade is rarely brought forward into the sixteenth century. For two exceptions, see Janet Arnold, *Queen Elizabeth's Wardrobe Unlock'd* (Leeds: Maney, 1988), 219–27; and Natasha Korda, 'Women's Theatrical Properties', in Jonathan Gil Harris and Natasha Korda (eds.), *Staged Properties in Early Modern English Drama* (Cambridge: Cambridge University Press, 2002), 213–15.

[61] Barron, 'The "Golden Age" of Women', 40.

[62] For example, Steven Barnham procured property in Kent from kinsman Richard Patrick; he transferred it to his mother Alice in November 1577, a few weeks before she sold it to a

Queen v. *Barnham* shows how useful it was to the family to have a retail branch, and how Alice's commerce in fine and imported ornaments complemented Francis's traffic in money. Silk was the pretended medium of exchange for the loans to both Rowland Searle and Sir Walter Waller. If it is true that Alice retrieved ferret silks that John Chapman held on consignment from Waller, and if, as also seems likely, these were her own wares, then it was her inventory that authenticated the ruses by which Francis represented his usurious loans as exchanges of merchandise. Francis Ardes had claimed, improbably, that Barnham sought counsel to subvert the Statute against Usury. William Martin deposed that he was concerned instead about regulations for buying and selling foreign merchandise. Because Francis's merchant activities involved export primarily, this appeared an equally implausible pretext for his strategic caution in early negotiations with Waller. But there may indeed have been foreign goods at issue—not Francis's home-county wools or Sir Walter Waller's provincially produced iron, but instead Alice Barnham's imported ferret silks.

When Francis Barnham died in 1576, his apprentices Thomas Hyll and Lawrence Manfield were still several years away from achieving their freedom. Had Alice remarried a man not a draper, they would have been 'set over' to another draper (as Francis had himself been transferred in 1539). But, like Trott, Alice remained a widow and protected her status as a free woman of the city. Hyll and Manfield worked out their apprenticeships with her until 1578–9 and 1580–1, respectively. In her own name, Alice then bound John Pamplyn, Ellis Watson, and Christopher Harbert, freeing them in 1586, 1598–9, and 1601–2.[63] The sheer length of her experience is informing, beginning as it does in the first years of her widowhood when her youngest son was still under age, continuing through Benedict's active career as a merchant and venturer, ongoing even after his premature death, and, because the Drapers' records are not exhaustive, perhaps encompassing other apprenticeships as well. Anne Sutton has pointed out the particular usefulness of male workers for women in business, because they could be assigned legal and administrative

---

fourth party; see *CPR: Elizabeth I*, vii. *1575–1578*, nos. 2061, 2502, and 2808. For others of Alice's property transactions (in widowhood), see GL Ms 977/1, fols. 53a–b and 56b, pp. 371–4; *CPR: Elizabeth I*, ibid. nos. 3106 and 3240; 'William Horne, Citizen and Grocer', *Abstracts of Inquisitions Post Mortem*, 193; SBT DR18/1/1226; ESRO HIC/319–22. Among her purchases were the Sign of the Two Legs and the Sign of the Eagle and Boy, both in Watling Street (1578).

[63] Drapers' W.A.5, 1578–9, fo. 5^v (Hill); W.A.5, 1580–1, fo. 6^v (Manfield); M.B.10, fo. 51^v and W.A.5, 1585–6, fo. 5^v (Pamplyn), W.A.5, 1598–9, fo. 8^r (Watson), W.A.5, 1601–2, fo. 10^v (Harbert). 'Spoon silver', the fee paid the Company by masters for apprentices, was set for 'every Sister whose husband has been of the aforesaid livery' in 1524 (cited by Johnson, *History*, i. 280). For regulations regarding the 'setting over' of apprentices when their masters died and the widow remarried outside the Company, see Drapers' M.B.5, fos. 32^v, 58^v.

tasks that were difficult for women to execute. It is not clear whether Alice trained men in her husband's public mold, as merchants, in her own silk business, or, like some other moneyed widows, in the occupation of lending at interest.[64]

She herself continued to move in the circles of silkworkers, negotiating a marriage there, after Francis's death, for her third surviving son. Martin had been placed in families with Draper connections (the Rudstons, the Wottons, and the Calthorps), but Benedict was matched to the daughter of the Queen's silkman, Ambrose Smith. Pioneering studies by Alice Clark and Marian K. Dale give silkwomen a fairly localized character: they were, first, London-based, as that was the center of the luxury trade, and, second, medieval, because they maintained their monopoly of decorative 'narrow ware' only until the end of the fifteenth century. Their later activities are relatively obscure except as a history of decline described by William Harrison: 'until the tenth or twelfth year of Queen Elizabeth'—that is, somewhere around 1568 or 1570—'there were but few silk shops in London, and those few were only kept by women and maidservants, and not by men, as now they are'.[65] Alice was one of the small group of women who continued to operate in what had over the course of her lifetime become a male-dominated profession. Her kin by Benedict's marriage represented the sixteenth-century regendering of the trade.

The traffic in ornamental textiles was vulnerable to male arrogation because silkwomen had never sought to make political capital out of their business prowess. Between 1368 and 1504, they six times proved their ability to take corporate action when they petitioned either the Mayor or the Parliament for protection from foreign competition. They were then, according to Barron, 'a guild in all but name'. And yet medieval silkwomen never organized formally. Dale suggests that because most were wives, the guilds of their husbands fulfilled their social, religious, and charitable interests. She also conjectures that, as 'more of an art than a craft', silkwork resisted the kind

---

[64] Sutton refers to a medieval silkwoman who in her will made her male servant responsible to collect her debts, 'a task which neatly explains the need any female merchant had for at least one responsible male servant if she was to operate successfully' ('Alice Claver', 138). Stone emphasizes the liquidity of merchants' widows, (*Crisis*, 628–9). See also Muldrew, *Economy*, 111–12; B. A. Holderness, 'Widows in Pre-Industrial Society: An Essay upon Their Economic Functions', in R. M. Smith (ed.), *Land, Kinship and Life-Cycle* (Cambridge: Cambridge University Press, 1984), 423–42; Robert Tittler, 'Money-Lending in the West Midlands: The Activities of Joyce Jeffries, 1638–49', *Historical Research* 67 (1994), 249–63 (and see *Townspeople and Nation*, 177–97); and Barbara Todd, 'Freebench and Free Enterprise: Widows and Their Property in Two Berkshire Villages', in John Chartres and David Hey (eds.), *English Rural Society: Essays in Honour of Joan Thirsk* (Cambridge: Cambridge University Press, 1990), 175–200.

[65] Harrison quoted by Janet Arnold, *Queen Elizabeth's Wardrobe*, 219. Francis Barnham encountered many male silkweavers and silkworkers in Bridewell; see e.g. BCB-01, fos. 92^r, 221^r; BCB-02, fos. 40^v, 42^v, 59^v, 72^v–73^v, 178^r, 208^v.

of trade regulations and manufacturing standardizations that were a principal concern of livery companies monitoring other, more easily quantified kinds of production. Natalie Zemon Davis argues that women were trained to self-identify primarily as wives, not as workers, and that their career interests had to be adaptable for changing marital circumstances. Grethe Jacobsen points out that any regular incorporation would have 'attracted men who would surely dominate it', and, indeed, in early modern Paris most all-female companies were headed by male governors.[66] Perhaps as important were practical concerns about expense and effort: a wife's guild membership would have required disbursements for admissions and quarterage fees over and above those already paid by her husband to his company, and a separate administration would have involved its own extensive bureaucracy. Like Francis, Alice already had a dual career. His was in business and civic governance, hers in business and household governance.

Because they had not incorporated themselves, however, women lost control of their craft amid the larger economic, demographic, and industrial currents of the later sixteenth and early seventeenth centuries. First, the luxury market boomed in an expanding economy, making the narrow ware too profitable a site not to attract merchants and craftsmen. Between 1559 and 1622, silks jumped from 4.4 per cent of all English imports to 12.6 per cent. There was also a move under James VI and I to develop a domestic industry, and, as a new science, silk growing appealed to gentlemen inventors and cultivators. Second, the focus of the industry shifted in mid-sixteenth century from narrow ware to fabric woven on a broad loom. Third, the methods for large-scale manufacturing that are associated with proto-capitalism jeopardized the smaller, more highly individualized modes of production most silkwomen practiced. And fourth, as London grew in population, so did its workforce; in a more competitive climate, female and foreign workers were targets for the protectionist policies of civic and company leaders, all men.[67] In 1555, silkworking came under the control of the Weavers' Company, which ruled that 'no manner of person or persons of the said craft of silk weavers shall take any women to his apprentice'. The penalty was prohibitive: a monthly fine of 3s. 4d. By 1577, the forfeit had doubled to 6s. 8d. for those who 'keep,

[66] Kowaleski and Bennett, 'Crafts', 480–1; Barron, 'The "Golden Age" of Women', 47; Dale, 'London Silkwomen', 335. Davis and Jacobsen cited by Kowaleski and Bennett, ibid. 484–5, 482; see also Lacey, 'Production', 187.

[67] Linda Levy Peck, 'Creating a Silk Industry in Seventeenth-Century England', *Shakespeare Studies* 28 (2000), 225–8. On silkweaving, Lacey, 'Production', 187. In 1607, Nicholas Geffe published a translation of Oliver de Serres, *The Perfect Use of Silk Worms and their Benefit, With the Exact Planting and Artificial Handling of Mulberry Trees Whereby to Nourish Them, and the Figures to Know How to Feed the Worms, and to Wind Off the Silk.* On the economic pressures of the sixteenth century, see especially Rappaport, *Worlds,* 88–90, 98–9.

teach, instruct, or bring up in the use, exercising, or knowledge of the same art or mystery of weaving any maiden, damsel, or other woman whatsoever'. After the fall of Antwerp in 1585, labor tensions were exacerbated by an influx of refugees representing a full third of the Dutch city's silk merchants and craftsworkers. The slow process by which women were excluded from a profession they had once monopolized marked further unhappy milestones in 1630 and 1631, when the male companies of Silkthrowers and Silkmen were constituted.[68]

The silkwork of women was appropriated in the interests of patriarchy as well as commerce. In 1595, Yeomen members of the Weavers' Company complained that women from immigrant French families sold silkwares door to door. This gave them an advantage over native Londoners who honored established customs by trading in common markets and who professed the belief that a wife's work was properly home-based. An even greater threat was known to be posed by that other form of female itinerancy, marriage. As the Yeomen Weavers wrote, strangers 'set women and maids at work, who, when they are become perfect in the occupation, do marry with men of contrary trade, and so bring that which should be our livings to be the maintenance of those that never deserved for it, and these likewise increase an infinite number'.[69] It was the ever-present awareness that women moved when they wed, threatening to take goods and children and specialized knowledge with them, that animated the gendering of so much property law in the period, made legal 'orphans' of children who lost only their fathers, and, in the case of the London silk trade, displaced women from the practice of their own craft.

Alice occupied the years of transition. She may have joined her sisters in an act of resistance as they shunned the common beam; the city scales represented an arm of the government which was becoming increasingly inimical to them. She would certainly have appreciated the marked delicacy of tone with which the Aldermen inquired why Rose Trott and others were 'not contented to weigh their silk' at the common beam. That same year, in 1560, the governors of Bridewell were presented with the case of Jane Weston, who had stolen 'from diverse silkwomen in London'. When her victims assembled in court—'the parties from whom she did steal the silk were also here present'—the Governors deferred their ruling 'till some of the

---

[68] Frances Consitt, *The London Weavers' Company*, i. *From the 12th Century to the Close of the 16th Century* (Oxford: Clarendon, 1933), 230, 292 (excerpting Ordinances of the Company); Kowaleski and Bennett, 'Crafts', 486; on Antwerp, Harris, *Sick Economies*, 66–7.

[69] Consitt, *London Weavers' Company*, 313. For the similarly protectionist policies of the Carpenters, Clothworkers, and Bakers, see Rappaport, *Worlds*, 38–9; he also discusses the Weavers, 37, 39, 57. Ward, *Metropolitan Communities*, 128, 133.

Aldermen come hither that their advice herein may be had'.[70] Among the complaining witnesses were undoubtedly aldermen's wives; others would have benefited simply from the aldermanic principle of treating earning power with respect.

But the traditional deference accorded the silkwomen was on the wane. Alice may also have known of another pivotal moment in the work history of women that came a decade later, in March 1570. A man named Calverley brought a young woman to the parlor at Drapers' Hall, observing the protocols of presentment. He was probably the Bryan Calverley who had achieved his freedom as a Draper in 1539, who was in due course elevated to the livery, who was elected Third Warden in 1566 (the year Francis Barnham was made First Warden), and who sold silk fringe to the Company in 1564–5. Calverley's request was a local sensation. Later that day, at a view dinner, the Drapers' officers were still talking about it, and some asked the year's First Warden 'whether a maiden servant willing to be bound apprentice to a master and mistress for term of years might not be presented in our Hall and also enrolled in the Chamber of London as other apprentices are and thereby to enjoy also the freedom of the city?' William Dummer, himself married to the silkwoman who sold the Drapers' Company twelve ornamental counterpanes (six with white bone lace and white buttons, six with gold lace and gold buttons), answered that indeed such a thing was possible. There were precedents going back more than a hundred years. But this was nothing more than an academic discussion. The Assistants had already refused Calverley's request to bind a female trainee 'for that they had not seen the like heretofore'.[71] The alternate history Calverley had been able to imagine for his silk trade was not to be.

The occlusion of Alice Barnham's entrepreneurship is part of this larger process of female disempowerment in the Tudor years. Had women throwsters, weavers, and fine needleworkers organized, they might have had a longer history and they would certainly have had a less hidden one. Because they did not form a guild, they did not leave behind institutional archives—another jeopardy of traffic in public records, with all their gender biases. Thus, a career that was not at all secret in its own time is barely recoverable in ours. There are important social and political processes at work in this story, but the story is not about personal privacy.

Alice Barnham's professional profile must be reassembled in patchwork. The evidentiary pieces include her silk sales to the Drapers' Company, her

[70] BCB-01, fo. 94^v. See also BCB-02, fos. 59^v–60^r: a servant who stole some of his master's goods with the intent of selling them was told to say he offered them 'in his mistress's name'; the goods were 'pointing ribbon, lace, and other things' associated with silkwomen.

[71] Drapers' M.B.8, fo. 97^r, also noted by Rappaport (*Worlds*, 36) and Girtin (*Triple Crowns*, 165–6). Drapers' W.A.5 1570–1, fo. 7^v (Dummer's wife; see also Ch. 3).

textual affinity with Rose Trott, her supervision of apprentices, her property transactions, the marriage of her son to the Queen's silkman, her contribution to the family's traffic in money—and also, as finally becomes clear, her portrait. Knowing what we now do about her working life, we should realize that we have had samples of her wares before us all along, unrecognized, in the painting with which we began. The material meanings of 'Alice Barnham and her Two Boys' include the blackwork edging her shirt collar and those of her sons, the ornamental ties of their sleeves, the olive ribbon around Martin's waist, the crimson lining at Stephen's neck, the remarkable table covering on which Alice writes, with its appliquéd ribbons, and the window behind her with a foreign landscape signifying international traffic.[72] As the representation of a sixteenth-century Englishwoman with the products of her industry, the portrait is even more important than we can first have appreciated. Now, we may also detect in it an unintended elegaic aspect. It was painted just two years after the Weavers gained control of the silk trade, and twenty years before William Harrison was to describe silk shops, 'kept by men, as now they are'.

---

[72] Lacey says that silkwomen generally did not practice or purvey embroidery ('Production', 192), which is, indeed, absent from Alice Barnham's portrait. Particularly noticeable is the plainness of Alice's white cap. Lacey notes also that 'Ribbons were the most important of silk women's products, as they could be made into many other items' and were, for example, 'used to decorate curtains' (p. 191). These seem to be the wares and the technique employed for the table covering in the portrait.

8

Closets

SEARCHING FOR the history of privacy in unfamiliar places, I have followed paths first traveled by a woman who, 450 years ago, commissioned a painting of herself and her children. As a 'speaking' portrait, 'Alice Barnham and her Two Boys' engages its viewers directly. The *trompe l'œil* plaques give off just enough information to allow their referents to be identified in the parish registers of St Mildred Poultry, London. Martin's book is represented merely in two short lines of verse—'My son, receive ye these my words, the which shall be right wise'—and yet these are traceable to a known translation of *The Proverbs of Solomon*. Then there is the third act of textual simulation. This chapter revisits the line Alice purports just to have penned: 'That we all may receive the same.'

It also returns to the painting's material meanings. The portrait shows as well as speaks, indicating visually that its subjects are members of a family, communicating their middling status. Alice is sufficiently wealthy to wear fur and velvet, and gold glints on her fingers and at her wrist, but she does not make an aristocratic display of embroidered satins, gemstone pendants, and roped pearls. As for the verbal vocabulary, so, too, for the material: evidence is required from the archives if the painting is to tell us all it can about the table covering and blackwork lace as indicators of Alice's profession. Again, though, there is yet more to attend to: here, the environment in which she has positioned herself.

The lower-left-hand corner of the painting seems to make a claim of actuality. We are encouraged to imagine that the ribbon-striped cloth is from Alice's sales inventory if not her home, that she herself made this early purchase of a Protestant primer, that she owned the gilded-leather writing box with its cunning cubbyholes, and that she unfolded a sheet of paper, opened an inkpot, dipped her quill, and recorded the message addressed to us as well as her sons. By contrast, the upper right-hand corner of the panel is fantastical. It may take its inspiration from Alice's contact with the Continent through her traffic in fancy goods, but the landscape is unparticularized, deriving more from painterly convention than direct observation. The opening to this view is an unframed window set in an unplastered wall of masonry, all the more stark when compared to such over-elaborated contexts as that of Mary Neville, Lady Dacre (see Fig. 1.7), all the more suggestive when compared to such vacant backgrounds as that of Joan Thornbury, Mistress Wakeman (see Fig. 1.11). As if in further testimony to the primacy of goods in the domestic realm of the middling sorts, Alice's objects seem real. The setting does not; she appears to inhabit a symbolic space.

What is it that this distinctive background is meant to convey? Because the bricks are of Flemish manufacture, we may conjecture that Alice had a brief exile in the Low Countries during the Marian years. But this is to identify the sorts of bricks shown, when the larger question is: why bricks at all? Perhaps Alice chose her austere setting as a suitable visual context for those genealogical plaques which laid the trail for her latter-day rediscovery. Or perhaps the bare walls were intended to suggest the underfurnished conditions of a domestic strong room. Were this the case, then Alice elected to position herself as if in a middle-class closet. The painting encourages us to wonder whether the woman not previously known to have had a name of her own—'Lady [given name withheld] Ingram'—thought of this as a room of her own.

Closets feature in any attempt to capture privacy, to give it a local habitation and a name. They are convenient conceptual containers for the subjectivities, genderings, and sexualities in which we persistently interest ourselves. Alan Stewart's argument that the sixteenth-century closet in England was a 'secret nonpublic transactive space between two men behind a locked door' is unusual for not emphasizing, as Mark Girouard does, that it was 'perhaps the only room in which its occupant could be entirely on his own'. But, like Girouard, Stewart otherwise joins the tradition that closets were places of high status and male privilege; the second person he imagines is the secretary whom only the wealthiest of men could have employed.[1] If Alice Barnham and her two boys are indeed sited in a closet, then the painting poses a forceful alternative to conventional associations with the space and especially to its widely presumed capacities for secrecy, isolation, and prerogative. She is a woman of the middling sort who portrays herself as educating her sons there.

A continuing argument of this book is that privacy was not always the object of desire we have assumed it must have been. What is true for privacy may also be true for its correlative, solitude. Derek Hirst has challenged the idea that Puritanism appealed to its believers primarily as a practice of the individual conscience; instead, he emphasizes the powerful attraction of godly fellowship,

---

[1] Alan Stewart, 'The Early Modern Closet Discovered', *Representations* 50 (1995), 83. Girouard, *Life*, 56. Some of the material in this chapter is derived from my 'Gertrude's Closet', *Shakespeare Jahrbuch* 134 (1998), 44–67.

especially in towns.[2] Although no Protestant of the 1550s could properly be called a Puritan, Alice Barnham was an ardent convert to the reformed religion which, in its time of persecution, necessarily created resistant communities. To the list of reasons the Barnham family moved from St Mildred Poultry to St Clement Eastcheap in 1559—proximity to Lombard Street and the Royal Exchange, the presence of draper neighbors, and the availability of a status residence with a gate, a garden, and a gallery—should be added the possibility that they found a sympathetic incumbent and congregation there, a parish population of like-minded believers. After all, the church's officers were later to give a foundling the pious name of Charity of God. For the last fifteen years of her life, Alice directly administered a dole of bread to those she found to be both deserving and full of 'godly conversation'.

She located her identity in other groups, as well. We can place her in the social worlds of her Sussex hometown (she commissioned a monument in Chichester Cathedral and was a philanthropist to the poor there), of mercantile London (she fostered the orphaned daughters of two clothworkers), of civic leadership (she joined in election, feast, quarter, search, view, and funeral dinners, both as a wife and then as a widow, and herself hosted shrieval, livery company, and other municipal events), of country gentility (she entertained Eleanor Wotton in London and in Kent participated in the masque celebrating her son's wedding). With the Wottons and the Rudstons, in particular, a kinship by marriage was reinforced by other ties such as those to the Drapers' Company, active Protestantism, and upward mobility. With the Smiths, birth family of Benedict's wife, she shared a career in the silk trade. With the Utleys and the Bennetts, draper families headed by men who left her their deathbed 'remembrances' of gold rings, she enjoyed a long intimacy.[3] One of the last and most unexpected of her archival appearances, in the diary of Richard Madox, is social, too. The Oxford-trained Madox was chaplain on an ill-fated expedition to China. As its crew prepared for departure in 1582, he met some of the London merchants and Muscovy Company members who backed the voyage. On 2 April Madox recorded:

Monday. The wind being slack, we weighed anchor and went to service, and or ever the first lesson the west wind was so large that at a quarter flood we went ahead with the

---

[2] Derek Hirst, *Authority and Conflict: England, 1603–1658* (Cambridge, Mass.: Harvard University Press, 1986), 75.

[3] In his will of 9 July 1579, George Utley, a draper of the parish of St Benet Gracechurch, bestowed upon 'Mistress Alice Barnham, widow, forty shillings to make her a ring' (PROB 11/61, fos. 236^r–237^r). On 2 January 1595, William Bennett, a draper of the parish of St Clement Eastcheap, left 'to Mistress Alice Barnham, widow, five angels of gold for to make her a ring for a remembrance' and also the same to Benedict (PROB 11/85, fos. 9^v–10^v). Benedict sold property to Bennett in 1581; see *CPR: Elizabeth I*, vii. *1575–1578*, no. 2808.

main topsail, and so lousing [getting under way] we towed down past [Blackwall] Reach and came to Woolwich, where we anchored about noon, three hours after we launched from Blackwall. I walked ashore into the woods and supped at Master Gilburn's with the Captain, with *Master Barnham and his mother*, Master Megs and his wife, Master Marsten the Chancellor of [blank], and had very good cheer.   [emphasis added]

The young Merchant Adventurer who, in advance of his wedding, partnered with his mother socially in Woolwich as well as commercially in the City was undoubtedly Benedict. William Gilborne, one of the men implicated in the usury investigation known as *Queen* v. *Barnham* and one who had practiced the 'double stoccado' with the assistance of Barnham brother-in-law John Chapman, wrote his will just a few months after this day of 'very good cheer', leaving 'my aunt Mistress Barnham a ring of gold of three pounds'. The Meggs and the Marstons were in the Barnham kinship network, too.[4]

The importance of fellowship to Alice Barnham's life is also present in her portrait. She displays rings that had probably been willed her as 'remembrances', and she poses not alone but with her older sons. She responds to the text set for Martin's reflection—'My son receive ye these my words, the which shall be right wise'—with her own act of volition: 'That we *all* may receive the same.' This is a statement of human community rather than spiritual withdrawal. It may seem at first blush that the textual and material messages of the painting are in conflict, the act of writing speaking to an inclusive hope and the choice of backdrop showing an exclusive room. But this is a contradiction only if Alice shared our notion of the closet. To test the prevailing associations of space and solitude is to revisit the Great Rebuilding a last time, in one of its most frequent manifestations, and to argue that the Tudor closet had its genesis in the accumulation of valuable goods rather than an aspiration for personal privacy.

WHAT RICHARD BELLASIS HID

Under the general editorship of Philippe Ariès and Georges Duby, the multipart *History of Private Life* laudably pursues the material dimensions of its subject. Orest Ranum's contribution to the volume on the Renaissance declares a central 'hypothesis' that, through 'emotions, actions, prayers, and dreams',

---

[4] *An Elizabethan in 1582: The Diary of Richard Madox, Fellow of All Souls*, ed. Elizabeth Story Donno, Hakluyt Society, 2nd ser., 147 (London: Hakluyt Society, 1976), 101. Will of William Gilborne (1 September 1582), PROB 11/64, fos. 265^r–266^v. Benedict was not to marry Dorothy Smith until 28 April 1583 (GL Ms 4429/1).

the persons of the past 'identified most intimately with certain particular places'. The 'souvenir-space', he says, might be a walled garden, a bedroom, or a study. Most historians of the subject quickly train their focus on the last, because of its new popularity in Renaissance homes, its presumed connection with textual residues, and its formulation in a classic excerpt from Leon Battista Alberti's *Della Famiglia*:

I kept only the ledgers and business papers, my ancestors' as well as mine, locked so that my wife could not read them or even see them then or at any time since. I never kept them in my [sleeve], but always under lock and key in their proper place in my study, almost as if they were sacred or religious objects. I never allowed my wife to enter my study either alone or in my company, and I ordered her to turn over to me at once any papers of mine she should ever find.

For Ranum, this is a meticulous record of social behavior in the quattrocentro and after: 'It tells us much about the division of space within the house, the classification of objects, and the role assigned to the wife.'[5]

As should be apparent by now, however, any formula for domestic divisions, classifications, and assignments must be presumed to represent a degree—if not more—of wishful thinking. And, in fact, the passage at issue is thoroughly self-deconstructing. There is no pretense that its voice is that of Alberti himself, speaking autobiographically; instead, he creates a character named Giannozzo, who is set in dialogue of a highly artificial sort with one Lionardo. Immediately after describing his household management, moreover, Giannozzo implicitly acknowledges how idealized the scenario is: 'To prevent her from ever wanting to see my papers or know about confidential matters, I often spoke against those bold, impudent women who try so hard to find out their husbands' or other men's affairs outside the home.' Although he portrays his wife as an exception, Giannozzo is aware of a world of wives who intermeddle, who resist confinement to what he believes to be their proper sphere, and who fail to fulfill Lionardo's observation that the female is 'almost universally timid by nature, soft, and slow'. Interposing that Giannozzo's wife is 'perhaps more virtuous than others', Lionardo re-emphasizes that outside the charmed

---

[5] Orest Ranum, 'The Refuges of Intimacy', in Roger Chartier (ed.), *A History of Private Life*, iii. *Passions of the Renaissance*, trans. Arthur Goldhammer (Cambridge, Mass.: Belknap Press of Harvard University Press, 1989), 207–63; see esp. 207, 218. Leon Battista Alberti, *The Albertis of Florence: Leon Battista Alberti's 'Della Famiglia'*, ed. and trans. Guido A. Guarino (Lewisburg: Bucknell University Press, 1971), 217, 216, 215. Guarino has 'I never kept them in my pockets', but notes that 'The original has "sleeve"', 338 n. 61. For Stewart, who importantly reminds us that 'Alberti is giving us a *topos*, taken from Xenophon, and not an unmediated account of household practice in quattracento Italy', the power of the formulation is nonetheless irresistible: 'a topos only functions insofar as it expresses something recognizable about the society to which it is applied' ('Early Modern Closet', 79). There is also slippage in *Della Famiglia*'s Giannozzo, remotely based on a kinsman of Alberti's but clearly a dramatic character.

confines of Giannozzo's house there are any number of women of less 'virtue'.

Giannozzo modestly admits that his wife's excellence is in part a product of her childhood upbringing. But there is also the matter of his own admirable tutelage, as he explains in the passage that leads directly into his discussion of the study:

When after a few days my wife began to feel at ease in my house and did not miss her mother and family so much, I took her by the hand and showed her the whole house. I showed her that upstairs was the place for storing grain and down in the cellar that for wine and firewood. I showed her where the tableware was and everything else in the house, so that she saw where everything was kept and knew its use. Then we returned to my room, and there, after closing the door, I showed her our valuables, silver, tapestries, clothes, and jewels, and pointed out their proper storage places. . . . I always thought it less dangerous to keep my valuables as secret as possible, locked away from people's hands and eyes. I always kept them in my room, where they would be safe from fire and any other danger. There I could often look at them for my pleasure or check them, locking myself in alone or with anyone I pleased, without giving those who remained outside any reason to try and find out anything about my affairs that I did not want them to know. It seems to me that no place is better suited for this than my own bedroom. There, as I told you, I kept none of my valuables hidden from my wife. I showed her all the treasures of my household. I kept only the ledgers and business papers . . . under lock and key in their proper place in my study.[6]

In a powerful undertow of association, and even as he goes immediately on to describe the Italian *studiolo* in one of its most elite forms, as a repository for property documents or 'evidences', Giannozzo by means of this narrative context betrays that the space participates in a family's strategies for organizing and protecting prized possessions. Safe storage was the dominant purpose of the room that in early modern England was known interchangeably as a closet or study. Its nature was betrayed by the first of its names: it was a room that was closed (and secured), even during daylight hours. 'To a closet', wrote Angel Day, in yet another influential formulation, 'there belongeth properly a door, a lock, and a key.'[7]

The medieval practice had been to stow valuables in chests, but Renaissance houses were increasingly furnished with variations on the form, including court cupboards, livery cupboards, dole cupboards, clothes presses, book desks, grain arks, and, in its most capacious variant, the closet. Under the impact of early modern accumulations of goods, chests grew either in number or in size. On her deathbed in 1596, a Kentish woman named Christian Sloden

---

[6] Alberti, *Della Famiglia*, 215–17.
[7] Angel Day, 'Of the Parts, Place, and Office of a Secretary', in *The English Secretary or Method of Writing of Epistles and Letters* (London: 1586), part 2, p. 103.

bequeathed a chest which, she admitted, 'is so great that it cannot be removed except the house be broken or the chest took in pieces'. For most, a more practical solution, and one that made access to household goods easier, was the closet. John Donne, describing his book-filled study as 'this standing wooden chest', testified to its not-so-distant derivation.[8]

In his *Dictionary* of 1611, Randle Cotgrave indicated that in England it was the cabinet, closet, 'little chamber', or wardrobe (not, as Alberti would have it for Italy, the householder's bedroom) 'wherein one keeps his best, or most esteemed, substance'. Contents varied with social and financial standing. For the tanner John Mathewe, for example, the assets itemized in his closet were 'two stone of wool and one chest'. By contrast, the closet of John Edolf, a gentleman, had 'two great saltcellars of silver and gilt with covers, two trencher saltcellars of silver and gilt with one cover, one nest of bowls of silver all gilt with one cover, two cups of silver parcel gilt with one cover, two great stone jugs covered and footed with silver and gilt, and four stone jugs covered with silver, half a dozen of spoons all gilt, one dozen of apostle spoons with the heads gilt, and eleven spoons of silver', along with two chests full of fabric. The closets inventoried at the death of Henry VIII were crammed with paintings, sculptures, gold flagons, spoons, cups, salts, chalices, clocks, scales, books, coins, exotic objects such as unicorn horn, purses, gloves, rings, combcases, caps, spurs, dog collars, and coffers and writing boxes covered with leather and velvet.[9]

Most often, closets contained bed linens, tableware, and what in inventory after inventory is called 'household stuff', 'implements of household', 'necessary particulars of household', or items 'for the use of the house'. Thus, in his 'little closet', John Russell of Canterbury kept his pewter platters, candlesticks, saucers, spoons, a salt, a basin, and a ewer, as well as 'certain old books'. As documented, closets belonged to women as often as men, though these, too, were rarely filled with personal goods. They might, as in the case of a Mistress Stanley, have nineteen dishes, a basin, a plate, nine 'salad or fruit dishes', and stores of flax, hemp, soap, and hops. Other women stocked saucers, potingers,

---

[8] CCAL X.11.5, fo. 66[r]. John Donne, *The Complete Poetry of John Donne*, ed. John T. Shawcross (New York: New York University Press, 1968), Satire 1. Peter Thornton points out that 'it had been a common medieval practice to store one's books in a chest and this continued well into the seventeenth century', in *Seventeenth-Century Interior Decoration in England, France, and Holland* (New Haven: Yale University Press for the Paul Mellon Centre for Studies in British Art, 1978), 306.

[9] Randle Cotgrave, *A Dictionarie of the French and English Tongues* (London: 1611), sig. N3[r]. Inventory of John Mathewe (1608), *Probate Inventories of Lichfield and District, 1568–1680*, ed. D. G. Vaisey, Staffordshire Record Society, 4th ser., 5 (1969), no. 6. Inventory of John Edolf (1576), Folger Ms X.d.64. *The Inventory of King Henry VIII: Society of Antiquaries MS 129 and British Library MS Harley 1419*, ed. David Starkey et al. (London: Harvey Miller for the Society of Antiquaries of London, 1998).

platters, candles, candlesticks, ewers, looking glasses, conserves, and preserves. Alice Towney kept three closets, one with two baskets and 'other household stuff'; a second with 'glasses and other like necessaries'; and a third with a table, seven shelves, two baskets, and 'other household stuff'.[10]

Fitted with table and shelves, Towney's third closet sounds like a working space rather than a storage area. It would be tempting to call it a 'study' rather than a closet, but in fact the terms were employed without apparent distinction. With an iron desk, a cupboard, a latten lamp, an iron candlestick, two writing stands, a clock, a 'pair' of compasses, balances, gold weights, and 'diverse books, small and some great', Thomas Cawarden's room fits our notion of a study or even a countinghouse, but his appraisers name it a 'closet'. Yeoman John Wright secured his pewter in his 'study'. William Glaseor's study had an evidence chest and a library's worth of books, but there were also books in his closet. We might think that gentlemen would be those most likely to have had rooms set aside for their books and papers, but many, like John Lisle, kept household closets in which they stored plate, glasses, 'and some other implements'. Because Jude Allin was a clerk, his study had books, a globe, a table, shelves, two joined stools, a chair, a desk, a candlestick, and some 'alchemical' spoons, but it also housed a salt and various pots and glasses. Especially surprising are the circumstances of a parson, Robert Hyndmer. A man who might have been expected to have had a small library, instead he kept the following objects in his 'study':

Sixteen cushions, a carpet of tapestry lined for a table, nine pillows of down, seven pairs and one odd blanket, two basins and two ewers, a press of wainscot, two dozen tin trenchers, nineteen ells of canvas, two fruit dishes, two basins, two chargers, one garnish of vessel lacking a saucer, six doublers and four dishes, six dozen trenchers, one little cupboard with a carpet, a garnish of vessel, two cupboards with two Kentish carpets, two lanterns, one study candlestick, a touchstone with case, a tin bottle, a cypress chess, fifteen yards of linen cloth, fifty-one yards of harden cloth, three chests bound with iron, one of fir, two featherbed ticks, two surplices, one dozen damask napkins, one dozen diaper napkins, seven plain napkins, three diaper tablecloths, three diaper tablecloths for the hall, nine plain tablecloths for the hall, three plain tablecloths for the parlor, three diaper towels, three long plain tablecloths for the hall, one fine napkin of damask work, five plain towels, four cupboard cloths.[11]

[10] Inventory of John Russell (1608), CKS DCb-PRC/27/1/72. Inventory of Henry Stanley, esq. (1598), *Lancashire and Cheshire Wills and Inventories from the Ecclesiastical Court, Chester, Part 2*, ed. G. J. Piccope, Chetham Society 51 (1860), 97. Inventory of Alice Towney (1598), CKS PRC 27/1/5.

[11] Inventory of Thomas Cawarden, knight (1559), Folger Ms L.b.328. Will of John Wright (1622), *Wills of the Archdeaconry of Suffolk, 1620–1624*, ed. Marion E. Allen, Suffolk Records Society 31 (1989), no. 676. Inventory of William Glaseor (1588), *Lancashire and Cheshire Wills and Inventories from the Ecclesiastical Court, Chester, Part 3*, ed. G. J. Piccope, Chetham Society

Early moderns inevitably worried about the prehension, stewardship, and redistribution of their moveables. Closets were less about keeping people preclusively *out* than about keeping goods safely *in*. The anxieties of ownership are the subtext for most wills, written and nuncupative; for probate inventories, legally mandated from 1529 on; for other, occasional catalogues of personal and household belongings; for dowry and dower negotiations; for laws of inheritance and sibling rivalries; for the corporal punishment of theft and housebreaking; and also for the construction of closets. An unusual testament to the disquiet associated with possession is the late sixteenth-century will of Richard Bellasis, a north country gentleman who died unmarried and childless.[12] He owned a modest collection of plate—a dish, nine drinking bowls, forty-two spoons, and various cups and salts—but he elected not to convert more of his discretionary wealth into pewter and silver. Instead, he kept a large supply of coin.

For his will of 6 February 1597, which distributed his goods and furnishings among a brother, a sister, five cousins, six nephews, eight nieces, and four servants, there were seven witnesses. Soon after completing it, however, he secretly added a codicil itemizing his hoards of cash. He described £500 'lapped up in one several thin piece of lead', £100 'within a little wooden box', and £200 'likewise lapped within a little thin piece of lead'. All three parcels were 'together walled upon the left hand and west side of the little dark stair that goeth down out of my bed chamber at Morton into my study there, about three quarters of a yard above the upper step or stair'. In addition, there was £200 'under the boards, betwixt two joists, and the ceiling of the chamber or room under that place . . . next to the wool house there, under the edge of the boards of the highest step towards the north window, but is hard under the first stepping up towards that window'. Another £200 was 'put edgeways into a wooden box' and 'walled up in a hollow place within the wall of the new great chamber at Morton called 'Sir William's chamber', about one yard above the floor on the south gavel end, betwixt the south window and the west side or corner'. Meanwhile, 'in the bottom of an old little barrel in the storehouse, where wine and much beer standeth' was another £100. The 'table chair' in his

54 (1861), 128–42. Inventory of John Lisle (1623), *Darlington Wills and Inventories, 1600–1625,* ed. J. A. Atkinson et al., Publications of the Surtees Society 201 (1993), no. 55. Inventory of Jude Allin (1631), *The Ipswich Probate Inventories, 1583–1631,* ed. Michael Reed, Suffolk Records Society 22 (1981), no. 72 (the study is the only room listed). Inventory of Robert Hyndmer (1558), *Wills and Inventories Illustrative of the History, Manners, Language, Statistics, &c. of the Northern Counties of England, Part I,* ed. James Raine, Publications of the Surtees Society 2 (1835), no. 122 (I have omitted appraised values for these items).

12 Will of Richard Bellasis (1597), *Wills and Inventories from the Registry at Durham, Part II,* no. 150. I have discussed this will in more detail in 'The Secret History of Richard Bellasis', in a Forum edited by Peter Stallybrass for *Shakespeare Studies* 28 (2000), 220–4.

bedchamber—that is, a chair with a hinged back that folded down to form a table top—'which standeth before the bedside and hath ever some books and papers and hour-glasses standing on it', held £100 more. In his study was a 'wooden box on the ground under the presser', with £100; 'a bag that lieth upon the middle floor of the same presser, in the west end, behind two books', with £60; and 'a little purse of silk ribbon within a little leather bag which is put within a white leather shoe and lieth in the west end of the highest floor of the presser', 'where the glasses stand', 'behind two books', with £64. Finally, Bellasis stored £100 in an iron chest in a second house at Jarrow. The last was the only cache not known exclusively to his servant Margaret Lambert, who either 'helped' him to secrete his stores or who 'was one time told of this money'.

In a second codicil, Bellasis recorded that he 'removed and otherwise disbursed' coins from the more easily accessed hoards. Later still, there was a third codicil documenting further deposits of funds in the barrel, in a desk, on his press, in a chest, and in Jarrow. In a fourth codicil Bellasis recorded that he had expended these funds, too. The moneys in Jarrow were eventually augmented by £129. 13s. 4d. from a debt repaid and, in February 1599, Bellasis restocked his study press with £400 divided among 'eight several leather bags'. At his death, the amounts of hidden cash totaled nearly £1,200. The trepidation that courses through the will of Richard Bellasis is more about security than secrecy—that is, secrecy is the method he employs in the overriding interest of protecting his assets.

Unmarried and childless, Bellasis shared his proprietary strategies with his testament and with a servant who was among his most richly rewarded legatees. It was otherwise not an unfamiliar problem, for anyone with surplus wealth faced the challenge of safeguarding it. Sir John Oglander, for another example, kept £220 readily available in a box in his study but also hid £2,400 by contriving a hole in the wall behind the head of his bed. Yeoman Hugh Wyatte placed £100 'in my quiver within my coffer at Wilnecote, which is locked with two locks and my quiver is locked, and roundabout the case and the hasp is tied a lute string and sealed on the knot on the keyhole'. (He adds the superfluous note that 'under the lute string shall you find this my will'.) Such private depositories had to be obscurely located but at the same time more readily accessible than the cache of Edward Underhill. His collection of reformist books predated the reign of Mary I; in 1554 he bricked them up in the chimney in his bedchamber, not to be broken out until Elizabeth came to the throne in 1558.[13]

---

[13] For Oglander, see Stone, *Crisis*, 509. Will of Hugh Wyatte (1556), *Essex Wills (England)*, i. *1558–1565*, ed. F. G. Emmison (Washington, DC: National Genealogical Society, 1982),

For most, however, solitude, secrecy, and closet doors were not the first solution. As Francis Barnham demonstrated with the loan evidences he kept in a capcase, coalition was. Many testators created an ad hoc partnership of guardians for their goods. The knight Original Babington dictated that 'all my evidence be locked in chests, and every chest to have two locks and several keys, that they cannot be opened without both the keys'. Yeoman James Richardeson required his chest full of 'household stuff' and evidences to have three locks and three keys; in a not-uncommon request, 'one shall always remain in the hands of my wife and two in those of my supervisors'. Alan Bellingham followed this familiar principal for his overgrown chest, his study, specifying that his property documents were 'to be safely kept under two locks and keys' there. His cousin was to have one key and his brother the second, so that one could not enter without the other.[14] These closet practices found the security afforded by numbers a more urgent priority than the self-expression possible in solitude.

LONDON'S CLOSETS

Ralph Treswell's surveys of tenanted properties owned by Christ's Hospital and the Clothworkers' Company are endlessly informing about the material conditions of London life. Most of his reports include drawings of ground-level plans (which he thinks of as 'first' floors), accompanied by verbal descriptions of the corresponding stories above. For upper levels he lists the rooms, gives their measurements, and mentions important amenities such as chimneys and privies (which he calls 'houses of office'). The surveys are full of evidence about the spaces most commonly associated with privacy. In reports on something like 225 tenancies (not all of them complete), Treswell catalogues twenty-six closets, twenty-three studies, two rooms which he says might be either a 'closet or study', and seven countinghouses (all named without any definition of

no. 377. For Underhill, see Philippa Tudor, 'Protestant Books in London in Mary Tudor's Reign', *London Journal* 15 (1990), 21.

[14] Will of Original Babington (1577), *North Country Wills . . . 1558 to 1604*, ii, ed. J. W. Clay, Publications of the Surtees Society 121 (1912), no. 65. Will of James Richardeson (1591), *Essex Wills: The Archdeaconry Courts, 1591–1597*, ed. F. G. Emmison (Chelmsford, Essex: Essex Record Office, 1991), no. 954; see also Will of Christopher Freebarne (1563), *Essex Wills (England)*, i. no. 498; and Will of Richard Boune (1572), *Essex Wills (England)*, iii. *1571–1577*, ed. F. G. Emmison (Boston: New England Historic Genealogical Society, 1986), no. 117. Will of Alan Bellingham (1579), *Wills and Inventories from the . . . Archdeaconry of Richmond*, ed. James Raine, Publications of the Surtees Society 26 (1853), no. 205.

terms).[15] These related spaces show the variety of sizes, shapes, and locations of which early modern closets were capable.

The measurements are occasionally obscure. Too often, Treswell lists 'a garret . . . with a study in it' (no. 13) or 'one other chamber . . . with a little closet in it' (no. 21), giving dimensions for the whole rather than each part. Where he is more explicit, however, he provides evidence that closed spaces were not always small rooms. Admittedly, there are three instances of closets or studies that were just 7 or 7½ ft long by 3½ ft deep (nos. 25, 35, and 43). One 'little study . . . being in the staircase'—presumably under it—cannot have been more than 3 ft wide and must have had limited head room (no. 31). But there are also others that were 9 by 7 ft (no. 15) and 13½ by 4 ft (no. 7). Many closets were square spaces, variously 4 by 4 ft (no. 3), 7 by 7 ft (no. 53), 8½ by 8½ ft (no. 38), 9 by 9 ft (no. 11), and 10½ by 10 ft (no. 13). The largest rooms, presumably working spaces, were those on the ground level, such as a study that was 15½ by 10 ft (no. 30). The chamber that was probably Treswell's own home office had 8½ ft of frontage on Aldersgate Street (no. 1; see Fig. 4.2).

Another property occupied by a member of the Treswell family included a large study with an irregular shape. Two sizable corners within it, one labeled a 'buttery', had been partitioned off for doubly secured storage (no. 2). William Campion's house had two adjoining studies, one accessed by means of the other (no. 40). Closets seem sometimes to have been positioned 'within' not only as an added precaution but also because this put them at the outer perimeter of a house, where they enjoyed ever-important natural light. The model 'countryman's' home drawn by Gervase Markham had 'an inward closet within the parlor' that was the same size as a guest chamber and possessed windows on three sides.[16]

Despite Markham's formulation, the closet is generally thought of today as a small contained area located within an upper-level bedchamber.[17] Indeed, Treswell shows that Master Parler had three such closets. At the same time, however, Parler also had two free-standing closets as well as a study off the gallery (no. 31). Master Backhouse's study was within the upper-level bedchamber, but his closet was an autonomous chamber near his first-floor parlor (no. 15; see Fig. 8.1). In other residences, there were a closet within

---

[15] *London Surveys*, ed. Schofield. For the convenience of the reader, I use Schofield's numbers to identify Treswell's plans in the discussion that follows. However, I rely upon my own transcriptions from GL Ms 12805 and the Clothworkers' Hall Evidence Book. With respect to the count of closets, for example, I include one from plan 11 which Schofield has transcribed as 'chimney' and one from plan 53 that Schofield omits.

[16] Gervase Markham, *The English Husbandman Drawn in Two Books* (London: 1635), sigs. D4ᵛ–E1ʳ.

[17] See e.g. Thornton, *Seventeenth-Century Interior Decoration*, 296.

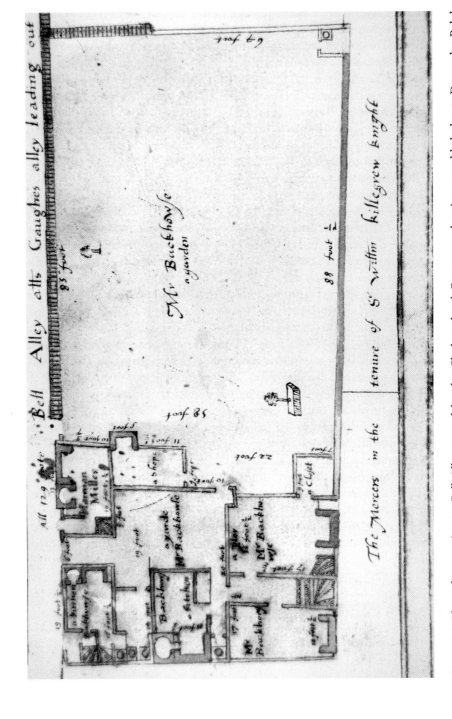

Figure 8.1 Plan of properties on Bell Alley owned by the Clothworkers' Company, showing an added closet. Drawn by Ralph Treswell, 1612.

'a dining chamber' (no. 2), another off a hall (no. 11), 'a hall with a closet or study taken out of it' (no. 34), and a gallery 'with a closet at one end' (no. 53). The property parceled out between Master Baber, Master Jackson, and Master Halles (no. 33; see Fig. 8.2) had two studies and a countinghouse tucked against staircases. (One may have incorporated space under the stairs; another opened directly off them.) Working spaces were especially likely to have immediate access from the street or yard when at ground level, although Treswell also lists an upper-level chamber 'with' countinghouses on the second and third floors of Clothworkers' Hall (no. 29).

Dorothy Parsons's house was six stories tall with just one room at street level; the 'study hanging over into the street' off the second floor was probably a fairly recent extension (no. 6). Jane Bruskett similarly had a house of seven floors, with a 'little closet hanging into the street' added off a third-floor chamber (no. 38). Other cantilevered spaces included Richard Bullman's third-floor closet over Fleet Lane (no. 22), William Jennyngs's second-floor 'little closet on the south side hanging over into the yard' (no. 20), John Domelaw's second-floor 'little closet hanging over into Minchin Lane', and also Domelaw's third-floor 'hanging closet' (no. 29). John Burduge's second-floor study, projecting 'over into the garden', had to be 'supported upon two posts', and on the floor above was a 'study over the study aforesaid of the like bigness' ($10\frac{1}{2}$ by 10 ft, no. 13). 'Some part' of Abraham Frythe's study was found 'lying on the stone wall next the gate' (no. 43; see Fig. 4.4). Renaissance retrofittings presumably included not only closets that were extruded overhead, such as these, but also those bumped out at ground level, such as Thomas Inche's countinghouse (no. 11) or Master Backhouse's closet (no. 15; see Fig. 8.1).

These added spaces constituted some of London's principal contributions to the Great Rebuilding. Closets that were newly appended represented supplemental square footage, but others were created by spatial reallocation. Many in London, as elsewhere in England, resulted from the subdivision of a room. Board or 'paper' walls were probably used to establish the 'closet or study taken out of' a hall (no. 34) and also the 'closet at one end' of a gallery (no. 53). In some cases, a corner or an odd area was closed off, as in a property called the Crowne in Aldgate. This had, in Treswell's words, 'a little void place or passage with a little closet' (no. 3).[18]

Closets and studies were among the most frequent additions to sixteenth-century inventories of rooms, not because household practices had changed so radically but because the household's possessions had increased. Thus, the elite home of Sir Edward Darcy had just one closet on the second story, but Darcy also possessed a 'long cellar' (14 by 70 ft) and two butteries, all spaces

---

[18] The 'little void place' is in text not transcribed by Schofield.

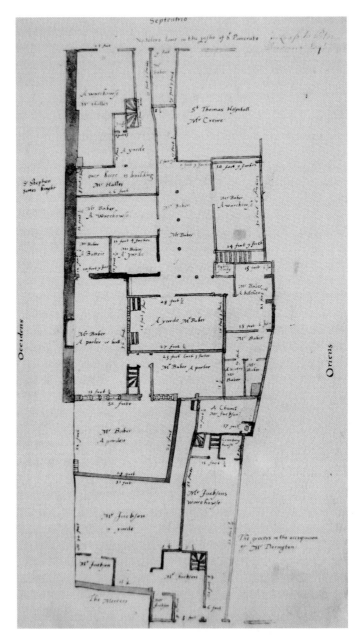

Figure 8.2 Plan of properties on Needlers Lane in St Pancras purchased by Christ's Hospital with the bequest of Peter Blundell. At the top of the plan near the staircase is the study of Master Halles; near one staircase to the right is the study of Master Baber and, near another, the counting house of Master Jackson. The bottom of the plan may show another closet in Master Jackson's tenure. Drawn by Ralph Treswell, 1611.

which provided goods storage (no. 21). With five storehouses and three studies at street level, as well as 'a study or chamber with a chimney' one floor up, clothworker William Campion seems to have kept vast stocks of various sorts (no. 40). Master Parler needed five closets and a study not as multiple *studiolos* but as ample storage space (no. 31).

In the sixteenth-century records of the Carpenters' Company, the most popular building projects involved the excavation and construction of cellars. As storage areas, these, too, were part of the process by which the Renaissance proliferation of goods and supplies was domiciled. Along with closets and studies, cellars and warehouses give further evidence for an argument made earlier: what lay behind many acts of Rebuilding was an aggregation of personal possessions. The need to keep goods securely, as also to display them on occasion, was perceptibly more urgent than a desire for privacy. The architectural anthropologist Amos Rapoport notes a related phenomenon: 'I have personally observed among the Bedouin that the first modern buildings are meant for safe storage of possessions rather than for dwelling.'[19]

CLOSET PRACTICES

Treswell's London surveys record three women with closets, two with studies, and one with both a closet and a study. Alice Barnham and Mary Neville, Lady Dacre, may have posed for their portraits in their closets. Alberti, however, observes a more segregative gendering of space. 'Off the wife's bedroom should be a dressing room,' he declares in *De re aedificatoria*, 'and off the husband's, a library.' He argues the need for separate bedrooms by attaching the cultural capital of classical history to his fantasy of private life. From Aemilius Probo, he says, he has learned that Greek women were 'not to be admitted to table' when guests were present, and that they were expected to dwell in areas of the house that were 'out of bounds to all but closest kin'. To his own mind, he adds, 'any place reserved for women ought to be treated as though dedicated to religion and chastity'. Young girls, especially, should be 'allocated comfortable apartments, to relieve their delicate minds from the tedium of confinement' in the Greek fashion. *Della Famiglia* is an even more conspicuously fictionalized work; there, Giannozzo and Lionardo agree that their property documents and their business activities are matters for men only: 'I never allowed my wife

[19] GL Ms 7784. Amos Rapoport, 'On the Attributes of "Tradition"', in Jean-Paul Bourdier and Nezar AlSayyad (eds.), *Dwellings, Settlements, and Tradition: Cross-Cultural Perspectives* (Lanham, Md.: University Press of America, 1989), 94.

to enter my study either alone or in my company, and I ordered her to turn over to me at once any papers of mine she should ever find.'[20]

In a brilliantly theorized essay, Mark Wigley suggests that Alberti demonstrates 'architecture's complicity in the exercise of patriarchal authority by defining a particular intersection between a spatial order and a system of surveillance which turns on the question of gender'.[21] It is important to remember, however, that agency in the matter is located not in the architecture of quattrocento Italy but instead in Alberti's gynephobic imagination—a distinction too rarely observed. His misogynistic utopianism has captivated many besides Wigley; Alberti was, after all, Burckhardt's Renaissance '*uomo universale*'. The story of Alice Barnham is a case study of a woman who did not heed the 'sacred' boundaries Alberti would have instituted between women and the worlds of commerce, fellowship, evidences, and closets, not because she was particularly remarkable but because real-world borders did not lie where Alberti drew them. Just as we should have anticipated that Francis Barnham was a moneylender, had we understood London's capital economy better, so, too, we would have expected Alice to be a business person in her own right, had we not fallen victim to false histories of 'the woman's place' in the past. The chief virtue of this accidental biography, the rediscovery of an obscure person located in public life through institutional records, is that, while it was surely not universal, it is unlikely to have been exceptional. And, indeed, such other anecdotal evidence as remains to us also suggests that neither the English closet nor early modern gender roles were as thoroughly coercive as was imagined by Alberti.

The investigation of Nicholas Williamson exemplifies this more complicated history. In 1595 Sir Robert Cecil demanded to know what access Williamson's wife had to documents that Williamson described as 'notes, surveys, or particulars touching lands'. Williamson cannot have known Alberti's *Della Famiglia*, which remained unpublished until 1734, but he could parrot patriarchal protocol when required: 'neither ever have I used to leave any writings in her custody, or to suffer her to come into my study among my writings but in my presence'. Just as Giannozzo's theoretically autocratic control was a function of his self-representation in conversation, so, too, Williamson declared of his alleged closet practice that 'this, many can testify that have conversed with me'. His attempt to validate his private affairs in

[20] Leon Battista Alberti, *On the Art of Building in Ten Books*, trans. Joseph Rykwert, Neil Leach, and Robert Tavernor (Cambridge, Mass.: MIT, 1988), 149. It is not often noted that even Alberti temporizes: 'in each case we should abide by whatever may be the ancestral custom', *Della Famiglia*, 217.

[21] Mark Wigley, 'Untitled: The Housing of Gender', in Beatriz Colomina (ed.), *Sexuality and Space*, Princeton Papers on Architecture (New York: Princeton Architectural Press, 1992), 332.

public knowledge was all the more strenuous because his wife had already been observed to 'deliver a good company of her husband's writings about January last past to the keeping of Master Pearsall of Staffordshire, as many as would go into two pillowberes'.[22] Like Alice Barnham, retrieving the ferret silks of the 'double stoccado', Mistress Williamson was undoubtedly her husband's closet partner. The secret of Nicholas Williamson's study was that, despite his open posturing on the subject, it was not an exclusive space.

The letters of Sir Edward Dering show his wife Unton to be the custodian of his closet in his absence. He wrote from London in early 1633, asking her to send him documents regarding some of their property in Kent. 'Upon the nearest corner of my study table next the door' she could expect to find 'a little fir box with a few papers and some evidence in it' as well as 'an old long book in my grandfather's hand of payments ... they do both concern our house in Dover'. (Advising that she should 'look not upon the messenger (for he doth squint fearfully)', Sir Edward reminded Unton to tip the man and send him 'speedily' on his way.) Certainly, the very fact that he is in London and she in Kent reflects upon the gendering of professional and public spheres, nor does Dering expect his wife to know his study well. And it seems likely, reading between the lines of the letter, that he had kept the key with him while travelling and thus was forced to send it back by the messenger carrying the letter. But nonetheless Sir Edward displays no hesitation in asking Unton to locate his papers, and he also suggests she 'keep the key of my study' for future use. A year-and-a-half later she again had need of it, when he wrote for 'a paper book wherein (you know) I write my justice matters' and also 'a Dutch book of arms, bound up like a song book but very thick'. The one was on his table and the other on his 'uppermost' shelf, 'among my printed books, not far from the window'. From this episode we learn that Unton was expected to have at least a working knowledge of the paper book in which her husband collected his legal records.[23]

There is a similar pattern in the letters of Thomas and Katherine Knyvett. In the 1620s Thomas sent home the 'key of my closet', having 'forgot' to leave it behind, and needing Katherine to 'look for two letters which my cousin Abrahall writ'. He again returned the key to her in 1642, when he required her to find a 'black box of writings' labeled 'Staffordshire', 'cord it up very safe',

---

[22] *Calendar of the Manuscripts of the ... Marquis of Salisbury ... Preserved at Hatfield House*, 24 vols. (London: 1883–1976), v. 224–5, 227–30.

[23] 'The Dering Love Letters', ed. Alison Cresswell, pamphlet published by Kent County Council Arts and Libraries (n.d.), 25 (Letter of 10 January 1633, CKS U350 C2/34), 31 (Letter of 2 June 1634, CKS U350 C2/43).

and dispatch it to him. He had been imprisoned as a royalist and, even when released, faced a long series of legal appeals to regain his property; he relied upon Katharine—not a secretary—as his home archivist and accomplice. He seems also to have been persuaded that his house was subject to invasion or search by the parliamentarians: 'My books and evidences are my chiefest care', he wrote, undoubtedly referring to his grandfather's library of Latin, Greek, Arabic, and English books and manuscripts (worth £700 when Thomas inherited them in 1618). 'How you will get them where we would have them I know not', he worried. Finally he concluded that Katherine should fill a 'little red gilded trunk' with his title documents and the two guns that were hidden 'behind the books' and should take the trunk to a friend. Also in his closet was 'an instrument to screw out a bullet out of a man's body'; this, too, she should remove. Having the freedom of the space, Katherine appears to have made use of it. In one letter, Thomas observed: 'You seem to be much frighted with something you found in my closet; if it be suspicion of any debt, let it not trouble thee.' While he was concerned with her reaction, he seems undisturbed that she had been reading his papers and drawing her own conclusions from them.[24]

Margaret Hoby is often cited as our best instance for the closet practices of a Tudor woman. Alan Stewart, for example, emphasizes that in her so-called 'diary', 'the (private) closet is placed in contrast to her (public) bedchamber'. In fact her spatial history seems to have been far more complex and eclectic than this. While it is often the case that she prays 'privately' in her closet, there are also instances in which she prays alone in her bedchamber, reads the Bible there, and makes notes in it. On one occasion, her meditations take place in the garden. In January 1600, she records that she has made herself 'busy' in her closet, a construct which usually refers to housekeeping responsibilities. She then goes to another, unspecified site, for 'private examination and prayer'. Even the keeping of the diary may not have been the sort of closet activity we usually assume, inasmuch as it seems to have been a record she kept and submitted to her chaplain Richard Rhodes, for his review. Stewart rightly emphasizes an entry for February 1600: 'To my closet, where I prayed and writ some thing for mine own private conscience.' The thing she recorded was too private for the journal that has survived. Perhaps it was informed, like its entries, by a spatial practice that was more opportunistic or whimsical than strictly routinized.[25]

[24] *The Knyvett Letters (1620–1644)*, ed. Bertram Schofield (London: Constable, 1949), nos. 5, 24, 48, 49, 52, 58, 60, 61, 77. For his grandfather's collection, see p. 17.

[25] Stewart, 'Early Modern Closet', 81. *The Private Life of an Elizabethan Lady: The Diary of Lady Margaret Hoby, 1599–1605*, ed. Joanna Moody (Phoenix Mill: Sutton, 1998), 9, 27, 50, 138,

Aaron Kunin revolutionizes our understanding of Anne Clifford's diary, too, as a process involving the 'collaboration of servants' rather than a product of solitude. The pages, he says, are not 'in her own hand'. Instead, 'she dictated them to an amanuensis, had them copied by scribes, and then wrote additions in the margin of the fair copy'. Kunin especially appreciates the significance of a journal entry in 1617: 'I went up to see the things in the closet and began to have Master Sandy's book read to me about the government of the Turks, my Lord sitting the most part of the day reading in his closet.' Stewart has emphasized this crucial passage, as well, summarizing that 'she goes to "see the things in the closet" and to be read to, he to read'. Against this, however, Kunin importantly recognizes that 'the segmentation of these spaces is obviously not absolute; since Clifford's diary has some access to what's going on in Sackville's closet'. Further, in a 'theatrical' way, the couple is 'demonstrating to one another an ability to function separately'. Most importantly, Clifford depicts herself not in a passive role, as Stewart implies, but in a powerful one. She is, Kunin says, 'directing not only her own activity as a reader but someone else's as well'.[26]

Clifford also records instances when her husband 'went up to my closet and said how little money I had left', and when she herself went 'down to my Lord's closet where I sat and read much' in books that were stored there, 'the Turkish history and Chaucer'. Neither space, these entries again suggest, was a preclusive one, as both husband and wife were familiar with the material circumstances of each other's private possessions and private practices. Elsewhere, Clifford describes an occasion with two household visitors; Sackville 'showed them the house and the chambers and my closet'.[27] Patricia Fumerton has pictured the elite cabinet as a place of display, but there is an even higher level of exposure here, where Clifford does not herself exhibit the space that was titularly hers. This representation of Clifford's closet largely accords with

---

142 (entries of 23 August 1599, 9 October 1599, 4 January 1600, 26 January 1601, 4 April 1601 on praying, reading, and writing in the bedchamber); 79 (29 April 1600, on meditating in the garden); 55 (25 January 1600, on business in the closet); 59 (4 February 1600, on writing too private for the closet). See also Mary Ellen Lamb, 'Margaret Hoby's Diary: Women's Reading Practices and the Gendering of the Reformation Subject', in Sigrid King (ed.), *Pilgrimage for Love: Essays in Early Modern Literature in Honor of Josephine A. Roberts*, Medieval and Renaissance Texts and Studies 213 (Tempe: Arizona Center for Medieval and Renaissance Studies, 1999), esp. 85.

[26] Aaron Kunin, 'From the Desk of Anne Clifford', *English Literary History* 71 (2004), 603, 590–1.

[27] *The Diaries of Lady Anne Clifford*, ed. D. J. H. Clifford, rev. edn. (Phoenix Mill: Sutton, 1990), 53 (5 April 1617), 54 (26 April 1617), 80 (25 October 1619).

Dora Thornton's argument that even the Italian *studiolo* was 'social' as well as private.[28]

'Inviting friends, fellow collectors and rivals into one's study', says Thornton, 'was a particular form of social communication, one which became increasingly significant in the course of the sixteenth century.' The *studiolo* may have had its nearest equivalent, in England, in the so-called 'painted closet' of Anne Drury, a collection of sixty-one wall panels ornamented with emblems and mottos. Although one sentence reads '*Nunquam minus sola quam cum sola*' — a feminization of the Ciceronian paradox 'Never less alone than when alone', which had become proverbial independently of its *De Officiis* context — the room is far too elaborate not to have been a showpiece space. In fact, it challenges its visitors to decode the riddling relationship of its texts and its images.[29]

Had closets been as preclusive as is generally believed, further, it is surely the case that the term would not have been applied to spaces used not for supplies and not for study, but simply as closed chambers. The single, fully fitted-out bed described in William Thomson's will ('my little feather bed in the closet, a mattress, two coverlets, two blankets, two pair of sheets, a bolster, two pillows, a covering of red say with the bedstead's curtains and hangings') would seem to have been in use rather than in storage. In London, the widow Hodges certainly employed her closet as a spare room; she took in and tended to the sick and dying there. Thomas Hanbury's closet, furnished with 'a little square table and a joined stool, a dozen and a half of round trenchers, two dozen of square trenchers, two voiding knives of wood, and a few cheese trenchers', sounds like the sort of private dining chamber described in Painter's *Palace of Pleasure*, which features a 'table ready furnished with exquisite confits and wines of the best' in a closet. 'My lady's closet' at Herstmonceux was a stillroom, with 'diverse sorts of glasses and some with

[28] Patricia Fumerton, *Cultural Aesthetics: Renaissance Literature and the Practice of Social Ornament* (Chicago: University of Chicago Press, 1991), 67–71. Dora Thornton, *The Scholar in his Study: Ownership and Experience in Renaissance Italy* (New Haven: Yale University Press, 1997), 175. See also William H. Sherman, *John Dee: The Politics of Reading and Writing in the English Renaissance* (Amherst: University of Massachusetts Press, 1995): 'The private (or privy) library was thus less asocial and apolitical than selectively social and political' (p. 50).

[29] Thornton, *Seventeenth-Century Interior Decoration*, 175. On Anne Drury's 'closet', see the forthcoming work of H. L. Meakin, which I am grateful to have read in draft. It is generally believed that the painted panels wainscotted a small room, and it is as a 7-ft-square closet that they are currently displayed at Christchurch Mansion in Ipswich, Suffolk. There is no record of their original configuration at Hawstead Place near Bury St Edmonds (*c*.1600), nor of their arrangement at Hardwick House (to which they were moved between 1610 and 1615).

stilled waters, some earthen and gallipots, some little pewter boxes, one stone mortar, one alabaster mortar, one little brazen pestle and mortar, four brass posnets or skillets, one iron trivet, four little boxes or little chests, one little still or limbeck, three books of accompt and certain shelves, one hair sieve, one little chain'.[30] Repeatedly, the records of actual closet practice return us to issues of shared space.

THE STANDISH IN THE CLOSET

Few early modern closets survive in their earliest states. A rare exception can be found at Boughton Monchelsea Place, near Maidstone in Kent.[31] The property was Rebuilt by Robert Rudston between 1567 and 1576, when he added three wings to convert a smallish timber-framed structure into an important courtyard house with a symmetrical main façade of local ragstone (see Fig. 1.2). The earliest, south range had been the site of the old great hall, but the new east wing, in Arthur Oswald's calculation, contained 'all the principal rooms of a virtually new house'. A fair amount of guesswork is required for Tudor Boughton because, in the mid-1700s, the west and north wings were torn down (eventually to be replaced by some low Georgian outbuildings) and, in 1819, the south wing was completely redone. On the back of the surviving east range, however, distinctly visible from the courtyard, there remains a gable-roofed staircase tower of Rudston's construction (see Fig. 8.3). The Elizabethan stairs still exist. At the top level of the tower is a reduced landing; the greater part of the area over the penultimate half-flight of stairs has been partitioned off to create a small closed room (see Fig. 8.4).

This closet occupies an area roughly 13 ft long by 7 1/4 ft wide. The door, with a veneer of linenfold paneling showing towards the stairs, square-paneling on the inside, and a heavy iron lock, is in the southeast corner of the room. On

---

[30] Will of William Thomson (1553), *Lancashire and Cheshire Wills and Inventories from the Ecclesiastical Court, Chester, Part 1*, ed. G. J. Piccope, Chetham Society 33 (1858), 90–3. For Widow Hodges: deposition of Thomas Kettyn regarding testament of Thomas Foorthe (1585), GL Ms 9585, fo. 175[v]. Inventory of Thomas Hanbury (1611), Folger X.d.65. William Painter, *The Palace of Pleasure*, ed. Joseph Jacobs, 3 vols., 4th edn. (London: David Nutt, 1890), novel 49 (ii. 23). For more on different configurations of the space, see my 'Gertrude's Closet'.

[31] The history of the house is derived from three different, undated guidebooks (one courtesy of Jill Harris) and from Arthur Oswald, 'Boughton Monchelsea Place, Kent', parts 1 and 2, *Country Life*, 20 June 1963: 1489–93 and 27 June 1963: 1552–5 (kindly copied to me by current owner Marice Kendrick). Description of the closet is from personal observation. I am grateful to George Way for dating the cupboard hardware to the seventeenth century (in private conversation).

Figure 8.3 The staircase tower at Boughton Monchelsea Place, near Maidstone in Kent, seen from the courtyard (and partially obscured by a later two-storied projection). The paired windows in the peak of the gable mark the location of the 'little stairhead closet'.

entry, there is an open area about 5 by 6 ft; then, to the north, two steps clear the top of the stairs below. The raised portion of the room is fitted out, on the eastern wall, with five cupboards, each about 22 in tall and provided with an interior shelf, and also two deep bins with hinged lids. Above the cupboards are two shelves supported by simply carved wooden corbels. The rest of the room is wainscotted with square panels surmounted, on the north and south, by small open storage niches; there is also a shelf over the door. On the west wall, overlooking the courtyard, is a high window finished, at its base, with the additional display surface of a deep stone ledge.

In a 1613 inventory completed at the death of Robert Rudston's heir Belknap Rudston, the 'little stairhead closet' is one of four closets at Boughton Monchelsea. None was an exclusive study space, for the impedimenta of learning were scattered through the house. In the closet 'by' the dining room were Sir Robert Brook's *Grande Abridgement* of English legal cases and 'threescore other small books', along with a table and an iron-bound chest.

Figure 8.4 The 'little stairhead closet' at Boughton Monchelsea Place, showing storage niches in the wainscotted wall on the left and cupboards, bins, and shelves fitted to the wall on the right.

A closet 'within' one of the principal bedchambers had a volume of Foxe's *Book of Martyrs* and a book of Chaucer's works, in addition to a table with a Turkey-work carpet, a chair with two Turkey-work cushions, a joined chair, and a joined stool. The 'little' closet 'within' a second chamber had just a table with carpet, a chest, a joined stool, and a lantern. In the great hall, meanwhile, was a Bible with its reading desk; in the room called 'Mistress Rudston her Chamber' were Erasmus' *Paraphrases* of the New Testament and a *Book of Common Prayer*; in the dining room itself were the second volume of Foxe, Jean Calvin's *Institutio* (also known as the *Institution of the Christian Religion*), Edmund Plowden's law *Reports*, John Rastell's *Abridgment of the Statutes in England*, and thirty-four other books, eighteen of which dealt with English statutes. The gallery had 'ten small books' as well as the countinghouse implement of a set of scales; there were also seventeen maps. The parlor displayed ten more maps and 'a little picture of the Parliament'.[32]

By tradition, inventories did not include fixtures and fittings. Their purpose was to list and appraise moveables, both to ensure that the estate remained unplundered until probate and also to record those assets which were attachable to offset debts. Thus, for the 'little stairhead closet' at Boughton there is no mention of the wainscotting, cupboards, and bins, of their iron hardware, nor of the window and door. In just this way, the inventory at Hardwick House omits reference to Anne Drury's painted panels. Probate inventories also neglected stores of food, which were assets only in the short term, and objects such as plate when designated as 'heirlooms'—these conveyed to the principal heir along with the house to which they were understood to be affixed. Other plate, pewter, and linen were gathered by genre rather than location because they were easily convertible to cash; they were customarily itemized without mention of the chest, cupboard, or closet in which they were stored.[33] These practices may account for the fact that the contents of the Boughton cupboards and bins go unacknowledged in the 1613 inventory and remain unknown. Or it may be that they were represented in the last, umbrella, designation of the inventory, 'certain plate and household stuff' worth £90. Whatever else may have been located there, the stairhead closet contained just four items that were listable for probate: one bench, two shelves (which were traditionally considered to be moveables), and a standish.

[32] I am grateful to Jill Harris for a transcription of the inventory. Some readings are deduced from the anonymous transcriber's apparent unfamiliarity with common paleographic abbreviations.

[33] See further my 'Fictions of the Early Modern English Probate Inventory', in Henry S. Turner (ed.), *The Culture of Capital: Property, Cities, and Knowledge in Early Modern England* (New York: Routledge, 2002), 51–83.

The standish was, as noted in a will of 1596, 'for writing', an implement containing ink, pens, and other scribal accoutrements.[34] It is the only object in the Boughton inventory to share a functional kinship with the writing box in the painting of 'Alice Barnham and her Two Boys'. It may have been held in the stairhead closet as a prized possession, or it may have been used simply for running accounts of the household supplies that were apparently kept there. The closet's built-in cupboards, as also its emptiness of table, chair, stool, and books, give evidence that the purpose of this space was storage. However, event could always overtake intent, and the standish may have found—or even inspired—other, more creative purposes. As the only closet not 'within' or near other chambers, this was the most removed and isolated of Boughton Monchelsea's closed spaces. Anyone who had access to it may have discovered privacy in it. In consequence of a convenient standish, that privacy could have been the kind history has always valued highly: that which manifests itself in a subjectivity made accessible to us through its articulation in authorship. The standish transformed this closet into an enabling space.

Was the Barnham family memoir a product of the accidental effects of an early modern storage closet? In 1613, through the failure of male heirs in his mother's family, Sir Francis Barnham inherited Boughton Monchelsea Place, with its 'little stairhead closet' as well as three others. His reminiscence of his father, written around 1630, survives in two copies. One was made for Sir Thomas Rider and is now found among the papers of the Barrett-Lennard family in the Essex Record Office. Another, since deposited in the Bodleian, was labeled in the seventeenth century as 'The Character of Sir Martin Barnham, Knight, written by his son Sir Francis, who was the father of the Lady Salkeld, in whose *closet* it was found after her death' (emphasis added).[35] The memoir is full of closet concerns, as well, in that its most lively interest involves property disputes and their closet-kept evidences. One controversy is centered on Alice Barnham.

Because of Francis Barnham's 'indulgence to his younger sons', says Sir Francis, Martin inherited 'no more estate but both the Bilsingtons'—the two manors of Bilsington Superior (or Bilsington Priory) and Bilsington Inferior. The Court Lodge of Bilsington was part of Alice's jointure, settled on her for

---

[34] Inventory of Robert Atkinson (1596), *Wills and Inventories from the Registry at Durham, Part II*, no. 117.

[35] T. Barrett Lennard's transcription for *The Ancestor* (9 (1904), 191–209) was based on the eighteenth-century copy now in the Essex Record Office, ERO Ms D/DL/229. I quote from my new transcription, which collates the seventeenth-century Salkeld copy, Bodley Ms 10. See 'The Character of Sir Martin Barnham, Knight, by his son Sir Francis Barnham', in James Dutcher and Anne Lake Prescott (eds.), *Renaissance Historicisms: Essays in Honor of Arthur F. Kinney* (Newark: University of Delaware Press, 2008).

her widowhood. While she 'was always to her eldest son a very loving and indulgent mother', she was not so indulgent as to transfer this holding into her son's name; she retained title. But she leased the lodge to Martin for £300 a year, an old rent which was something under its real market value. Thus Martin received 'some small benefit' from the difference between the rents he took in and those he paid to his mother. There was also promise of better revenues when, with the expiration of old leases, he would be able to raise the rates. The arrangement was threatened, however, during Alice's courtship by 'a very rich Alderman of London'. Sir Francis calls his grandmother's suitor 'Sir John Ramsey', undoubtedly referring to the grocer Sir Thomas Ramsey. Ramsey enjoyed the career trajectory that in Francis Barnham's case was cut off by premature death: Ramsey was Sheriff of London in 1567, became Lord Mayor in 1577, and was rewarded with a knighthood in 1578.[36]

The 'treaty' of marriage was 'almost concluded', writes Sir Francis, 'upon such terms as were very advantageous to my grandmother'. But negotiations foundered on the matter of Bilsington Lodge. Ramsey had discovered that Alice's jointure property 'was leased out to her prejudice', because she was not herself receiving all the rents. 'Pressing hard', he urged her to recall the lease. It was increasingly the habit of wealthy merchants to keep second homes in the provinces, and Ramsey suggested they might rebuild the lodge for the seasonal use of her children and friends. This was a ruse, according to Sir Francis; 'the truth was that his aim in getting in of my father's lease was only to improve my grandmother's jointure to the full value', even though, without it, she was already wealthy enough to be 'a very good marriage to him', owning in addition to her annual rental incomes of £300 'a very good personal estate' that probably included goods, ready money, merchandise, bonds for funds out on loan, even shares in voyages.

Alice and 'Sir John' having achieved 'a full agreement on all other conditions', she put the proposition to her son. Martin resisted, making 'answer in such sort as might have been fully satisfactory had not the importunities of a loving mother prevailed against all the reasons a dutiful son could urge'. Finally, however, he acquiesced. Alice told her suitor of the date agreed upon so that Ramsey could be present for the 'surrender' of the property documents. 'My father kept his time', said Sir Francis, and 'the covetous old knight' did, too. 'As soon as he saw my grandmother possessed of the lease by my father's

[36] For Ramsey see Alfred B. Beaven, *The Aldermen of the City of London*, 2 vols. (London: E. Fisher for the Corporation of the City of London, 1908–13), i. 101, 123; ii. 37. Ramsey and his eventual wife, Mary Dale, featured in Stow and Anthony Munday's *Survey of London* as civic philanthropists ((London: 1617), 202–3, 209).

delivering thereof into her hands, he told her that now the marriage between them should be consummated, and named a speedy day for it.' But, 'nay', said Alice,

Good Sir John, be not so hasty, except it be to appoint your wedding day with some other wife, for on me I assure you you must not reckon. For I shall never think my self happily bestowed upon a husband that setteth so small a value on me as you have done in making this little improvement of my jointure (for that I know was indeed your aim) a necessary condition of your match with me. But it hath fallen out well and given me two satisfactions, the one of your nature, which is surely so set upon covetousness as would have given me but small comfort in you; the other, that of my son's duty and good affection to me, which made him comply with my desires though to his own prejudice. For which I bless him, and in retribution of my love do here give back his lease again, wishing it were of much better value than it is that so it might make a full expression of my love to him and my just acknowledgment of his loving and dutiful carriage towards me.

'And so', concludes Sir Francis, 'Sir John Ramsey and she parted.' With this, Alice Barnham disdained the title 'lady' which her descendants were to assign to her portrait. In its own way, finally, the episode is as revealing of her interiority as is the painting. It, too, shows her keeping her own council. Then, as was so often the case in this period, she celebrated her privacy by staging it publicly before her son and her disappointed suitor.

As suggested by the title 'The Character of Sir Martin Barnham, Knight', Sir Francis Barnham meant to produce a garden-variety memoir about the progenitor of his own gentility. Indeed, the second lively and dialogic scene in the account concerns Martin's defense of the greater part of his estate against the claims of others to the property, including Sir John Perrot. Sir Francis is aware of the shift of focus in telling the 'true story' of how Martin's mother also protected his land and station: 'though it relate principally to my grandmother's goodness, yet my father hath so great a share in it as maketh it I think not unfit for this discourse'. In other words, he had intended to give us the sort of masculinist report which is most recognizable to us. This last account of Alice Barnham resists the familiar kind of history-making that Sir Francis set out to perpetuate. But then, so much of her story involves defiance: not only that she thwarted Randall Hurleston and refused Sir Thomas Ramsey, but also that she adhered to the Protestant religion and, as a silkwoman, withstood the forces of industrial change. From our first encounter with her, and the name she suppresses and the 'turn' she leaves unspecified, her interiority is constituted in resistance—as privacy so often had to be in the early modern period.

IN CLOSING

Privacy was sometimes a product of serendipity; sometimes, of a standish. In the discourse of the archives, solitude and secrecy were inevitably described as accidental in order to inoculate them from the stigma of sinister intent. Sasha Roberts defines privacy as 'a controlling act—the ability to choose your own companions, or to be alone'. But in the sixteenth century domestic sphere, privacy did not have a coherent history of control. More importantly, it had a history of competing priorities, of overriding suspicions, of social prohibitions, and of compulsory betrayals.

In the unreceptive environment of the early modern house, privacy also lacked a sustained locational history. For Roberts, control is 'enabled by material conditions: the creation of withdrawn, hidden, personal or secure spaces'; her subject is the elite closet and reading practices within it.[37] Unarguably, the privileged status of the closet features strongly in the more esoteric discourses of imaginative and prescriptive literature. There, the closet achieved a focused meaning in common culture as a space of solitude, and privacy itself acquired an unexceptionable rationale. James Bankes counseled his children: 'every morning when you rise, serve God privily in your closet or chamber before you have any conferences with any man whatsoever, yourself alone'. And Lady Katherine Paston wrote, 'I pray thee, do not fail to render most humble thanks unto his majesty on thy bowed knees from the ground of thy heart, in thy closet privately by thy own self, when none may hear or see thee, but he alone who searcheth the heart and the reins.'[38] In both cases, the advice was conventional.

It is no accident that this notion of the closet—as a space disburdened of all its associations with goods storage and proofs of possession—intersected so often with the privacies of the Protestant religion. The closet's persistent connotative life followed from its prehistory as a late-medieval space with devotional functions. Private chapels lining the side aisles of churches were also called 'closets'; they appear in last testaments as a desire 'to be buried in Myton Church in the closet', or 'hard at the outside of the wall of my closet', or 'in my closet in the church of Alne'.[39] Perhaps more important for

---

[37] Sasha Roberts, 'Shakespeare "creepes into the womens closets about bedtime": Women Reading in a Room of their Own', in Gordon McMullan (ed.), *Renaissance Configurations: Voices/Bodies/Spaces, 1580–1690* (Basingstoke: Macmillan, 1998), 33.

[38] *The Early Records of the Bankes Family at Winstanley*, ed. Joyce Bankes and Eric Kerridge, Chetham Society 3rd ser., 21 (1973), 17. *The Correspondence of Lady Katherine Paston, 1603–1627*, ed. Ruth Hughey, Norfolk Record Society 14 (1941), 80.

[39] Will of Edmund Watson (1596), *North Country Wills*, ii. no. 137. Will of Robert Forster (1583), *Wills and Inventories from the Registry at Durham, Part III*, ed. J. C. Hodgson, Publications

our understanding of the conceptual life of the closet is a royal variation, the small room placed near a chapel, equipped with its own altar or prayer stand, and also provided with a small latticed interior window—a built hole—so that the monarch could enjoy a private hearing of chapel services. Lady Margaret Beaufort, mother of Henry VII, was famously represented in this pious setting.[40] The prayer closet had an essential connection to Catholic observance, but the symbolic identity of the space was to survive religious reformation as an object of the cultural imaginary, of those 'emotions' and 'dreams' about which Orest Ranum hypothesized. It inhabited a fiction of privacy in its most extreme form, isolation.

Alberti was not unique in purveying a cultural fable that, even if out of step with social circumstance and the closet's variable uses, nonetheless had some salience in Renaissance culture. William H. Sherman recognizes the distance between experience and spatial mythology; dialogues of space and solitude 'are less representations of early modern reality', he says, 'than rhetorical strategies by which early modern subjects negotiated their place in society'.[41] What we learn about privacy from Alberti and his contexts, then, is that it may not have been actual but could be aspirational. While the material life of privacy was a contingent one, it had that persistent mental life which has long dominated our understandings of the Renaissance.

In actuality, even the prayer closet had a public function. Henry Machyn knew when Philip and Mary heard mass in their closet; he noted it in his so-called 'diary'. Elizabeth had a 'private closet' as well as a 'great closet', and Robert Carey was aware when she used one rather than the other. Anne Clifford 'went to the Court thinking that the Queen', Anna, 'would have gone to the chapel, but she did not, so my Lady Ruthen and I *and many others* stood in the closet to hear the sermon' (emphasis added). The prayer closet was not free of stigma, either. For Richard Brathwait, for example, it was a room in which one might find oneself alone and dangerously exempt from the usual inhibitions of social surveillance. 'Task yourselves then privately, lest privacy become your enemy', he advised. 'Be you in your chambers or private

of the Surtees Society 112 (1906), 99–100. Will of Richard Ellerker (1583), *North Country Wills*, ii. no. 88.

[40] On the prayer closet, see esp. Thurley, *Royal Palaces*, 125–7. For the circumstances of particular palaces, see the several volumes of *The History of the King's Works*, gen. ed. H. M. Colvin, 5 vols. (London: HMSO, 1963–82). Furnishings and ornaments are detailed in *The Inventory of King Henry VIII*, e.g. 217, 380, 383. Some private houses had prayer closets adjoining their private chapels; see 'A View of Petworth House, 1574', in *The Household Papers of Henry Percy, Ninth Earl of Northumberland (1564–1632)*, ed. G. R. Batho, Camden Society 3rd ser., 93 (1962), 105. Drapers' Hall also had 'a closet sealed and matted with a bay glass window and lattice windows to look in to the chapel', Drapers M.B.1/C, fo. 377ʳ.

[41] Sherman, *John Dee*, 50.

closets, be you retired from the eyes of men, think how the eyes of God are on you. Do not say, the walls encompass me, darkness o'ershadows me, the curtain of night secures me . . . do nothing privately which you would not do publicly.'[42]

Brathwait's unease testifies to the capacities of the closet and the possibilities of privacy. It occurred in intrigues and intents, and in interiorities such as those displayed in 'Alice Barnham and her Two Boys', where the principal subject pauses in the act of writing, leaves her next thought unknown, and reminds us that there are limits to how far we can follow her. There remain secrets that got away, as she suggests. Despite all the impediments that have been the subject of this book, privacy sometimes happened.

[42] *The Diary of Henry Machyn, Citizen and Merchant-Taylor of London, from A.D. 1550 to A.D. 1563*, ed. John Gough Nichols, Camden Society 42 (1848), 129. *The Memoirs of Robert Carey*, ed. F. H. Mares (Oxford: Clarendon, 1972), 58. *The Diaries of Lady Anne Clifford*, 66 (19 January 1617). Richard Brathwait, *The English Gentlewoman* (London: 1631), 48–9.

Works Cited

Manuscript Sources

Bethlem Royal Hospital Archives and Museum (BCB):

> BCB-01: Minute Book of the Bridewell Court of Governors, April 1559–June 1562
>
> BCB-02: Minute Book of the Bridewell Court of Governors, March 1574–May 1576
>
> Ms 10: Sir Francis Barnham, 'The Character of Sir Martin Barnham, Knight', *c.* 1630

British Library (BL):

> Harl. Ms 6019: Account of Sir Francis Barnham's connection to Boughton Monchelsea Place, Kent
>
> Ms Add. 28330: Lucas de Heere, 'Corte Beschryuinghe van Engheland, Schotland, ende Irland'

Canterbury Cathedral Archives and Library (CCAL):

> X.11.1: Deposition Book of the Consistory Court of Canterbury, 1585–1589
>
> X.11.3: Deposition Book of the Consistory Court of Canterbury, 1598–1600
>
> X.11.5: Deposition Book of the Consistory Court of Canterbury, 1594–1598
>
> X.11.6: Deposition Book of the Consistory Court of Canterbury, 1592–1594

Centre for Kentish Studies (CKS):

> Dcb-PRC/27: Consistory Court of Canterbury Probate Inventories
>
> Q/M/SB: Sessions Papers for the West Kent Quarter Sessions
>
> Q/M/SI: Indictments for the West Kent Quarter Sessions
>
> Q/M/SR: Sessions Rolls for the West Kent Quarter Sessions
>
> Q/M/SRc: Recognizances for the West Kent Quarter Sessions

Clothworkers' Company of London:

> Clothworkers' Plan Book: Surveys of lands belonging to the Worshipful Company of Clothworkers of London, 1612

The Corporation of London Records Office (CLRO):

> Hustings Roll 248 (CLA/023/DW/01/247): Court of Hustings deeds and wills, 1555–1558
>
> Hustings Roll 250 (CLA/023/DW/01/249): Court of Hustings deeds and wills, 1561–1562
>
> Hustings Roll 255 (CLA/023/DW/01/254): Court of Hustings deeds and wills, 1566–1568
>
> Journ. 17 (COL/CC/01/01/017): Journal of the Court of Common Council, September 1556–June 1561

Journ. 18: (COL/CC/01/01/018): Journal of the Court of Common Council, August 1563–May 1566

Journ. 19: (COL/CC/01/01/019): Journal of the Court of Common Council, August 1567–August 1572

Journ. 20: (COL/CC/01/01/020): Journal of the Court of Common Council, November 1572–June 1575

Misc. MSS Boxes 91 and 93 (COL/SJ/27/464, 470): Certificates of the Sworn Viewers of the City of London, 1508–1558

Rep. 13 (COL/CA/01/01/014 and 015): Repertory of the Court of Aldermen, December 1552–January 1558

Rep. 14 (COL/CA/01/01/016): Repertory of the Court of Aldermen, January 1558–October 1561

Rep. 15 (COL/CA/01/01/017): Repertory of the Court of Aldermen, November 1561–January 1566

Rep. 16 (COL/CA/01/01/018): Repertory of the Court of Aldermen, January 1566–March 1570

Rep. 17 (COL/CA/01/01/019): Repertory of the Court of Aldermen, March 1570–April 1573

Rep. 18 (COL/CA/01/01/020): Repertory of the Court of Aldermen, April 1573–October 1575

Rep. 19 (COL/CA/01/01/021): Repertory of the Court of Aldermen, November 1575–October 1579

Rep. 46 (COL/CA/01/01/050): Repertory of the Court of Aldermen, November 1631–October 1632

Drapers' Company of London (Drapers'):

A.III.151: Miscellaneous Letters to the Masters and Wardens, 1537–1611

D.B.1: Dinner Book, 1563–1602

M.B.1/B: Minute Book of the Court of Assistants, Repertory 7, 1530–1542

M.B.1/C: Minute Book of the Court of Assistants, Repertory 7, 1543–1553

M.B.4: Minute Book of the Court of Assistants, Repertory A, 1547–1552

M.B.5: Minute Book of the Court of Assistants, Repertory B, 1552–1557

M.B.6: Rough Minute Book of the Court of Assistants, 1553–1555

M.B.7: Minute Book of the Court of Assistants, Repertory C, 1557–1561

M.B.8: Minute Book of the Court of Assistants, Repertory E, 1567–1574

M.B.9: Minute Book of the Court of Assistants, Repertory F, 1574–1584

M.B.10: Minute Book of the Court of Assistants, Repertory G, 1584–1594

M.B.11: Minute Book of the Court of Assistants, Repertory H, 1594–1603

M.B.13: Minute Book of the Court of Assistants, Repertory I, 1603–1640

O.B.1: Ordinance and Oath Book, 1460–1560

R.A.4: Renters' Accounts, 1539–1560

R.A.5: Renters' Accounts, 1560–1604

W.A.3: Wardens' Accounts, 1541–1542

W.A.4: Wardens' Accounts, 1547–1562

W.A.5: Wardens' Accounts, 1562–1603

East Sussex Record Office (ESRO):
  HIC/319-22: Conveyance, deed, final recovery, and exemplification of a common recovery relating to the manor of Ockley, 1602
Essex Record Office (ERO):
  Ms D/DL/229: 'A Copy of an Original Manuscript of Sir Francis Barnham, Knight', c. 1630
Folger Shakespeare Library (FSL):
  L.b.38: Letter of George Carey, 2nd Baron Hunsdon, to Sir William More, 1596
  L.b.328: Inventory of Thomas Cawarden, 1559
  V.b.232: Thomas Trevelyon, Pictorial Commonplace Book, c.1608
  X.d.64: Inventory of John Edolf, 1576
  X.d.65: Inventory of Thomas Hanbury, 1611
Guildhall Library of London (GL):
  Ms 204: Nehemiah Wallington, 'A Record of God's Mercies, or a Thankful Remembrance', 1630
  Ms 977/1: Churchwardens' Accounts for St Clement Eastcheap, 1636–1740
  Ms 977/4: Churchwardens' Accounts for St Clement Eastcheap and St Martin Orgar, 1841–1875
  Ms 981/2: Churchwardens' Accounts for St Clement Eastcheap, 1864–1888
  Ms 2463: William Smythe, 'A Brief Description of the Royal City of London', 1575 (with manuscript additions to 1633)
  Ms 3047/1: Search Book of the Tilers' and Bricklayers' Company, 1605–1650
  Ms 3656: 'Account of the bread given away . . . by Alice and Benedict Barnham', 1834–1835
  Ms 4071/1: Churchwardens' Accounts for St Michael Cornhill, 1455–1608
  Ms 4072/1: Vestry Minute Book of St Michael Cornhill, 1563–1697
  Ms 4384/1: Vestry Minute Book of St Bartholomew Exchange, 1567–1643
  Ms 4429/1: General Register of St Mildred Poultry, 1538–1724
  Ms 4783/1: General Register of St Clement Eastcheap, containing baptisms, 1539–1812; marriages, 1539–1754; burials, 1539–1812
  Ms 4887: The 'Ancient Vestry Book' of St Dunstan in the East, containing churchwardens' accounts, 1494–1509, and vestry minutes, 1515–1651
  Ms 6152/1: Court Minute Book of the Tallow Chandlers' Company, 1549–1585
  Ms 7164/1: Inventories of the Cutlers' Company, 1586–1664
  Ms 7784/1: Various records of the Carpenters' Company, 1600–1632
  Ms 7971: Deeds and papers relating to property of the New England Company situated in Bucklersbury in the parishes of St Stephen Walbrook and St Mildred Poultry, 1548–1791
  Ms 9056: Deposition Book of the Archdeacon's Court of London, 1566–1567
  Ms 9064/14: Acta Quoad Correctionem Delinquentium of the Commissary Court of London, 1593–1599
  Ms 9189/1: Deposition Book of the Consistory Court of London, 1622–1624
  Ms 9189/2: Deposition Book of the Consistory Court of London, 1627–1628

Ms 9234/1–7: Memorandum Books of the Parish Clerk of St Botolph Aldgate, 1583–1598

Ms 9585: Deposition Book of the Bishop's Commissary Court of London, 1581–1593

Ms 12805: Evidence Book of Christ's Hospital, 1611

Ms 12806/1: Minute Book of the Christ's Hospital Court of Governors, 1556–1563

Ms 12806/2: Minute Book of the Christ's Hospital Court of Governors, 1562–1592

Ms 12918: Leases, surveys, and other documents relating to Francis Barnham's gift to Christ's Hospital of land and tenements in the parish of St Olave Southwark, containing bundle 1 for 1494–1604, bundle 2 for 1604–1663, bundle 3 for 1667–1782

Ms 12919: Conveyances and other documents relating to Francis Barnham's gift to Christ's Hospital of fourteen messuages (formerly six) in the parish of St Olave Southwark, 1559–1603

Ms 21096: Bargain and sale of an upper room in the parish of St Martin Ludgate, 1573

Ms 34010/1: Court Minute Book of the Merchant Taylors' Company, 1562–1574

Lambeth Palace Library (Lambeth):

Ms 1485: 'Monumental Inscriptions from London Churches', *c.*1638

Leicestershire, Leicester, and Rutland Record Office (LRO):

ID 41/4 Boxes 23, 26, 27: Interrogatories and Depositions for the Archdeacon's Court of Leicester, 1638–1640

London Metropolitan Archives (LMA):

DL/C/211/1: Deposition Book of the Consistory Court of London, April 1572–February 1574

DL/C/214: Deposition Book of the Consistory Court of London, June 1591–November 1594

DL/C/215: Deposition Book of the Consistory Court of London, October 1597–June 1600

H01/ST/A/001/001: Minute Book of the General Court of Governors of St Thomas's Hospital, January 1557–July 1564

H01/ST/A/001/002: Minute Book of the General Court of Governors of St Thomas's Hospital, August 1564–September 1568

H01/ST/A/001/003: Minute Book of the General Court of Governors of St Thomas's Hospital, September 1568–August 1580

H01/ST/A/024/001: Book of the Government of St Thomas's Hospital, 1556, with Treasurers' Yearly Accounts, 1561–1582

H01/ST/D/01/001: St Thomas's Hospital Treasurers' Week Books, September 1559–September 1565

H01/ST/D/01/002: St Thomas's Hospital Treasurers' Week Books, October 1565–November 1572

H01/ST/D/33/001: St Thomas's Hospital Workmen's Accounts, October 1565–October 1586

H01/ST/E/065/A/001/001: Book of Evidences for St Thomas's Hospital, 1618

Public Record Office, The National Archives (PRO):

E 123/5: Exchequer Records of the Queen's Remembrancer: Entry Books of Decrees and Orders, Series 1, 1572–1578

E 123/6: Exchequer Records of the Queen's Remembrancer: Entry Books of Decrees and Orders, Series 1, 1572–1580

E 133/1/188: Exchequer Records of the Queen's Remembrancer: Barons' Depositions *in re Queen* v. *Slanye*, 1573

E 133/1/190: Exchequer Records of the Queen's Remembrancer: Barons' Depositions *in re Queen* v. *Slanye*, 1574

E 133/1/205: Exchequer Records of the Queen's Remembrancer: Barons' Depositions *in re Queen* v. *Barnham*, 1574

E 133/1/210: Exchequer Records of the Queen's Remembrancer: Barons' Depositions *in re Queen* v. *Barnham*, 1574

E 133/2/221: Exchequer Records of the Queen's Remembrancer: Barons' Depositions *in re Queen* v. *Barnham*, 1574

E 133/2/230: Exchequer Records of the Queen's Remembrancer: Barons' Depositions *in re Queen* v. *Barnham*, 1574

E 133/2/233: Exchequer Records of the Queen's Remembrancer: Barons' Depositions *in re Queen* v. *Barnham*, 1574

E 133/2/234: Exchequer Records of the Queen's Remembrancer: Barons' Depositions *in re Queen* v. *Barnham*, 1574

E 133/2/238: Exchequer Records of the Queen's Remembrancer: Barons' Depositions *in re* lease to Sir John Sentleger, 1575

E 133/2/269: Exchequer Records of the Queen's Remembrancer: Barons' Depositions *in re Queen* v. *Barnham*, 1575

SP 15/12: State Papers Domestic of Secretaries of State, Letters and Papers, 1564–1565

SP15/27A: State Papers Domestic of Secretaries of State, Letters and Papers, 1580

SP 46/32: State Papers Domestic, Supplementary: Exchequer, 1580–1582

SP 46/33: State Papers Domestic, Supplementary: Exchequer, 1583–1587

SP 46/37: State Papers Domestic, Supplementary: Exchequer, 1589–1590

SP 46/38: State Papers Domestic, Supplementary: Exchequer, 1591–1593

STAC 5/L3/30: Court of Star Chamber Proceedings: Plaintiffs' Papers *in re Lambert* v. *Quarles and others*, 1568

STAC 5/L7/21: Court of Star Chamber Proceedings: Plaintiffs' Papers *in re Lambert* v. *Quarles and others*, 1569

STAC 5/L8/28: Court of Star Chamber Proceedings: Plaintiffs' Papers *in re Lambert* v. *Quarles and others*, 1569

STAC 5/L11/27: Court of Star Chamber Proceedings: Plaintiffs' Papers *in re Lambert* v. *Quarles and others*, 1569

STAC 5/L16/29: Court of Star Chamber Proceedings: Plaintiffs' Papers *in re Lambert* v. *Quarles and others*, 1570

STAC 5/L26/27: Court of Star Chamber Proceedings: Plaintiffs' Papers *in re Lambert* v. *Quarles and others*, 1570

STAC 5/L32/29: Court of Star Chamber Proceedings: Plaintiffs' Papers *in re Lambert v. Quarles and others*, 1569

STAC 5/L40/5: Court of Star Chamber Proceedings: Plaintiffs' Papers *in re Lambert v. Quarles and others*, 1569

STAC 5/L47/4: Court of Star Chamber Proceedings: Plaintiffs' Papers *in re Lambert v. Quarles and others*, 1569

STAC 7/13/26: Court of Star Chamber Proceedings: Addenda, 1558–1603

PROB Various: Copy wills registered in the Prerogative Court of Canterbury

Shakespeare Birthplace Trust Records Office (SBT):

DR18/1/1226: Assignment of lease at Leighton Buzzard, Bedfordshire, 1585

West Sussex Record Office (WSRO):

CHICTY/AY/122: Chichester City Archives, deed of 1577

STC 1/5, fo. 90: Will of William Bradbridge, 1543

STC 1/10, fo. 326ᵛ: Will of Augustine Bradbridge, 1567

STC 7, fo. 57: Will of Nicholas Bradbridge, 1548

Primary Sources

Abstracts of Inquisitions Post Mortem Relating to the City of London, Part III: 19–45 Elizabeth, 1577–1603, ed. Edward Alexander Fry. Index Library 36. London: British Record Society, 1908.

The Accounts of the Churchwardens of the Parish of St Michael, Cornhill, in the City of London, from 1456 to 1608, ed. William Henry Overall. London: Alfred James Waterlow for the Vestry, 1868.

Acts of the Privy Council of England, ed. John Roche Dasent. 32 vols. London: HMSO, 1890– .

ALBERTI, LEON BATTISTA. *The Albertis of Florence: Leon Battista Alberti's 'Della Famiglia'*, ed. and trans. Guido A. Guarino. Lewisburg: Bucknell University Press, 1971.

—— *On the Art of Building in Ten Books*, trans. Joseph Rykwert, Neil Leach, and Robert Tavernor. Cambridge, Mass.: MIT Press, 1988.

Allegations for Marriage Licences Issued by the Bishop of London, i. *1520–1610*, ed. Joseph Lemuel Chester and George J. Armytage. Publications of the Harleian Society 25 (1887).

ARCHER, ISAAC. *Two East Anglian Diaries, 1641–1729: Isaac Archer and William Coe*, ed. Matthew Storey. Suffolk Records Society 36 (1994).

BACON, FRANCIS. *The Essayes or Counsels, Civill and Morall*, ed. Michael Kiernan. Cambridge, Mass.: Harvard University Press, 1985.

BANKES, JAMES. *The Early Records of the Bankes Family at Winstanley*, ed. Joyce Bankes and Eric Kerridge. Chetham Society, 3rd ser., 21 (1973).

BARLOW, EDWARD. *Barlow's Journal of his Life at Sea in King's Ships . . . from 1659 to 1703*, ed. Basil Lubbock. London: Hurst & Blackett, 1934.

BARNHAM, FRANCIS. 'The Character of Sir Martin Barnham, Knight, by his son Sir Francis Barnham', ed. Lena Cowen Orlin. In *Renaissance Historicisms: Essays in*

Honor of Arthur F. Kinney, ed. James Dutcher and Ann Lake Prescott. Newark: University of Delaware Press, 2008.

—— 'A Copy of an Original Manuscript of Sir Francis Barnham, Knight', ed. T. Barrett Lennard. *The Ancestor* 9 (1904), 191–209.

Book of Examinations and Depositions, 1570–1594, ed. Gertrude H. Hamilton. Publications of the Southampton Record Society 16 (1914).

BRATHWAIT, RICHARD. *The English Gentlewoman*. London: 1631.

BROWN, JOSEPH. *The Trial of Thomas Duke of Norfolk by his Peers, for High Treason against the Queen*. London: J. Morphew, 1709.

Calendar of the Manuscripts of . . . the Marquess of Salisbury . . . Preserved at Hatfield House. 24 vols. London: 1883–1976.

CAREY, ROBERT. *The Memoirs of Robert Carey*, ed. F. H. Mares. Oxford: Clarendon, 1972.

CAVENDISH, GEORGE. *The Life and Death of Cardinal Wolsey*. In *Two Early Tudor Lives*, ed. Richard S. Sylvester and Davis P. Harding. New Haven: Yale University Press, 1962, 1–193.

Certayn Chapters taken out of the Prouerbes of Salomon . . . translated into metre by J. Hall, Which Prouerbes of late were imprinted and vntruely entituled to be of T. Sternhold. London: 1550.

Certayne Chapters of the Prouerbes of Salomon drawen into metre by Thomas Sterneholde, late grome of the Kynges Majesties Robes. London: 1549–50.

CHAMBERLAIN, JOHN. *The Letters of John Chamberlain*, ed. Norman Egbert McClure. 2 vols. Philadelphia: American Philosophical Society, 1939.

Child-Marriages, Divorces, and Ratifications, &c. in the Diocese of Chester, A.D. 1561–6, ed. Frederick J. Furnivall. Early English Text Society, os 108 (1897).

Christ's Hospital Admissions, i. *1554–1599*. London: Harrison, 1937.

Civil and Uncivil Life: A Discourse Where is Disputed What Order of Life Best Beseemeth a Gentleman. In *Inedited Tracts: Illustrating the Manners, Opinions, and Occupations of Englishmen during the Sixteenth and Seventeenth Centuries*, ed. William Carew Hazlitt. 1579; London: Roxburghe Library, 1868, 3–93.

CLIFFORD, ANNE. *The Diaries of Lady Anne Clifford*, ed. D. J. H. Clifford. Rev. edn. Phoenix Mill: Sutton, 1992.

COE, WILLIAM. *Two East Anglian Diaries, 1641–1729: Isaac Archer and William Coe*, ed. Matthew Storey. Suffolk Records Society 36 (1994).

COKE, EDWARD. *The Third Part of the Institutes of the Laws of England: Concerning High Treason and Other Pleas of the Crown*. London: 1660.

A Collection of State Papers Relating to Affairs in the Reign of Queen Elizabeth from . . . 1571 to 1596, ed. William Murdin. London: William Bowyer, 1759.

A Collection of State Papers Relating to Affairs in the Reigns of King Henry VIII, King Edward VI, Queen Mary, and Queen Elizabeth from . . . 1542 to 1570, ed. Samuel Haynes. London: William Bowyer, 1740.

A Compleat Collection of State-Tryals . . . From the Reign of King Henry the Fourth, to the End of the Reign of Queen Anne. 4 vols. London: Timothy Goodwin et al., 1719.

COOKE, ROBERT. *Visitation of London 1568*, ed. H. Stanford London and Sophia W. Rawlins. Publications of the Harleian Society 109 and 110 (1963).

COTGRAVE, RANDLE. *A Dictionarie of the French and English Tongues*. London: 1611.

County Genealogies: Pedigrees of the Families of the County of Kent, ed. William Berry. London: Sherwood, Gilbert & Piper, 1830.

County Genealogies: Pedigrees of the Families in the County of Sussex, ed. William Berry. London: Sherwood, Gilbert & Piper, 1830.

CULPEPER, THOMAS. *A Tract against Usury*. London: 1621.

Darlington Wills and Inventories, 1600–1625, ed. J. A. Atkinson et al. Publications of the Surtees Society 201 (1993).

DAVIS, JOHN. 'The Imprisonment of John Davis, a Boy of Worcester, Written by Himself in After Life'. In *Narratives of the Days of the Reformation*, ed. John Gough Nichols. Camden Society 77 (1859), 60–8.

DAY, ANGEL. *The English Secretary, or Method of Writing of Epistles and Letters*. London: 1586.

DEE, JOHN. *The Diaries of John Dee*, ed. Edward Fenton. Charlbury: Day Books, 1998.

—— Preface to *The Elements of Geometry of the Most Ancient Philosopher Euclid of Megara*, trans. H. Billingsley. London: 1570.

—— *The Private Diary of Dr. John Dee*, ed. James Orchard Halliwell, Camden Society 19 (1842).

Depositions and Other Ecclesiastical Proceedings from the Courts of Durham Extending from 1311 to the Reign of Elizabeth, ed. James Raine. Publications of the Surtees Society 21 (1845).

Devonshire Wills: A Collection of Annotated Testamentary Abstracts, ed. Charles Worthy. London: Bemrose, 1896.

A Dictionary of the Proverbs in England in the Sixteenth and Seventeenth Centuries, ed. Morris Palmer Tilley. Ann Arbor: University of Michigan Press, 1950.

DIGGES, DUDLEY. *The Compleat Ambassador: or Two Treaties of the Intended Marriage of Qu: Elizabeth . . . Comprised in Letters of Negotiation*. London: 1655.

DOD, JOHN, and CLEAVER, ROBERT. *A Godly Form of Household Government*. London: 1598.

DONNE, JOHN. *The Complete Poetry of John Donne*, ed. John T. Shawcross. New York: New York University Press, 1968.

Essex Wills: The Archdeaconry Courts, 1583–1592, ed. F. G. Emmison. Chelmsford: Essex Record Office, 1989.

Essex Wills: The Archdeaconry Courts, 1591–1597, ed. F. G. Emmison. Chelmsford: Essex Record Office, 1991.

Essex Wills: The Bishop of London's Commissary Court, 1558–1569, ed. F. G. Emmison. Chelmsford: Essex Record Office, 1993.

Essex Wills: The Bishop of London's Commissary Court, 1569–1578, ed. F. G. Emmison. Chelmsford: Essex Record Office, 1994.

Essex Wills: The Bishop of London's Commissary Court, 1578–1588, ed. F. G. Emmison. Chelmsford: Essex Record Office, 1995.

Essex Wills (England), i. *1558–1565*, ed. F. G. Emmison. Washington, DC: National Genealogical Society, 1982.

Essex Wills (England), ii. *1565–1571*, ed. F. G. Emmison. Boston: New England Historic Genealogical Society, 1983.

Essex Wills (England), iii. *1571–1577*, ed. F. G. Emmison. Boston: New England Historic Genealogical Society, 1986.

The Famous Historie of Fryar Bacon. London: T. Bensley, 1816.

FOXE, JOHN. *Foxe's Book of Martyrs Variorum Edition Online*, version 1.1. <www.hrionline.ac.uk/johnfoxe>, accessed 4 May 2007.

GASCOIGNE, GEORGE. *George Gascoigne's A Hundreth Sundrie Flowers*, ed. C. T. Prouty. Columbia: University of Missouri Press, 1942.

—— *A Hundreth Sundrie Flowers*, ed. G. W. Pigman III. Oxford: Clarendon, 2000.

GERBIER, BALTHAZAR. *Counsel and Advice to all Builders*. London: 1663.

GERSCHOW, FREDERIC. 'Diary of the Journey of Philip Julius, Duke of Stettin-Pomerania, through England in the Year 1602', ed. Gottried von Bülow. *Transactions of the Royal Historical Society* NS 6 (1892), 1–67.

GOLDING, ARTHUR. *A Brief Discourse of the Late Murder of Master G. Saunders*. In *A Warning for Fair Women: A Critical Edition*, ed. Charles Dale Cannon, Appendix D. 1573; The Hague: Mouton, 1975.

Grantees of Arms Named in Docquets and Patents to the End of the Seventeenth Century, ed. Joseph Foster and W. Harry Rylands. Publications of the Harleian Society 66 (1915).

HAKLUYT, RICHARD. *The Principal Navigations, Voyages, Traffiques, and Discoveries of the English Nation*. 12 vols. Glasgow: James MacLehose, 1903–5.

HARINGTON, SIR JOHN. *A New Discourse of a Stale Subject Called the Metamorphosis of Ajax*. London: 1596.

HARRISON, WILLIAM. *The Description of England*, ed. Georges Edelen. Ithaca, NY: Cornell University Press for the Folger Shakespeare Library, 1968.

HARSNETT, SAMUEL. *A Declaration of Egregious Popish Impostures, to Withdraw the Hearts of her Majesty's Subjects from their Allegiance and from the Truth of the Christian Religion Professed in England, under the Pretense of Casting Out Devils*. London: 1603.

HASTED, EDWARD. *The History and Topographical Survey of the County of Kent*. 4 vols. Canterbury: Simmons & Kirkby, 1778–99.

HEYWOOD, THOMAS. *If You Know Not Me, You Know Nobody, Part II*, ed. Madeleine Doran. Malone Society Reprints. Oxford: Oxford University Press, 1935.

HOBY, MARGARET. *The Private Life of an Elizabethan Lady: The Diary of Lady Margaret Hoby, 1599–1605*, ed. Joanna Moody. Phoenix Mill: Sutton, 1998.

HOLINSHED, RAPHAEL. *The Chronicles of England, Scotland, and Ireland*. 2 vols. London: 1577.

HORMAN, WILLIAM. *Vulgaria*. London: 1519.

Household and Farm Inventories in Oxfordshire, 1550–1590, ed. M. A. Havinden. Historical Manuscripts Commission 10 and Oxfordshire Record Society 44. London: HMSO, 1965.

Howes, John. *A Brief Note of the Order and Manner of the . . . Three Royal Hospitals*, ed. William Lempriere. 1582; London: privately printed, 1904.

'Inquisitions Post Mortem. Temp. Henry VII, James I and Charles I', ed. F. W. T. Attree. *Sussex Archaeological Collections* 52 (1909), 100–31.

The Inventory of King Henry VIII: Society of Antiquaries MS 129 and British Library MS Harley 1419, ed. David Starkey et al. London: Harvey Miller for the Society of Antiquaries of London, 1998.

'Inventory of Sir Henry Sharington: Contents of Lacock House, 1575', ed. Thelma E. Vernon. *Wiltshire Archaeological and Natural History Magazine* 63 (1968), 72–82.

'An Inventory of the Goods of John Cuerden of Cuerden, 1601', ed. R. Sharpe France. *Transactions of the Historic Society of Lancashire and Cheshire* 91 (1939), 193–204.

The Ipswich Probate Inventories, 1583–1631, ed. Michael Reed. Suffolk Records Society 22 (1981).

Jacobean Household Inventories, ed. F. G. Emmison. Publications of the Bedfordshire Historical Record Society 20 (1938).

Knox, John. *A Brief Exhortation to England for the Speedy Embracing of the Gospel*. London: 1559.

Knyvett, Thomas. *The Knyvett Letters (1620–1644)*, ed. Bertram Schofield. London: Constable, 1949.

Lancashire and Cheshire Wills and Inventories from the Ecclesiastical Court, Chester, Part 1, ed. G. J. Piccope. Chetham Society 33 (1857).

Lancashire and Cheshire Wills and Inventories from the Ecclesiastical Court, Chester, Part 2, ed. G. J. Piccope. Chetham Society 51 (1860).

Lancashire and Cheshire Wills and Inventories from the Ecclesiastical Court, Chester, Part 3, ed. G. J. Piccope. Chetham Society 54 (1861).

Leicester's Commonwealth: The Copy of a Letter Written by a Master of Art of Cambridge (1584), ed. D. C. Peck. Athens, Ohio: Ohio University Press, 1985.

Letters and Papers . . . of the Reign of Henry VIII, ed. J. S. Brewer et al. 21 vols. London: HMSO, 1864–1932.

Lincolnshire Pedigrees, ed. A. R. Maddison. Publications of the Harleian Society 51 (1903).

London Assize of Nuisance, 1301–1431, ed. Helena M. Chew and William Kellaway. London Record Society 10 (1973).

London Consistory Court Depositions, 1586–1611: List and Indexes, ed. Loreen L. Giese. London Record Society 32 (1995).

London Marriage Licences, 1521–1869, ed. Joseph Foster. London: Bernard Quaritch, 1887.

The London Surveys of Ralph Treswell, ed. John Schofield. London Topographical Society 135 (1987).

London Viewers and their Certificates, 1508–1558: Certificates of the Sworn Viewers of the City of London, ed. Janet Senderowitz Leongard. London Record Society 26 (1989).

Lowe, Roger. *The Diary of Roger Lowe of Ashton-in-Makerfield, Lancashire, 1663–74*, ed. William L. Sachse. New Haven: Yale University Press, 1938.

MACHYN, HENRY. *The Diary of Henry Machyn, Citizen and Merchant-Taylor of London, from A.D. 1550 to A.D. 1563*, ed. John Gough Nichols. Camden Society 42 (1848).

MADOX, RICHARD. *An Elizabethan in 1582: The Diary of Richard Madox, Fellow of All Souls*, ed. Elizabeth Story Donno. Hakluyt Society, 2nd ser., 147. London: Hakluyt Society, 1976.

MANNINGHAM, JOHN. *The Diary of John Manningham of the Middle Temple, 1602–1603*, ed. Robert Parker Sorlien. Hanover, NH: University Press of New England for the University of Rhode Island, 1976.

MARKHAM, GERVASE. *The English Husbandman, Drawn into Two Books.* London: 1635.

MASSINGER, PHILIP. *A New Way to Pay Old Debts*, ed. T. W. Craik. New Mermaids. London: Ernest Benn, 1964.

MOULSWORTH, MARTHA. *My Name was Martha: A Renaissance Woman's Autobiographical Poem*, ed. Robert C. Evans and Barbara Wiedemann. West Cornwall, Conn.: Locust Hill, 1993.

MULCASTER, RICHARD. *Positions: Wherein those Primitive Circumstances be Examined, Which are Necessary for the Training Up of Children.* London: 1581.

MUNDAY, ANTHONY. *A View of Sundry Examples Reporting . . . All Memorable Murders Since the Murder of Master Sanders by George Browne.* London: 1580.

NASHE, THOMAS. 'The Unfortunate Traveller'. In *Thomas Nashe: Selected Writings*, ed. Stanley Wells. Cambridge, Mass.: Harvard University Press, 1965, 187–278.

North Country Wills . . . 1558 to 1604, ii., ed. John William Clay. Publications of the Surtees Society 121 (1912).

The Order of my Lord Mayor, the Aldermen, and the Sheriffs for their Meetings and Wearing of their Apparel throughout the Whole Year. London: 1568.

PAINTER, WILLIAM. *The Palace of Pleasure*, ed. Joseph Jacobs. 4th edn. 3 vols. London: David Nutt, 1890.

PASTON, KATHERINE. *The Correspondence of Lady Katherine Paston, 1603–1627*, ed. Ruth Hughey. Norfolk Record Society 14 (1941).

PEACHAM, HENRY. *The Complete Gentleman, The Truth of Our Times, and the Art of Living in London*, ed. Virgil B. Heltzel. Ithaca, NY: Cornell University Press for the Folger Shakespeare Library, 1962.

PHILIPOT, THOMAS. *Villare Cantianum: or Kent Surveyed and Illustrated.* London: 1659.

Plymouth Building Accounts of the Sixteenth and Seventeenth Centuries, ed. Edwin Welch. Devon and Cornwall Record Society NS 12 (1967).

The Port and Trade of Early Elizabethan London: Documents, ed. Brian Dietz. London Record Society 8 (1972).

The Practise of the Sheriff's Court. London: 1657.

Probate Inventories of Lichfield and District, 1568–1680, ed. D. G. Vaisey. Staffordshire Record Society 4th ser., 5 (1969).

The Progresses and Public Processions of Queen Elizabeth, ed. John Nichols. 2 vols. London: John Nichols & Son for the Society of Antiquaries, 1823.

The Progresses, Processions, and Magnificent Festivities of King James the First, ed. John Nichols. 4 vols. London: J. B. Nichols for the Society of Antiquaries, 1828.

Queen Elizabeth and Some Foreigners, Being a Series of Hitherto Unpublished Letters from the Archives of the Hapsburg Family, ed. Victor von Klarwill, trans. T. H. Nash. London: John Lane, 1928.

The Register of Admissions to Gray's Inn, 1521–1889, ed. Joseph Foster. London: Hansard Publishing Union, 1889.

Register of Freemen in the City of London in the Reigns of Henry VIII and Edward VI, ed. Charles Welch. London: London and Middlesex Archaeological Society, 1908.

RICH, BARNABE. *Barnabe Riche His Farewell to Military Profession*, ed. Donald Beecher. Ottawa: Dovehouse Editions for Medieval and Renaissance Texts and Studies, 1992.

ROGERS, RICHARD. *Two Elizabethan Puritan Diaries by Richard Rogers and Samuel Ward*, ed. M. M. Knappen. Chicago: American Society of Church History, 1933.

Roll of the Drapers' Company of London, ed. Percival Boyd. Croydon: J. A. Gordon at the Andress Press, 1934.

ROPER, WILLIAM. *The Life of Sir Thomas More*. In *Two Early Tudor Lives*, ed. Richard S. Sylvester and Davis P. Harding New Haven: Yale University Press, 1962, 195–254.

SCOTT, WILLIAM. *An Essay of Drapery (1635)*, ed. Sylvia L. Thrupp. Kress Library of Business and Economics 9. Boston: Harvard Graduate School of Business Administration, 1953.

SHAKESPEARE, WILLIAM. *The Norton Shakespeare Based on the Oxford Edition*, gen. ed. Stephen Greenblatt. New York: W.W. Norton, 1997.

SHUTE, JOHN. *The First and Chief Groundes of Architecture*, ed. Lawrence Weaver. 1563; London: Country Life, 1912.

SMITH, HENRY. *A Preparative to Marriage*. London: 1591.

SMITH, THOMAS. *A Discourse of the Commonweal of This Realm of England, Attributed to Sir Thomas Smith*, ed. Mary Dewar. Charlottesville: University Press of Virginia for the Folger Shakespeare Library, 1969.

'A Speke Inventory of 1624', ed. E. B. Saxton. In *Transactions of the Historic Society of Lancashire and Cheshire* 97 (1945), 106–43.

STOW, JOHN. *The Annals of England*. London: 1592.

—— *A Survey of London*. London: 1598.

—— *A Survey of London*. Rev. edn. London: 1603.

—— and MUNDAY, ANTHONY. *A Survey of London*. London: 1617.

STRYPE, JOHN. *A Survey of the Cities of London and Westminster . . . Written at First in the Year MDXCVIII by John Stow*. 2 vols. London: 1720.

STUART, ARBELLA. *The Letters of Lady Arbella Stuart*, ed. Sara Jayne Steen. Women Writers in English, 1350–1850. New York: Oxford University Press, 1994.

TAYLOR, JOHN. *The Carriers' Cosmography*. London: 1637.

TRESWELL, RALPH. *See* under *The London Surveys of Ralph Treswell*.

Tudor Royal Proclamations, ii. *The Later Tudors (1553–1587)*, ed. Paul L. Hughes and James F. Larkin. New Haven: Yale University Press, 1969.

Two Tudor Subsidy Assessment Rolls for the City of London: 1541 and 1582, ed. R. G. Lang. London Record Society 29 (1993).

'A View of Petworth House, 1574'. In *The Household Papers of Henry Percy, Ninth Earl of Northumberland (1564–1632)*, ed. G. R. Batho. Camden Society, 3rd ser., 93 (1962), 103–7.

The Visitations of Kent, ed. W. Bruce Bannerman. Publications of the Harleian Society 74, 75 (1923, 1924).

WARD, SAMUEL. *Two Elizabethan Puritan Diaries by Richard Rogers and Samuel Ward*, ed. M. M. Knappen. Chicago: American Society of Church History, 1933.

A Warning for Fair Women: A Critical Edition, ed. Charles Dale Cannon. The Hague: Mouton, 1975.

WENTWORTH, WILLIAM. 'Sir William's Account of the Providences Vouchsafed his Family'. In *Wentworth Papers, 1597–1628*, ed. J. P. Cooper. Camden Society, 4th ser., 12 (1973), 25–35.

—— 'Sir William Wentworth's Advice to his Son'. In *Wentworth Papers, 1597–1628*, ed. J. P. Cooper. Camden Society, 4th ser., 12 (1973), 9–24.

WHEATCROFT, LEONARD. *The Courtship Narrative of Leonard Wheatcroft, Derbyshire Yeoman*, ed. George Parfitt and Ralph Houlbrooke. Reading: Whiteknights, 1986.

WHETSTONE, GEORGE. *A Critical Edition of George Whetstone's 1582 An Heptameron of Civill Discourses*, ed. Diana Shklanka. The Renaissance Imagination 35. New York: Garland, 1987.

WHYTHORNE, THOMAS. *The Autobiography of Thomas Whythorne*, ed. James M. Osborn. Modern Spelling Edition. London: Oxford University Press, 1962.

Wills and Inventories from the . . . Archdeaconry of Richmond, ed. James Raine. Publications of the Surtees Society 26 (1853).

Wills and Inventories from the Registry at Durham, Part II, ed. William Greenwell. Publications of the Surtees Society 38 (1860).

Wills and Inventories from the Registry at Durham, Part III, ed. J. C. Hodgson. Publications of the Surtees Society 112 (1906).

Wills and Inventories from the Registry at Durham, Part IV, ed. Herbert Maxwell Wood. Publications of the Surtees Society 142 (1929).

Wills and Inventories Illustrative of the History, Manners, Language, Statistics, &c. of the Northern Counties of England, Part I, ed. James Raine. Publications of the Surtees Society 2 (1835).

Wills of the Archdeaconry of Suffolk, 1620–1624, ed. Marion E. Allen. Suffolk Records Society 31 (1989).

WILSON, THOMAS. *A Discourse upon Usury*. London: 1572.

'The Woeful Lamentation of Mistress Anne Sanders'. In *Old English Ballads, 1553–1625, Chiefly from Manuscript*, ed. Hyder E. Rollins. Cambridge: Cambridge University Press, 1920, 340–8.

A World of Wonders, A Mass of Murders, A Covey of Cozenages. London: 1595.

WOTTON, HENRY. *The Elements of Architecture by Sir Henry Wotton*, ed. Frederick Hard. Charlottesville: University Press of Virginia for the Folger Shakespeare Library, 1968.

Secondary Sources

600 Years of British Painting: The Berger Collection at the Denver Art Museum. Denver: Denver Art Museum and the W. M. B. Berger Charitable Trust, 1998.

ADAMSON, NANCY LEE. 'Urban Families: The Social Context of the London Elite, 1500–1603'. University of Toronto Ph.D. dissertation, 1983.

AGNEW, JEAN-CHRISTOPHE. *Worlds Apart: The Market and the Theater in Anglo-American Thought, 1550–1750*. Cambridge: Cambridge University Press, 1986.

AIRS, MALCOLM. *The Tudor and Jacobean Country House: A Building History*. Phoenix Mill: Alan Sutton, 1995.

ALCOCK, N. W. *People at Home: Living in a Warwickshire Village, 1500–1800*. Chichester: Phillimore, 1993.

ALFORD, B. W. E., and BARKER, T. C. *A History of the Carpenters' Company*. London: George Allen & Unwin, 1968.

ALFORD, STEPHEN. *The Early Elizabethan Polity: William Cecil and the British Succession Crisis, 1558–1569*. Cambridge: Cambridge University Press, 1998.

ARCHER, IAN W. 'The Charity of Early Modern Londoners'. *Transactions of the Royal Historical Society*, 6th ser., 12 (2002), 223–44.

—— *The History of the Haberdashers' Company*. Chichester: Phillimore, 1991.

—— *The Pursuit of Stability: Social Relations in Elizabethan London*. Cambridge: Cambridge University Press, 1991.

ARIÈS, PHILIPPE. 'Introduction'. In Roger Chartier (ed.), *A History of Private Life*, iii. *Passions of the Renaissance*, trans. Arthur Goldhammer: Cambridge, Mass.: Belknap Press of Harvard University Press, 1989, 1–11.

ARNHEIM, RUDOLF. *The Dynamics of Architectural Form*. Berkeley: University of California Press, 1977.

ARNOLD, JANET. *Queen Elizabeth's Wardrobe Unlock'd*. Leeds: Maney, 1988.

ASLET, CLIVE, and POWERS, ALAN. *The National Trust Book of the English House*. Harmondsworth: Viking in association with the National Trust, 1985.

BARLEY, MAURICE W. *The English Farmhouse and Cottage*. London: Routledge & Kegan Paul, 1961.

—— *Houses and History*. London: Faber & Faber, 1986.

—— 'The Use of Upper Floors in Rural Houses'. *Vernacular Architecture* 22 (1991), 20–3.

BARNES, THOMAS G. 'The Archives and Archival Problems of the Elizabethan and Early Stuart Star Chamber'. In Felicity Ranger (ed.), *Prisca Munimenta: Studies in Archival and Administrative History Presented to Dr. A. E. J. Hollaender*. London: University of London Press, 1973, 130–49.

BARRETT-LENNARD, SIR THOMAS. *An Account of the Families of Lennard and Barrett Compiled Largely from Original Documents*. Privately printed, 1908.

BARRON, CAROLINE M. 'The "Golden Age" of Women in Medieval London'. *Reading Medieval Studies* 15 (1989), 35–58.

BEAVEN, ALFRED B. *The Aldermen of the City of London.* 2 vols. London: E. Fisher for the Corporation of the City of London, 1908–13.

BELLAMY, JOHN. *The Tudor Law of Treason: An Introduction.* London: Routledge & Kegan Paul, 1979.

BENBOW, MARK. 'Index of London Citizens Involved in City Government, 1558–1603', deposited at the Corporation of London Record Office.

BENNETT, JUDITH. *Ale, Beer, and Brewsters in England: Women's Work in a Changing World, 1300–1600.* Oxford: Oxford University Press, 1996.

BERGER, HARRY, JR. 'Artificial Couples: The Apprehensive Household in Dutch Pendants and *Othello*'. In Lena Cowen Orlin (ed.), *Center or Margin: Revisions of the English Renaissance in Honor of Leeds Barroll.* Selinsgrove, Pa.: Susquehanna University Press, 2006, 114–57.

—— *Fictions of the Pose: Rembrandt Against the Italian Renaissance.* Stanford: Stanford University Press, 2000.

BOULTON, JEREMY. *Neighbourhood and Society: A London Suburb in the Seventeenth Century.* Cambridge: Cambridge University Press, 1987.

BREARS, PETER. *All the King's Cooks: The Tudor Kitchens of King Henry VIII at Hampton Court Palace.* London: Souvenir, 1999.

BRENNER, ROBERT. *Merchants and Revolution: Commercial Change, Political Conflict, and London's Overseas Traders, 1550–1653.* Princeton: Princeton University Press, 1993.

BRIGDEN, SUSAN. *London and the Reformation.* Oxford: Clarendon, 1989.

BROOKS, E. ST. JOHN. 'A Pamphlet by Arthur Golding: The Murder of George Saunders'. *N&Q* 174 (12 March 1938), 182–4.

BROWN, FRANK E. 'Continuity and Change in the Urban House: Developments in Domestic Space Organisation in Seventeenth-Century London'. *Comparative Studies in Society and History* 28 (1986), 558–90.

BUNTEN, ALICE CHAMBERS. *Life of Alice Barnham (1592–1650), Wife of Sir Francis Bacon.* London: Page & Thomas, 1919.

BURNETT, DAVID. *Longleat: The Story of an English Country House.* London: Collins, 1978.

CAPP, BERNARD. 'Life, Love and Litigation: Sileby in the 1630s'. *Past and Present* 182 (2004), 55–83.

CARLIN, MARTHA. 'Four Plans of Southwark in the Time of Stow'. *London Topographical Record* 26 (1990), 15–56.

CARLTON, CHARLES. *The Court of Orphans.* Leicester: Leicester University Press, 1974.

CHAMBERS, DOUGLAS. ' "A speaking picture": Some Ways of Proceeding in Literature and the Fine Arts in the Late-Sixteenth and Early-Seventeenth Centuries'. In John Dixon Hunt (ed.), *Encounters.* London: Studio Vista, 1971, 28–57.

CHAMBERS, E. K. *The Elizabethan Stage.* 4 vols. Oxford: Clarendon, 1923.

CHARTIER, ROGER. 'Introduction' to 'Forms of Privatization'. In Roger Chartier (ed.), *A History of Private Life*, iii. *Passions of the Renaissance*, trans. Arthur Goldhammer, Cambridge. Mass.: Belknap Press of Harvard University Press, 1989, 163–5.

CLARK, ALICE. *Working Life of Women in the Seventeenth Century.* London: Routledge & Kegan Paul, 1919.

CLARK, PETER. *English Provincial Society from the Reformation to the Revolution: Religion, Politics and Society in Kent 1500–1640.* Hassocks: Harvester, 1977.

CLODE, CHARLES M. *The Early History of the Guild of Merchant Taylors.* 2 vols. London: Harrison, 1888.

COLVIN, H. M., RANSOME, D. R., and SUMMERSON, JOHN (eds.). *History of the King's Works,* iii. *1485–1660 (Part I).* London: HMSO, 1975.

—— SUMMERSON, JOHN, et al. (eds.). *The History of the King's Works,* iv. *1485–1660 (Part II).* London: HMSO, 1982.

COMITO, TERRY. *The Idea of the Garden in the Renaissance.* New Brunswick, NJ: Rutgers University Press, 1978.

CONSITT, FRANCES. *The London Weavers' Company,* i. *From the 12th Century to the Close of the 16th Century.* Oxford: Clarendon, 1933.

COOK, OLIVE. *The English House through Seven Centuries.* 1968; Woodstock, NY: Overlook, 1983.

COOPE, ROSALYS. 'The Gallery in England: Names and Meanings'. In *Design and Practice in British Architecture: Studies in Architectural History Presented to Howard Colvin. Architectural History* 27 (1984), 446–55.

—— 'The "Long Gallery"': Its Origins, Development, Use, and Decoration'. *Architectural History* 29 (1986), 43–72.

COOPER, NICHOLAS. *Houses of the Gentry, 1480–1680.* New Haven: Yale University Press for the Paul Mellon Centre for Studies in British Art in association with English Heritage, 1999.

—— 'Rank, Manners and Display: The Gentlemanly House, 1500–1750'. *Transactions of the Royal Historical Society,* 6th ser., 12 (2002), 291–310.

COOPER, TARNYA. 'A Painting with a Past: Locating the Artist and the Sitter'. In Stephanie Nolen (ed.), *Shakespeare's Face.* Toronto: Piatkus, 2002, 229–41.

COOPER, WILLIAM DURRANT. 'Former Inhabitants of Chichester'. *Sussex Archaeological Collections* 24 (1872).

COX, MONTAGU H., and NORMAN, PHILIP (gen. eds.). *The Survey of London,* xiii. *The Parish of St. Margaret, Westminster, Part II (Neighbourhood of Whitehall,* i). London: B. T. Batsford for London County Council, 1930.

CROFT-MURRAY, EDWARD. *Decorative Painting in England, 1537–1837.* 2 vols. London: Country Life, 1962–70.

DALE, MARIAN K. 'The London Silkwomen of the Fifteenth Century'. *Economic History Review,* 1st ser., 4 (1933), 324–35.

DAVIDSON-HOUSTON, C. E. D. 'Sussex Monumental Brasses, Part II'. *Sussex Archaeological Collections* 77 (1936), 130–94.

DENT, JOHN. *The Quest for Nonsuch.* London: Hutchinson, 1962.

DIETZ, BRIAN. 'Overseas Trade and Metropolitan Growth'. In A. L. Beier and Roger Finlay (eds.), *London, 1500–1700: The Making of the Metropolis.* London: Longman, 1986, 115–40.

DILS, JOAN. 'Deposition Books and the Urban Historian'. *The Local Historian* 17 (1987), 269–76.

DUNLOP, IAN. *Palaces and Progresses of Elizabeth I*. London: Jonathan Cape, 1962.

DURANT, DAVID N. *Arbella Stuart, a Rival to the Queen*. London: Weidenfeld & Nicolson, 1978.

—— *Bess of Hardwick: Portrait of an Elizabethan Dynast*. New York: Atheneum, 1978.

DYER, ALAN. 'Urban Housing: A Documentary Study of Four Midland Towns, 1530–1700'. *Post-Medieval Archaeology* 15 (1981), 207–18.

EDWARDS, FRANCIS. *The Marvellous Chance: Thomas Howard, Fourth Duke of Norfolk and the Ridolphi Plot, 1570–1572*. London: Rupert Hart-Davis, 1968.

EMMISON, F. G. *Archives and Local History*, 2nd edn. Chichester: Phillimore, 1974.

—— *Elizabethan Life: Home, Work and Land*. Chelmsford: Essex Record Office, 1991.

—— *Elizabethan Life: Morals and the Church Courts*. Chelmsford: Essex County Council, 1973.

—— *Tudor Secretary: Sir William Petre at Court and Home*. Cambridge, Mass.: Harvard University Press, 1961.

ETHERTON, JUDITH. 'New Evidence—Ralph Treswell's Association with St. Bartholomew's Hospital'. *London Topographical Record* 27 (1995), 103–17.

FAIRCLOUGH, OLIVER. *The Grand Old Mansion: The Holtes and Their Successors at Aston Hall, 1618–1864*. Birmingham: Birmingham Museums and Art Gallery, 1984.

FEYNMAN, RICHARD P. *The Pleasure of Finding Things Out: The Best Short Works of Richard P. Feynman*, ed. Jeffrey Robbins. Cambridge, Mass.: Perseus Books, 1999.

FILDES, VALERIE. 'Maternal Feelings Reassessed: Child Abandonment and Neglect in London and Westminster, 1550–1800'. In Valerie Fildes (ed.), *Women as Mothers in Pre-Industrial England: Essays in Memory of Dorothy McLauren*. London: Routledge, 1990, 139–79.

FINLAY, ROGER. *Population and Metropolis: The Demography of London, 1580–1650*. Cambridge: Cambridge University Press, 1981.

FOSTER, FRANK FREEMAN. *The Politics of Stability: A Portrait of the Rulers in Elizabethan London*. London: Royal Historical Society, 1977.

FOUCAULT, MICHEL. *Discipline and Punish: The Birth of the Prison*, trans. Alan Sheridan. 1975; New York: Vintage Books, 1979.

—— 'The Eye of Power'. In Colin Gordon (ed. and trans.), *Power/Knowledge: Selected Interviews and Other Writings, 1972–1977*. New York: Pantheon Books, 1980, 146–65.

FRENCH, SARA. 'A Widow Building in Elizabethan England: Bess of Hardwick at Hardwick Hall'. In Allison Levy (ed.), *Widowhood and Visual Culture in Early Modern Europe*. Aldershot: Ashgate, 2003, 161–76.

FRIEDMAN, ALICE T. *House and Household in Elizabethan England: Wollaton Hall and the Willoughby Family*. Chicago: University of Chicago Press, 1989.

FUMERTON, PATRICIA. *Cultural Aesthetics: Renaissance Literature and the Practice of Social Ornament*. Chicago: University of Chicago Press, 1991.

Gent, Lucy. *Picture and Poetry, 1560–1620: Relations between Literature and the Visual Arts in the English Renaissance*. Leamington Spa: James Hall, 1981.

George, C. H. 'Parnassus Restored, Saints Confounded: The Secular Challenge to the Age of the Godly, 1560–1660'. *Albion* 23 (1991), 409–37.

Girouard, Mark. *Hardwick Hall*. Rev. edn. N.p.: National Trust, 1989.

—— *Life in the English Country House: A Social and Architectural History*. New Haven: Yale University Press, 1978.

—— *Robert Smythson and the Elizabethan Country House*. New Haven: Yale University Press, 1983.

—— 'Suitable for all men of dignity: Domestic Architecture and the Reaction against Elizabethan and Jacobean Individualism' (review), *Times Literary Supplement*, 16 June 2000, 20–1.

Girtin, Tom. *The Triple Crowns: A Narrative History of the Drapers' Company, 1364–1964*. London: Hutchinson, 1964.

Glanville, Philippa. 'Cardinal Wolsey and the Goldsmiths'. In S. J. Gunn and P. G. Lindley (eds.), *Cardinal Wolsey: Church, State and Art*. Cambridge: Cambridge University Press, 1991, 131–48.

Godfrey, Walter H. *The English Staircase, an Historical Account . . . to the End of the XVIIIth Century*. London: B. T. Batsford, 1911.

Gowing, Laura. *Domestic Dangers: Women, Words, and Sex in Early Modern London*. Oxford: Clarendon, 1996.

Greenwood, M. A. *The Ancient Plate of the Drapers' Company*. London: Humphrey Milford, Oxford University Press, 1930.

Griffiths, Paul. 'Contesting London Bridewell, 1576–1580'. *Journal of British Studies* 42 (2003), 283–315.

—— 'Meanings of Nightwalking in Early Modern England'. *The Seventeenth Century* 13 (1998), 212–38.

—— *Youth and Authority: Formative Experiences in England, 1560–1640*. Oxford: Clarendon, 1996.

Gristwood, Sarah. *Arbella: England's Lost Queen*. London: Bantam, 2003.

Grove, L. R. A. 'Archaeological Notes from Maidstone Museum'. *Archaeologia Cantiana* 86 (1971), 220–5.

Harding, Vanessa. *The Dead and the Living in Paris and London, 1500–1670*. Cambridge: Cambridge University Press, 2002.

Harris, John. *The Design of the English Country House, 1620–1920*. London: Trefoil and the American Institute of Architects Foundation, 1985.

Harris, Jonathan Gil. *Sick Economies: Drama, Mercantilism, and Disease in Shakespeare's England*. Philadelphia: University of Pennsylvania Press, 2004.

Harte, N. B. (ed.). *The New Draperies in the Low Countries and England, 1300–1800*. Oxford: Oxford University Press, 1997.

Hasted, Edward. *The History and Topographical Survey of the County of Kent*. 4 vols. Canterbury: Simmons & Kirkby, 1778–99.

Haynes, D. E. L. 'The Arundel Marbles'. Oxford: Ashmolean Museum, 1975.

HEAL, FELICITY. 'Clerical Tax Collection under the Tudors: The Influence of the Reformation'. In Rosemary O'Day and Felicity Heal (eds.), *Continuity and Change: Personnel and Administration of the Church in England, 1500–1642*. Leicester: Leicester University Press, 1976, 97–122.

HEARN, KAREN (ed.). *Dynasties: Painting in Tudor and Jacobean England, 1530–1630*. London: Tate Publishing, 1995.

HELMHOLZ, R. H. *Marriage Litigation in Medieval England*. Cambridge: Cambridge University Press, 1974.

—— *Roman Canon Law in Reformation England*. Cambridge: Cambridge University Press, 1990.

HERRUP, CYNTHIA B. *A House in Gross Disorder: Sex, Law, and the 2nd Earl of Castlehaven*. New York: Oxford University Press, 1999.

HIRST, DEREK. *Authority and Conflict: England, 1603–1658*. Cambridge, Mass.. Harvard University Press, 1986.

HOBBS, MARY (ed.). *Chichester Cathedral: An Historical Survey*. Chichester: Phillimore, 1994.

HOLDERNESS, B. A. 'Widows in Pre-Industrial Society: An Essay upon Their Economic Functions'. In R. M. Smith (ed.), *Land, Kinship and Life-Cycle*. Cambridge: Cambridge University Press, 1984, 423–42.

HONIG, ELIZABETH. 'In Memory: Lady Dacre and Pairing by Hans Eworth'. In Lucy Gent and Nigel Llewellyn (eds.), *Renaissance Bodies: The Human Figure in English Culture c. 1540–1660*. London: Reaktion Books, 1990, 60–85.

HOSKINS, W. G. *The Age of Plunder: The England of Henry VIII, 1500–1547*. London: Longman, 1976.

—— 'The Rebuilding of Rural England, 1570–1640'. *Past and Present* 4 (1953), 44–59.

HOULBROOKE, RALPH. *Church Courts and the People during the English Reformation, 1520–1570*. Oxford: Oxford University Press, 1979.

—— (ed.). *English Family Life, 1576–1716: An Anthology from Diaries*. Oxford: Basil Blackwell, 1988.

The House of Commons, 1558–1603, ed. P. W. Hasler. 3 vols. London: HMSO for the History of Parliament Trust, 1981.

HOWARD, MAURICE. *The Early Tudor Country House: Architecture and Politics, 1490–1550*. London: George Philip, 1987.

HUNT, T. F. *Exemplars of Tudor Architecture*. London: Longman, 1830.

HUTCHINS, JOHN. *The History and Antiquity of the County of Dorset*. 4 vols. Westminster: John Bowyer Nichols, 1861–70.

HYDE, PATRICIA, and ZELL, MICHAEL. 'Governing the County'. In Michael Zell (ed.), *Early Modern Kent, 1540–1640*. Rochester, NY: Boydell & Brewer, 2000, 7–38.

IMRAY, JEAN M. 'The Merchant Adventurers and their Records'. In Felicity Ranger (ed.), *Prisca Munimenta: Studies in Archival and Administrative History Presented to Dr. A.E.J. Hollaender*. London: University of London Press, 1973, 229–39.

—— 'The Origins of the Royal Exchange'. In Ann Saunders (ed.), *The Royal Exchange*. London Topographical Society 152 (1997), 20–35.

INGRAM, MARTIN. *Church Courts, Sex and Marriage in England, 1570–1640.* Cambridge: Cambridge University Press, 1987.

INGRAM, WILLIAM. *A London Life in the Brazen Age: Francis Langley, 1548–1602.* Cambridge, Mass.: Harvard University Press, 1978.

JARDINE, DAVID. *Criminal Trials: Supplying Copious Illustrations of the Important Periods of English History during the Reigns of Queen Elizabeth and James I.* London: M. A. Nattali, 1847.

JARDINE, LISA, and STEWART, ALAN. *Hostage to Fortune: The Troubled Life of Francis Bacon, 1561–1626.* London: Phoenix Giant, 1998.

JENKINS, FRANK. *Architect and Patron: A Survey of Professional Relations and Practice in England from the Sixteenth Century to the Present Day.* Oxford: Oxford University Press, 1961.

JENKINS, R. B. *Henry Smith: England's Silver-Tongued Preacher.* Macon, Ga.: Mercer University Press, 1983.

JOHNSON, A. H. *The History of the Worshipful Company of the Drapers of London.* 5 vols. Oxford: Clarendon, 1914–22.

JOHNSON, MATTHEW. *Housing Culture: Traditional Architecture in an English Landscape.* Washington, DC: Smithsonian Institution Press, 1993.

JOHNSON, PAUL. *Elizabeth I.* New York: Holt, Rinehart & Winston, 1974.

JONES, ANN ROSALIND, and STALLYBRASS, PETER. *Renaissance Clothing and the Materials of Memory.* Cambridge: Cambridge University Press, 2000.

JONES, NORMAN. *God and the Moneylenders: Usury and Law in Early Modern England.* Oxford: Basil Blackwell, 1989.

JONES, P. E. 'Orphanage'. Unpublished Corporation of London Record Office Research Paper 7.33.

JONES, WHITNEY R. D. *The Tudor Commonwealth, 1529–1559.* London: Athlone, 1970.

JOURDAIN, MARGARET. *English Decoration and Furniture of the Early Renaissance (1500–1650).* London: B. T. Batsford, 1924.

—— *English Decorative Plasterwork of the Renaissance.* London: B. T. Batsford, 1926.

JUPP, EDWARD BASIL. *An Historical Account of the Worshipful Company of Carpenters of the City of London.* London: Pickering & Chatto, 1887.

KEENE, DEREK. 'Material London in Time and Space'. In Lena Cowen Orlin (ed.), *Material London, ca. 1600.* Philadelphia: University of Pennsylvania Press, 2000, 55–74.

—— 'A New Study of London before the Great Fire'. *Urban History Yearbook* (1984), 11–21.

KING, DONALD, and LEVEY, SANTINA. *The Victoria and Albert Museum's Textile Collection: Embroidery in Britain from 1200 to 1750.* London: V&A Publications, 1993.

KINGSFORD, CHARLES LETHBRIDGE. 'A London Merchant's House and Its Owners, 1360–1614'. *Archaeologia* 74 (1925), 137–58.

KITCH, M. J. 'The Reformation in Sussex'. In M. J. Kitch (ed.), *Studies in Sussex Church History.* London: Leopard's Head, 1981, 77–98.

KORDA, NATASHA. 'Women's Theatrical Properties'. In Jonathan Gil Harris and Natasha Korda (eds.), *Staged Properties in Early Modern English Drama*. Cambridge: Cambridge University Press, 2002, 202–29.

KOWALESKI, MARYANNE, and BENNETT, JUDITH M. 'Crafts, Gilds, and Women in the Middle Ages: Fifty Years after Marian K. Dale'. *Signs* 14 (1989), 474–88.

KUNIN, AARON. 'From the Desk of Anne Clifford'. *English Literary History* 71 (2004), 587–608.

LACEY, KAY. 'The Production of "Narrow Ware" by Silkwomen in Fourteenth- and Fifteenth-Century England'. *Textile History* 18 (1987), 187–204.

LAMB, MARY ELLEN. 'Margaret Hoby's Diary: Women's Reading Practices and the Gendering of the Reformation Subject'. In Sigrid King (ed.), *Pilgrimage for Love: Essays in Early Modern Literature in Honor of Josephine A. Roberts*. Medieval and Renaissance Texts and Studies 213. Tempe: Arizona Center for Medieval and Renaissance Studies, 1999, 63–94.

LEHMBERG, STANFORD E. *The Reformation Parliament, 1529–1536*. Cambridge: Cambridge University Press, 1970.

LEVIN, CAROLE. *The Heart and Stomach of a King: Elizabeth I and the Politics of Sex and Power*. Philadelphia: University of Pennsylvania Press, 1994.

LEWALSKI, BARBARA KIEFER. *Writing Women in Jacobean England*. Cambridge, Mass.: Harvard University Press, 1993.

LEWIS, THOMAS. *On the Constitution, Jurisdiction, and Practice of the Sheriffs' Courts of London*. London: A. Maxwell, 1833.

LINGELBACH, W. E. 'The Internal Organisation of the Merchant Adventurers of England'. *Transactions of the Royal Historical Society* NS 16 (1902), 19–67.

LLEWELLYN, NIGEL. *Funeral Monuments in Post-Reformation England*. Cambridge: Cambridge University Press, 2000.

LLOYD, NATHANIEL. *A History of the English House from Primitive Times to the Victorian Period*. 1931; London: Architectural Press, 1975.

LUBBOCK, JULES. *The Tyranny of Taste: The Politics of Architecture and Design in Britain, 1550–1960*. New Haven: Yale University Press for the Paul Mellon Centre for British Art, 1995.

McCANN, JOHN. 'Dissatisfaction with Builders in the Sixteenth Century'. *Historic Buildings in Essex* 4 (November 1988), 9–10.

McINNES, E. M. *St Thomas' Hospital*. London: George Allen & Unwin, 1963.

McINTOSH, MARJORIE KENISTON. 'The Benefits and Drawbacks of *Femme Sole* Status in England, 1300–1630'. *Journal of British Studies* 44 (2005), 410–38.

—— *Controlling Misbehavior in England, 1370–1600*. Cambridge: Cambridge University Press, 1998.

—— 'Money Lending on the Periphery of London, 1300–1600'. *Albion* 20 (1988), 557–71.

MACHIN, R. 'The Great Rebuilding: A Reassessment'. *Past and Present* 77 (1977), 33–56.

MANZIONE, CAROL KAZMIERCZAK. *Christ's Hospital of London, 1552–1598: 'A Passing Deed of Pity'*. Selinsgrove, Pa.: Susquehanna University Press, 1995.

MARSHBURN, JOSEPH H. ' "A Cruell Murder Donne in Kent" and its Literary Manifestations'. *Studies in Philology* 46 (1949), 131–40.

MASTERS, B. R. 'The Mayor's Household before 1600'. In A. E. J. Hollaender and William Kellaway (eds.), *Studies in London History Presented to Philip Edmund Jones*. London: Hodder & Stoughton, 1969, 95–114.

MERCER, ERIC. *English Art, 1553–1625*. Oxford: Clarendon, 1962.

—— *English Vernacular Houses: A Study of Traditional Farmhouses and Cottages.* London: HMSO, 1975.

—— *Furniture, 700–1700*. The Social History of the Decorative Arts. New York: Meredith, 1969.

—— 'The Houses of the Gentry'. *Past and Present* 5 (1954), 11–32.

MONTROSE, LOUIS. 'Shaping Fantasies: Figurations of Gender and Power in Elizabethan Culture'. *Representations* 2 (Spring 1983), 61–94.

MOWL, TIMOTHY. *Elizabethan and Jacobean Style*. London: Phaidon, 1993.

MUKERJI, CHANDRA. *From Graven Images: Patterns of Modern Materialism*. New York: Columbia University Press, 1983.

MUKHERJI, SUBHA. 'Edmunds vs. Edmunds 1596'. *Queens College Record* 16 (2004), 14–17.

MULDREW, CRAIG. *The Economy of Obligation: The Culture of Credit and Social Relations in Early Modern England*. Houndmills: Macmillan, 1998.

MULLANEY, STEVEN. *The Place of the Stage: License, Play, and Power in Renaissance England*. Chicago: University of Chicago Press, 1988.

NELSON, ALAN H. *Monstrous Adversary: The Life of Edward de Vere, 17th Earl of Oxford*. Liverpool: Liverpool University Press, 2003.

NELSON, BENJAMIN. *The Idea of Usury: From Tribal Brotherhood to Universal Otherhood*. 2nd edn. Chicago: University of Chicago Press, 1969.

NEWTON, WILLIAM. *The History and Antiquities of Maidstone, The County-Town of Kent*. London: privately printed, 1741.

NICOLSON, NIGEL. *Great Houses of Britain*. New York: Putnam, 1965.

O'DONOGHUE, EDWARD GEOFFREY. *Bridewell Hospital: Palace, Prison, Schools*, i. *From the Earliest Times to the End of the Reign of Elizabeth I*. London: John Lane, the Bodley Head, 1923.

O'HARA, DIANA. *Courtship and Constraint: Rethinking the Making of Marriage in Tudor England*. Manchester: Manchester University Press, 2000.

ORLIN, LENA COWEN. 'Fictions of the Early Modern English Probate Inventory'. In Henry S. Turner (ed.), *The Culture of Capital: Property, Cities, and Knowledge in Early Modern England*. New York: Routledge, 2002, 51–83.

—— 'Gertrude's Closet'. *Shakespeare Jahrbuch* 134 (1998), 44–67.

—— 'Rewriting Stone's Renaissance', *Huntington Library Quarterly* 64 (2001), 189–230.

OSWALD, ARTHUR. 'Boughton Monchelsea Place, Kent'. *Country Life*, 20 June 1963: 1489–93; 27 June 1963: 1552–5.

PARSONS, F. G. *The History of St Thomas's Hospital*. 3 vols. London: Methuen, 1932.

PEARL, VALERIE. 'Change and Stability in Seventeenth-Century London'. *London Journal* 5 (1979), 3–34.

PECK, LINDA LEVY. 'Creating a Silk Industry in Seventeenth-Century England'. *Shakespeare Studies* 28 (2000), 225–8.

PLATT, COLIN. *The Great Rebuildings of Tudor and Stuart England*. London: UCL, 1994.

POLLACK, LINDA. *With Faith and Physic: The Life of a Tudor Gentlewoman, Lady Grace Mildmay, 1552–1620*. New York: St Martin's Press, 1993.

PORTMAN, DEREK. 'Vernacular Building in the Oxford Region in the Sixteenth and Seventeenth Centuries'. In C. W. Chalklin and M. A. Havinden (eds.), *Rural Change and Urban Growth, 1500–1800: Essays in English Regional History in Honour of W. G. Hoskins*. London: Longman, 1974, 135–68.

PRIESTLEY, URSULA, and CORFIELD, P. J. 'Rooms and Room Use in Norwich Housing, 1580–1730'. *Post-Medieval Archaeology* 16 (1982), 93–123.

QUAIFE, G. R. *Wanton Wenches and Wayward Wives: Peasants and Illicit Sex in Early Seventeenth-Century England*. London: Croom Helm, 1979.

RABB, THEODORE K. *Enterprise and Empire: Merchant and Gentry Investment in the Expansion of England, 1575–1630*. Cambridge, Mass.: Harvard University Press, 1967.

RANUM, OREST. 'The Refuges of Intimacy'. In Roger Chartier (ed.), *A History of Private Life*, iii. *Passions of the Renaissance*, trans. Arthur Goldhammer. Cambridge, Mass.: Belknap Press of Harvard University Press, 1989, 207–63.

RAPOPORT, AMOS. 'On the Attributes of "Tradition" '. In Jean-Paul Bourdier and Nezar AlSayyad (eds.), *Dwellings, Settlements, and Tradition: Cross-Cultural Perspectives*. Lanham, Md.: University Press of America, 1989, 77–105.

RAPPAPORT, STEVE. *Worlds within Worlds: Structures of Life in Sixteenth-Century London*. Cambridge: Cambridge University Press, 1989.

READ, CONYERS. *Lord Burghley and Queen Elizabeth*. New York: Alfred A. Knopf, 1960.

REYBURN, SCOTT. 'The High Price of Falling for Lady Ingram'. *Antiques Trade Gazette*, 7 February 1998, 24–5.

RICHARDSON, WALTER C. *History of the Court of Augmentations, 1536–1554*. Baton Rouge: Louisiana State University Press, 1961.

RIDLEY, JASPER. *A History of the Carpenters' Company*. London: Carpenters' Hall, 1995.

ROBERTSON, MARY L. 'Profit and Purpose in the Development of Thomas Cromwell's Landed Estates'. *Journal of British Studies* 29 (1990), 317–46.

ROBINSON, JOHN MARTIN. *The Dukes of Norfolk: A Quincentennial History*. Oxford: Oxford University Press, 1982.

SALZMAN, L. F. *Building in England Down to 1540, A Documentary History*. 2nd edn. Oxford: Clarendon, 1967.

SAWYER, WILLIAM PHILLIPS. 'The Drapers' Company'. *Transactions of the London and Middlesex Archaeological Society* 7, pt. 1 (1888; printed as an appendix to vol. 6, 1890), 37–64.

SCHOFIELD, JOHN. *Medieval London Houses*. New Haven: Yale University Press for the Paul Mellon Centre for Studies in British Art, 1995.

SEAVER, PAUL S. *Wallington's World: A Puritan Artisan in Seventeenth-Century London.* Stanford: Stanford University Press, 1985.

SHAW, DIANE. 'The Construction of the Private in Medieval London'. *Journal of Medieval and Early Modern Studies* 26 (1996), 447–66.

SHERIDAN, ALAN. 'Translator's Note'. In Michel Foucault, *Discipline and Punish: The Birth of the Prison.* New York: Vintage, 1979.

SHERMAN, WILLIAM H. *John Dee: The Politics of Reading and Writing in the English Renaissance.* Amherst: University of Massachusetts Press, 1995.

SINFIELD, ALAN. *Faultlines: Cultural Materialism and the Politics of Dissident Reading.* Berkeley: University of California Press, 1992.

SKIPP, VICTOR. *Crisis and Development: An Ecological Case Study of the Forest of Arden, 1570–1674.* Cambridge: Cambridge University Press, 1978.

SPUFFORD, MARGARET. 'First Steps in Literacy: The Reading and Writing Experiences of the Humblest Seventeenth-Century Spiritual Autobiographers'. *Social History* 4 (1979), 407–35.

STANILAND, KAY. 'Thomas Deane's Shop in the Royal Exchange'. In Ann Saunders (ed.), *The Royal Exchange.* London Topographical Society 152 (1997), 59–67.

STEWART, ALAN. 'The Early Modern Closet Discovered'. *Representations* 50 (1995), 76–100.

STONE, LAWRENCE. *The Crisis of the Aristocracy, 1558–1641.* Oxford: Clarendon, 1965.

—— and STONE, JEANNE C. FAWTIER. *An Open Elite? England, 1540–1880.* Oxford: Clarendon, 1984.

STONEHAM, EDWARD T. *Sussex Martyrs of the Reformation,* 3rd edn. rev. by G. Seamer. Burgess Hill: Protestant Alliance and Sussex Martyrs Commemoration Council, 1967.

STRONG, ROY. *Hans Eworth: A Tudor Artist and his Circle.* Leicester: Museums and Art Gallery, 1965.

—— 'Sir Francis Carew's Garden at Beddington'. In Edward Chaney and Peter Mack (eds.), *England and the Continental Renaissance: Essays in Honour of J. B. Trapp.* Woodbridge: Boydell, 1990, 229–38.

SUMMERSON, JOHN. *Architecture in Britain, 1530 to 1830.* 7th edn. Frome: Penguin Books, 1983.

—— 'The Building of Theobalds, 1564–1585'. *Archaeologia* 97 (1959), 107–26.

SUTTON, ANNE F. 'Alice Claver, Silkwoman (d. 1489)'. In Caroline M. Barron and Anne F. Sutton (eds.), *Medieval London Widows, 1300–1500.* London: Hambledon, 1994, 129–42.

—— 'The Merchant Adventurers of England: Their Origins and the Mercers' Company of London'. *Historical Research* 75 (2002), 25–46.

TARGOFF, RAMIE. *Common Prayer: The Language of Public Devotion in Early Modern England.* Chicago: University of Chicago Press, 2001.

THIRSK, JOAN. *Economic Policy and Projects: The Development of a Consumer Society in Early Modern England.* Oxford: Clarendon, 1978.

—— 'England's Provinces: Did They Serve or Drive Material London?' In Lena Cowen Orlin (ed.), *Material London, ca. 1600.* Philadelphia: University of Pennsylvania Press, 2000, 97–108.

THOMPSON, FRED. *Sons of Joyce Frankland: Some Record of the Boys of Newport Grammar School, Essex,* i. *1588–1945.* Saffron-Walden: Old Newportian Society, 1979.

THORNTON, DORA. *The Scholar in his Study: Ownership and Experience in Renaissance Italy.* New Haven: Yale University Press, 1997.

THORNTON, PETER. *Seventeenth-Century Interior Decoration in England, France, and Holland.* New Haven: Yale University Press for the Paul Mellon Centre for Studies in British Art, 1978.

THURLEY, SIMON. *Hampton Court: A Social and Architectural History.* New Haven: Yale University Press for the Paul Mellon Centre for Studies in British Art, 2003.

—— *The Royal Palaces of Tudor England: Architecture and Court Life, 1460–1547.* New Haven: Yale University Press for the Paul Mellon Centre for Studies in British Art, 1993.

—— *Whitehall Palace: An Architectural History of the Royal Apartments 1240–1698.* New Haven: Yale University Press in association with Historic Royal Palaces, 1999.

TITTLER, ROBERT. 'An Actor's Face? The Sanders Portrait in Context'. In Stephanie Nolen (ed.), *Shakespeare's Face.* Toronto: Piatkus, 2002, 212–28.

—— 'For the "Re-edification of Townes": The Rebuilding Statutes of Henry VIII'. *Albion* 22 (1990), 591–605.

—— 'Money-Lending in the West Midlands: The Activities of Joyce Jeffries, 1638–49'. *Historical Research* 67 (1994), 249–63.

—— *Townspeople and Nation: English Urban Experiences, 1540–1640.* Stanford: Stanford University Press, 2001.

TODD, BARBARA. 'Freebench and Free Enterprise: Widows and Their Property in Two Berkshire Villages'. In John Chartres and David Hey (eds.), *English Rural Society: Essays in Honour of Joan Thirsk.* Cambridge: Cambridge University Press, 1990, 175–200.

TUDOR, PHILIPPA. 'Protestant Books in London in Mary Tudor's Reign'. *London Journal* 15 (1990), 19–28.

TYACK, GEOFFREY. *The Making of the Warwickshire Country House, 1500–1650.* Warwickshire Local History Society Occasional Paper 4 (July 1982).

VEALE, ELSPETH M. *The English Fur Trade in the Later Middle Ages.* 2nd edn. London Record Society 38 (2003).

WARD, JENNIFER C. 'The History of Old Thorndon Hall'. In *Old Thorndon Hall.* N.p.: Essex County Council, 1972, 1–12.

WARD, JOSEPH P. *Metropolitan Communities: Trade Guilds, Identity, and Change in Early Modern London.* Stanford: Stanford University Press, 1997.

WARNICKE, RETHA M. 'A Dispute among the Freemen of the Drapers' Company in Elizabethan London'. *Guildhall Studies in London History* 1 (1974), 59–67.

—— *William Lambarde, Elizabethan Antiquary, 1536–1601.* London: Phillimore, 1973.

WATERHOUSE, ELLIS (ed.). *The Dictionary of 16th and 17th Century British Painters.* Woodbridge: Antique Collectors' Club, 1988.

WAYNE, DON E. *Penshurst: The Semiotics of Place and the Poetics of History*. Madison: University of Wisconsin Press, 1984.

WEST, TRUDY. *The Timber-Frame House in England*. Newton Abbot: David & Charles, 1971.

WIGLEY, MARK. 'Untitled: The Housing of Gender'. In Beatriz Colomina (ed.), *Sexuality and Space*. Princeton Papers on Architecture. New York: Princeton Architectural Press, 1992, 327–89.

WILLAN, T. S. *The Early History of the Russia Company, 1553–1603*. Manchester: Manchester University Press, 1956.

—— *The Muscovy Merchants of 1555*. Manchester: Manchester University Press, 1953.

—— *Studies in Elizabethan Foreign Trade*. Manchester: Manchester University Press, 1959.

WILLIAMS, NEVILLE. *Thomas Howard, Fourth Duke of Norfolk*. London: Barrie & Rockliff, 1964.

WILSON, ADRIAN. 'The Ceremony of Childbirth and its Interpretation'. In Valerie Fildes (ed.), *Women as Mothers in Pre-Industrial England: Essays in Memory of Dorothy McLaren*. London: Routledge, 1990, 68–107.

WUNDERLI, RICHARD M. 'Evasion of the Office of Alderman in London, 1532–1672'. *London Journal* 15 (1990), 3–18.

YOUINGS, JOYCE A. *The Dissolution of the Monasteries*. London: George Allen & Unwin, 1971.

—— *Sixteenth-Century England*. The Pelican Social History of Britain. Harmondsworth: Penguin Books, 1984.

Index